SOME CALLED HIM

"MAVERICK"

Memoirs of 33 years in
Africa

"God, I don't even know who you are! How can I tell anyone about you? You can't call me!" But He did! …and He gave me such an incredible time and ministry in Africa that it blew my mind. I couldn't believe I was actually getting paid to do something I enjoyed so much!

Jim Sawatsky

"Even though Jim and I have been friends since high school, I found myself drawn into this book. Cleverly woven through the narrative are fables and adventure stories. This is a fascinating read for family, friends, and strangers alike. This book reads like a novel"
-Rudy Raabe BSc., BEd., Math and Science High School Teacher for 33yrs.

✦

I've known Jim for some 40 years and still haven't heard all his stories. For me this book was a page turner and my wife and I had a friendly race to see who would finish reading it first. Jim has always been a "free range" visionary and you will see that the term "maverick" fits him well as an out-side-of-the-box thinker. As I reflect on his ministry, I believe this acrostic describes his memoirs in the best manner: **M**usician, **A**mbassador, **V**isionary, **E**vangelist, **R**ighteous, **I**nside **C**hrist's **K**ingdom!
-Merl Francis, retired MIT

✦

There's no double about it! In many ways, being so much alike, those High School years with Jim were a definite challenge. Of course, we took our studies "seriously": music, sports, girls and English 30! So, it was with considerable interest that I read Jim's memoirs, "Some Called Him Maverick".

I wasn't disappointed! I found Jim's openness and clarity refreshing as he recounted how God used many of our youthful experiences to ready him for future major challenges in the heart of Africa over the next 30 some years.

Jim (and his dear wife Dawn), has long since retired from mission activity, but clearly many of those memories are still strong within him. During recent chats, I have been amazed and at the same time challenged in my own faith by some of the incredible stories of how God had repeatedly intervened in answer to prayer. I was delighted when I heard that Jim was finally putting his life experiences into a book of memoirs so that they could be shared with everyone ...before these memories could slip away.

So finally, here it is, and it is a great read! I'm sure it will draw you in as well...enjoy!
-Gracen Beutler BSc. BEd. Math and Science High School Teacher for 30 yrs.

Some Called Him "Maverick"
Memoirs of 33 years in Africa

Author:

James R Sawatsky

Editors and Contributors:

Bev and Merl Francis,
Dawn Sawatsky
Raymur Downey,
Ruth Wylie Cannemeyer

Copyright © 2017 by James R Sawatsky

First Printing: 2017

ISBN #: 978-1-387-33263-2

Content ID: 21750752

Book Title: Some Called Him Maverick, Memoirs of 33 years in Africa

Published by:

James R Sawatsky
18638 – 56B Ave
Cloverdale, BC, Canada V3S 7N2

JRS
mancavepub@shaw.ca

Cover design by Rodney J Sawatsky

Title Page Photo by R Raabe and J R Sawatsky

Dedication

To our wonderful 11 grandkids without whom
there probably would be no book…
If it weren't for you, to whom would I write?
And
To my lovely wife, your Gramma.
Thank you Gramma, for without your loving support and
patience, I would have never achieved this monumetal task.

Foreword

Mavericks. We need them. The world needs them. Bold and unconventional risk-takers, they make things happen. They stir things up. James R. Sawatsky wears the "maverick" label well. I've witnessed that through what has now been close to six decades of friendship.

We first met in the Fall of 1960, as first-year students at Canadian Bible College in Regina. I grew up in Regina, where the CBC community was our second family. My father, Murray Downey was a founding faculty member. Jim hailed from Chilliwack, BC. Our friendship quickly grew as classmates, teammates on the College basketball team and members of a freshmen quartet.

I owe a huge debt to Jim for facilitating my introduction to a very special lady from his Fraser Valley region in BC, a classmate named Viola. The first time I saw her that fall of 1960, I had this strange feeling that one day she would be my wife. The rest is history! Jim's family and ours spent the better part of our professional careers as International Workers with the Christian & Missionary Alliance in the Democratic Republic of Congo.

I felt greatly honored when Jim invited me to write a "Foreword" after previewing his detailed autobiographical reflections, prepared for his grandchildren. The more I read, the more I became convinced that this exceptional document deserved a much wider audience than his immediate family.

Granted, writing with his grandchildren as the target audience has biblical precedence. Prior to entering the Promised Land, Moses impressed upon the emerging Hebrew nation the importance of the generational transmission of their divine history and calling.

"These commandments that I give you today are to be upon your hearts. Impress them on your children. Talk about them when you sit at home and when you walk along the road. ...Write them on the doorframes of your houses and on your gates". (Deut. 6:6-9 NIV).

Words, when written, facilitate a permanence that insures transmission to children, grandchildren and future generations.

Mavericks function best when surrounded by wise counselors who know how to ask the hard questions. Jim has been blessed with such a person in his life – Dawn, his life partner, aka "Gramma". Referring throughout the document to Dawn as "Gramma" is a creative and characteristically "maverick" touch to the document. Appropriate too.

In addition to Dawn, Jim acknowledges a host of other people who have had the privilege and courage to speak into his life, including ministry colleagues, supporters and others whom Jim has himself mentored. Mavericks are often misunderstood, especially by those to whom they report. Jim documents with honesty and humility several times when he was a surprised victim of misunderstanding. And there was a price to pay, unfair though it seemed to be at the time.

Mavericks may give the impression that they are unreceptive to others' opinion. I never felt this way with Jim. I have often turned to him for advice, especially in times of transition myself. The fact is that we had built, over time, a climate of mutual trust and respect. In my role as Field Director in the DRC, I learned to give Jim a long rope. At times it meant that we just had to agree to disagree. Mavericks are visionaries. They have an innate sense of what to do, where they want to go and how to get there.

Be amazed and blessed as you read Jim's autobiographical reflections, prepared especially for his grandkids, but for us as well. Together, Jim and Dawn and their family have touched thousands of lives for God's glory. Their gifting and calling are exceptional. The miraculous permeated their lives. Admittedly, their greatest ministry impact came through what continues to function today as Studios Sango Malamu Ministries (SSMM). Well-equipped and multi-gifted, they are right at the top of my list of effective missioners. May their tribe increase!

Dr. Raymur J. Downey

Preface

While the family was home on and extended home assignment 1987-89, we were "Missionaries-in-Residence" at Peace Portal Alliance Church. That wasn't too extraordinary as we had been there already on our home assignment in 1982-83 and it seemed a good fit. We helped in many areas, not the least of which was leading in worship. It was a passion of mine to see people worshiping, not just singing. It seemed to me, anybody could announce a song, a page number and then start the people singing after the piano introduction, but I wanted to do more than that. I didn't want to be a "song leader", but one who led people in worshiping the Lord in song. My goal was first to prepare my heart, then worship Him before the people and then bring others along with me in worship while singing new songs and the glorious old hymns. As "worship leaders" we aren't just calling people to sing, but to worship our Savior in singing, in playing, in taking the offering and even in preaching.

I loved the people at PPAC and it was a treat to be able to use the gifts that God had given me and to use them in ENGLISH. While we were home for those two years '87 to '89, people of the church were hinting (and to the pastor obviously) that I should be asked to come on staff as their worship pastor. So, it wasn't surprising to me that the Pastor called me to his office for a chat.

After the niceties were done he began with, "Many people have suggested that I ask you to come on staff as our worship pastor for the next few years. You may be aware of this."

I responded, "Yes, some people have suggested that to me."

But his next statement really caught me off guard. He immediately followed through with, "But we can't work together!"

I was stunned. Why not? It seemed to be going well so far, where was the problem?

Pastor Bubna said that I wouldn't be able to follow his direction. I objected, politely of course, and intimated that I had never had a problem working with those in authority over me. I followed up by saying that if he gave me a job to do I would get it done. And then he said something that really floored me.

"Yes, I know you'll get the job done, but you won't do it my way! You're a maverick, Jim, and it would be too hard for you to minister here the way I want you to. Now don't get me wrong. The term 'maverick' in my understanding has no negative connotation; it just means that you don't necessarily run with the pack. I need someone here who will follow my lead right down to the letter."

I was devastated for I felt that God had definitely indicated that I would be on staff there. It wasn't that I was pushing for it; I just felt that this was what God wanted me to do for the next few years while our children acculturated and integrated themselves into Canadian society, the Canadian school system and then after graduation launch out on their own. Now, I was refused the position because I was a "maverick!" I really didn't understand. But as I thought about it, I began to realize that Pastor Bubna had great insight and really understood my character. He had hit the proverbial "nail" on the head and had really tagged me correctly. Maybe he was right. He knew how t he could be and he knew what a free runner I was. He didn't want er of us to have to change.

However, for the two years that I was on home assignment as missionary in residence at PPAC the pastor continually asked me to lead in worship and even give a worship seminar to other potential leaders. It seemed that both of us were happy with this arrangement. On Sundays he didn't try to fit me into his mold for I was free to lead as I felt lead by the Holy Spirit in the allotted time he gave me. But the rest of the week I was a missionary on home assignment. And yes, I did a lot of travelling and ministering with the Trio Sango Malamu right across Canada and then with my daughter Loralee on different "Missionary Tours".

"Maverick!" That term got me thinking as to how God had directed my life, even before I was a confirmed believer. In high school I saw the opportunity one day to play the bass fiddle in the jazz band that Mr. Steele was leading. I didn't know how to play but had a vision of how to do it and requested permission to try out. He was astounded at how I played, never having had an upright bass fiddle in my hands before. That led to him arranging for me to have a few free lessons and that gave ris( ) me putting a musical group together in high school—with voices and instruments. Interestingly, this kind of thing had never been done before.

My thoughts then jumped to Kitimat B.C. and our pastorate position there. I was on my own; no other Alliance leader around me. It was my first church plant as the official pastor and I could do things the way I thought was good for my people. The Alliance "law" stated that no divorced person could sit on the board, but one of the founding members, a spiritual leader in the church, was a divorcee. We had no choice; he had to be on the board of elders. Even before that, I was pastoring in Wild Rose North Dakota (during my last year at CBC). The Alliance "law" stipulated that there would be no women on the board of elders, BUT there was no person more suited to be on the board than this fine Christian woman; a leader in the church and in the community. So, she was on the board. Not only that, she was the chair person.

God seemed to give me the liberty to run a little outside of the "pack" with no repercussions. Many times though, when "it just wasn't done that way," my Heavenly Father allowed me to slip under man's imposed "laws" with his leading and blessing. After all, didn't Jesus do something similar when he told Peter to cast his net on the "other" side. Peter could have said, "But Lord, it just isn't done that way!" But he did say, "OK, whatever you say, Lord!" *(Personal interpretation of John 21:3-6)*

When we went to Kinshasa, I was made pastor of two churches by the District Superintendent, Pastor Mabiala Mavungu, and at the same time became the treasurer of the district. I said the Alliance Mission "law" (policy) didn't allow for either of those things to take place, but because he was my superintendent I would comply for a time. Being a pastor in Kinshasa certainly helped me learn the Lingala language fast. I don't think that there could have been a better language learning program for me. But it certainly wasn't the norm, quite the contrary.

When I was reprimanded for an innovation, thinking and moving outside of the CMA field "box", I was subjected to disciplinary action by the Area Director of the CMA in the USA. I was given no responsibilities and almost thought of going home. However, the Lord gave me a vision for a new ministry. He directed me to begin TEE (Theological Education by Extension) for the Alliance church leaders in Kinshasa. It became a wonderfully exciting ministry, never done before with the Alliance in Kinshasa, and I had all the room to envision and innovate as I felt directed by the Holy Spirit. He blessed the effort and soon we had 7 centers with over 100 students. At this point I trained other leaders, translated and printed new materials (God marvelously supplied new printing machines) and even held conferences with leaders. The TEE ministry mushroomed.

As this ministry was being given to the national church leaders, I felt directed by the Lord into full time evangelism. Two young men were available to work with me in music and the Trio Sango Malamu was born. With Sango Malamu (meaning "Good News") we started a music ministry that I would like to call "music and worship evangelism". What we did as a group in music and evangelism was not a new concept in the western world, but it was in the Congo. We ministered together for ten years. We sang and preached in front of hundreds of thousands of people, from lowly rural villages to stadiums, from seemingly inconsequential surroundings to elite expensive hotel forums and from banquets to TV platforms across Central and West Africa, in the USA, Canada and eventually Europe. Although it had never been done quite like that before in the Congo Alliance, we felt it as God directed.

Earlier, the Lord had given this maverick a vision of bringing what had been done in the Congo, through years of missions giving and sending, to the rest of the world through worship evangelism, and personal testimony. And that vision became a reality in the Kinshasa Trio (as we were known in North America). This Sango Malamu ministry also birthed many other Christian musical groups and worship bands to the end that worship leading became the norm in almost all the churches in the Congo.

The Lord began to give vision for other ministries that had not yet been tapped, at least not for over the 30 years that President Mobutu was in power. From the ministry and influence of the group Sango Malamu came a professional Christian recording studio—which became known as *Studios Sango Malamu*. Our studios were the first of its caliber in Christian sound production in Kinshasa—maybe in all of the Congo. In the first 5 years, we recorded over 100 cassette albums each year (2 a week, one shift during the day and another at the night) and fulfilled another vision the Lord had given—to make Christian cassettes as available on the market as Bibles.

Out of that ministry came:

1. A Christian cassette reproduction and distributing house for Christian music—multiplying tapes in mass, conceiving and making cassette jackets and labels for the artists, and distributing the product to many outlets around the city and to the entire Congo.

2. A three-camera video studio in Kinshasa for Christian Artists.

3. A Music and Worship Academy, teaching the basics of music, worship and sound reinforcement.
4. A radio station, Radio Sango Malamu, in Kinshasa. This vision then spread to many parts of Central and West Africa.
5. From these ministries came the Sango Malamu TV station and eventually "SSM Ministries", a radio/television network of 4 radio stations in other parts of the Congo and the one TV station. Still other sister stations were birthed in Pointe Noire, Republic of Congo, and Libreville, Gabon. Other stations were set up in Guinea, Mali, Burkina Faso, Cote D'Ivoire and encouragement for others was given in Niger, Benin, and other areas across Africa.

It seemed like the Lord was constantly giving this "Maverick" vision for new ministries and what was so pleasantly surprising was that the Christian and Missionary Alliance allowed me to "run" with these visions. I learned early on that if I would receive a vision for ministry, I needed to give that vision immediately back to God and wait on Him. If He would begin to open doors, then I would understand that it was definitely from HIM[1]. These "visions for ministry" scared Gramma almost half to the death (for what did I know about recording studios and radio or video production?), yet when the Lord would give them back to me and open doors, I would run like the wind with them. **Eric Liddell said, "I believe God made me for a purpose... And when I run I feel His pleasure."** When I ran with the vision that God had given back to me, I too could feel "His pleasure". I also think that is what mavericks do. They run, but not necessarily with the pack! I believe that the CMA not only allowed me to run, but encouraged me to run and many times (if not all the time) they ran with me, even though much of what was done or accomplished was on the borderline of CMA policy.

---

[1] *If I could get the vision passed my wife, I pretty much knew it was from God. Then, if the Lord convinced the CMA and it was endorsed by them, I was home free!*

Acknowledgements

I want to thank all (and you are many) who contributed to our ministry in prayer and financial support. I thank Pastor Ron Gifford of the Peace Portal Alliance Church who first encouraged The Christian and Missionary Alliance (CMA) to run with me on my first year back home in Canada on Home Assignment. And thanks to the CMA (USA and Canada) for taking his advice (or so it seemed) and being so good to us in so many instances, even when I took the bit in my mouth and ran (albeit with projects that I felt were God given and subsequently "approved" by the mission). I especially thank the CMA in Canada for standing by us when Dawn took so sick and was near death. They kept us on allowance for much longer than they needed to. We praise God and thank Him for their compassion and understanding. Their unending support made a big difference in our ministry. We could not have ministered with and for a better mission/church organization.

I also want to give a huge ovation to our three kids for travelling this journey with us and with me, especially, as their father. Like the song says, "It's not an easy road, we are travelling together and many are the thorns on the way..." All of you kids joined us in Kinshasa after you had already flown the nest which was so meaningful. You were always so supportive of all that we were involved in. One of my great joys was to visit the Ivory Coast Academy and see all of you "in action", whether singing, studying, relating to other students or being active in sports. Rod, it was pure joy to have you with us a couple of times working hard in the SSM ministry in the Congo and doing video and graphics for us, even before you became a bona fide graphic designer. Also, it was a real treat to travel on tour with you, Loralee, singing and ministering together in our CMA churches before you launched out with your husband in a more profitable and blessed music ministry. Jon-Marc, our youngest and our athlete, you gave us the greatest compliment ever when he said, "I couldn't have had a better up-bringing anywhere. Thanks for how you made it all happen." (Or words to that effect.) You did so well at ICA and at TWU and I am proud of you, the only one of our three who actually graduated from a University. Wow! Thanks kids for your great support in life and in the writing of these memoirs.

And Dawn, Whew! What can I say? Dawn (Gramma) you have been an incredible life partner. Without you I would not have grown in many areas of my Christian life. Without you I could never have gained the trust and friendships of our Congolese colleagues as I had. Without you, our home would never have had that open-door policy that it had to all Congolese and "mundeles" (whites) with whom we worked. Without your initiative we would not have been blessed by all those whom we helped along their way and even by those who stayed in our home for a weekend or for a month or for several years. Your gracious hospitality helped so much in showing love to our Congolese family and friends. God planted in you a caring heart and love for people, especially for those who were hurting or alone. You were God's answer to me for ministry and although you didn't get involved in church planting, or in singing with the Sango Malamu Trio (although you did a little bit), or all other ministries that kept popping up, I couldn't have done anything without your support. I thank God for you every day for you surely have the heart of a servant , which went a long way in keeping us true to His calling in our lives. Thank you also for contributing in every way to the writing of these memoirs and for your expert help in critically reading and rereading all these pages.

And by the way, having Pastor Charles Yangu, his wife Elise and then little son Joshua in our home over a stint of several years was a great honor and blessing to us. You, Gramma Dawn, sent me on this path of "opening our home to strangers" and what an exciting adventure that became for us. Charles and Elise have both passed on now, but their lives had made an indelible impression on us, on me. They opened many doors of ministry to us and helped us understand the difficult areas of ministering in a different culture. I loved them dearly. They were our adopted children. In remembrance, a big thank-you to Charles who always ran interference for me at Sango Malamu, in a good way; who always counselled and prayed with all at Sango Malamu Studios as their beloved Chaplain. I believe Sango Malamu weathered many early storms and is still a viable ministry today due to his ministry and later on due to Elise's input. I just want to thank God for them and all the wonderful people whom they brought into our lives. Without them, many areas of this book could not have been written.

I also want to thank all the CMA missionaries of Zaire (and the Congo) who were our leaders and colleagues over many years, for doing all they could to work in harmony with this "maverick". I realize now that it must have been difficult at times, but you all hung in there and I still consider you all our "missionary family". One "buddy" especially, Ray Downey, friends from our freshman year at Canadian Bible College (1960-61), has been a great encouragement to me in our ministry together and now in the writing of these memoirs. Thank you, Ray, for your valuable input. And to all, thanks for displaying love at every turn.

Friendship is a prized possession and without these personal relationships life would be hard, maybe unbearable. From time to time, the Lord brought to us wonderful friendships outside of our "mission", both in the white and black communities. I recognize now how important these relationships were to me (to both of us and to all of us as a family) and how these friendships and interactions with each other really helped us "do life" in the Congo. As I reflect on our lives and past experiences in Africa, I am truly grateful for all the good friends we made who enriched our lives, benefited our ministry, and broadened our world view.

Two long lasting friendships that I need to acknowledge (that continue till today) are those of Paul and Joe Tsasa and their families. I spent 30 plus years as a missionary in Africa and one third of that time was spent in very close relationship with these two young men. Those 10 years were, for me, the best years of ministry in my life. I loved every minute of the time we spent together in ministry and couldn't believe that missionary life could be so enjoyable. I need to thank you guys for "hanging in there" with me. Because of your musical talents and the many sacrifices you made, there have been innumerable ripples of "Good News" spreading across not only the Congo but also all of Africa, North America and other parts of the world. I can't imagine you guys not being at the base of all Sango Malamu ministries. I am so grateful for you both.

The friendship of the Peace Portal Alliance Church and that of Bev and Merl Francis and their two girls were also God-sent friendships for us. Our 2nd time on home assignment we were asked to be missionaries in residence and PPAC. This was a wonderful experience and it became our home church for years to come. The church not only loved on us, but they also always prepared a home and transportation for us! When we asked what they wanted from us in return they simply said, "Nothing! We just want to love on you while you are at home this year!" That is exactly what they did. What an impact that made on our lives.

Bev and Merl were part of that love. The Francis family became almost like our family and after my parents died it seemed like their place became our home away from home (in the Congo). Loralee had prayed for a special friend and their daughter Tanya filled the bill. I thank God for their friendship since the early '80s until this day. Their kids were good friends with our kids; Bev looked after our finances as needed; they were in on the beginnings of GNI and looked after the books; they played host to the Kinshasa Trio on numerous occasions and were always at the ready. Thank you, Bev and Merl and kids for being such gracious and generous friends! You were certainly part of our ministry and the experiences written in the following pages. Thank you too for all the effort you put into reading and correcting and publishing these pages.

I especially need to thank 4 key men: Daryl, Ted, A.T. and Byron (chairman of Good News International), who played a great part in financially supporting our visions. They and all the members of the board of GNI[2] not only contributed enormously to our ministry in the Congo, but also here at home, standing by us in every situation. Without them, their counsel and financial support, we could not have done what we felt God leading us to do. I am eternally grateful to God for you men.

There is another small group of guys who have stuck with me in my early years and now also in my latter years. Without their friendship, I must say again, these pages probably would never have been written. Their influence in my teen years kept me out of a lot of trouble and they were very instrumental in showing me not only that a Christian guy can have a lot of fun, but also that there is a line to be drawn. Without their influence in my life I may have never turned my life over to Jesus. In later years, especially when Dawn (Gramma) was so ill, they again came to the fore with unrelenting support and then again, as in high school, became my best friends. We call ourselves the BBB's or the Best Biking Buddies. Gracen and Rudy, you have been such a great support to me for some 60 years of friendship. You guys know me better than most anybody, yet you have stuck with this maverick through all the years. What an inestimable value your

---

[2] *GNI was started as a non-profit extension ministry here in Canada to help support the Kinshasa Trio while in Canada, but soon became an integral part of the whole of The Studios Sango Malamu Ministries in Zaire and then in the Congo. It was mainly through GNI Ministries that all funds were raised for all the projects involving SSM Ministries.*

friendship has been to me personally. Thanks so much for your encouragement and support in my trying to write these memoirs.

Just before I get to the final group, I need to say that I owe a deep debt of gratitude to (Auntie) Ruth Wylie Cannemeyer. She and her husband, John, left the comforts of their condominium near Toronto to spend over a week with us editing this manuscript (day and night). She caught what others left behind. She cut, slashed and burned what wasn't necessary, reworded and rephrased the best she could with what I gave her! She did what others didn't have the heart to do or this volume would have even more pages. Thank you, Ruth and John, for taking so much time out of your schedule to help this poor fledgling brother-in-law try out his wings in writing, in putting down these memoirs. Not only did you edit and send out all our "prayer letters" throughout the years, but you have now come to our aid in these memoirs. I am forever grateful!

I am deeply grateful for all the people mentioned above, but there is a small group of eleven who have surely conquered my heart, from the youngest to the oldest and for whom I am actually putting down on paper all of these memories—OUR GRANDKIDS! It is to you that grandpa is writing this story. I have enjoyed so much walking with my Savior through all the mountains and valleys of life that I felt I just had to leave you my memoirs as a legacy. I trust that these writings will encourage you to really know God, through His Son Jesus; to really understand how much He loves you and how you can prove Him true to His Word in every situation. I am hoping that through my life's experiences you will see, as the old hymn states, "…There is no other way to be happy in Jesus, but to trust and obey."

If in the reading of my accounts of life you too will say (as I have said), "I will trust in Him no matter what!" Then, I think I have accomplished my goal. Gramma and I pray for you always and some of the older ones even more specifically. May God open your eyes to see more of the spiritual realities behind the accounts and experiences than just the physical.

When thinking of a title for my memoirs, the term Pastor Bubna used to describe me came to mind. I wasn't sure it would be a good title, so I ran it by friends and family. To my surprise, most of them immediately agreed that this would be the best title. I don't see myself as that, but it looks like others do, so "Maverick" it is.

Disclaimer

I refer to those that live in the Democratic Republic of the Congo as Congolese and sometimes as Zairian. Those who lived during the name change to Zaire were called Zairians, but in actual fact they were always Congolese. The people never changed, the country never moved. President Mobutu just decided to change the name to further his own interests. It is hard for me to call the people that I served and worked with two different names while I view them as one group, the "Congolese people" or simply, "The Congolese".

In fact, the **Bakongo**, or the **Kongo people**, also referred to as the **Congolese**, are a Bantu ethnic group who live along the Atlantic coast of Africa from Pointe Noire (the Republic of Congo) to Luanda, Angola.

It is most likely the Kongo people arrived in the region of the mouth of the Congo River before 500 BCE, as part of the larger Bantu migration. The region that is now the Democratic Republic of the Congo was first settled about 1400 years ago. It is supposed that Bantu migration arrived in the region from Nigeria in the 7th century AD. The Kingdom of the Kongo remained present in the region between the 14th and the early 19th centuries. In time the spelling was changed to "Congo". [3] When I refer, then, to the people of Zaire or the DRC as Congolese, I refer to them as historically named and as an ethnic group which doesn't change even though the country name may change.

In France, 1972

In Canada 2015

---

[3] *https://en.wikipedia.org/wiki/Kongo_people*

Table of Contents

SECTION ONE

My Grandpa in his mid-50s and my dad in his mid-20s.

TO THE READER:
You will soon realize that in the telling of my story I refer to my wife, Dawn, as "Gramma" and my children (Loralee, Rod and Jon Marc) as Auntie and Uncle. My original target audience was my eleven grandchildren. But as the book grew and took shape, my friends and family suggested that I should put the book out there for other friends and the general public to read. This I have done, but have not changed the target audience. All are welcome to read and share these stories according to your own interest level.

Part I -The Early Years

Chapter One: An African Fable

Fifakio (Pronounced fee-fa-key-oh)

It all began when there was much hunger in the animal village deep in the rain forests of Central Africa. But this particular year the rains had refused to come. Mr. Turtle due to his longevity, his wealth of knowledge and his inexhaustible wisdom had become not only the chief of this village but also of the whole region. Being the oldest and wisest chief in the area, he was also the village counselor and judge. No one was older, wiser or more knowledgeable.

However, during this serious time of drought, not even he had much counsel or advice for the starving animals in the village. They all simply had to tie in their belt strings and simply wait it out. Yet there was one in the village who could not abide by the idea of doing nothing. Along with all the other inhabitants of the village, he was told not to stray far from his home in this time of crisis. Many were on the lookout for food and he might just end up on someone's table! Above all, if anyone chanced upon some food, he should share it with all—as was always their custom

Fifakio [fee-fa-key-oh] was his name. He was a young snake, but an upstanding member of the village counsel. Every day, along with all the other animals, Fifakio became thinner and thinner. His stomach began to growl so loud that it was hard for him to sleep at night. He would often go out of his hut in the middle of the night, wandering around, seeking any morsel of food that might have dropped from a tree or from some other villager that just might have had a crumb or two to eat. One night as he was gazing into the darkness of the thick African forest, with only the lights of the stars to illuminate his path, he saw in the distance a thin flicker of light, on the hill side, far from his village.

Curiosity got the best of him and although Chief Turtle repeatedly warned him not to stray from the village during these extremely hard times, he put his mind to seeing where that flicker of light had come from and began to slither up the nearside of the hill for a better look.

Of course, the closer he got to the light, the brighter it became until he could see that it was not just a light, but a complete compound with house, yard, and chicken coup. Ah, he thought, one of the feared humans must live here and the light that I see comes from his lamps keeping out the darkness of the jungle. He must be guarding something of value burning that light all night.

Sure enough, as Fifakio slithered closer he began to hear the soft noises of chickens roosting in their coup. He looked around the coup but there was no way in as the door was tightly closed. However, as he circled the coup he chanced upon a knothole just big enough to allow him to gain entrance into the shed.

He pulled himself through. As he began to make his way stealthily among them, the chickens did not feel at all comfortable. He was not about to make much noise and arouse the whole compound, but these chickens were not of his village and began to cackle and cause a great noise. Soon the light outside became brighter. Fifakio quickly went to the nesting areas and swallowed an egg and then darted toward the knothole. Now with the egg bulging in his body, he could not make it through the hole that was just big enough to let him pass. So, he quickly backed out, threw himself against the ground this way and that until the egg inside was broken and then he slipped away through his opening just as the light came so near as to almost blind him.

He slithered down the hill to his village and silently into his house where in the morning he was the most content of all the animals in the village. This was recognized by not a few of his neighbors and soon he was accused of finding food and not sharing it with all. He complained bitterly that they were falsely accusing him and so they ceased from their railings against him for after all, due to their emaciated condition, they did not have that much strength for this sort of thing.

The next night, Fifakio did the same thing. He slithered up the hill, in through the knot whole, swallowed an egg, threw himself on the ground, broke the egg and slithered through the hole down the hill and silently into his house, disturbing no one, not even the chickens. This continued for several days until the neighbors recognized that as they were getting thinner and weaker Fifakio was getting fatter and stronger. There was certainly something wrong here and the villagers knew it. He was immediately accused before Chief Turtle. Fifakio was called to present himself before the chief and the council.

Although Fifakio vehemently denied that he was getting any nourishment on the side, the evidence was strongly stacked against him by the fact that he was stronger and healthier than any of the others in the village. At the insistence of Chief Turtle, Fifakio finally capitulated and told the story of seeing the light in the forest, finding the eggs and how he would steal away each evening and swallow one and then return to his home.

Chief Turtle knew about the human who lived on the hill and he, along with the whole village, reprimanded Fifakio severely. The Chief also gave him wise counsel. He said that he was glad to see Fifakio looking so good and he realized that this was a source of nourishment that could not be shared with others, but he also stipulated that indeed it was not wise to take from the human that which he deemed most precious. For the human is cunning and wise even more so than the serpent and in the end the human will have his retribution. Chief Turtle forbade him from ever going there again, though all understood it was a great temptation and a way of escaping the suffering of the great famine.

Fifakio, now warned, was all the more on the alert, but did not heed the advice of the Chief. He went even later in the dark of the night and got his egg, repeating his ritual of breaking the egg once inside him and then making it home without being detected.

Not long after the counsel of the villagers and Chief turtle, the human began to understand what was happening and why he was losing so many eggs. So, early one evening he gathered all the eggs and put several of them in boiling water for many minutes. He then took them and planted them in the nests of the chickens. Fifakio, deeming himself more intelligent than all his neighbors, even his Chief and the human, made his usual trek up the hill in the dead of night. He found his favorite knothole, slithered through, found an especially warm egg and this time took another. He began his usual ritual, but the eggs did not break. The chickens began to squawk and make a great noise. He threw himself against the ground, then against the side of the coup and then tried to make it through the knothole, all to no avail. All of a sudden, the door of the coup opened, the light shone bright, he heard the humans say, "There you are, you thief!" Quietly and swiftly there was a flash of the machete and immediately the eggs were broken, but Fifakio was no more. The animals of the village saw him no longer, but the rains did come and soon the famine was broken.

An African Understanding

One should always follow wise counsel. One cannot just look after himself and ignore the sentiments, the well-being, the counsel and the wisdom of his family, friends and neighbors for in the end, if he does, it will bring about his destruction.

A Scriptural or Moral Understanding

Obeying the counsel of many is the beginning of wisdom. To disobey is the beginning of destruction. God admonishes us to obtain counsel. Proverbs 12:15 states, "The way of a fool is right in his own eyes, But a wise man is he who listens to counsel" (NASB), and Proverbs 15:22 reads, "Plans fail for lack of counsel, but with many advisers they succeed."

Chapter Two: The Ambition

My Youthful Fifakio Patterns of Thought

A sugar cube went whizzing past my head. I looked up and saw this bulk of a young man sneering at me. My friend Bob and I were coming home from Cultus Lake, not too late, and stopped to have a burger. We had fun listening to the Liechtensteiner Polka on the jute box at this roadside stand. I guess Bob really liked it as he, for the second time, put a quarter in and pressed the button 5 times so the song would play over and over again. The fairly inebriated "bull" or "bully" couldn't stand our laughing every time the same song kept on repeating itself, so he thought he would let me know. The sugar cube was thrown hard and fast, but hit the wall behind be. Mine was thrown a tad more accurately and hit the top of his head. That was the end of it all.

Lots of guys were there and we had a fun time, I was about 17 at the time. Bob had the family car and it was time to go home. The drunk bully (older and heavier than I) was leaning against the front of a car when we went out.

"Come over here," he slurred. I ignored him.

"Hey, come over here, c'mon, I've got som'thin' to tell ya." He gently mumbled.

"OK" I said, and went over to him. He indicated that I step closer and I did.

"You know wha' I think of you?" he blurted. He then got all his beer spittle together and spit full force right into my face. "That's what I think of you!"

All my parents counsel from my Christian up bringing went out of my soul in a flash; no wise advice had time to calm down my spirit. My fist went hard and fast and landed in an instant on the side of his face. The brawl began! He got in a few licks, but I backed him up so hard against the stucco wall of the restaurant that I thought his head would break, but he really was hard headed! With a last hard hit to his temple, I finally knocked him down and then he thought I was a good guy and kept on repeating that as he got up and staggered to his friend's car. My head was throbbing; I thought I would have some explaining to do when I got home. I was in deep doodoo! I crept into the house and into my bed while the house was silent. "The next morning will be soon enough to account for my actions," I thought. But the next morning there was not a sign on my face. I guess my thick wool Indian jacket that he pulled over my head had softened the blows and no explanation was needed. "Fifakio" was not found out… this time!

My Youth

I was brought up in a Christian home. My dad was born into a Mennonite family in Canada in 1903, in a sod hut in the area of Aberdeen, Saskatchewan.

And somewhere in a Mennonite community in the Ukraine (Russia) my mother was born a few months earlier that same year. Dad was reared on a farm in Aberdeen, Saskatchewan, where I was born (in 1941). My mother came to Canada with her parents in 1910-11. They settled in Vanderhoof, BC, but it wasn't long before her whole family moved to Winkler and Morden, Manitoba.

My earliest recollection of going to church was in Chilliwack where my folks, along with a few other families, started a new church plant called the Chilliwack Alliance Church. As a little boy of 3 or 4 I remember meeting in the hall of the United Church in Chilliwack and listening to my dad sing in a quartet. My parents' background was with the Mennonite Brethren Church, but along with 4 or 5 other former Mennonite families decided that the CMA was a better fit for them. There were a lot of Mennonite believers in the area, so much so that when the Christian and Missionary Alliance planted their churches in Chilliwack, Abbotsford and Yarrow some referred to the churches as the Christian and Mennonite Alliance.

Jimmy – age 5

I went to church every Sunday with my parents and even during week days when there was a special speaker for the week or a missionary conference. During the school year of 1948-49, I went forward for prayer while attending one of these week day special meetings and prayed with Pastor Paul Edwardson. I expected lights to flash, but nothing really happened. In my mind it didn't "take" and

I began looking in another direction for fun and excitement, often skipping church to ride on the bus or later going out with friends in their little British car for a cruise around town. Then we would slip into church during the last prayer, go to the basement washroom and ascend when everyone was coming out—acting as if I had been there all the time. Like Fifakio, I was attempting to fool the whole "village", not taking the advice of my elders or my parents. But it had to come to an end!

In my "muddled" (middle) teen years this whole charade became monotonous to the point where I told my mom one day that Sunday School was a drag; I wasn't going to do my Sunday School lessons anymore. I didn't want to go to church and I didn't want her to ever speak to me of Jesus again! This broke my mother's heart, but I couldn't live a life of hypocrisy any longer.

Jimmy age 11, Alf age 16

My Future in the Field of Jazz

Music was always a big part of my life. My parents and all my siblings were musical and so were my grandparents—on both sides. The Sawatsky family, my dad's parents and his siblings all sang and/or played an instrument (including the piano). At least four of the Bauman brothers, on my mother's side played violin and other stringed instruments. During family visits or reunions, it was not uncommon for the families to gather around the piano, pick an instrument or two and have a good song fest of gospel music. It wasn't strange that I grew up singing parts and hearing good harmonies in my head. I had heard that since birth! At an early age, I had a strong boy soprano voice. So much so that in grade school the teacher always wanted me to sing in front of the class. I even sang a solo over the church radio broadcast when I was about 4 or 5.

My grandpa, Henry Sawatzky, told me how he had learned to play the trumpet as a young man living in the Ukraine farm lands of Russia. He was forced to join the Russian Military, but being a conscientious objector, he was sent to Siberia to build railroads as part of his military training. One day coming to the barracks, tired and dirty after a hard day's work, he heard a band playing and soon found out it was the military band of his company. He thought to himself, "I can do this" and immediately requested to join the band to learn to play trumpet. He was granted that request and made such good strides in playing that soon was playing the 1st trumpet parts.

Not long after that he became band master and began writing/composing his own band music for the military. Because the Russian military was so poor, grandpa said that he would send away for the 1st trumpet part only, of a march he liked, and then he would compose all the other parts for the rest of the band. And even sometimes he would write his own music including all the parts for all the other instruments.

In the process of immigrating to Western Canada, just before my dad was born, he was sitting in the railway station in Canada (waiting for his ticket to come west) when his name was called to go to the wicket. Being on the ready, he jumped up and went to where he was called, leaving his precious brief case and all his music where he had been sitting. When he got back, his brief case was gone! He was devastated! He recounted with great sadness how that many years later when he was in a hotel room on July 1st in Saskatoon, he heard his music being played by a marching band on the official Independence Day of Canada.

It wasn't surprising then to my family that I wanted to join the junior high beginner's band and learn how to play the trumpet. My parents agreed and I began my first personal adventure in music. I did so well in the first months of the beginner band that the conductor said he wanted me to come and join the junior band which would be more of a challenge for me. I agreed, but when I tried to play with the junior band the music went so fast that I could only read one note in six or 10, even though I was only playing 3rd trumpet. Riding my bike on the way home, after that first Junior Band practice, at age 12, I cried most of the way, thinking that I would never be able to play such complicated music. I wasn't going back! But somehow, I went back to the next practice and it didn't seem quite so hard! Before long, I too, like my grandfather, was playing first trumpet in the junior band, then in the senior band and in the Chilliwack city band—being then in my mid-teens.

Two Significant Events

Around this same time, there were two significant "happenings" in my life. One, I had asked to join the jazz band because they requested someone to come and play the bass (fiddle). I thought I could do that and tried out. The Art teacher, Robert Steele, a great jazz pianist, thought I was a

Jim

natural and gave me the position. I began playing by ear, but soon he requested that I take a few lessons from a friend in the military band stationed near Chilliwack. I said I would be glad to as he had arranged that these lessons would be free. To my surprise the "teacher" turned out to be my trumpet teacher, so we knew each other well and he was

Louis "Satchmo" Armstrong

only too willing and keen to help me on the bass. From that point on I learned hand positions and learned to read notes in the bass clef. The high school band director found out about this and no longer allowed me to play trumpet in the high school band—only the bass. The trumpet was relegated to the city band and the rube band at sports events and city hockey games!

I really enjoyed playing the bass in the high school jazz band and even played for dances, sock hops etc.—of course without my parents' knowledge or consent. I began thinking of making a career in music. Musicians like Harry James and Louis "Satchmo" Armstrong were my heroes. My ambition was to join the military band in Chilliwack (Sardis area), learn to play the trumpet really well and then go on to Toronto Conservatory of Music to learn theory, composition and whatever else would be helpful. Then I would work on setting up my own band. Trumpet would be my primary instrument. The bass and guitar would be my secondary instruments. Both my music teacher and the jazz band leader thought this a good goal and encouraged me in it.

I tried playing my trumpet like them. A plan was forming!

At the same time, however, because of my love for music and singing, I had joined the church choir. I had also started a quartet group in high school, singing at different functions, which was great fun. Actually, we were four guys left singing in the showers after basketball games and it just developed from there. Also, I was playing instrumental duets in church with my buddy Gracen (trombone and trumpet). I loved music and would sing or play anywhere.

The second event was not so praise worthy or enjoyable. One day, during this involvement in jazz and other music (during my Junior year

Dennis, Gracen and Jim in the center. Vic

in High School), the pastor of the church came to see me and said he would like to chat. "OK," I said, thinking that he too would acknowledge my prowess in music— not thinking that anything was wrong. He said that he had heard that I was playing in the jazz band and playing for dances on Saturday nights, but on Sunday morning I was singing in the choir. I agreed, thinking this was pretty cool. Then he dropped the bomb and told me that I couldn't do both! I had to choose. Well, I immediately thought of how my life was going to be in the jazz field, so it was an easy choice. I would drop the choir—not the answer he wanted to hear. But for me at the time it wasn't a difficult choice. I thought it strange, a bit humiliating, and I was a bit disgusted with the pastor, but it wasn't a hard decision to make. He went away sad. I was an arrogant and cocky maverick, but deep down inside, I respected his principles and respected the fact that he had the guts to let me know that as a non-believer I couldn't sing things I didn't believe in—living as I pleased the rest of the week. I needed to come clean... and so I did—on the other side of the fence. I heard his advice, but like Fifakio I didn't change my ways.

No Time for Church and Religion

The rebuke from the pastor gave me respect for him and the things that he stood for, but it was a further indication to me that I didn't need the church and what it stood for. By this time, I had seen how the church had hurt my dad—he wasn't attending anymore—and now it was my turn to shun what I thought were legalistic rules that should have no authority in my life. During this time, I began doing a lot of things on my own. I experimented with different kinds of alcoholic drinks and different cigarettes. I snuck out at night, took my dad's car and drove out to the country to see my girlfriend. We had a secret signal when I approached her house, so that she knew it was me and then she too snuck out and joined me as we rode around the country side, or just parked.

As I look on it now, it was foolish and haughty on my part to be driving all over East Chilliwack late in the evenings without a license. Thankfully for me at the time my dad never found out for he always left the keys in the car and didn't pay attention to the mileage or gas indicator—which wasn't so accurate in the cars in those days anyhow!

Severing ties with the choir meant severing ties with the church. I only went on Sunday mornings to please my parents. One Saturday night Gracen, Rudy and I were going to play a prank on some guys who were visiting "our" girlfriends while they were having a pajama party. Things got a little out of hand and when we met them outside in the dark trying to find their car, which we had pushed out of the driveway and down the road, having heard them say what they were going to do to us, we obliged them. Gracen broke his hand on one and I helped the same guy and his friend run into a brick outhouse, or so they put it. That night we were bad dudes!

Later we apologized, but the next morning I saw the guys in church and was really afraid that we were going to be called into the police station and suffer the consequences. Their faces were a mess. I must have been a bad influence on my buddies as they would never have done that on their own. The next day too I had to skirt around what actually happened when Mrs. Beutler called me on the phone and demanded to know why they had to take Gracen to the emergency to have his hand put in a cast. I don't think I ever told her what really happened. I left that up to Gracen himself, but I don't know if he ever told her the real story either.

Fortunately for us, no one ever pressed charges even though I didn't pay the dry-cleaning charges of the expensive coat one of the guys was wearing. I wanted to, but didn't have the money. That whole incident cured all of us from ever fighting again.

Tobacco, Alcohol and Girls

I used to babysit a lot to get some spending money. I was always good with kids and enjoyed looking after them. I guess I got that characteristic from my mom. One night I needed to look after my cousin's young boy, as I had often done in the past. But this night my cousin and military captain husband where going to be out late and told me that I could stay overnight if I liked. That night I decided to experiment some more with the alcoholic beverages that they had in their cupboards. A little gin, a little something else and a little smoking of his pipe with cigarette tobacco (I couldn't find his pipe tobacco). I thought I was having an exciting time until, suddenly, I didn't feel so good!

I ran to the bathroom and threw up profusely, had a terrible headache and couldn't walk straight! The room was spinning. What a horrible experience. I finally went to sleep on the couch and when the parents came home, I must have talked silly as they began laughing at me and the things I was saying. I went back to sleep and didn't move until late next morning. I think they too were sleeping off a hangover. Neither they nor I told my parents of either of our actions, but that experience turned me off alcohol once and for all. I think the Lord allowed me that experience to get me sick of the "stuff" before I really got into it. I thank Him for it.

We played hooky together. Once the 3 of us rode on Gracen's BSA twin motor bike to Cultus lake!

Girls on the other hand were another story. I enjoyed relating to them. At one point, I had a "steady" and she was also in the church, so my parents felt it was OK, I guess. However, I rarely went on a "single" date (except that of sneaking off with my dad's car). We always double dated or dated in groups and later I dated together with Gracen and/or Rudy. Sometimes Gracen and I would even exchange girlfriends. We never thought about how the girls felt. We were just having fun.

In my senior year in high school I knew what it felt like to have one's heart broken over a girl, but I had my jazz and my buddies, so I got over it. At the time though, I thought the world had come to an end!

After high school graduation I really didn't date again, until I met your Gramma. And the rest is history. I will always thank my parents for instilling in me a profound respect for the opposite sex and I thank God that I never violated that respect for my parents, nor for the girls I dated.

Chilliwack High School graduation, 1959

Chapter Three: The Vision and Call

[6] "Alas, Sovereign LORD," I said, "I do not know how to speak; I am too young." [7] But the LORD said to me, "Do not say, 'I am too young.' You must go to everyone I send you to and say I am with you and will rescue you," declares the LORD. Jeremiah 1:6-8(NIV)

The "Missionary Call"

Earlier I mentioned that there were two significant "happenings" in my life. One was the fact that I was able to learn the bass and join the jazz band. The other, around the same time, **I was asked to leave the church choir and in my thinking, I was also leaving the church and "that way of life." Yet during that same time there came a vision and a call.** Some might say that it was a "missionary call."

I was sleeping in on a Saturday morning, as most teens (of 15 or 16 yrs.) love to do. The previous night, I had just snuck into church after a missionary meeting had started and sat in the back seat as the missionary slide presentation was about to begin. I wore my black leather jacket, collar up to hide my identity, but was powerfully drawn to the missionary presentation. Before the meeting was over, I left and walked home. I don't remember what was said or any of the pictures, nor the identity of the missionary, but as I was in a lethargic slumber late the next morning, God gave me a vision.

I saw myself standing near water, perhaps a large river, and I saw that I was handing out Christian literature and telling people about God. They weren't white people, but people of another culture and race. When it came to me what was happening, I immediately sat up in bed (sleep was gone) and said aloud, "God, this is ridiculous! I don't even know who you are, how can I tell anyone about you? What's more, I can't even tell a joke straight to my parents and get them to laugh, how can I explain to anyone the complexities of You and Your Story (the gospel)?!"

The gifts and callings of God are irrevocable[4]

It's a funny thing about God, He doesn't make mistakes! And His "call" isn't just temporary. His call is for life. I knew about God, but

---

[4] *Romans 11:29*

didn't know God at the time. How dare He, how could He, in fact, give me such a vision and call me to be a missionary? Yet, I knew He had! At the moment that I recognized his call on my life, I started running— not toward Him, but away from Him.

Later, when I explained to my parents what I thought was a great ambition and plan for my life—to join the military band, then study music at Toronto Conservatory and eventually have my own big band as did another young man from Chilliwack—they were dead set against it.

"Join the army?" they responded stupefied at the suggestion. "Not on your life!"

"But why not," I immediately responded. "It is a great way to spend a lot of time learning how to play well and even get paid for it! I'm not joining up to fight, but to play in the best band in BC, perhaps even in all of Canada!" The military band in the Sardis Army Camp had a great reputation.

"After all," I reminded them, "my grandpa played in a military band in Russia (Siberia) and he did well. That is how he got all his musical training, that is where he had time to learn how to play the trumpet well and even write new music for the military!"

But the answer was still an emphatic, "No!"

My oldest brother joined the military and he was taken away from the family at 17, never to return (that is, for any length of time). His life principles changed and that wasn't going to happen again to my parents' youngest. I looked for support from my music teacher and from my jazz teacher who agreed with me on the imagined trajectory of my life, but when they heard my parents were not in agreement, they backed right off and said I needed to listen to them. I continued playing my instruments and even got a high school group together, singers and instruments. I played my trumpet in the Chilliwack Senior Band, even marched with them in parades. I played the Bass Violin (bass fiddle) in the High School band and in the jazz band. And, as mentioned, I played trumpet and trombone duets with Gracen who had a good mellow sound on the trombone. We both played in the Chilliwack city band and an ad hoc band for hockey games. My trumpet was my ticket to get in for free as we always had a standing invitation to play. Sometimes not many of us showed up, but we still played. We also played in the high school "rube band" at basketball games, especially when there was a lull in the game.

I loved sports: I did track and field and played basketball for the high school, but if I had a choice, music always came first.

Yet at 17, I was an angry young man—angry at God and my parents! No way could I be thwarted like that! In my mind, I was already running, but now I really upped the energy: running away from God, away from my parents, away from Chilliwack that held these restrictions. I couldn't wait to graduate, so I could take off and be on my own!

1960

Chapter Four: The Escape to Fichtner Lumber

A trip to Prince George

Towards the end of the school year of 1959, I heard my buddies, Gracen and Rudy, talk about an opportunity to go north of Prince George B.C. to work for a logging and sawmill operation. I asked to join them and immediately after graduation the three of us headed up north in Rudy's little Morris Minor convertible. Whoopee, get away from Chilliwack, parents, church and God! I couldn't wait to leave Chilliwack and left high school even before I had finished some of my final government exams. I could write my final math exam in Prince George.

I would lose myself among the rough and tough loggers of the north. I didn't mind that my buddies were much more serious about their relationship with God. One was a preacher's kid and the other a member of a Mennonite Church in Greendale. They had a godly influence on me, but they also knew how to have fun. We had dated together (sometimes the same girls), we rode motor bike together, we sang together, we played our instruments together, we played sports together, and we played hooky from school together. We generally got into mischief together. Yet, they both

Jim   Gracen   Rudy

On the way to Prince George

had certain principles and convictions that would not be broken or traversed. This was a powerful unspoken message to me who abandoned most of the Christian principles of my upbringing. But, they were cool guys, good friends and they both had motor bikes--Rudy a very early-dated Harley and Gracen a relatively up to date BSA twin that flew like the wind—or so we thought.

Rudy also had a Morris Minor convertible and was ready to take it to Prince George, so we piled all our stuff in the trunk and the back seat and the three of us took off. And, I did write my final math exam in Prince George! I passed it too! We didn't have much money and we were too cheap to pay the full price for the three of us to stay in a room, so we always sent at least one guy to rent the room, sometimes two, and then snuck the other one or two in after finding the back door or the fire escape. We stayed in the poorest, cheapest rooms for rent we could find and sometimes all three of us slept in one bed!

Several times we made so much noise (laughing and fooling around) that the proprietor would knock on the door, asking us to open up so he could check to see how many were in the room. We always managed to show only the persons who had rented it while the others were adept in finding some space to hide without being detected! It never occurred to us that we were cheating or misrepresenting ourselves. We just felt we couldn't pay more and did our own thing, of course behind the backs of those running the "rooms for rent". It must have been a little different in those days! In any case, we made it to the lumber camp north of Prince George, where I thought I would meet up with the "rough and tough" loggers and lumber jacks and begin doing my own thing. Little did I know that God has a great sense of humor!

Lumber Camp Church Group

In that one lumber camp and sawmill operation, about 90 miles north of Prince George, deep in the BC forest, HE had invited (it seemed like to me) a delegate or two from every Bible College in the nation and there was no way for me to escape HIS presence. These guys formed a camp church, held prayer meetings, prayed before meals, and even took turns preaching on Sundays. I couldn't believe it! Christians surrounded me! Guys who lived to please God, guys who gave their whole lives to God and encouraged us to do the same. Well, so much for the rough and tough loggers! Oh, there were a few, but you couldn't really get near them, they were doing their own thing and wouldn't come near these Bible thumpers who I hung with because of my buddies Gracen and Rudy.

I didn't go to all their meetings, but did play in a brass ensemble—a group of four. Gracen and I had brought our instruments along, and

so did a couple of other guys. We had a quartet of two trumpets and two trombones and sounded not too badly—actually, we were asked to play in a kids' camp and at church (again!) on some weekends. Music always drew me in to the church. I couldn't say no to music! I loved to play …and sing!

Gracen is on the left and I am standing in the center on the jack ladder.

In my solitary moments, I had somber thoughts that nothing was going right. I couldn't pursue my music dream as I wanted, I couldn't even run from God— "The Hound of Heaven".[5] And on top of that, this vision of being a missionary kept coming back to me. I wasn't a terrible guy, or so I thought, thanks to my parents and my friends' influence on me. They sneered at my smoking, saying that athletes, as in basketball and track and field, can't perform well while filling their lungs with smoke! So, the cigarettes went out the window. They frowned on swearing and alcohol, so I didn't do that. And we only took out girls to have fun, not to get into a sexual relationship of any kind (thanks to all our parents)! BUT nothing was working out for me. I felt like I had no future and I would end up a bum on skid row—a homeless, worthless social outcast! Yet, I wouldn't give in to "the vision"!

A Bleak Future

They say that if you aim at nothing in life, you'll hit it every time! Up till now my goals had all been shot down, I really had no purpose in life. Now I was aiming at nothing and was successful in hitting it. During this time, my mind would fly back on occasion to an interview I had with the school counselor. We called him Pappy Orme. When he asked of my plans for the future I gave a very vague answer but also

---

[5] *"The Hound of Heaven" is a poem written by English poet Francis Thompson (1859–1907). Thompson's work was praised by G.K. Chesterton and it was also an influence on J.R Tolkien -* https://en.wikipedia.org/wiki/The_Hound_of_Heaven

included that I might even go to university one day (just to rub him a bit). It worked! He immediately jumped on me (verbally) and said that I was too insincere (for lack of a "better" word) and that I would never even darken the door of a university. I didn't have the brains or the jam to make it! Well, at that put-down he got my dander up.

Although I didn't say anything I certainly thought of a few words, including, "I'll show you! Wouldn't you be surprised if I graduated from UBC and came back to rub your nose in my BA degree?" (In looking back on that incident many years later, I was thinking that my reaction was exactly what he desired from me. I'm only sorry that I wasn't able to let him know how he motivated me at the time!)

But now in the logging camp, at age 18 it seemed like he was right and I had no future. I knew in my heart that I was headed in the direction of being that homeless guy in a squalid district inhabited by derelicts and vagrants. Nothing was going right! I was hitting the target of "nothing!"

Rudy left early to go to grade 13 in Chilliwack. Gracen and I hitch hiked home. While in the countryside around Penticton, it just happened that I got a ride all the way home. We took turns "thumbing" and while Gracen was sleeping this young man stopped for me. I shouted for Gracen, but the guy wouldn't wait. He took me right to Chilliwack. Gracen followed shortly after.

When I got home there was no one there and the house was locked solid. Only an experienced inhabitant of the house knew how to break in and I did. By crawling into the cemented crawl space that could be entered through the carport, I came into the house via a trap door in the floor. My first thought was that the Lord had come and my parents were taken. I was left. But then I saw a few other people who should have been taken if that had happened and I was consoled. I found out in the next few days that my parents had found an apartment in North Vancouver, dad had a construction job there and they were going to move there in the next few days. I had no other place to go, so eventually I went with them, leaving even my best friends behind. Everything seemed to be pulled out from under my feet and I had nothing to stand on. And that is when there was an about turn in my life, when "heaven came down and glory filled my soul!"

A Complete Turn Around

One evening in my brother Alf's front room after singing together with him and some other guys, just for pure enjoyment, I suggested that we form a Sawatsky brothers' quartet. Our eldest brother, Larry, who was living in the Vancouver area at the time, had a great tenor voice and we had a cousin that sang bass. We could do it! But my brother's response was, "Yeah… and where would we sing?" Well, I guessed we could start in church. What a mixed-up mind I had! He straightened me out fast. He said, "Our brother Larry is not a professing Christian and neither are you and you think we could sing in church, not having the faintest idea of what we are singing about!" He continued with, "It doesn't work that way! You'd be singing a lie every time you stood up in church to sing as you don't believe a word you're singing!" That stopped me cold in my tracks. He was right! Again, another disappointment!

"But", he said, "It doesn't have to be that way," and he began sharing the good news of the Gospel with me. After much talk--it was already getting quite late and my sister-in-law had already gone to bed--I just sat gripping the piano bench with white knuckles, experiencing conviction. There was a great inner struggle going on. I couldn't pray, I couldn't ask God to forgive me, but I knew in my heart it was now or never. Finally, unlike "Fifakio" I took the counsel given me. I needed to make a change or I would experience certain death of soul. After what seemed like a long time of silence, I blurted out, in a loud voice, "Lord be merciful to me a sinner" …a phrase my brother suggested and a phrase we knew from the Bible! Well, immediately God acted. I felt what the song writer penned--that **"Heaven Came Down and Glory Filled My Soul!"**[6]

After having cried out this phrase, after confessing my sin and receiving His forgiveness, the flood gates of heaven were opened and I spent a good part of the rest of the night on my knees in prayer. My experience that night in my brother's front room, while my sister-in-law was praying in the bedroom, is best described in the words of this song written by John Peterson (on the next page).

Immediately my understanding of the future changed. I knew the next morning that I was no longer going to end up on skid road. I had

---

[6] *John Peterson https://austinbhebe.wordpress.com/2013/01/08/heaven-came-down-and-glory-filled-my-soul/*

a vision to fulfill; a calling to which I was now saying, "Yes, I hear you. I'll be right there!" And the first step I felt I needed to take was to get to Bible College to start my Bible and Theology training. I told my dad the next morning of my salvation experience as I came to work (I was working for him on a warehouse construction project). I told him that now I had a reason for being and that I would now be saving my money for Bible College. I don't remember my dad or my mom saying too much, but I could tell they were well pleased.

It was the fall of '59 and they were praising God that their "wayward son," their youngest, had returned home to his Heavenly Father.

Heaven Came Down and Glory Filled My Soul

O what a wonderful, wonderful day, Day I will never forget;
After I'd wandered in darkness away, Jesus my Savior I met.
O what a tender, compassionate friend,
He met the need of my heart;
Shadows dispelling, with joy I am telling,
He made all the darkness depart!
CHORUS:
Heaven came down and glory filled my soul,
When at the cross the Savior made me whole;
My sins were washed away, and my night was turned to day-
Heaven came down and glory filled my soul!

Born of the Spirit with life from above,
Into God's family divine,
Justified fully through Calvary's love, O what a standing is mine!
And the transaction so quickly was made
When as a sinner I came,
Took of the offer, Of grace He did proffer-
He saved me, O praise His dear name!

Now I've a hope that will surely endure
After the passing of time;
I have a future in heaven for sure.
There in those mansions sublime.
And it's because of that wonderful day
What at the cross I believed;
Riches eternal and blessings supernal
From His precious hand I received.

Part II – The Preparation Years

Chapter Five: The Preparation Begins
I now entered what I call, my "10 Year Boot Camp"

My father's construction job was all too soon completed and I had to look for another job that would get me to Bible College in Regina-- that is, to pay for my tuition, meals and lodging. My aim was to follow the call of God and get started as soon as possible. By the beginning of the school year of 1960, I wanted to be at Canadian Bible College. Little did I know that I would be starting this new life right from the nuts and bolts up, quite literally, for my next job was in a "nuts and bolts" factory! A good "Boot Camp" experience for this novice. I did not in the least suspect that God was going to put me through ten years of it before He gave me the green light to be His "sent one".

At the same time, I felt I needed to discover a church and a youth group where I could find Christian fellowship. I had had a Christian girlfriend in Chilliwack, but once I left there for Fichtner, I wasn't going back and besides I was now living for a brief time in North Vancouver with my parents. Gracen's dad was called to a new church in Oroville, Washington, so he was going to grade 13 in the Okanagan and Rudy was doing grade 13 in Chilliwack. We would still remain friends, but our lives were now tracking in different directions.

Being brought up in a C&MA[7] church, my attention was drawn to the 10th Avenue Alliance Church, near Broadway and Main in Vancouver. I enjoyed Pastor Brooks' preaching on Sundays, but needed friendship with young adults my own age who were interested in following Jesus. I looked for the youth group, which I found quite quickly, and started attending their meetings. Always being interested in the opposite sex, I scanned the group for a girl that might be interesting for me to get to know. Not a one, and no one really befriended me! My first experience there in the youth group was uneventful. Fortunately, I had come with a friend from Chilliwack and we stuck together. He too was seeking more of God.

However, not seeing anyone of interest didn't deter me from attending the youth group again. Girls or no girls I was committed to getting involved with Christian peers and soon was even asked to take part in a play that the young people were doing. I was to play opposite

---

[7] *The Christian and Missionary Alliance*

the leading role, a girl named Ruth, who was a very pleasant and a good-looking gal, but way too old for me—somewhere in her mid-twenties, or so I thought. Unbeknownst to me, Ruth went home and told her younger sister that she had met this "cute" new guy at youth group and that she should come next time. So, she did!

A Jaw-Dropping, Good-Looking Gal!

It happened that on a subsequent visit to the "Young People's Group", as they called it, I saw a gal that really interested me and decided that at the very least I should get to know her.

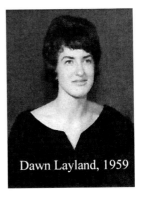

Dawn Layland, 1959

I had just come out of the men's washroom and who should be walking in through the basement doors on this Friday evening but the most striking girl I had seen since I started attending that church. I said to myself, "That's her! That's the one I've been looking for! Oh yeah, I need to get to know her!" Actually, she was "jaw-dropping" good looking and elegant! I thought that she was way above my pay grade and social level, but that didn't stop me!

It was the custom that after the youth meeting, we all went up to the gym to play volleyball. Well, I had to get on the same team as this slim, trim beauty (about my age to boot)! No "ifs" or "buts" about it! And, I managed it somehow! But that wasn't enough. I had to get to play next to her, so I could strike up a conversation. And it happened! At one point we were talking so much that the volley ball fell right between us and we didn't even see it coming! Boy, were we scorned! But it was worth the scorn and I never looked back!

After the volleyball game, I was determined to give her a ride home, but she was nowhere to be found. I went to my hot rod '49 Ford dejected, but as I was walking to my car I saw in the darkness of the night a figure walking briskly up the hill beside the church. It was her!

"Hey", I said, "Do you need a ride home?" By this time, I was standing beside my sleek automobile, under the street light, with my front door open revealing the maroon and white pleated leatherette upholstery and I knew that if she caught a good view of the complete package (the car that is), she could not resist saying yes. My thinking was that if she didn't care much for me, she would at least be enticed by the blanked out and lowered, metallic sky blue "hot-rod" with oversized tires and twin exhausts! But she simply said, "Oh, I already have a ride, thank you!" and kept on walking. Little did I know that she had arranged for a young man, a six foot something athlete, with another shiny car to come and pick her up after youth group to take her home.

I surely felt disappointed, but again not daunted. I

knew her name was Dawn Layland and in time I would be able to "take her home" all the way to Coquitlam. Early in the New Year of 1960 I had set it up so that after a skating party the youth were putting on I would take her home. We would meet at the rink. Normally I wouldn't have gone to an ice skating party as I really didn't know how to skate that well, but her sister Ruth also encouraged me. So, we all met at the rink.

I saw how effortlessly they glided around the skating rink and thought, "There is no way I'm going to get out there and fall on my tush in front of them and everyone else!" But they had pity on me and they grabbed me by the arms, one on each side and away we went. Hey, a bit of humiliation, but two cuties, one on each arm, what was there to lose! I "suffered" until it was time to leave and then I finally could take this gal with the wonderful name home. Being alone with "Dawn" for the first time was a real treat. She really didn't notice the car, but now I didn't care much about it either. My attention was completely diverted and I soon had this sneaky feeling that she was the one that would be with me the rest of my life!

That night I found out that she was only 15; I was only 18 (the same age as her sister Ruth!). I also found out that she felt called to be a missionary--I couldn't believe it! Well that almost sealed the deal for me! But it wasn't until five years later that by God's plan we found ourselves at the altar of 10th Avenue Church, in front of Pastor Brooks repeating our wedding vows. Incidentally, the wedding celebration was August 1st, 1964, together with Gramma's sister Auntie Ruth and Uncle Norm Wylie, in a double wedding ceremony. It was also the day of your great grandparents' 25th wedding anniversary, George and Florence Layland.

Humbling Experiences—Total Confirmation!

A lot happened during those 5 ensuing years after our first date. I would take her home from church most of the time, often together with her sister and on the way home we began to sing. That was the beginning of our trio and we sang together all through our Bible College years. We even travelled a bit for the College, but we never had a special name. When we were introduced once by uncle George's brother, Jack Schroeder (pastor of the Kelowna Alliance Church at the time), he mentioned that I was his brother's brother-in-law and Dawn was my wife. Then he came to introduce Ruth who was, and I quote, "my sister-in-law's, sister-in-law's sister." We all had a good laugh and later figured out that he was right!

After the construction job with my dad was completed, I was a "government fresh air inspector" for a few grueling months (on Unemployment Insurance, as they called it then). I definitely needed to get employment and save for Bible College, so I hunted high and low for anything that would bring in some money! I finally got a job in a "nuts and bolts" factory, putting nuts on bolts all day long—a great study in perseverance and good lessons in patience and humility (the Lord knew I needed that). This was also where I learned to praise God and sing at the top of my voice. It was so loud in the factory no one could hear me—or so I thought. I later found out that they did hear me and were puzzled about this young man who was singing his way through the day doing such menial tasks?

It was during this time, coming home from seeing my new girlfriend late one night, that God spoke to me through John 15:16 and confirmed his call on my life. In this new decision I had made, this newly-found life *I had chosen*, **I** was happy that **I** had finally made the right choice! **I had chosen** to give in to this "Hound of Heaven." Right from the start, I had begun the habit of reading a passage from the Bible before hitting the sheets at night and praying. That night was no exception. Although I was sleepy, with eyes half closed I read the following:

*"**You did not choose me**! **But I chose you** and **ordained you**, **s**o that you might go and bear fruit—fruit that will last—and so that whatever you ask in my name the Father will give you."* Jn.15:16

This verse was a real shocker to me, another humbling experience. Wow! It really woke me up, immediately! Up till this point I was thinking how glad I was that I had finally chosen to follow Christ and then in my reading I came to this verse which hit me like a knock-out blow. "YOU didn't choose ME, I chose YOU!" It was God all the way. But He didn't stop there. He said "…and furthermore, I ordained or 'appointed' you for a reason and that reason is that you should go and bear fruit!" That was total confirmation right there that I was on the right track, but **I** wasn't at the helm. It was all HIS doing, I wasn't in charge; I was just following HIS lead! In doing that—confirming His call, confirming the "Vision" all the while knocking the wind out of my sails—HE also gave me a promise for encouragement: "Whatever you ask in His Name, the Father will give it to you." Wow again! What a promise! I knew enough by then, through my upbringing, that this wasn't a "carte blanche" for new cars and houses and lands and whatever else I wanted. No, this promise was for a higher purpose. The message to me was that He would provide all that I needed in "bearing fruit." He would provide through His Father all that I needed for ministry and for the glory of His Name. And He did just that!

Not straightaway, but not long after this He also showed me His thoughts on cars, houses and lands, brothers and sisters: His solid lay away plan for the future. He directed me to Mark 10:28-30 where it says, [28]*Then Peter spoke up, "We have left everything to follow you!"* Peter spoke for the other disciples, but it was a message for me as well—to leave everything behind and follow Jesus! At the thought of leaving everything behind—family, friends and ownership—I definitely felt a sense of remorse. This was life without anything at all! Yet, with this self-denial, His encouragement also came.

[29]*"Truly I tell you," Jesus replied, "no one who has left home or brothers or sisters or mother or father or children or fields for me and the gospel [30]will fail to receive a hundred times as much in this present age: homes, brothers, sisters, mothers, children and fields—along with persecutions—and in the age to come eternal life.*

As I look back over the years of ministry, in Canada and in Africa, I certainly have found this Word to me to be true. Persecution and tough times have always raised their ugly heads. He didn't promise an easy time, but through the years in Africa God has given us "family" members who are now all over the world. Even now in our home group in Cloverdale we have family outside of our nuclear family. And what's more we have a beautiful house/home that we never in our wildest imaginations could have thought we would have! Throughout these pages you may recognize how the Father has given what we have asked for in the context of bearing fruit and you will also recognize how he has not failed in replacing many times over who and what we had left behind.

Another Trip to Fichtner Lumber Co.

Toward the end of May of that year, 1960, I sold my '49 hot rod Ford, jumped on the back of Gracen's motorbike and went for another stint with Fichtner Lumber—sawmill and logging operations. As I recall we almost killed ourselves a couple of times on the way there and riding around the Prince George area. I think our angels were working overtime. We were even in a serious accident involving a pickup truck in which we were both riding (neither of us driving), but other than a few minor injuries, we made it through the summer safe and sound.

We worked hard, many times 18 hours a day, or should I say night. We opted for the night shift, from 18h00 to 02h00, but if we were all in agreement, the mill could work until dawn! And we generally agreed! We often worked until 6 the next morning, so that gave us a 12-hour shift right there. But often, someone was sick or didn't show for the day shift, so we would sub in at least until noon making it an 18-hour shift.

At one point we were transferred to the planer mill. My job was to feed the lumber into the planer (the machine that would smooth the lumber on all sides). There too we worked our own hours, but I always got a reprieve. The foreman found out that I could fix meals, so he always sent me away before noon and before supper to prepare the meals for the small crew of 4 while he took my place. We were a fair distance away from the main sawmill and well isolated. I shot (with a borrowed .22) a wild rabbit one day to make rabbit stew, but when I got to see the poor thing dead in its tracks, I couldn't bring myself to skin it and dress it. I just buried it and found other meat to use.

Due to fire hazards, the planer mill operation didn't last too long and we were back at the main mill doing night shift! Towards the end of August, I had had enough. My strength was waning, my head wasn't clear for lack of sleep, I missed my girl (Gramma) and I needed to recuperate before leaving for Regina.

Gracen carried on a bit longer, but I quit, got my pay and hitch-hiked home. I had made enough money to pay for all my first-year expenses (tuition and dorm fees etc.) with a little left over for extra activities. I hitch-hiked all day, but only made it half way home. I was in the middle of nowhere and about to crawl into an old abandoned railroad car I spotted to sleep the night away, when I saw in the dusk the lights of a distant car coming. "OK," I thought. "I might as well give it one last try." To my surprise, the car stopped and picked me up. An ex-serviceman from the USA was driving from Alaska to Mississippi and wondered if I knew the way to the nearest border. Well, I wasn't thinking very clearly. I told him that I knew of the border crossing at Sumas, just south of Abbotsford and he agreed to take me there, but wanted me to drive. So, I drove all night and ended up in Abbotsford around 5 in the morning. He took off for Sumas and I went to sleep on a park bench in the then rural town. (Had I been thinking clearly, I would have directed him through the Okanagan and at least down through Osoyoos. However, we did have a great chat about the Lord and I believe the Lord gave me that opportunity to witness to him. And it got me closer to home in North Vancouver.)

Not long after he let me off, I fell asleep on an Abbotsford park bench. A big semi changing gears woke me and I thought of trying to get a ride with him. I jumped up, ran to the side of the road and stuck out my thumb. Again, oddly enough, the truck stopped and picked me up, but the driver told me that he was going to go through Mission and Coquitlam instead of Vancouver. Well, he was my man! My girl lived in Coquitlam, I could go there! When I got to your Gramma's house it was about 6:30 am and no one was stirring. I knocked on the door, woke up the household and collapsed into my girlfriend's arms... well almost. I was so tired, skinny and looked so much like a homeless person that they fed me and put me to bed! Later that day I made it to my parents' home in North Vancouver—but I don't remember how I got there.

"CBC, here I come!"

I do remember though, after I had another good day's rest, my father took me out for coffee and said we needed to chat. He said that he had fallen into very tough times. Mom was working, but they couldn't really make ends meet. Would I be able to loan him $500 until he got work and could pay me back? What to do?! That was almost the entire amount I had saved to pay for my first year's tuition and expenses at Canadian Bible College (close to $10,000.00 or more today). If I loaned him the money, I couldn't go to CBC, but how could I refuse. This was my first big test in trusting God for all my needs. I gave my dad the money and with what was left I made it to CBC and was able to put a little down on my account for the year, trusting the Lord for the rest

I travelled with a carload of five guys from the 10th Avenue Alliance Church youth group. As all of us had only one little suitcase there was no problem stuffing them into the trunk. We called ourselves the 5 Irish Men. There was Joe Ottom (formerly Otomosky or Ottomachuk or something like that), he owned the car and was about 7 years older than the rest of us. Then there was Peter Brucenowsky (now Peter Bruce), Frank Horodyski, Jim Sawatsky and Fred Eldred. Fred was the only real Irishman in the group. The rest of us were all "...sky's!" We had a wonderful time getting there. It took us 19 hours of straight driving, but it sure didn't cost us all that much.

I asked CBC if they could wait a bit for the complete tuition, which they did, and I trusted God to provide the rest for me. They were good at waiting, but also God was great in providing. My mother was able to send some funds, little by little, and often I would find money in my mail box from anonymous donors. By miracle after miracle, money came in and I got through that first-year debt free.

It was a great year! I got to know Ray Downey, who would be a future missionary colleague in the Congo. Ray and I sang in a quartet together that freshman year—not a very good one, but we enjoyed it! While we were out on an assignment one weekend I found out that he had his eye on Viola Wiens from Yarrow. I knew Vi from the Chilliwack/Yarrow area and in fact she was my co-host for the upcoming youth conference. We were one of many couples that would co-host youth on that weekend. We had fun planning …and during the planning I mentioned that a certain young man was interested in her.

That was the spark that started the fire burning and the next thing I knew, they were an item! What fun that was!

I wasn't dating. I had a girl back home. In fact, before I left (at age 19) I had told her that I knew what I wanted in our relationship, but she was young yet (still in high school) and maybe didn't want to commit to a long-distance relationship, so she was free to date and I would be too. She did. I didn't. But we sent many letters back and forth and when she came to that youth conference at CBC, your Gramma and I both found out for sure that this relationship was in for the long haul!

Being sure of a future relationship with this special girl, I enjoyed a lot of friends at CBC, both male and female. We went on day trips together and tried to make the most of the barren lands of Saskatchewan. We pulled a lot of stunts, got caught a few times, but never got caught sneaking out the window of my first-floor room, going out on the town after hours (10pm) having a pop and a burger, if we could afford it! We didn't think of it as breaking the rules, only bending them a little. I always cut hair for a little extra cash—not enough to pay down on my tuition, but enough to buy a burger, sometimes.

My roommate, Mel Dick, was a 2nd year student (we used to call him Mel-keze-Dick after the Old Testament King, Melchizedek) and often throughout the year received care packages from his mom that included butter, peanut butter, jam, cheese and good Mennonite buns. Some of the guys in our residence weren't very happy when my roommate and I shut our door, locked it by pulling out the dresser drawer and then had a feast from his care package from home--with just one or two other guys down the hall. What a feast that would be and we would pile everything on one bun! First came a slab of butter, then a slab of cheese, then peanut butter and at last came the jam! With the door barred, the dorm seemed to know we were feasting. They complained quite loudly and bitterly, but we didn't have enough to feed the whole dorm! Mel was a good roommate!

I remember my first public speaking class. We all had to stand up in front of the auditorium and give, what for many of us was our first speech in front of a group of people. We were all nervous and it didn't help that Mr. Kincheloe would be there grading us. I gave my speech about something innocuous, with "great" gestures (for we were graded on those too). Unbeknownst to me I repeatedly used only one gesture. I would spread out my fingers on both hands in front of me at the same time, in making a good point (like time lapse photography of the opening of a budding flower). Students were snickering. The speech had some funny parts to it, so I thought they were reacting to my sense of humor, until I got Mr. Kincheloe's remarks. "You could vary your gestures," he wrote. My freshman friend across the hall in the men's dorm (Abe Sandler) never let me forget that gesture. He would knock on my door, throw it open, stand there with poker face and give me that same gesture, then close the door and leave me to my humiliation. It was a fun time! …and I never used that gesture again!

Crusaders
Back: Ken McGann, Don Scott, Ray Downey. **F r o n t** Abe Sandler, Jim Sawatsky, Co-captain; Don Sylvester. Captain, Al McVety.

---

[8] Captain Al McVety wasn't able to be present for the picture

Chapter Six: Back to High School
The Continuation of the Ten-Year Boot Camp

A Three-Year Program Crammed into Six.

Throughout my life, I often took consolation in I Corinthians 1:26 – 31.

> [26]*For consider your calling, brethren, that there were not many wise according to the flesh, not many mighty, not many noble;* [27]**but God has chosen the foolish things of the world to shame the wise, and God has chosen the weak things of the world to shame the things which are strong,** [28]**and the base things of the world and the despised God has chosen, the things that are not, so that He may nullify the things that are,** [29]**so that no man may boast before God.** [30]*But by His doing you are in Christ Jesus, who became to us wisdom from God, and righteousness and sanctification, and redemption,* [31]*so that, just as it is written, "LET HIM WHO BOASTS BOAST IN THE LORD."*[9]

I wasn't a dummy, but I knew I wasn't the brightest light in the harbor either. I saw that God was more concerned with an increasing commitment to Him rather than a great intelligence quotient. It seems like your IQ is a ceiling. In other words, when you reach your full potential that's it. It is what you were born with. But you can always be on the growing edge in the faith and commitment arena. When we see wonderful answers to prayer occur we know it wasn't because of our high IQ that things worked out, it was all Him. The greater our commitment the more we can trust Jesus for His intervention and outcome. Then, when we see His miracles take place (in our workaday world), it increases our faith and in our commitment to Him. That is when we understand that we can only boast in Him and not in our IQ!

Up to this point, I had never really applied myself to learning. I didn't really graduate from high school (as seen in the picture) even though I went through the ceremony and received a diploma (false, in fact). My first year at CBC in Regina was starting to wake me up to the world of academia. I realized that I had to make up time for all my tomfoolery in high school. I had to complete my high school university entrance courses if I was to go anywhere. That I did, but I had to work

---

[9] *1 Corinthians 1:26-31New American Standard Bible (NASB)*

Dawn and Ruth Layland fall of 1961, off to Canadian Bible College, Regina

an extra year to catch up in the finance department before getting back to CBC.

After my 2nd year, when we got married, I needed another year of university to graduate with a Bachelor of Religious Education degree. I started at CBC in 1960 and finally graduated (together with Gramma) in 1966. So began the saying that "I crammed a 3-year Bible College program into 6."

I really needed to get those mandatory high school credits to finish my university entrance status, so I went back to high school in North Vancouver. That didn't turn out so great! I was 20 years old by this time and really didn't fit in with the antics of the younger teens, even though they thought I was their same age. During those 3 months that I managed to stay there, I learned to type, which turned out to be a great blessing for the rest of my life, but I just couldn't hang in there for the rest of the stuff. I needed to make trips to Coquitlam to see my lovely girl, but I never had enough money for gas to get there! I was working part time bagging in a local grocery store, but I had to help out with my room and board at home. When some guys and gals around me thought that I was only 16 that was the last straw. I immediately transferred to night school, got a full paying job in a service station, bought a '51 Plymouth coupe and started paying my own way in life!

So, night school it was, for the next school year—working during the day at a Chevron service station, pumping gas, doing lubes and oil changes, repairing tires and studying at night. I still roomed with my parents in North Vancouver and went to see my future wife as often as gas would permit. She lived about 20 miles away in Coquitlam and there was no freeway!

We got to know each other well that year. In the spring of '62 while stopped for a red light in the middle of the city of

Saying good-bye

Vancouver with the ring hot in my pocket, I popped the question. I asked Gramma if she would commit to a very long-term relationship and she said yes. I couldn't contain the excitement in my chest any longer, so I gave her the ring right in the middle of traffic.

Although she was only 17 at the time and still in high school, she accepted the engagement ring. She didn't wear it all the time while in class (I found out later), but she always had it on when we went out. And she wore it when she and her sister Ruth went off to CBC that fall (at age 18).

Chapter Seven: The Tahsis Experience

The Continuation of the Ten-Year Training Camp

After getting my high school diploma, I needed funds big time, for Bible College and marriage. So as Gramma and Ruth found their way to Regina, I secured a job working with a lumber company in Tahsis on Vancouver Island, in the heart of Nootka Sound—another great preparation for future ministry. I had the privilege of sharing Christ with office and mill workers alike. Practical jokes were played on me in the bunk house, like stealing my clothes from the shower room, just to see how I would respond as a Christian—as I streaked buck naked across the public lobby to my little square room. I was always aware of the tests and always tried to respond good-naturedly. I live in a private 7x9 foot square bedroom on the top floor of a

In my 7' x 10' bunk house room in Tahsis, 1961

three-story square bunk house with a center lobby full of diverse kinds of furniture for sitting, lounging and eating. Even though I worked in the office, I had the privilege of living with some of the mill management and eating with them in the mess hall. We had separately prepared food--always good and lots of it!

I found a small protestant chapel there and soon became friends with the lay pastor and family who lived in the basement. I soon found out what it meant to work interdenominationally. I began working with the pastor going out to a mission station hospital called Esperanza on Nootka Sound. Soon I was asked to teach Sunday School in the larger United Church in the town--mainly to junior high girls. We had good interaction and I enjoyed making up my own lessons until feedback came to the attention of the minister. I took the Bible seriously, believed in all the miracles of Jesus, and in His divinity. At that point, the pastor suggested I take a break from teaching the kids over the Christmas vacation. That was good timing as I had requested time off to go home for a week at Christmas. I was very anxious to meet up with Gramma again. However, I was never asked to teach again for the rest of the year that I was there. I felt a bit slighted, but chalked it up to good preparation in becoming a "full-fledged" missionary.

In Tahsis I set up an informal Barber Shop, for I had learned cutting hair at Fichtner Lumber, practicing on my buddies, and then cut hair during my freshman year at CBC. Office workers, mill workers and many first nations young men came to me for their haircuts. Just

Jim cutting Gracen's hair in the lumber camp

for fun, I put up a barbershop sign until the RCMP came around and wanted to fine me for setting up a business without a license. I quickly apologized, took the sign down and said it was just a joke. They didn't think so, but didn't fine me and I still kept on cutting hair. This gave me good opportunity again to get to know my indigenous neighbors. I went to grade school in the '40's in Chilliwack with first nations kids and enjoyed their friendship. Now in Tahsis in the '60's, I again began to make friends with them and was asked to play basketball on their team. I began to learn their culture, their understanding of time and their values. At almost 5'8" I was one of the tallest on the team, but also the lightest and could jump the highest (I couldn't dunk, but could get up to the rim), so they put me in as center! We played other local teams and teams that were made up of the merchant marines off the boats. It was good recreation.

However, I was isolated from family and friends, especially my fiancée, for by this time I had popped the question and got a very positive response. Gramma was in her first year in Bible College in Regina with an engagement ring on her finger and I was aching and "sleepless" in Tahsis.

I began to understand in part how God was preparing me for future ministry by showering me with many different life experiences; that of leaving home and family (dearly loved ones), that of relating to different cultures (not only to the first nations people but also to all the merchant marines that came off the boats, not to mention the multinational groups who were present in that little company town) and that of working interdenominationally. I found that most of the few believers in the town of Tahsis didn't even know who the C&MA was. Of all things! Although, I did meet the sister of the man who would one day become the president of the CMA in Canada, Dr. Mel Sylvester. His sister and her husband lived in Tahsis and we became friends.

The Proposed Elopement

A plan was forming in my mind and it definitely included getting married after this year of separation. I couldn't stand the separation; I needed the love of my life to be right beside me. I promised myself that from the day we would be together again there would be no more separation (oh, little did I know)! But there were a few obstacles in the way. By the time we would get married I would be almost 22 and Grammaalmost 19, yet pastor Brooks and the Laylands weren't that keen on our getting married so young. My parents were fine with it, but then they both got married at 19, so did my Grandpa Sawatsky and my two older brothers. I was much older than them! I even had enough money! Where's the problem?

But Mom and Dad Layland both knew there was a long row to hoe ahead of us before we could be missionaries—they both understood our calling. Therefore, they insisted that we wait at least another year, which we did, but nearly eloped! Gramma had her dress ready, I had made an appointment with a judge in Blaine, Washington and my sister Rose and her husband George were ready to witness. However, when my Dad got wind of it, through Godly and wise counsel, he persuaded us not to do it! He pointed to all the problems of lying when signing our names, not declaring our true status when at the college etc. etc. He convinced us not to elope, but suggested we get married with the full blessing of each of the sets of parents. Well, that wasn't going to happen that year, so we went to our 2nd year at CBC as an engaged couple, not married.

The Trip to Regina

We set off for CBC in our little yellow 1954 Vauxhall, a British made GM car, with everything we could pack into it. Ruth and Norm had his Volvo of about the same year and we set off together. In the

Okanagan we separated, Norm and Ruth driving to Edmonton to see his parents and Dawn and I were going taking the southern route straight to Regina. We would drive straight through the night and get there the following day. That was the plan. But things don't always go as planned.

We got to somewhere near White Fish, Montana when a gasket burst in our little engine. I didn't really know what the problem was with the car, but I did know that I had to stop every few miles to fill up the radiator with water or it would over heat... and we had very little power. There was no way that we could make it through the mountain pass to a larger city that could perhaps help us out. I happened to stop at a restaurant (of beautiful log construction, but in a very deserted area) thinking that someone there may be able to give me some direction in finding a mechanic who could help. It turned out that there was nothing in the area at all. But among the few customers in the place, who were immediately made abreast of the story, was a couple who was travelling to Great Falls, that very same evening. They had a pickup truck and they offered to pull us through the mountain pass and over to Great Falls where they lived. I couldn't believe it. "Are you sure?" I asked. They indicated that they would be glad to. It was a very difficult journey over gravel roads on a short rope up and down steep inclines, but we made it with no mishap and got to Great Falls in the middle of the night. We thanked them, but didn't know exactly what we were going to do next. Perhaps stay in the car until a garage opened when we could get help.

They saw our plight and offered to put us up for the night as they had plenty of room for the both of us. We graciously accepted their grand hospitality. They gave us breakfast in the morning, phoned around to found us a good garage and gave us directions. We gave the family our thanks with deep gratitude in our hearts and off we limped in our little yellow "lemonzine".

At the garage they gave us the sad news after only a few minutes of examination. Old yeller had blown a head gasket and it would take a week for them to order the part and fix it up road ready. Well, we couldn't wait that long of course. By now we were already way behind schedule and at CBC the teachers (and students) would be beginning to wonder what had happened to us. We had no phones to contact anyone and anyhow long-distance phoning was way too expensive. We bit the bullet, filled containers with water and again limped off north and east into the sunrise. Fortunately, there were only a few hills in Montana and fewer in Saskatchewan. We had to stop frequently to fill the radiator and to replenish our water supply, but we were going to make it.

At one point going up a long hill, I told Gramma to hold her foot on the gas pedal and I got out of the car and began running and pushing the car uphill, so we could finally make that incline. We laughed at the sight of it, but it got us over that last hurdle and we even reached 50 miles an hour on the way down. We were lucky if we could make 35 to 40 mph on the straight stretches, which of course were many. We made it late that same day to Regina and finally found our respective rooms in the men's and women's dorms. The next day we found out that the whole school was praying for us as we now were a couple of days late, without word! They were so encouraged to see us both well and happy that no one really was concerned about our being on the road so long by ourselves. We did explain that we were graciously hosted by an "angel" family and the rest of the time we were on the road, filling up our radiator every 30 minutes or so. CBC did, however, put on us the same restrictions of no talking in the halls and no dating (except for special privileges), just as those who were meeting each other for the first time. It seemed to me a bit ridiculous, but we complied—the best we could.

Chapter Eight: Life at CBC

The Ten-Year Training Camp Continues…

As single students in the fall of '63, at Canadian Bible College, we suffered through the strict dating rules even though we had been engaged for two years. Nevertheless, since Gramma and Auntie Ruth and I sang in a trio, often representing the College, we had plenty of "practice" and "singing together" time which kept us in touch and in close "harmony" …if you get what I mean! I did get the car fixed in Regina (somehow) and if we really needed to be together to talk something out, I just pulled up in front of the main building with my little yellow Vauxhall and took Gramma for a ride—and let the chips fall where they may. We figured it was easier to ask for forgiveness than to ask for permission. We did get a few "deportments"[10] but oddly enough never for that.

Dating Privileges Suspended

One Saturday morning we really wanted to spend some time together, but did not have the permission of the Dean of Men or Women. We thought we could get away with pretending to practice in one of the music cubicles in the basement of the old administration building. We left the door open and began singing at the top of our voices, duets of some renown at the time—even tried a little of the Messiah by memory! Unbeknownst to us, the choir director had come to his office for something special and heard us. He didn't come to check on us, he just gave us both deportments for being in the cubicle together. He heard only two voices!

Well… that was the 4th deportment we had received thus far. That same Saturday, the Dean of Men (Mr. Willoughby) called me into his office and sadly said, "This is going to hurt me probably more than its going to hurt you!" He said this knowing full well that we were engaged but also that he had no choice but to take away all our "dating" privileges for a whole week. I took it like a man and told him not to worry, I understood.

"Them's the rules!" I said. But, I mentioned that we had to sing next Friday night for missionary meeting. Should we cancel or should we continue to practice?

---

[10] *Notes of reprimand. Four notes and all privileges would be taken away.*

"Oh, well, you must sing," was Willoughby's reply. "It will be alright for you to practice together with Ruth!" I think he was looking for a way out of this restriction, just as I was.

Needless to say, we did a lot of practicing that week and we saw more of each other, legitimately of course, than we generally did—just not alone. But Ruth was already a bon-a-fide sister-in-law, so there was no problem. If I hugged my fiancé after (and during) a good practice, she understood.

To finish off things in style, my brother-in-law, Uncle George, phoned on Friday night and said he was in Regina on business and asked if he could take us out to dinner around 8 pm. We told him the sad story of our "confinement" and he took it upon himself to call the Dean of Women, who surprisingly gave her consent. After all, family was visiting from afar (Vancouver) and that really should be grounds for an exception. She gave us a curfew of 11 pm—an hour later than was the norm for something like that! So, during this time of "punishment" we not only spent more time together during the week than normal, we sat together at "Mish"[11] meeting, sang together and went out to dinner together and got in later than anyone else. The next day was Saturday and the "sanction" was lifted! The many other experiences will be left for us to recount to you, our grandkids, in person in the here and now or in eternity.

One of the best experiences about our years at CBC was the music ministry that we were involved in. In my first year, I was devastated that I didn't make the men's ensemble. I couldn't believe it! The music director, David Tarr, after an audition, told me that my voice had not yet finished changing and for that reason I couldn't keep singing an extended note without waving! What??? I never heard of anything like that before! My voice hadn't finished changing? But he was right; I couldn't hang onto a note in a stable fashion for any great length of time. It was a very humbling experience! But my buddy Ray Downey and I did get a quartet together that first year. You can imagine that it wasn't the greatest, but we did some travelling together in ministry for the College as a freshman quarter (Hughes, Warner, Downey and Sawatsky).

---

[11] *Every Friday night we had a dress up for a missionary emphasis meeting after dinner which we called, "Mish Meeting." Known couples were not allowed to sit together during the meeting, but were able to hook up after the meeting, if you had permission.*

The Layland girls' first year, while I was in Tahsis, was also a good music experience for them. By this time Gramma, her sister Ruth and I had been singing a fair bit together, so when they went together to CBC they found a replacement in Viola Wiens (now Downey). They had a very rich quality to their singing as all their voices were rather low and full. And that summer they toured for a month together with Professor Bob Willoughby. They all had a tremendous tour. (Maybe that's why it hurt him so much to put those restrictions on us the next year!)

Quartet Ministry

Jim   Dean   Gene   Ron

Although we had those few problems in our second year together, a highlight for me was singing with the CBC Kingsmen Quartet.

Gene French, from Washington State, Deane Downey (son of professor Downey at CBC and Ray's older brother) from Regina, Ron Schroeder and I from B.C. formed this quartet. I thought we had a great sound. Ron and I were originally from Chilliwack and had sung together from time to time with our brothers for the pure joy of harmonizing. Here we were as roommates at CBC and singing together in a quartet making melody from our hearts to God! How great was that!

Sadly though, Ron developed a kidney problem and had to leave his studies, never to return. We were completely depressed to lose him and especially like that! Yet God provided another bass, with a deeper voice. It gave us a different sound, but we all gelled together. That spring and summer we travelled together representing the college, first with the choir, our trio (Gramma, Auntie Ruth and I) and our quartet. After the choir tour, then the Kingsmen continued until the end of July with our pianist Franklin Thomas. What a great ministry we enjoyed!

We travelled all over Ontario and the New England States putting a lot of miles on in that blue CBC Pontiac. had many hilarious

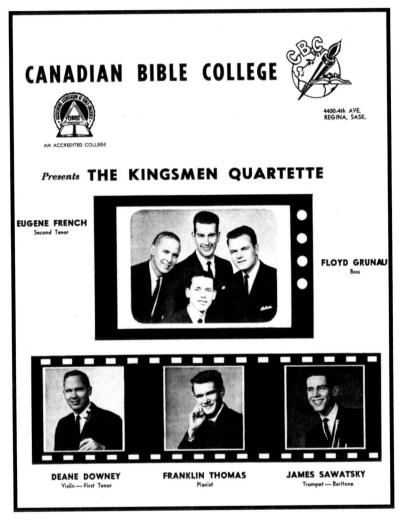

The flyer sent to churches announcing our tour in 1964

experiences due to 5 guys on our own with not a few having their funny bones well in place!

That CBC year went by rather quickly and we got married right after summer quartet tour for the College. In fact, I didn't even make it back in time for the rehearsal. I arrived at the church directly from the bus station after the rehearsal was finished.

When I met Gramma, she was pretty cool towards me as she hardly recognized me due to my tan, being in the sun a lot during our travels. But she finally warmed up! She said, "Everything will be OK. Just follow Norm and everything we will be just fine!" I did just that and everything went well. Our marriage, August the 1st, 1964, was a double wedding on the Laylands 25th anniversary. It was a gala event with over 400 in attendance. Pastor Brooks conducted the wedding ceremony without a hitch. Gramma, Auntie Ruth and I sang a trio, without

Jim and Dawn; Norm and Ruth;
"Let us exalt His Name together"

practicing, "Savior, Like a Shepherd Lead Us". It wasn't hard to sing as we knew the song well and Glen Hoskins on the organ put it in the right key for us, a couple of steps lower than in what key it was generally written. We didn't turn around; we sang facing the pastor and everybody thought that it was a quartet.

Our wedding day, August 1, 1964

We didn't get any money for going on tour, but I sure got good ministry experience and enjoyed the great friendship of the other 4 guys in the group. We did get a small bursary for the next year's studies.

Fifty years later, Floyd called from Toronto and said that he had a brainwave. He was going to be in the Vancouver area that summer and wondered if it would be possible to get together for a 50th anniversary reunion. I thought it might just work. Dean and Marg lived in Abbotsford and Gene and Betty French lived on the Washington Peninsula area, some 3-4 hours' drive away. And we lived in Surrey. We opened our home for the "gathering" and it seemed like God granted us this gift of being together again.

It "just so happened" that Franklin and Donna were also going to be in the Surrey area at the same time visiting relatives. It was a very special time at our house in Cloverdale. Of course, we took pictures and we even recorded a song of two!

2014, a mock presentation of what was
taken 50 years earlier.

Chapter Nine: "Le Couple Sawatsky"

The Continuation of the Ten-Year Boot Camp—now as a couple

More Education Needed

After a 2000-mile honey moon in my brothers little Triumph Spit Fire Convertible[12], the Lord helped us begin together our journey to Africa (although we didn't know it was going to be Africa at the time). Now there were two of us in on my 10-year training camp.

It felt as if the Lord was again saying to get more education. For me to graduate from CBC

After graduation from CBC in 1964, we got married August 1st and went on our honeymoon with $90 in our pocket and my brother's Triumph Spitfire and his gas credit card. What a great wedding gift!

with a degree in Religious Education, I needed to have at least one year of university under my belt. That became the plan.

The honeymoon over, I needed a job in Vancouver to get me through my first-year university training. Both of us needed to get jobs before university started, but first we needed a place to live. We hunted high and low for a little apartment or basement suite, but couldn't find anything that was decent and at the same time affordable. We prayed hard and so did our families and God provided a beautiful little

---

[12] *My brother Alf gave us, for our wedding present, his little sports car and his credit card and said, "Don't put on more than 2000 miles." Well that is exactly what we did. What a fun time we had. I have always been so grateful to my brother for such a wonderful present!*

furnished basement suite with telephone and laundry facilities, so we didn't even need to buy furniture. It was the nicest place we had seen anywhere.... and it was only $55 a month. The young couple upstairs were great Christian people and became good friends. They were just starting a family.

Gramma had worked hard during the summer and had saved $90.00. I had no money at all. That is all that we had to go on our honeymoon! Well, when my brother offered his car and credit card I was beside myself with joy, but knew we still had to be frugal or we wouldn't make it past that first month. We must have spent, of our own resources, something like $40.00 and had something like 50 bucks to our name on our return home. Thankfully, there was a little cash money that had come in as wedding presents, so that helped us immensely.

As I prayed for God to supply work, I had no idea what He could do for us. I had no car and no money for transportation, just enough to pay the rent. However, the day after we moved in, a man in our church who was involved in building houses and remodeling approached me after the morning service. My dad knew him and so I kind of knew him as well. He asked me what I was doing these days and I said looking for a job but not too sure where. I mentioned that I didn't have a car or much money for transportation. He said. "Well I have a job for you and you don't need a car and you don't need transportation." He continued, "I'm building an extension on the house in which you are living and all you need to do is walk outside your door and you will be on the job site. Would you help me for a month?" **Well that was exactly the time that I had available--**one month before classes were to start. I thanked him (and the Lord) profusely and started work the next day (Monday) and worked for the rest of the month. At the end of the month he paid me $1000 which was exactly what I needed to pay the tuition for my year of university at Vancouver City College.

That year was a lesson in trusting God for all our needs. We had a friend who sold our Vauxhall for us (after fixing it up again) in Regina and sent us the money just when we desperately needed some funds as we had absolutely nothing to go on. But most of the time we were flat broke! Gramma was working in a restaurant with just pittance for a salary. People at church often would press a 5 or 10-dollar bill in our hands when we had no food or money for transportation for the next week. Five dollars would buy us 3 lbs. of hamburger. It was amazing how God provided. And then a couple of apartment blocks became available for me to look after in the West End of Vancouver. I couldn't believe I actually got the job. It was too good to be true. Regretfully we said goodbye to the people upstairs and their little daughter, but the transition was perfect for us. We moved to the "West End" and really enjoyed the time there—taking care of two self-owned apartment blocks. Gramma got a new job with All State Insurance and together with what I made looking after the apartment buildings we earned enough money for transportation and food and even some savings.

During this time, I learned from my sister and brother-in-law never to deny a gift from God through people, no matter how humiliating or embarrassing it may be. When God puts it in the hearts of people to give to us, we must be willing to accept it as from God and not as mere charity for the poor!

One day, Uncle George and Auntie Rose wanted to come and take us out for dinner. They thought it would be great to go to a restaurant and spend some quality time together without kids and family around. We did just that and had a wonderful time. During dinner, we were explaining how God was wonderfully supplying our needs when sometimes we didn't even have bus fare for the next day. Unbeknownst to us God spoke to them and prompted them to give us 20 dollars (enough at that time for us to live on for the next couple of weeks). We had already said our goodbyes, but before they actually left the yard, George came back, knocked on the door and handed me a twenty-dollar bill saying that both he and Rose felt that they should do this.

I, in my pride, refused to take it saying that the stories we told were not to coerce them into giving us some money. We will get by and God will provide. Well, he didn't take no for an answer and threw the bill in the door and shut it as he left. I opened the door immediately and threw it back to him (a stupid gesture on my part). He was offended, picked up the bill and left. Later, Rose called and said that God had told them to give it to us and it no longer belonged to them, if we didn't accept it then they would give it to someone who would. It wasn't theirs to keep.

I felt like a real idiot. I missed the badly needed 20 bucks and I messed up with my sister. I apologized. The apology was accepted, but I didn't get the $20 back. It had already been given to someone else. The Lord then made it very clear to me that from that point on when He moves people to give to us, no matter what the situation, no matter how much or how little, I needed to swallow my pride and take it as from Him.

Uncle George had an Austin Healey Sprite which he wanted to sell that spring, so I said I would help him sell it. He gave me the keys and I agreed to advertise it in the papers and drive it around with a nice big "For Sale" sign on it, which I did. But try as I might, I couldn't sell it and ended up driving it all summer long. That beautiful little white convertible became our mode of transportation for that spring and summer. At the end of the summer when we were about to leave for Canadian Bible College again, the car sold. Uncle George said he was convinced that the Lord had his car made available especially for me to drive for that summer before it sold.

Collectively, with Gramma's work, the apartment blocks I looked after and with my dad needing help on his construction and painting projects during the summer months, we were able to save enough funds to pay for our next year's rent and tuitions at CBC. The two of us graduated together from Canadian Bible College in 1966.

That final year at CBC, my practical assignment was pastoring a little church in Wild Rose, North Dakota! The first thing we did when we arrived in Regina was to pay the whole year's rent for our little basement suite, one block from the campus, right up front. We got that out of the way, so didn't have to worry about having a roof over our heads for that school year! We had sent our wicker furniture from Vancouver via train. Because it was so light it was really cheap to send. For our bedroom, we bought a beautiful old three-piece suite from a prof at CBC who couldn't store it for his mother any longer. I think we paid $40 for it, fixed it up beautifully and later sold it for $350.00. There was a pool table just outside our door that the proprietor said we could use anytime. Even though I wasn't in the dorm, I still cut hair for many. The guys would come over, give me 50 cents for a haircut and then we would have a game of pool. I used to say that while I was pastoring in the USA, I was running a barber shop and pool hall in Canada!

The transportation (car and gas) to Wild Rose every Sunday was paid for by the college and all funds for pastoring were directed back to the College as well. I would get up at 5:30 a.m. on Sunday mornings, leave shortly after 6 a.m. and arrive in Wild Rose somewhere around 10:30 or 10:45 just in time for the 11:00 a.m. service. Gramma had other responsibilities, so I often went alone or with someone else from the college who needed to put in some hours of practical work. It was a good 9 months of pastoring with the farmers and ranchers of the area.

I even got to ride horseback out in the rolling hills and check on the cattle, if I came in on a Saturday and stayed overnight. I loved riding horse out on the grazing lands and even saw a calf being born while checking on the cattle.

It was a tough decision for me, when the district superintendent of that area called me to come be the pastor of that little church of 30 (including dogs). I loved the people and the area, but there was no future there. There were no young people in the church, just a few kids and some hard working, weather beaten older farmers/ranchers, most of whom fell asleep in a warm church on Sunday mornings. During the spring and fall seasons, most of the congregation (men at least) were out seeding, working the land, or harvesting. BUT if God wanted me there, I had to say yes! And that is exactly what HE wanted to hear. He wanted me to be willing to go and when I was, He said, "I have

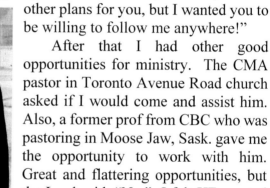

other plans for you, but I wanted you to be willing to follow me anywhere!"

After that I had other good opportunities for ministry. The CMA pastor in Toronto Avenue Road church asked if I would come and assist him. Also, a former prof from CBC who was pastoring in Moose Jaw, Sask. gave me the opportunity to work with him. Great and flattering opportunities, but the Lord said, "No." I felt HE wanted us to go back to Vancouver and that I needed more maturing and more education.

Therefore, after graduation we sold the wicker furniture and whatever else we could, bought a '53 Chevy for $70 and we packed everything that remained

We both graduated in 1966

into that car. We took out the back seat and made the trunk and backseat space available for all our belongongs and drove to Vancouver. The car was stuffed! We sent our bedroom suite home via rail. Surprise of all surprises we actually made it over the mountains with the car, but when we got to Vancouver the car developed some problems, so we sold it for junk and got our 70 bucks back. We didn't do too badly on that deal.

God Closed a Strategic Door

We found a cute and new apartment, 30 East 15th Ave., just a few blocks up from our home church on 10th Avenue and Ontario Street. This time we were again looking for work and looking for a University. Simon Fraser was a new university campus, had a good Anthropology department, used the trimester system (which I was used to from CBC) and wasn't that far away on Burnaby Mountain. I applied, knowing that there was no reason I wouldn't be accepted, but prayed and asked the Lord to shut the door if I wasn't supposed to be there. University of British Columbia was a little too large and intimidating for me.

It wasn't long, while I was helping my dad in some renovation jobs, before I received a formal letter of acceptance from Simon Fraser—or so I thought! When I read it, they said that I was an out of the province student and I had not applied early enough and therefore I was refused entry. Try again next year!

That was ridiculous. I had lived in BC all my life. I only went out of the province for 9 months of that year and now was back living in Vancouver. How was I an "out of the province student?" Nevertheless, they didn't budge and I had to look elsewhere--UBC of course. I didn't really want to go there, but had little choice. I applied, albeit a little late, but was immediately accepted. I couldn't believe that God had really shut the door on me, as I had prayed, and Simon Fraser University was now out of the question.

The neat part about this whole experience of being dejected was that during the year there was a hippy uprising of some kind, among the Anthropology students and SFU was completely shut down by the government. It was in fact black balled by other universities that year. How fortunate was I that God had shut the door and directed me to UBC where I graduated in three years, without losing a whole year as I would have done at SFU. God was again directing my path.

Fraser View Alliance

In Vancouver, we started working with Tenth Avenue Alliance Church as youth sponsors and really enjoyed the work there while going to university. But at one point the Lord was indicating to us that we should go to Fraser View Alliance Church on East 54th Street which is now the Filipino Christian Alliance Fellowship. Pastor Ted Colley invited us to serve there after Auntie Ruth and Uncle Norm Wylie left. They lived just down the street from us while Ruth went to UBC to finish some teaching courses and had been volunteering at Fraserview for the past school year.

Not really wanting to go, but trying to listen to what the Lord was saying, I said, "OK Lord I'll visit the church and if I hear your voice telling me stay and work there, we will." Gramma didn't go with me that morning due to other responsibilities, but said that whatever the Lord indicated to me to do she would be happy to comply. So I visited the church, looking for some kind of sign. Nothing happened during the morning worship nor during the pastor's preaching nor during the greetings in the foyer with church people, some of whom I already knew. I had worked there some years ago with Christian Boys Brigade, but no sign, nothing! At the last minute, as I was about to leave, the pastor came over, and shook my hand and said something to me that was quite routine, trying to make conversation! There was nothing in what he said that lit up a light bulb, but when he shook my hand, in saying good bye, the Lord spoke. He spoke in the handshake! He said very clearly, "This is where I want you." I was sure I heard His voice, so we gently told 10th Avenue we were moving to work with Fraserview Alliance Church and began volunteering as the assistant pastor. We were there for a little over two years while I was finishing up my university training at UBC.

We were both involved in many ways. I acted as the Worship Pastor, Choir Director, Sunday School Superintendent and Sunday School teacher. Together we were the Youth Pastors and did whatever else they could throw our way. Gramma took more of the leadership with the youth which helped me enormously. Of course, we didn't get any money for this as it was volunteer work, but it was another great experience (the church did give us some gifts from time to time which was very kind of them and also sent us off with a good love gift).

God was supplying all our needs. Gramma was working at a fairly good job, I was going to university and working as well at different jobs during the year, especially in the summer. I worked again in a lumber/sawmill operation during that first summer and partly during the year of studies. That was good, but I didn't like the dust and dirt, so the next summer I sold Encyclopedias! That worked well until I ran out of contacts, so got a job as a waiter on the Canadian National Railway Trains—working the Vancouver-Winnipeg run. It was supposed to be 3 days on, 3 days off, but I needed the funds so I often took only one day off or sometimes when I got back in the morning I turned around and went out that same afternoon. I would come home with a sack full of change, up to 30 bucks a trip. These tips, added to my regular wage, in 1967, gave me a well-rounded income.

However, I spent too much time away from a young, good looking wife and that wasn't good for either of us. So, the next year God provided a great summer job in an office with BC Hydro and Gas. That turned out to be a blessing not only for the summer, but also during my final year at UBC. After the summer office job working in the controlling office, I worked in their drafting department for around 15 hours a week. I worked at least 20 hours a week for the church and the rest of the time I worked on my studies. One philosophy class was in the way of my work, so I attended only a few lectures. I got all the notes from a friend, wrote my paper and passed with good marks. Actually, I did well in all my studies getting bursary grants from the BC government because of my high marks. That was a surprise to us all!

God blessed us with all that we needed. He gave us many wonderful experiences of sharing Christ with fellow students and fellow office workers, the youth of the church, special teenage kids of the youth group, Sunday School classes and other young and older church members. Leading the church choir and leading the people in worship were special ministries to me. We also saw God working in many wonderful ways in the young people of our church and that was a great encouragement to Gramma and I as young budding pastors/missionaries.

Learning to Love

There was a group of young boys at Fraserview that really got under my skin. They were about the age range of 12 to 13, not yet in the youth group that Gramma and I were working with. It seemed like nobody had control of these boys and they were running roughshod over the church area and its buildings—and me! They would tap me on my shoulder and then hide or flip up my tie while I was in an important conversation with people in the foyer after the church service. It was usually crowded, so they would bend down pretending to pick something up from the floor and tie my shoe laces together while I was talking or saying goodbye to people. Then of course they'd watch me as I tried not to fall on my face after finishing the conversation. And they generally created "hoopla" in the basement and around the church yard, always running, yelling and making a disturbance of some kind!

One Sunday after church I finally found them all together outside the church building and gruffly called them to me. I lit into them for acting so immaturely, doing all that crazy stuff they did and really let them know what I thought of their antics and their overall behavior! It felt good getting that off my chest and they went away with their heads down. "Good," I thought to myself, "I hope they have learned their lesson!"

When I got home, I was feeling pretty happy that I finally got to them and let them have it. But in my quiet time the Lord seemed to say to me, "Do you think I love those kids?"

"Well… I guess You do," was my reply.

"Then how will they know it, if you don't show it!" was His counter.

That really shut me up quickly, brought me quickly down from my high horse and caused me to think. My immediate reaction was, "I can't love them, Lord. They are complete brats!" His response was silence. But then I prayed earnestly, "I can't love them, but I give You the responsibility to love them through me. Give me a love for them." It would have to be nothing short of a miracle.

One day at work, during conversation, a colleague said that his dad had just died and left him an old 39 Dodge Desoto, a bit banged up, but still in good running condition. He really needed to sell it and would give it to me for fifty bucks. Immediately I thought of the mischievous boys at church and the thought came to me to redirect their energy. I scraped together an extra fifty dollars and bought the car, put insurance on it, just enough to get it on the road and drove it to church one day. I called the guys together and told them I had a "club car" and wanted to know if they wanted to join the club. They would have to bang out the dents, sand it down, mask it out and then we could have it painted by my mother's cousin who had his own auto-body repair shop. Until got it painted, it would be our "club car" and we could go for pizzas and ice cream together and stuff like that! We could even go on little excursions together.

They were in like a flash! God gave me a love for those guys and we did all kinds of goofy things together, including skipping out of church early, just before the benediction, and riding over to get an ice cream. We even went to the Cloverdale Rodeo and had an outing to

Harrison Hot Springs. We worked on it on Saturdays and finally got it painted for 20 bucks—a nice dark green metallic color. Whenever we went anywhere, the car was full. It needed a 3-foot-long 2x4 to hold up the front seat, which could squeeze in 4 of us and the back seat could hold at least 5, sometimes 8. The more there were, the more fun it was and one or two sisters of the group came along as well. But the car was for the core group that stuck together like glue.

I never preached to them, but I shared my life and life principles with them. The neat thing about this was that when I returned home from Africa some 8 years later (3 years in Kitimat and 5 years on our first missionary assignment) I found these guys all married to Christian girls, all were working in the church and some even elders. That ministry was a very rewarding experience in learning to listen, to love, and to be obedient to God; to do something with His help that I couldn't do by myself. Seeing His reward for that obedience was very gratifying.

Our 1939 green Dodge Desoto

The Call to the Congo

It was at Fraserview Alliance Church that we received the call or the green light from God to go to the Congo, Africa. It seemed that whenever we heard a missionary challenge, whether at Bible College or in our home church, we always felt interested in going to that field. We would ask the question, "Is this where you want us to go, Lord?" The call was always there, but each "field" when considered, with all its allurement, never really stuck until missionary Arnie Shareski came to speak at our church about his ministry in the Congo! He personally challenged us to consider the Congo and that challenge stuck. God placed a passion for the Congo in our hearts and it never left.

I was just about to graduate from UBC and we were looking towards full time ministry, so we asked the CMA if we could go to the Congo immediately, perhaps to teach in their high school at Maduda. The CMA replied that if we were sure that this was God's place of ministry for us they would be happy to consider sending us there, but first we should get in at least two years of home service pastoring a local church. Well we were hyped and wanted to go yesterday, if not sooner, but we listened to their advice. In retrospect, that was a very wise decision. Soon we were called to plant a church in Kitimat, BC and what we learned there as a young pastor and wife gave us the foundation for ministry that we needed to see us through the rest of our years in God's service.

Country Overview[13]

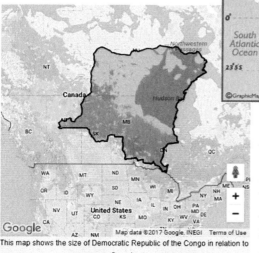

This map shows the size of Democratic Republic of the Congo in relation to Canada

The Democratic Republic of the Congo (DRC), the largest country in Francophone Africa, has vast natural resources and spans a surface area of 2.3 million square kilometers. Fewer than 40 percent of the nearly 77 million inhabitants live in urban areas. With 80 million hectares of arable land and over 1,100 minerals and precious metals identified, the DRC has the potential to become one of the richest economies on the African continent and a driver of African growth, provided the country manages to overcome political instability.

---

[13] *http://www.worldbank.org/en/country/drc/overview*

Chapter Ten: Pastor in Kitimat BC
The Continuation of the Ten-Year Training Camp

Planting a Church

I knew of a couple young men who had planted churches or had gone to small existing churches that really couldn't support them financially, so they had to work part time in another job (outside the church) to supplement their income. After talking to them and thinking ahead to a ministry that I might be involved in, I thought that there would be two things that I would NOT like to do as a young pastor—especially in planting a church. In fact, I went so far as to say I would NOT do them. I would NOT teach Sunday school, the parishioners could do that, and I would NOT work out side of the church—that is, I would devote all my attention to the ministry, not to working at another job to support myself.

As consequence, this is what I tried to gently bring up to the few who had gathered to interview us as their new prospective pastor and wife of the CMA church in Kitimat. This was a new group forming just over 60 kilometers south of Rev. Henry Young's Terrace Alliance Church, that he had begun to shepherd. Pastor Young would take the 45-minute drive to Kitimat Sunday afternoons to lead them in an afternoon meeting, but now that they had at least 8 families they felt that they could call their own pastor and plant their own church. In fact, they agreed with me that I would not have to do these two things and that they would like to call me to be the

JAMES SAWATSKY, a student minister affiliated with the Christian Missionary Alliance, has arrived in Kitimat to act as pastor for the Kitimat Alliance Church. Mr. Sawatsky, is a graduate of UBC in anthropology and sociology and of the Canadian Bible College, Regina, in religious education.

Last year he was assistant to the pastor of the Alliance Church, Vancouver, and the Kitimat church will be his first full charge. He and his wife have taken up residence at the church property, 1417 Cormorant.

founding pastor. That was the summer of 69 and by the end of August we would be there to begin our new ministry... this time as solo pastor and wife!

Two things happened during the month and a half that we were away preparing to wrap up our ministry at Fraserview and getting our meagre belongings together to move to Kitimat. Gramma got pregnant and at least 4 families left Kitimat (a very transient town). By the time we got there to settle in, the few families who were left (only 4) had just enough funds to rent a building for our church and pay all the utilities. It actually was a house in which we lived with a 50 ft. long by 15 ft. wide front room. And in that room, we started Kitimat Alliance Church. It was a good house for our purposes for it had two bedrooms downstairs—one for a front office and the other a master bedroom—with two more upstairs. All rooms were used for Sunday School class rooms and the big front room was our sanctuary.

Well, God has a great sense of humor. The first thing the board said to us, as when we sat down together for their welcome, was that they could not support me with only 4 families and pay the rent and utilities for the church-house as well. Would I consider allowing my wife to work? "Uh, Okaaayy. I said slowly, "Normally that would have been fine, but she is pregnant now and not feeling that well. I didn't think that would work."

"Well then," was their thoughtful reply. "Would you try to find an outside job?"

"Was I what? Did I hear you right?" I thought to myself as I looked straight at them, speechless for a moment! What was I supposed to say? It took me about 3 seconds to compose myself and then I said with a big smile that I would be happy to work at an outside job. My heart changed in a flash, but I immediately followed that up with a question. I asked them if they would help me find that job as I was very new to the area and didn't even know where to begin.

"And oh, by the way," they asked, "would you also teach Sunday School as a lot of the teachers were among the families that left!" Like I said, God has a good sense of humor. Never say "never" to God or to his people!

Well, they did find me a job and a good one at that! Our treasurer, a bank manager, Ron Thiessen, knew the Eaton's Manager in town and asked him if there was an opening for his new, young pastor. There was, and before we even got settled I was working for Eaton's selling home furnishings of every kind. I worked hard 6 days of the week until January and made the most money I had ever made in my life, before or after Kitimat, which allowed me to pay off all University debts, all my credit card debts, pay off the car (a little red '65 Mustang) and any other debt that we might have had at the time. I was able to buy stuff for the new baby, Loralee Dawn, who arrived on June 1st, 1970, and generally was able to contribute financially as well to the ministry of the church. God blessed.

By January the church had grown to the point of demanding more of my time, so the Lord opened the door for me to change jobs from salesman to substitute teacher, in all the schools in Kitimat—from high school to the elementary schools. This gave me a little more free time for church related activities. As I was a grad of UBC, substitute teaching also gave me good money! Although my major was in Anthropology, the Kitimat school district was hard pressed for substitute teachers and I was accepted. I was thrown into every kind of class, every subject possible, some of which I knew nothing about, but faked my way through, pretending to know and understand what I was to teach. Most often I was called to substitute for the Physical Education and the French class! (I ground through two years of university French, but when I got to France for language study, I really found out how little I knew!)

The school kids soon learned that I was a local pastor and began asking me all kinds of questions about why I was a pastor, what it meant to be Christian etc., so instead of teaching we had some great discussions! I was warned that I was definitely not to initiate any conversation about my religious beliefs, not to propagate my religion, but if I was asked I could respond honestly and directly. Oddly enough, I didn't have to initiate any discussion. The students, especially the high school kids, initiated all the good conversations we had. Off campus, I was even able to lead a few to faith in Jesus Christ.

It didn't take long before my supply teaching schedule was almost full days, 5 days a week. That wasn't what I had bargained for. I didn't want to say no, when the principle called, so after a few months, just before school ended for that year (1970), I started looking for another job that would give me more time for shepherding. It didn't take too long and I found a job driving buss. The manager of Far West agreed to train me and it didn't take long before I was holding a full license of class 4. The switch was quite interesting. One day I was teaching the high school kids in their classrooms and the next day I was driving their school bus—usually to the First Nation's village up the channel. It was a humbling experience, but paid enough and gave me regular hours so I could do church work and study on a regular schedule. Although, I was often called for extra hours to drive the tour bus through the Kitimat smelter and/or other unscheduled tours and charters. Several times I was called to drive to Prince Rupert and pick up all the air plane passengers headed for Terrace and Kitimat as the plane was not able to land at the Terrace/Kitimat airport due to severe weather.

Doubts

Early in my ministry in Kitimat I needed to come to grips with doubts of my salvation. Oh, I believed all the "right stuff" but in the back of my mind there were still question about my personal salvation. I was even reading books in preparation for my ordination at the time. It was during that ministry period of my life that we were invited to a Bill Gothard seminar in Seattle and was really encouraged to come by a Presbyterian couple who would host us for the few days. We weren't sure for we also had a 3-month-old baby and two foster girls to take care of. But people of the church offered to take the foster girls and the family in Seattle said they would be happy to babysit Loralee. It was one of the best decisions we had made during our 3 years in Kitimat! We took our little new born baby, Loralee Dawn, and the couple with whom we stayed had kids who loved to look after her while we attended the seminars.

I was drawn to an illustrative story of how Bill Gothard had dealt with doubts. That particular story went something like this: A man was plagued with doubts about his Christian life. Was he really saved or was this just a thing imagined?! The man in question decided to put a stake in a small plot of land that he had designated for a grave. On the stake he had written, "Here lies the old Jon Doe, died ___." …and put in the date of his accepting Christ into his life on that stake. The man then said that after this act, if doubts came, he would say to the Devil, "Come with me!" He would walk behind the barn and show him the stake and then declare that the old Jon Doe was dead and here was the evidence! He declared his new life in Christ to have started on that same date. The application was that when we drive a stake, literally or figuratively, into the ground, no one can refute that. The stake would be a testament and evidence to the enemy of being dead to the old life, and alive to a new life in Christ. There could be no more doubts!

I went home and after a great reception that was given by the church, a grocery shower, and things began to settle down, I went into my office one day and prayed, "Lord if I have never given my life to you, I do it now! (I knew I had, but made a recommitment that day). Forgive my sin; forgive my unbelief and my doubts. I give my life completely to you and receive you as my Lord and Savior, AMEN!" I drew a stake driven into the ground, then drew a placard nailed to that stake and on that placard I wrote,

"HERE LIES THE OLD JIM SAWATSKY,
DIED AUGUST 19TH, 1970"

I signed it and put the piece of paper under my blotter on my desk. We still had those large rectangular framed blotters to cover the desk— a desk I had made in high school and kept it with me right to Kitimat. I went home satisfied that the action was definitely done and there would be no more doubts. BUT, wouldn't you know it, a few days later while I was studying, preparing for a Sunday message, the enemy again came with doubts. I said out loud, "Satan, come with me!" I stuck my hand under the blotter and pointed my finger to the sign that I had made and read it, out loud. I said something like, "The old Jim Sawatsky has passed away and there is a new Jim now! I have made the decision to accept Christ and He has saved me and accepted me and there is the date of the death of the old Jim Sawatsky!" I figuratively rubbed his nose into the "stake" and "sign" and then continued studying. The doubts never returned for the rest of my life and even today I can still see in my mind's eye the sign and the paper that I placed under my blotter, which stayed there until we left for language study in France and then the Congo.

Our Father in heaven knew I needed that for after knowing His wonderful peace in my heart, unknown to me, a spiritual storm was brewing!

A Love Note…

Not long after this experience, my heart burned within me to know how to express my love to God. How did He know of my love for Him? I was down on my knees in my study agonizing in prayer for the proper expression when I wrote this poem.

As a young pastor, it was the only way I knew how to express my love for my heavenly Father. I realize now that it was the Holy Spirit who was moving me to a more concrete and demonstrative love for my Heavenly Father. He knew the difficult path that was ahead of us and He knew I needed that

A LOVE NOTE...

I love You, Lord…
I long to love you more,
I want to tell you that I love You,
But it seems I don't know how…
And yet,

If being available before you and you alone
Each day, dear Lord,
Is loving You,
Then, I love You.

If placing myself as a bond slave before you
Is loving You,
Then, Master, I love You.

If delighting to do Your will,
And nothing else,
Is loving You,
Then, I love You Father.

If praising and worshipping You
Is loving You,
Then, Jesus, how I love You.

If trusting You completely for everything I need
Is loving You,
Then, I do love you Lord!

If denying self;
Longing for Your full life manifest in me
Is loving You,
Then, blessed Holy Spirit,
I love you.

If rejoicing over the victory You secured by the giving
Of Your Blood
Is loving You,
O how I love You, Jesus!

If loving people,
Lost and found,
Means loving You,
Then I long to love more.

If looking for your glorious return,
Means loving You,
Give me a greater love,
O Lord, for You!

solid love relationship with Him.

Foster Parents

We were in Kitimat almost a year when we both felt that we should be more active in our community (outside the church), at least in some significant way. We both thought of helping as foster parents—perhaps that might work. Dawn was already at home with a baby, a couple of months old, and being able to help with another young child would not be a problem. The secretary of the social welfare department in Kitimat was a member of our church and the wife of one of our Elders. Why not? So, we gave her a call and the response was very affirming and she said that she would be in touch with us soon!

It didn't take long and we got a call from the social worker who said, "We have two girls, sisters, who desperately need a home right now!"

"Well... we had thought of only one! But, OK. How old are they?"

"Twelve and fourteen!" was the reply.

Gulp, we weren't thinking of teenagers (or soon to be). But we talked it over briefly and said, "Yes".

The next thing we heard was a knock on the front door and there stood two of the most forlorn, spindles of young girls I had ever seen. We took them in, loved on them and soon they loved on little Loralee and then on us.

In order to show love to the younger one, Debbie, I would wrestle with her and we had fun doing that! The older one, Cathy, was already 14 and too old for that ...and it wasn't her thing. We knew immediately that Cathy had some serious issues, but couldn't figure out exactly what it was. The social worker suggested some ideas, but we didn't agree. They thought she would never make it out of grade 10. Again, we didn't agree!

With the addition of two "teenagers", there were more adjustments made in our home than we thought might occur. Space wise, the house was big enough so the girls had their bedrooms (but they had to share them with Sunday school classes on Sunday mornings). In many other ways, we and both girls, had to make mental, emotional and behavioral changes. All the while, we earnestly prayed that they would accept our faith and make it their own. What we didn't know then was that an older woman in the community had been holding a children's weekly Bible meeting in her home and that Kathy was among the kids from that group who actually prayed with her to accept Jesus into her heart and life. Not long after that, Kathy and Debbie's father died and with their mom having a serious addiction to alcohol, Kathy prayed to God and asked Him to send her some new parents.

After we came back from the Gothard seminar, the church gave us a grocery shower (such a blessing) as a welcome home gift. The girls noted that the items which were bought had them in mind—fours of everything, which included them! They began to ask about that gesture and Dawn shared the love of Jesus with them in a personal way and what a difference His life makes in us. They had not known that kind of love before and both accepted Jesus shortly after we came home (for Kathy this was a definite recommitment of her life to Jesus as she had had absolutely no home encouragement). It was a very happy occasion when we could announce to the church that their gifts of love initiated a wonderful response in our "girls" and they had accepted the Lord as their Savior.

But there was still a problem in completely understanding Kathy.

Lessons in Gaining Victory over the Enemy

We had heard of a revival going on in Saskatoon and spilling over in many areas of Saskatchewan. I often sang the song on my own, and in church, "While on others Thou art calling, do not pass 'us' by." And He didn't. Often on a Sunday morning or evening, the Lord would be moving in our midst. I would get up to speak, but invite others, if God had given them a message for us, to share it. I can remember that for many Sundays God spoke to us through the people of the church. I was always ready with a message, but God chose others and it was the exact message for us at that time, that week! We loved to hear from Him; He was not passing us by.

During this time, in the fall of 1970, a single missionary woman came to our church for a missionary conference. She had had a "devil" of a time getting to us and almost fell in a heap in my Gramma's arms when she arrived. She felt definite spiritual opposition. Her name was Susan Dyck from Japan. I noticed that Kathy would make herself scarce whenever she was around, even at the Youth Group gathering. So I mentioned it to Kathy and asked her why. Her immediate response was, "I hate her, I hate her, I hater her!"

"Kathy," I said, "you don't even know her, how can you hate her so?"

Her response was immediate, "I don't know, I just hate her!"

I couldn't understand this outburst, so we asked Susan, who had had experience in dealing with evil spirits, if Kathy could have a problem with that kind of oppression due to her rough and uncertain childhood. Susan took it one step further and said it certainly was, but not only with her. She sensed there were a number of people in our church who were being seriously attacked by the enemy.

She was right! There was a former Austrian circus actor who had delved into dark stuff; there was a former Hitler SS man who had serious addictions; there was a couple, who had taken in and adopted first nations children, who was seriously harassed in the home and in their person; there was another German family who had delved into the occult and other religions and who were totally harassed in the home (knocking in the walls, lights flicking on and off). The wife of this latter family went completely berserk with demon oppression and possession and as pastor and wife we bore the brunt of her attacks on us and the church.

Earlier in the ministry, there were some lies that were circulating around about me and the Lord whispered in my heart, *"Don't try to get to the bottom of this, it is completely from the enemy. Humble yourself before me and I will lift you up at the right time."* I followed His instructions, even to the point of visiting and apologizing to a family for something that I really didn't understand, but took the position of being wrong. That act in itself helped clear the atmosphere of the church and brought a lot of solidarity to us as a church family. Nevertheless, there were issues brewing that I had no idea how to handle until Susan came along and "fell" into Gramma's arms.

Susan did not mess around in dealing with the enemy and his hordes of evil spirits. She had learned a lot during the great revival and awakening in Saskatoon with the Sutera Twins in the late 60's early 70's. She got right down to business. Her method was simple;

She first set the stage with prayer for the covering of ourselves, the person who was seeking deliverance of any kind and for the area, praying God's protection over us, placing us under the protective covering of the blood of Jesus (1 Peter 1:19, (Hebrews 9:22, Exodus 12:13).

She next claimed her authority, in Jesus' Name, over the enemy and all his demons that would seek to bombard us, using scripture from various passages. At strategic times she would say to the enemy, out loud in a booming voice, "All that Jesus was here on earth, I am by the power of His Holy Spirit residing in me!" (Ephesians 1:15-23, Ephesians 2:6)

She next addressed the evil spirits that were present in the person and commanded them to reveal themselves by giving us their names and their assignments! If they were there, under the authority of Jesus, they had to respond. She would then bind them all together in the Name of Jesus and command them to leave and often cast them out to the pit (of hell)! The person always knew when they had left. Sometimes there would be a struggle and the evil spirits would refuse to leave. Then Susan would say "alright we will torment you with praise of our Lord Jesus Christ!" We would then sing. She had such a loud booming voice that it would scare any opposition whatsoever! While singing, the evil spirits would often leave. (Matthew 28:18, Acts 16:23-26)*

Then she would test to see if they all had left, by commanding them to reveal themselves, always stipulating that they were under the authority of Jesus Christ and there would be no overt action, but a calm response. Of all the cases that we dealt with there was never a writhing, a convulsing or a foaming at the mouth as is often depicted (even in the Bible). If all was quiet with no response at all in the person, then we could praise God and perhaps wait until another day for a follow up if necessary.

If there was no sign of infestation at the very beginning, then she would suggest that we were dealing with oppression and nothing else. We would then take a stand in the Name of Jesus, always using scripture, claiming our rightful place in Christ and claiming defeat over the enemy. We would then, together, command the enemy to leave the oppressed person alone, claiming the covering of the blood of Jesus.

We prayed with many. After Susan left, we did the same thing that we learned from her and saw that all who came to us wanting complete deliverances from oppression or infestation were totally freed. Sometimes it was a one-time session of prayer, other times there were repeated sessions as activity and new elements were revealed, but in Jesus Name and in His authority, all were freed from the enemy's harassment.

At one point it took an elder and myself getting up very early in the morning and praying together for at least a full two weeks to see complete freedom for a lady--claiming deliverance, commanding the enemy to leave, binding him out and away from this particular lady's life and that of her family, in Jesus' Name all the while quoting scripture and doing all in and under the authority of Jesus.

At the end of that two-week period this lady called me. "Pastor," she said, "I just want to tell you that I have had an awesome experience." She then began to relate how she had been so harassed by demons that there was a constant knocking in the walls of her house, laughing could be heard and lights were going on and off. She mentioned that at one time she even saw Satan at the foot of her bed. Her hair stood straight up and she couldn't comb it down, so she never went anywhere. Then one morning as she looked in the mirror she said, "I saw them leave!" She wasn't sure what she saw, but some kinds of forms leaving from the top of her head, then her hair fell down, her face relaxed and she knew she was free! Her voice was calm; she was no longer antagonistic, but gentle and grateful for all our intercession on her behalf and on behalf of her family. Her husband never came to church (maybe once), but she and her boys were re-integrated into the fellowship with us. When we as a board tested her and her family to see what residual effects may have still been there, we found nothing.

At another time we needed to have many sessions, dealing with many evil spirits in another person. When at one point in the midst of a prayer and deliverance session, the evil spirits refused to leave, I ask the elders present if anyone had a word from the Lord or a scripture. Immediately Ron Thiessen read Rev. 12:10-11

*"Now the salvation and the power and the kingdom of our God and the authority of his Christ have come, for the accuser of our brothers has been thrown down, who accuses them day and night before our God. [11] **And they have conquered [overcame] him by the blood of the Lamb** and by the word of their testimony, for they loved not their lives even unto death."*

When the Word was read and the reader came to the phrase, "overcome by the blood of the lamb" the evil spirits responded with, "Okay, Okay, you win, we leave!" and they were gone completely. This was the fourth session with this person and now there was complete freedom. What a sense of praise we all had and it exploded in song!

All the details of these experiences and individual stories have not been told, but we were so grateful that Susan came by and not only told us of what God was doing in Japan in and through her ministry, but also what God was doing in Canada through revival. Most of all, we were grateful for her understanding, her authority in Christ and for her passing on her knowledge, "discipling" us in this ministry and helping us understand the authority we have in Jesus. In His name we can overcome the enemy of our souls. All who came to us were set free; including Kathy, but her story is for her to tell.[14]

After Susan left (we really didn't want her to leave, feeling alone and left out on a limb), we discovered our own authority in Jesus and we discovered the power and efficacy of praise and the power in the precious blood of Jesus. These experiences greatly encouraged our hearts (and the whole congregation) in praise and worship. We had often sung "There's Power in the Blood" but now we sang it with a deeper, fuller understanding. We sang the Doxology with new vigor and comprehension of the importance to always begin our meetings with praise. I could not and will not ever forget the image of Susan lifting her hands in praise, singing praises at the top of her lungs with her booming voice and being more than a conqueror! I took that image of overcoming power and authority with me right to Africa and for the rest of my days!

God's Blessing

One more thing that would set the stage for Africa was our tithing habits. I have already mentioned that when we first got to Kitimat and I started working, I was making more money than I had ever made in my life. I was doing well in sales. God, with His sense of humor, was blessing my "outside" job as well as the ministry of pastoring. I immediately began giving to the church, at least a 10th of my income (that's what I was used to), but after Christmas things started to die down quite a bit and I felt I was wasting valuable time at the Eaton's store when I could be doing important ministry/church work. Shepherding this little group was exacting more of my time as it began to grow. It began to gnaw at me, so when the opportunity was given for me to go into substitute teaching I jumped at the chance. The positives were I would be working fewer days, fewer hours, but the negative aspect was that I would be making less money. We could handle it as we lived in the church and the people of the church paid for the rent of

---

[14]*We couldn't take the girls with us to Africa for many reasons (we felt very sorry about that), but God opened doors for them to live with their Aunt Phyllis--a God fearing woman. Debbie came to visit us in France and Kathy came to visit us in Africa. We are so grateful that they (and God) have allowed us to be in continual contact even though often many miles apart. We are really proud of" our" girls and how they love the Lord today!*

the house/church. That worked out fine until the Lord asked me to give more, perhaps 15%. I wrestled with that a bit, but said, "OK Lord, you know what you are doing." Fifteen per cent is nothing really to write home about, but stepping down in income and stepping up in giving was a little difficult, but that is what God was asking of me.

Soon the substitute teaching became too demanding. I was called almost every day and once a full week, substituting for a principle of an elementary school. At this point I felt I needed a change, so began driving bus. As mentioned, that was a bit humiliating; having been the kids' high school teacher one day then the next their bus driver, but it gave me steady "part-time" employment. It was also a sizeable cut in pay. Nevertheless, we thought we could get by seeing all our debts were paid. Again, with less money coming in, the Lord indicated to me to give more. Now, I knew it was the Lord for I would have never thought of that myself, being of good frugal Mennonite roots. (Everyone knows that the only person who can buy from a Scot, sell to one of God's chosen people and still make a profit is a Mennonite.) Again, I argued with God. This time a little stronger, but the insistence was still there. I talked it over with Gramma and she agreed that if God was indicating this increase, then we should do it. He would provide! So we upped it, to around 20% of our meagre income and continued with that amount until the day we left.

Now I realize that many people have given a lot more than 20% of their income as their tithe to the Lord for it is not so great an amount, yet it was more than I had ever given before. But, I was just following the Lord's direction. One day the treasurer approached me and said that we shouldn't give so much. We were giving more to the church than the church was putting out for us. "Well then," I said. "That's good isn't it?" Again, in God's sense of humor, when I said I wasn't going to have an "outside" job, He not only gave me the jobs I needed, but had me working at an "outside" job during the whole time we were in Kitimat, paying our own way and then some! I chuckle when I think of it now.

But I became really excited when God whispered in my heart that He was going to bless me! My immediate emotion was gratitude and surprise! Then I thought, "A blessing from you Lord, I can gratefully receive."

The communication came back to me, "No you don't understand, I am going to bless you for the rest of your life!"

"Oh no, Lord, you can't do that! Not for the rest of my life!" was my response. "I'm not worthy."

Of course, I wasn't worthy, but I didn't know how to handle God's grace. In refusing His "lifelong" blessing, I immediately felt that I had rejected Him. He was silent. I felt that He was saying in His silence that if I didn't accept His blessing then He would not give it. His blessing was not in just one area, or just for a short time, His blessing was in every area, for the rest of my life. It was not a matter of being worthy; it was a matter of being faithful and obedient in what He had asked me to do.

While this whispering communication was happening, I was looking out the front window of our newly acquired home that the church had purchased for us. The house-church had become too small for our home and the church combined, so the church purchased a new home for us with a basement suite which we finished off and rented to help pay the mortgage. I was watching the snow fall in great quantity; I had no pressing commitments and was savoring the moment enjoying the new warm carpet under my feet. In refusing this blessing, I had wounded His Spirit and I immediately got on my knees and repented. I said, "I don't understand it Lord, but if you say you will bless me and that blessing will endure the rest of my life, I will accept it. Thank you, Lord, for your blessing on this undeserving servant!"

I've learned over the years that God often comes to one of His children and makes that one feel so special by His whisperings that what He says seems so sacred and so intimate that one even hesitates to share those intimacies with another for fear of betrayal or for fear of being misunderstood in the sharing, fostering the thinking that you are more holy than the next person in being so intimate with God. Yet I found He does this with all His children who desire that intimate relationship with him. What I thought he had said only to me, I found out later that He has said much the same to many others (if not all of His children). A good example of this is written in 1 Chronicles 17, about King David and his conversation at one point with his Lord. My heart's response was very much like the prayer of the King, but not nearly so eloquent.

16 Then King David went…and sat before the LORD, and he said:

"Who am I, LORD God, and what is my family, that you have brought me this far? *17 And as if this were not enough in* *your sight, my God, you have spoken about the future of the house of your servant. You, LORD God, have looked on me as though I were the most exalted of men.*

18 "What more can David [Jim] say to you for honoring your servant? For you know your servant, LORD. 19 For the sake of your servant and according to your will, you have done this great thing and made known all these great promises.

20 "There is no one like you, LORD, and there is no God but you..."

It was an awesome holy moment which I will never forget, but I went about my ministry without further questioning it or even anticipating it. My thoughts were, if He said it, He will do it and I will see it along the way. And, in looking back over my life from that point on, I realize that I have experienced His blessing on my life in multiple ways throughout our ministry and even in retirement—the blessing of a fruitful ministry, of great and faithful friends, of His protection and healing, of children who love God, of home and housing that we could never afford (inherited), of good transportation all along the way, including motor bikes for ministry and even a cruiser motorbike in my retirement years! However, one of the greatest blessing in my life is having had the opportunity to work with young Christian men (and one or two women along the way), being intentionally involved in their lives as a disciple maker, some to a lesser degree than others, and now seeing the fruit of all that "labor" being distributed throughout the world. Young men and women with whom I have worked are now in pastoral ministry, in media production, in music and worship and in radio in many countries in Africa, in Europe, some in Asia and also in the United States.

About the same time this "blessed conversation" was happening, I was working late one Saturday night in my office at the church and was having a tough time finishing off my message for Sunday. I was finally finished around 11:00 p.m. and was packing up when I sensed the Lord telling me to drive by a certain family's town house, right on my way home, and share the gospel with the man of the house. I argued with the Lord that it was too late, I couldn't disturb them at this hour, but I felt He persisted with the request. I finally said, "OK Lord, I'll drive by their place and if I see a light on I'll stop and knock."

Now these people were very new to the church and only the wife had come a few times, but I had seen the husband before and had met him once. We were praying for him. So I drove by and sure enough the light was on and saw her through the kitchen window. I stopped, got out of the car and went to the door and knocked! When she opened the door and saw me, she smiled broadly and hollered to her husband, "It's pastor Jim, come to the door." Well, he was about to get up, but by this time I was in the front room, told him not to bother getting up, but also asked if I was disturbing him. "Oh no, nothing really interesting on TV anyhow." Immediately after a few niceties, I got down to business and told him why I had come. Let's say his name was Bob. I said, "Bob, I have felt a real urging from the Holy Spirit to come to you this evening and to talk to you about your spiritual life and your relationship with Jesus Christ." He was surprised, but I didn't let that slow me down.

I said, "Bob, your wife has been coming to our church a few times now and we have missed you. Have you ever accepted Jesus into your life as your personal savior?" It wasn't like me to be so bold.

"I have wanted to do that and I have tried," Bob gently said, with his eyes looking to the floor, "but I could never say the name of Je… well you know, that name that you just mentioned!"

"Jesus?"

"Yes," he said. "Every time I want to pray, I just can't say His name. I don't know what the matter is, but just can't say the name!"

"Well, I know," I immediately answered him. "Could I pray for you right now and see if that makes a difference?"

He agreed. Right then and there, I prayed for Bob and bound the enemy out and away from his life, from his family's life and from his home. I asked the Lord Jesus to cover Bob and us all with his precious blood and replace the bondage in Bob's life with His peace. By this time his wife was quite silent in the kitchen. All movement had stopped!

Bob looked up and his face had a different look to it.

I asked, "Do you think you could pray now in Jesus' Name?"

He answered, "Yes, I think I can!"

"Would you like to invite Him into your life now?"

Again, he agreed and I led him through a prayer, inviting Jesus to forgive his sins, his past life and to come into his life and make him a new person in Christ Jesus. With tears in his eyes, he could easily say the name of Jesus and accepted the Lord that night into his heart and life. Something he had wanted to do for a long time, but just couldn't. I knew the struggle as I had had the same problem many years before. That next day the whole family was in church and we were praising God again with new vigor! What an encouragement a new birth brings to the body. I was so glad I had agreed with the Lord to do the "drive by". He had the brother already prepared. It was a stark reminder to me to always obey the promptings of the Holy Spirit.

Kitimat in Perspective

In hind sight, Kitimat was an excellent training ground for me as a budding pastor and missionary. The whole three years was definitely a school of learning. I learned about "defending the faith" (how to speak of what I believed) before my neighbors and associates in the community, before those who brought me both spiritual and social opposition and even before my fellow pastors in the Ministerial Association of the

THE NORTHERN SENTINEL

Sawatsky Clergy Leader

James R. Sawatsky, minister, Kitimat Alliance Church, recently was elected president of the Kitimat Ministerial Association.

Father M. Reville, CP. Church of Christ the King, was elected vice-president and treasurer. R. K. Webb, pastor, Pentecostal Tabernacle, was elected secretary.

Welcomed as new members of the local clergy were: Rev. Keith Young, Christ Church; Rev. Irvine Ross McKee, Presbyterian Church and Father MacDonald.

President of the Kitimat Ministerial Association at age 30, but I looked like 21. I can't believe that the ministers of Kitimat had confidence in me!

... President: James R. Sawatsky

community. In spite of that and in spite of my youthful looks they somehow voted me president of the Association at age 30.

I learned how to play the sax in our youth band and how to lead a community choir singing the major portions of the composition "Elijah". I was learning big time how to be a good dad—which is still ongoing! I began learning what it took to work well interdenominationally with men and women of different theological backgrounds. I began learning how music was another "key" in sharing the faith and put several music groups together, even singing at trade fairs and in open air inter-denominational gatherings. This school was called the "Kitimat Practical Training Center" and the courses were "Ministry in the Community 101, "Missionary-in-Training 101" and "Our Authority in Jesus 101". Courses of infinite value!

We tried to adopt our "girls" as we call them, but at that point the CMA said that if we did, they couldn't send us as missionaries. We were in a quandary, knowing that God had called us to be missionaries, but it was no accident either that these two girls ended up under our care. While we were in prayer over this whole issue, their aunt, unknown to us, (sister of their father) called saying she would love to have the girls and would give them a good Christian home. She desired to have a positive influence on their lives. That seemed very much like an answer to our prayers, so they went to live with Aunt Phyllis. A lot happened in their lives, but today I can say they both love the Lord with all their hearts and both have wonderful children. Kathy is a wonderfully successful homemaker. She and Gary have 3 great girls and 3 grand kids (and counting). Debbie, still a business woman, also living a vibrant Christian life, has one girl and 2 grandkids, with hopes of more to come.

I also want to present to you two special families. Rev. Henry Young, former missionary to New Guinea, then pastor of the Terrace Alliance Church, about 60 km inland to the north of Kitimat, had been meeting with a few families on Sunday afternoons--families who were interested in planting a CMA church in this multinational town. When they called us to candidate, Pastor Young was among the people we first met when we arrived. Many years earlier, as a missionary to New Guinea, he had delivered a fiery challenge to us students at CBC which had really got my heart pumping and my mind considering his field of service. As young students, we were spellbound, listening to every word of his accounts of reaching the once cannibalistic culture of the Dani tribe for Jesus. Now here I was, having to preach my first sermon to these young families, in the presence of this respected missionary/pastor. No pressure!

Pastor Young and his family, including Paul Young, the author of *The Shack*, were a great encouragement to us in that first year in Kitimat; their home, a haven of rest from the struggles of ministry in this new area for us. We also enjoyed their children and I remember that Paul was fun to interact with as a young teenager. I knew that he had a lot of potential.

Another family that meant a lot to us while in Kitimat was the Sutherlands. I had met them at the Esperanza Mission Hospital when we would visit there from Tahsis. Now we found them in Terrace. They were a busy family. Both Shirley and Bob worked in the hospital as nurse and orderly and they had four children. But they always had room for us in their home when we needed to kick back and hang out—away from Kitimat! Their ministry to us was invaluable.

In the Kitimat Alliance Church, there were two men who really stood by me, befriended me and in fact became my mentors in many respects. They were Chuck Wirth (chairman of the board) and Ron Thiessen (treasurer). These were godly men, of mature character in Christ. Had it not been for them, their spiritual leadership, their support in every way, we would not have lasted in Kitimat. The enemy of our souls was bound to get us discouraged and put us to flight. Susan Dyck certainly helped us, but so did these men and their families. God alone will give them their reward.

A passage of scripture we memorized as a family during our years there is from the first chapter of James Chapter one,[15] quoted below. We were about to see just how often that scripture would come to mind!

"The Christian can even welcome trouble"

[2-8] *When all kinds of trials and temptations crowd into your lives my brothers, don't resent them as intruders, but welcome them as friends! Realize that they come to test your faith and to produce in you the quality of endurance. But let the process go on until that endurance is fully developed, and you will find you have become **men of mature character** with the right sort of independence. And if, in the process, any of you does not know how to meet any particular problem he has only to ask God—who gives generously to all men without making them feel foolish or guilty—and he may be quite sure that the necessary wisdom will be given him. But he must ask in sincere faith without secret doubts as to whether he really wants God's help or not. The man who trusts God, but with inward reservations, is like a wave of the sea, carried forward by the wind one moment and driven back the next. That sort of man cannot hope to receive anything from God, and the life of a man of divided loyalty will reveal instability at every turn.*

---

[15] *James 1 J.B. Phillips New Testament (PHILLIPS)*

Chapter Eleven: Transitioning to Albertville, France

The Final Year of Boot Camp Training

Our son Rod's first birthday was celebrated at 36,000 feet over the Atlantic on our way to France for nine months of language study. Two of our three children, Loralee and Rod, were born in Kitimat; Loralee arrived on June 1st, 1970 and Rod was born on Sept 19th, 1971. It was around the end of August 1972 when we had packed what we could in our suitcases and a cardboard 40-gallon barrel and brought it all with us as we were now flying to Paris. The barrel (150 lbs.) went as cargo and arrived with us on the same plane. Once we arrived at our destination, we rented a Renault hatch back with a roof rack on top, picked up our barrel, hoisted it up top, borrowed some strong string and secured it as best we could, got a map to Albertville, Haute-Savoie and made it out of the maze of Paris to the country. We travelled as far as Lyon, but then had to rest for the night, not having had any sleep on the plane with two little ones in diapers. Somehow, we found an inexpensive "Pension" for the evening with one large bed and we all slept in it--except the kids were wide awake in the middle of the night wanting to play. We made it through the night, got the included

JIM   DAWN
LORALEE   RODNEY
SAWATSKY

THE REPUBLIC OF ZAIRE, AFRICA

"This is the ministry which God in His mercy has given us and nothing can daunt us. We use no hocus-pocus, no clever tricks, no dishonest manipulation of the word of God. We speak the plain truth and so commend ourselves to every man's conscience in the sight of God . . . It is Christ Jesus as Lord whom we preach, not ourselves, we are your servants for Jesus sake."

−2 Cor. 4 (Phillips)

Our first "Prayer Card" as missionaries to Zaire, 1972

"continental breakfast" and asked the best way to Albertville. I used my best French pronunciation, but no one understood??

In my limited French I said, "Pouvez-vous nous montrer the way to Al-bear-t-veel (spelled Albertville). No one knew about "Al-bear-t-veel". We all (the inn keeper, the waitress and us) finally found the town on the map and they said, "Oh 'Al-bear-veel!'" (they did not pronounce the "t"). "Ah oui nous le voyons maintenant!" and began to show us on the map the best roads to use. That was helpful, but I couldn't understand why they couldn't get their "Al-bear-veel" out of my "Al-bear-t-veel"! This was our first introduction to the precision of the French in the pronunciation of their language!

Language School

Once in Albertville, we found the administrative staff very cordial and willing to help. We were so happy to flop down on the beds prepared for us in our two-bedroom apartment, right on campus. The next day, we left our children in the provided day care nursery, with a number of other children, and started our French studies. It wasn't that difficult at first, as our past studies in French had helped us quite a bit (Gramma had taken four years of French in high school; I had done my best at passing the French requirement in university). But as we continued throughout the year we found ourselves wading through something like a mud hole trying desperately to get to the other side.

In the small village of Albertville, we certainly were seen as foreigners and that was a shock to our system as we were "white". We thought that we would experience "culture shock" later among the "blacks". Not so, in fact, thanks to previous missionaries, we weren't really treated as "foreigners" as much in Africa as we were in France! I felt shunned in France just because I didn't speak the language correctly or had an accent that wasn't French. Now, I really understood what it meant to be an immigrant or a foreigner. Several things rose to the surface throughout those nine months at that missionary language learning institution.

Culture Shock

The first thing that hit me, and I think Gramma too, was the fact that we had to deal with "culture shock". Although we were white, there was a definite change in culture and we found out what "culture shock" was all about. We tried to dress like the French, but we couldn't communicate with anyone outside of the school. Coming from a life in Canada, as a pastor, my days were filled with communication--sharing what God was saying to me through my quiet times and personal study, counselling, casting vision for ministry and performing all the daily duties of a pastor. Here I could share nothing! I was reduced to baby-like talk at best. Although we went to the community church, on campus, all was in French and we couldn't understand a thing, nor could we communicate with the local members. We couldn't even participate in the church service in any way as we did not understand the prayers nor did we know many of the hymns they sang. If we did know the tunes we couldn't sing them in the French language even though they were printed out before us. For me at the time, French was the most unmusical language. How to sing in it was even more difficult. English was great, Spanish was beautiful, German seemed to have a natural flow, but French was just plain difficult—or so it seemed to me at least!

The Fiat

What rose to the surface immediately, in my thought process, was the fact that we needed to figure out some ways to help cushion the blow of culture shock and help us learn the language and culture outside of the classroom! I remembered that we had been counselled by former missionaries to buy a car if possible so that we could take our family on outings during the days off and after class hours. We had enough money saved, so we did that and found great solace in visiting the beautiful countryside. We found the farmers or country people much more willing to help us communicate than folks in the small "city" of Albertville. The Lord gave us a great little Fiat not too new, but in good condition, bought from a farmer. We could travel up to the chalet that they called "la Rocher" which belonged to the school. What a magnificent view!

Facsimile of "La Rocher"

We also visited Geneva several times, travelled through the mountains to Italy (with a beautiful view of Mount Blanc) and even visited some wonderful friends in

Schaffhausen, Switzerland, who were studying there, preparing for missionary service. These friends Gramma had the privilege of leading to the Lord in a small town on the upper coast of BC while she was on assignment for the foundation she worked for during our ministry at Fraserview. We just had to visit Paris and Marseille, so we made a

Loralee on the Fiat overlooking Albertville in Winter

special trip there to see the sites while visiting my cousin in Tours. At the end of the school year we sold the car and recuperated our money.

Incidentally, I sold the Fiat to a family from Tunisia who could speak little French, but a lot of Arabic, while I spoke a lot of English and a little French, yet somehow, we managed to barter and make a satisfactory deal, for us both. They motioned that we needed to seal the deal with a drink and poured out a small portion of beer in two glasses. The best I could, I told them I didn't drink beer, but they wouldn't hear of it and looked discouraged. Thinking that they might back out of the deal, I asked the Lord to forgive me (also the CMA) and drank the beer. The deal concluded happily for all.

In fact, that beer tasted pretty good to me. Everyone in France drank, wine and beer, Christian or not, so the next day I decided to identify with the culture and went out and bought a large bottle. One day, after a hard-played volleyball game, which we did on campus for fun and exercise after class, I came up to the confines of my apartment and pulled out of the fridge this nice big, cold bottle of beer and poured out a half of glass. It tasted terrible—so terrible in fact that I couldn't finish the glass. I poured what were the remaining contents of down the drain and gave the rest of the bottle away to the French couple that lived upstairs. The Lord seemed to say to me, "I allowed you to drink a glass so it wouldn't offend your neighbor in something that was very meaningful to him, but you don't need to drink for pleasure. In fact, you signed an agreement that you wouldn't, so stick to it!" And I did from that point on, all through my missionary career.

Simple Music and a TV

The other thing that we did was bought a TV. We wanted to surround ourselves with the French language and pick up the news on local broadcasting. This didn't help us as much as it helped our friends next door who already new French. They were an American couple, but she had grown up in Tunisia and spoke French like a native. He on the other hand, knew the vocab, but had such a southern drawl to all his French words that one could hardly understand him. She was an assistant teacher; he was a student, trying to perfect his Grammar and pronunciation. We became good friends and we spent a lot of time together discussing our lessons while playing Rook. They too had two little ones.

Another issue that arose was how playing simple music became a personal retreat to replenish my resolve to finish out the year. That year there were a few student casualties that couldn't handle the shock and the studies. I found a saxophone somewhere so went often to the chapel alone to worship and play what songs I could manage without having had any lessons. Oddly enough this became my quiet time with God which fed my soul when nothing else could. In general, that year in Albertville was a dark time for me spiritually. For us both I think.

Another MK

The biggest surprise greeting us in Albertville was that Gramma was carrying another child. She had become pregnant before we left Canada, but we didn't realize it at the time. She finally suspected something was up. A trip to the doctor confirmed that she was several months pregnant. With all the anxiety of packing and moving from Canada to France and then culture shock, no notice was given to how she was feeling. But after things had settled down a bit she began to suspect it while chatting with another mother—a CMA missionary heading for Gabon. Feeling embarrassed, due to the fact that the CMA did not send new missionaries over 30 with 3 children to language school, she wrote a letter to our African Director, explaining the situation in which she found herself. His response was that it was too late to have a special board meeting over this issue. Seeing it was already a done deal, they would just accept it and we would have to make the most the situation. Even though Gramma missed a total of about a week of classes, she still got a higher mark than I did at the end of the term (by one point) which put her in the Honorable Mention category, while I remained in the "Mention". That didn't make me too happy, so I got out and began using my French as much as possible.

On the beautiful spring day of May 14th, 1973, I assisted in the birth of our 3rd child, Jean-Marc (Jon-Marc). When a mid-wife jumped on the delivery table, straddled Gramma and began pushing on her stomach, I knew something was not right. I almost passed out seeing Gramma having real difficulties. I needed to sit down and put my head between my knees for a few minutes and then I took in the whole birth. Jon-Marc didn't make a sound when finally appeared and I thought there was something definitely wrong as they rushed the little guy away. But soon, I heard a cry and then the midwife presented to us a little package, neatly wrapped, breathing and wiggling in his little cocoon.

The next day I visited Gramma in the hospital and assessed the situation. Somehow I had to bring up the other two children who were dying to see their little baby brother. I noticed that there was a large window sash that could be raised and lowered to let in fresh air but also to serve as a fire escape. There were stairs on the outside with a small walkway all around the building. I got the idea of climbing up the fire escape stairs with the kids to Gramma's room and let the children in through the large window for a little family visit.

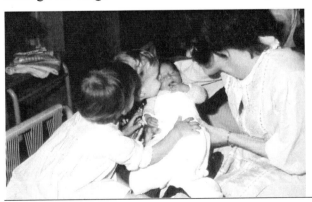

I very quickly and quietly opened the large window, scurried down to the Kids in the car and took them by the hand up the fire escape and through the window for a little family time!

Few nurses were around and the orderlies that were there said nothing! (In my earlier years with my buddies I had gained lots of experience climbing up fire escapes!)

Honorable Visitors

Gramma's sister, Auntie Joy, and our foster daughter Debbie, came out to visit us right after classes were over in the late spring of '73. We all piled into the Opel station wagon that we borrowed for doing our friends a favor and we set off to visit France, including tent and sleeping bags. We first headed for Paris and then the Cote d'Azur of southern France, camping along the way. It was a good experience and opportunity for us to use our French and see the country. After Joy and Debbie left, we drove back to southern France to drop off the vehicle. We even got to stay some days in Nice and in Monte Carlo before flying out from Nice to Kinshasa.

New Found Family

One wonderful surprise in being away from home is that we found "family" in France. I connected with a cousin and her husband (Ken and Bernice Frenzel) who, with their children, were missionaries in France, in the city of Tours in the famous Loire valley. We visited them a couple of times and learned to eat snails (we didn't know what we had ordered, but in butter and garlic everything tastes good). They took us around to see the castles of Tours but we most enjoyed interacting with new found family.

At Christmas, we joined them for over a week. Unfortunately, all of us, except Ken, were hit hard with the English Flu. Our heads were swirling like we were on a tilt-a-whirl, our throats were raw and extremely sore and we had a fever with heavy duty upchucks. Christmas

day was great for everyone and we thought it was over, but the next day it came back with a vengeance. I can remember Roddy staggering down the hall like a little drunk, weaving from side to side holding his little body up by his hands against the walls. It wasn't a pleasant time, but we all struggled through it and then we had to leave for Albertville. They were great hosts and did everything they could for us, but the flu just had to run its course. Perhaps it was a foreshadowing of sickness to come in the Congo (Zaire, at the time).

Turning the Other Cheek!

I thought that I would just add in this space a little lesson learned in France, on the way home from the Frenzels. One thing you don't do is serve yourself (self-serve) when you come to a gas station. We were running low on gas and it was around the noon period when most things shut down (which had not yet registered in my noggin). We pulled off the main road into a small town and found one gas station that had a gas pump, gravity feed, like I used to see when I was a little boy. When I drove up to the pump no one came out to serve me. I honked, like I would in Canada, to let someone know I was there—a couple of times, which must have gotten on the owner's nerves (as unbeknownst to me, he was having a siesta!). No one came, so I thought while I was waiting I would just put in 10,000 francs worth of gas. I figured out how the pump worked and started pumping with the 10,000-franc note ready in my pocket. Suddenly, the shutters flew open from an upstairs room across the narrow street and a man hollered something that I hadn't yet come across in my learning French! The next thing I knew, he was stomping hurriedly towards me.

Unsuspecting any real trouble, I was relieved that someone was finally there. I had just finished pumping and about to take a 10,000-franc bill from my pocket when he came right up to me and hit me as hard as he could with his fist on the side of my head. I looked at him, stunned! Not so much from the blow, but from the fact he would hit me. Then he hit me again as I didn't react. French didn't come to me as quickly as English, but he didn't understand that. I muttered something in French about just waiting for him, but he was too angry to even hear me. He took the hose and pump nozzle from me as I handed it to him and was going to hit me again—this time with the metal nozzle itself. I knew about turning the other cheek, but not about letting someone beat you up with a metal object. That was when I was ready for a fight and began to defend myself. When he saw that, he calmed down a bit and at the same time I explained what I was doing (the best I could in my limited French) and gave him the franc note. It was raining slightly and the kids were crying in the car because daddy was getting beat up. I quickly realized he thought that I was stealing his gas. He calmed down just a bit with the franc note in hand and I quickly went not so merrily on my way thanking God I had presence of mind to turn "the other cheek!" This was simply another example of not understanding the culture I was living in and ending up with a total case of "Culture Shock!" In more ways than one!

We did revisit France on one trip home when the kids were teenagers. This time we could communicate in French and were a little more culture savvy. We spent some great family times going up the Tour Eiffel, walking down the Champs-Elysées, visiting l'Arc de Triomphe and the Louvre. We even got to include a trip to all the glitter

and gold of Marseille. Those were wonderful experiences, but in '73 we had no premonition of that. We were soon to arrive at our "final destination" –the Republic of Zaire. We could hardly wait!

Gramma's Prayer Letters

Once we got to France, Gramma began noting little incidents of interest and including them in what we called a "Prayer Letter". These "Prayer Letters" started in Albertville and carried on until we retired in 2003. Sometimes only two a year, but we needed to keep in touch with those who prayed for and supported us. Here on the next pages are letters and notes of how Gramma saw things. The "happenings" from her perspective.

CENTRE MISSIONNAIRE
50 RUE DES GALIBOUDS
F-73 ALBERTVILLE
FRANCE.

Dear Ones at Home:

Before the novelty of being in a "foreign country" wears off, we thought we'd write and just share with you some of the things we've been experiencing. There is one thing that you will be most happy that we cannot share with you - a friendly bug named TOURISTA who has been faithfully making his round to all the newcomers to his country.

After our fourth week in Albertville we feel like we've been here a long time, except when we're reminded to the contrary on our trips downtown. It is relatively easy buying meat, yummy French pastries and fresh vegatables, because all you need are a few refined grunts, a talent for playing charades, numbers, and a pocket full of change. Trying to buy bathroom air freshner turned out to be a different matter. The best we could do was end up with some underarm deadorant: well it was pretty close, but we still felt like D.P.'s (translation for non-Canadians -"displaced persons.")

Actually every day after classes we praise the Lord for the little French that we've had, and, that way back at school the Lord guided our decisions to take French. We thought we had forgotten everything we had ever learned but surpringly enough, learning something for the second time around is just much less difficult. We knew it will get much more difficult, but right now we're thankful for the calm before the storm, so that we can all get adjusted to the new way of life here in France.

The children are really happy in the nursery, In fact with all those new toys and playmates, Loralee isn't at all anxious to leave when we come to pick her up after our classes. Roddy just takes everything in his stride. He doesn't care too much what country he's living in as long as there ~~is~~ an ample supply of food and someone to administer it.

We know that many of you have been remembering us to Jesus because we have sensed our minds being renewed and quickened. We continue to value your prayers more than we could ever tell you, as our studies get more difficult, pressures grow, and the longing for familiar faces and loved ones creeps in. It's so good to hear from home, so any news is good news!

Yours in France,
because of Jesus,
Jim, Dawn
Laralee & Rodney
Sawatsky.

Our last picture in Nice just before boarding the airplane for Kinshasa, Republic of Zaire.

Dear Ones at Home:

Today was especially frustrating! It is Saturday, and we were given time off from
our regular studies for a "Spiritual Life Retreat." After having the flu for the
whole ten days of our Christmas vacation, we felt in need of a bit of refreshing--
and then what? The speaker was giving an animated talk on the prayer life of
Elijah. He was getting so excited, speaking faster and faster (all in French of
course). There we were, sitting on the edge of our seats, straining every nerve
and catching only a few familiar words here and there--mostly conjunctions, adverbs,
and prepositions--things that only hold the meat together! One thing is certain, we
cannot depend on outside sources for our spiritual nourishment. Oh, am I ever glad
God can speak English in France! His personal communications to us are so precious,
and the reminders of your remembrances of us to Him take on a very special value here.

As soon as we started getting your Christmas cards and letters, we wanted to sit
right down and write back to each one, but it happened to be right before exams.
It's so good to hear from home and to hear your family news.

This Christmas, it seemed that all the frills were stripped away, and we were left
with only the essentials. We were really thrilled to receive an invitation to spend
our holidays with Jim's cousin and her family, who are missionaries at Tours, not
too far from Paris. (Wasn't the Lord good to find us relatives this far from home?)
Anyway, the day after we arrived, our whole family came down with a flu that has
spread all over France. We managed to have a nice Christmas day, going over the
Christmas story for the children and singing together. In the evenings the fevers
and nausea would subside somewhat, and we had some wonderful times of singing, talking, and praying together. Have you ever noticed that when you're sick, your heart
is very tender toward the Lord, and not cluttered up with thoughts of scurrying
around on sight-seeing trips, shopping sprees, or anything else? We were just very
thankful that there was someone to look after us, and that we weren't missing class
time.

On our days off from classes (Wed.) we have been able to do a bit of sight-seeing.
One day we went to Italy through the famous Mt. Blanc tunnel (only 2½ hr. drive).
Strangely enough, it felt like we were in a foreign country! The proprietor of the
restaurant we ate at spoke a little French, but he went away thinking that we were
French, and that Canada was a small village in southern France! Well, E for effort!
By the way, the ravioli was much better than any canned variety. When we got back
to France, we almost felt like we had "come home." It is most humiliating to be in
the process of being cheated out of money because you forget how many thousand lira
there are to the franc, or dollar, and not be able to do a thing about it.

As you have gathered, language learning is sort of a non-spiritual exercise, something like the confusing experience at Babel. On Saturday morning though, before
classes, something beautiful happens here. The frustration factor is noticeably
absent and we all bring our needs to the Lord in prayer, each in his own tongue.
It's really amazing how you can pray along with a sister in Christ in Japanese,
and a brother in German, and yet not understand a word they are saying. Somehow
the name of Jesus, understood in any language, makes the whole thing make sense.
No wonder there are so many songs written about "That Beautiful Name."

Sister, Ruth, said that seeing most of you are personal friends, we need not worry about keeping the letter short, so we have taken her advice. Besides, there just seems like a lot to say this time!

Because we got 86% and 87%, I was about to say that comparatively speaking, we are doing fairly well in our language study; but then again, it depends on whether you want to compare yourself to a Frenchman or another language student. How we covet your continued prayer support, as we have already experienced the quickened pace of this second trimester.

Loralee and Rod continue to feel right at home in the nursery and Loralee is starting to spice up her ever-expanding vocabulary with a bit of French.

Another newsworthy item is the forthcoming arrival of another M.K. (missionary kid), in early June (right before exams). Although our former doctor assured us that such a possibility was adequately cared for, it has become obvious that we are not in control of such plans. Although sometimes we feel we could have chosen a more appropriate time and place, the Lord has given a wonderful peace and assurance that He has a definite purpose in all of this. In the meantime, we will function on "borrowed strength," and wait for His plan to unfold.

Yours in France, because of Jesus,

Jim and Dawn,
Loralee and Rod.

P.S. We're almost adjusted to French cheeses. (But I think that 3 packages of Cheddar smuggled in from Canada had something to do with making that transition somewhat easier!) Maybe you could send a little snow our way, everything is still disgustingly green!

Dear Ones at Home:

Well I just found out that one of the best ways to pick up idiomatic expressions and colloquial French is to hang around a French hospital for awhile. Mind you, in the maternity ward, the vocabulary is rather specialized and limited in one sense, but it is also very practical and "earthy". OUR LITTLE FRENCHMAN ARRIVED ON MAY 14; 11:15 P.M. He was a bit ahead of schedule, but we were really happy for that as it gives us all a bit more time to get adjusted before leaving for another country. He has lots of dark hair and dark skin like Daddy, so he suits his name, Jean-Marc. We chose one that would "marche" in French as well as English--both Loralee and Rodney are sort of foreign sounding names to the French. Don't worry, we'll spell it the English way on his Canadian birth certificate, so he won't develop a complex about being "Jean" when he comes home to Canada!

I realize some missionary prayer letters say "we" and refer to Dawn and Jim doing such and such, so that you are never quite sure which one is writing the letter. In this case I guess it is sort of obvious! Although it is true that we were in the hospital, only one of us was constrained to stay! Anyway, for the ladies, I thought I'd include a few things that are different about having a baby in a French hospital. There is no doctor present, but the "sage-femme" (mid-wife) and her assistant really know their business. While the midwife was stretching and pulling, her little Italian assistant was on top, pushing--not at all like the Doctors at home who just tell you what to do and wait! Seeing they did half the work for me, it was accomplished in record time--4 hours from start to finish. Instead of stitches, they used "TIN CLAMPS." Sounds a bit barbaric? Actually they didn't feel very good either. Oh, and here's a bit of advice to save you from an embarrassing situation If you ever come to Europe and land up in a hospital. When the nurse comes in the room and hands you a thermometer, be imaginative and creative, but don't put it in your mouth. The French have a thing about taking even pills orally! Almost every type of medicine comes in the form of suppositories. I just bet nobody ever took the time to tell you that before!

It still seems a bit strange to encounter an older, dignified, refined little French lady in the grocery store, then later see her hop on her bicycle or motor bike and head for home with her round bread hung over the handle bars. Many other things though are so much like home: the beautiful mountains, lakes and trees. And the other things that used to be strange, like figuring in kilometers instead of miles, kilos instead of pounds, Francs instead of dollars, have become more familiar now. Spring came suddenly, accompanied by a mass of blossoms. Our province of Savoie is a famous fruit growing area, about like the Okanagan valley in B.C.

Even with all the conveniences of pure mountain running water, moderate weather, doctors around the corner, etc., we really are getting excited about getting to Zaire, (which should take place in the first part of August if visas etc. come through). Although the government has made some disturbing moves in the past year, the real move has been made against the Roman Catholic church and any neo-colonialism, as the Catholics in the old Belgian regime held political as well as religious power. All churches have been affected by some of the new stipulations, but our good friends there, the Ray Downeys, sent us a tape reassuring us that they have not been restricted at all in sharing the gospel and working with church and Y.P. groups. For the first year, to use our French, we will probably be teaching either in the Bible Institute or high school. We're excited about the possibility of being involved with real people again, instead of just books! In the high schools, there is a religion course scheduled into the curriculum, so with many of the students being non-Christians, this is a really great opportunity for sharing Christ on a personal, experiential level. The national church is mainly responsible for our placement, so maybe that can give you direction as you pray--that we will be put in that "pre-planned" spot that He has for us.

One more item! The Alliance takes good care of their missionaries and their basic needs, but about once a term, there arises a need that can't be met by ordinary scrimping. Mr. Klein, our director, assured us that soon after arrival we would find that we need a car, and that it is a necessity, not a luxury. Jim mentioned that a "greenhorn missionary" with a new car might seem a little pretentious, but again was assured that this is almost essential as "used" cars in Zaire are just too well used. I'm not too sure how to put this, but to avoid beating around the bush, we're asking you, over the next few months to pray about sharing this burden with us (the burden being about 4,000 dollars worth). The amount seems staggering, but the Lord has promised to supply all our needs...that is why we needed to be assured that a car is a definite need there. This item, classified as the SAWATSKY CAR, is on the list of approved specials that went through a system of approvals by the board of managers in New York etc. This all just means that your gifts, if sent to our C&MA headquarters, specially designated for the Sawatsky Car, will receive receipts for income tax purposes.

Final exams are only two weeks away. Jim jokingly said if we don't make it as missionaries, we should open up an A & W Root Beer stand here in Albertville! I'm sure it would be a success as the French love eating, but there just aren't "snacky" places here. You have to be hungry enough for a full course meal when you go out to eat. No such thing as a hamburger and chips!

Actually we are not worried about failing, but we do want to do our best. In such real and practical ways the Lord has showed us His love and care. We haven't had many hard times in our relatively short lifetimes, but this year has been one of the most difficult. It is a precious thing to learn that Jesus' love is just as real and active towards us when we are discouraged, sick or exhausted, as when our circumstances make living a pleasant, easy experience. Thank-you for praying. Many times we have literally felt "lifted" and strengthened by the prayers of those of you who have set aside that extra time.

May the experienced knowledge of His love open our eyes afresh to see the world from God's perspective. Yours in this part of the world....

Because of Jesus

Jim, Dawn and "gang"

P.S. Rod and Loralee think their new brother is really neat!

Part III – Introduction to Africa

Chapter Twelve: An African Fable

There was a time, a long, long time ago, when animals and humans could speak to each other. At that period, as the story goes, there was  a lion in dire need of food. The lion found out that when humans were in their gardens or on the outer limits of the village that he need not fear them, especially if one was alone. The one alone was easy prey and he began to assuage his hunger by eating the villagers one by one.

Of course, the villagers could not abide this killing and soon formed a hunting party to search for and kill the lion that was troubling all the villagers. The hunting party was ready and early one morning they set out to find the lion.

The lion himself was up and about looking for whom he may devour. The lion came upon a woman in her field. Having cleared a good parcel of land, she had gathered all the debris at the side of the garden and kept what she could use as fire wood in a clump under a large piece of cloth together with her harvest of manioc roots.

Just as the lion was approaching the woman, he heard the voices of the hunters coming from the village towards the gardens. The lion, cunning as he is, crept up to the woman, greeted her gently and said that he needed a place to hide from the oncoming hunters. The woman of course was very much afraid and said that she couldn't hide him; there was no place for her to hide him and she was frightened that he would do her harm.

"Oh no," said the lion, "I will leave you alone, absolutely alone. I will even help you with your garden, if only you could give me a place to hide from the hunters." Understanding that the lion was strong and that he could indeed help her greatly in the clearing of more land for the planting of a larger garden, she finally agreed to hide him. But he had to promise not to harm her. He promised.

The woman then said, "Quickly, get under this large piece of cloth with which I have covered some fire wood and some vegetable roots that I will take home to eat." The lion made himself as small as he could, crouched down and the woman covered him completely with the large piece of cloth.

The hunters soon approached and asked the woman if she had seen the lion. They said that he was a vicious and ferocious lion and that he had already eaten many of the villagers. He did not deserve to live any longer. The woman, thinking that the lion really wasn't that bad or perhaps it could be a different lion, lied and said that she had not seen a lion at all. When the hunters asked her what was under the cloth, she also thought of the help the lion was going to be to her and lied again, saying that it was fire wood and some cassava root she was going to take home to the village.

The hunters believed her. As they started on their way to continue the search they entreated her to call out to them immediately if she would catch a glimpse of the lion. She bade them good bye and promised to call out to them if she saw a lion.

 After the hunters had left and were gone into the forest to continue their search, the lion crawled out from under the cloth. He began to stretch, shake himself and then said to the woman, "I am hungry". The woman said that she had no food, but the meager collection of the cassava roots under the cloth. The lion said, "I don't eat cassava root. Woman, I am hungry, and I must eat!"

The woman in her frustration said that if he began clearing the land for her, she would look for some food for him after he helped her. The lion, coming closer, and closer, said, "Woman, I am hungry and I must eat now!" At that moment the woman began to tremble and began to cry out, but it was too late for the lion pounced on her and devoured her in a brief moment.

An African Understanding

Do not harbor danger of any kind; do not lie to protect wickedness for in the end it will be your demise. The inhabitants of the village always have benevolence in mind for the whole village. It is not yours to go against what the whole group has seriously considered and decided, nor is it wise.

A Scriptural or Moral understanding

A good portion of scripture that would apply to this story is found in 1 Peter 5:8-11 in the English Standard Version (ESV)

[8] Be sober-minded; be watchful. Your adversary the devil prowls around like a roaring lion, seeking someone to devour. [9] Resist him, firm in your faith, knowing that the same kinds of suffering are being experienced by your brotherhood throughout the world. [10] And after you have suffered a little while, the God of all grace, who has called you to his eternal glory in Christ, will himself restore, confirm, strengthen, and establish you. [11] To him be the dominion forever and ever. Amen.[16]

Our adversary the devil presents himself often as a gentle and friendly lion (a wolf in sheep's clothing), but his intent is always to gobble us up! If we are not grounded in God's Word, if we do not have a daily vibrant life of conversation with our Father, if we are not listening often to the "Shepherd's" voice, if we are not seeking direction of His Holy Spirit, we are in danger—especially in a foreign country. We must listen to the "community" of the Holy Trinity and the community of believers in which we find ourselves. Our "community", brothers and sisters in Christ, is seldom wrong. It is wise for us to be in community and to listen to its voice, for the "lion" is always ready to pounce.

And by-the-way, trying to cover him up will only work for a while and after that we always get a "raw" deal! He's out to destroy every believer, no matter how gentle he comes on in the beginning. I learned that in Kitimat and again in Maduda!

---

[16] *1 Peter 5:8-9 English Standard Version (ESV)*

Chapter Thirteen: Maduda–A Great Awakening!

Welcome to Boma and the Mayombe

The blast of the hot, humid air almost took my breath away as we stepped out of the DC-3 passenger plane on to the red dirt runway. In 1973, the President of the CMA church in Zaire, Pastor Joel Kuvuna, was at the airport to meet us, along with some other leaders of the CMA

church in Boma and a few missionaries. We were quickly whisked away to the Boma Guest House where President Kuvuna gave us a message. He first welcomed us to the Republic of Zaire and the Bas-Zaire area and then more specifically to Boma and the Mayombe, where the headquarters of the CMA in Zaire was located. He said that he had the same advice for all missionaries, "...love the people, love the country and love your work!" He also added that the church people will quickly recognize if you love all three or not. They will not be fooled! If you don't love all three, you will not have an effective ministry! After that he disappeared into the surroundings. We were officially welcomed and initiated!

His words were taken to heart and we knew he was right. We set about putting this advice into practice from day one! It next became apparent that we would live as a family on a mission station in the heart of the Mayombe forest and in this Bas-Zaire Province—one of 26 provinces in the whole country. The next day we were off to our new home. Our "barrels" hadn't come yet to the port of Boma, but the single ladies on the station had prepared the "house" and had enough stuff placed in there to help us get started in our new role as "missionaries". Wikipedia says, "Mayombe (or Mayumbe) is a geographic area on the western coast of Africa occupied by low mountains extending from the mouth of the Congo River in the south to the Kouilou-Niari River to the north. The area includes parts of the DRC, Angola (Cabinda Province), The Republic of Congo and Gabon. In the Democratic Republic of the Congo, Mayombe is part of the north-western province of Bas-Congo on the right bank of the River Congo, and contains the cities and towns of Lukula, Seke Banza, Kangu, and Tshela.[17] "Our village", Maduda, was at least a 40-minute drive from Tshela, the nearest center which was about 2 hours north of Boma (depending on the condition of the road).

The Mayombe is watered by many rivers with swift currents in its hilly and mountainous regions. The three largest are the Shiloango River and two of its main tributaries, the Lukula River and the Lubuzi River. It was in the heart of this lush forest area that began our first periences in the Congo!

The "Bayombe" of the Mayombe

The beautiful drive from Boma to Tshela (driven by our Field Correspondent, Jane Raffloer) was on a twisty snake like black road through the Mayombe forest. In '73 it was still a good asphalt road, made by the Belgians, which allowed us to make pretty good time. But we were about to have our first TIA[18] experience. A tree had fallen across the road blocking all traffic. We parked in front of it, on our side of the road and a taxi bus, coming toward us, parked on the other side—in his right lane.

"What do we do now?" I asked.

"A good question," Jane remarked, and then added, "we just wait!"

After a while more cars and trucks started piling up behind us and on the other side behind the taxi bus. Finally, out of nowhere, appeared men with axes and began chopping the tree. It took at least an hour to get a small passage way chopped through. They were good at what they were doing, but the tree was hard wood and there was no quick way to solve the problem. In the meantime, another taxi bus from our side went into the left lane where the passage way was opening and parked right in front of the tree and directly in front of the oncoming taxi bus. Now when a passage way was about to be freed up, the two

---

[17] http://wikivisually.com/wiki/Mayombe
[18] This Is Africa

taxi bus drivers began to discuss who would get to go first, for each were facing the other, head on, through the one lane that was being opened (on our left side). I soon learned that there were really no right lanes, no right of way, only if you had the loudest horn and the most animated personality, the loudest voice and the most people on your side, could you win the argument and go through first, no matter what side of the road you were on! After the tree was chopped through and a single lane was cleared we waited another good twenty minutes while the taxi drivers had it out! But we finally got going again and arrived at Maduda in good time! The single gals, four of them, had dinner waiting for us!

The road from Tshela to Maduda went through very rural Africa. We had arrived towards the end of the cool season—no sun and no rain for five months. As we scurried on through to our destination on the compact dirt, red dust flying everywhere, we drove through village after village which engulfed the road as little knots on a string at various intervals. It was hot and very humid, but not as hot as it was going to get as we still had about three more weeks of cool season. All along the way children, and a few adults, would run to the roadside hearing the car coming through the rain forest, and wave, calling out "mundele" or "miss-ee-ownee" (white man or missionary). We thanked the Lord for previous missionaries who had gone before us, who had gained the respect of most of the people in the area and left us a good legacy. It seemed to me all were excited to see us even if they didn't know us. The Bayombe were very pleasant people and most hospitable… much like our rural people of the mid-west.

Our Home

The temperature I'm guessing would have been 70-80 F degrees with 95% humidity! Those are my figures and I'm sticking to them! That's what it felt like to me. "And this is the cool season??" I thought to myself. For me, the humidity was almost unbearable. My mind flashed back to when I was in the Toronto area, on summer tour with our Kingsmen Quartet. I remembered thinking at the time, "Oh, I can't stand this humidity, this is terrible! Please, Lord, don't send me to a place that is as clammy and sticky as this is. I can hardly breathe!"

And here I was, in the heart of it. It was so humid that my shoes soon had sprouted so much mold that they were completely covered in the white stuff! After our arrival at Maduda, I didn't wear shoes for a couple of weeks, only sandals. When I went into the closet two weeks later to get shoes for a more formal meeting, my black shoes had turned completely white! (But I'm getting ahead of myself.)

We had finally arrived at our new home in Maduda. The "girls" as we called them (single women missionaries, Norma Hart, Trudy Hawley, Ruth Stanley and Gretha Stringer, all older than us and much more experienced in the ways of the forest-village of Maduda) were all there to meet us. They all lived in a long, white rancher type fourplex building with comfortable furnishings. The common front room, dining room and kitchen separated the two spacious bedrooms and two offices on either side. Each office had an access from the long veranda that stretched the entire length of the at least 90-foot-long building. After the introductions, a coke and a cookie, they all took us to our "new home"—a mud brick house fully furnished with two large bedrooms, two offices on opposite sides of the house with a large middle room and a good-sized fire place. That seemed odd when the temperature never got below 72 F, or so I thought. The house had a front and back veranda, both running the length of the house, all screened in just like the "girls' place." However, our kitchen was not attached to the house, but was a separate little room off the back veranda, all 6 to 8 feet off the ground at the back with an area underneath the kitchen for the gas motor operated wringer washer that we had purchased for washing all our clothes.

The stove in our kitchen was what my first recollection of our stove in Canada looked like—a wood burning, hutch type cooking stove of cast iron. My first reaction to the stove was, "Awesome!" Then I quickly realized why it was in a kitchen separated from the rest of the house! The heat in that little kitchen when the stove would be "fired" up would be almost unbearable, but the cook that was assigned to us seemed to take it all in good stride… and he was a very good cook! He cooked all our meals on that wood stove and did all the baking in the oven. He baked great bread and buns, delicious cookies and cakes for special occasions and he did the roasts, if we could buy local beef, chicken or game.[19]

The local fired and cured mud brick house with the high ceiling of 1-meter squares of plywood and the even higher pointed tin roof would keep the hot sun from scorching us and the open screened in verandas, front and back, kept us comfortable when a slight breeze would filter through from front to back. Because of the screens (including all the windows) all doors and windows were always open. There was plenty of room for all of us. It was a much better house than we had ever anticipated and again we thanked the Lord for the missionaries who had gone before us and had the forethought and insight to build such durable and effective housing which kept the mosquitos at bay and made our living most bearable, to say the least!

Gramma and I each had an office that had a separate entrance at opposite ends of the front veranda where we could receive visitors for private consultations when necessary. Our veranda became our dining room, where we ate all our meals, and it was also our receiving room, where we received all of our guests—which turned out to be quite a few. We hired a young girl to take care of young Jon-Marc, only three months old when we arrived, and we had other young boys, around 10 to 12 years of age who befriended our two and kept them occupied in many ways.

We both taught in the high school, trying to use our French as best we could. We both had our responsibilities at the school and on the station—although Gramma's first priorities were our children. I soon became in charge of station maintenance, taking care of the diesel-powered generator, the water reserve tank that supplied us with limited running (gravity feed) water. Yes, we had electricity from 6 to 9 every evening, which was a real blessing, and we had running water, but mostly when we would hire young students to run back and forth to fill up our big 50-gallon water barrels. We had 5-minute showers that would run from a tank on a stand higher than the down spout and sometimes very warm, heated by the sun, if we timed it just right. If

---

[19] Our Maduda house: Gramma, Loralee & Roddy on the steps with Paku, Poba and Emily (holding Jon-Marc, behind Poba). Emily was officially hired as our baby sitter, but Paku and Poba appointed themselves as playmates and guardians of our kids. They even came to church with us as a family. Poba was the son of the village thief. His father was reputed to have carried away a cow on his back to feed his children.

we really wanted a good shower, we waited until it rained and then ran out under the end of the eaves of the house where the water came cascading down upon us. Gramma didn't do it that much as it wasn't too becoming for a woman, but the kids and I did, when there weren't too many watching.

In this area, just below the equator, there were only two seasons: the dry season, which was hot, but cooler than the wet season and very humid, no sun, no rain which lasted for about 4 or 5 months of the year, and the rainy season, very humid and hotter, lasting for 7 to 8 months of the year, depending on where you lived. There wasn't however that much variation in Maduda. The dry season started the 15th of May and the rains came the 15th of October. There was nothing like a tropical, torrential down pour to cool things off a little and settle the dust. We looked forward to them. You could hear the rains coming through the forest, especially in the still of the evening, until they finally burst in upon you. With the tin roof amplifying the sound of the rain throughout the house and the thunder and lightning display of fireworks, we had our own 3D multiplex theater show of God's power. The sound was spectacular and the show was awesome!

By the time the cool season came around again we were becoming acclimatized to the heat. However, I never could stand the humidity. We found, too, that the fireplace came in very handy during the cool season drying out the dampness of heavy humidity which generally kept the house clammy and cool. The house was especially dark during the cool season as there was no sun at all, so we had a fire in the fireplace mostly all day long not only to stave off the humidity but also to keep a welcoming sign in the front room. That was most pleasant.

Our 1st Church Service

The "girls" had told us that the church service itself started at 9 am, but it wasn't necessary to be there at the very beginning for the service could go on for several hours. We could come late and go home early due to the fact that we had 3 little ones, all less than 3.5 years of age.

So we came late, our little ones in tow. By this time the sun was well risen and the trees along the ravine, carved out by the torrential rains, gave us welcomed shade as we descended the "mission" hill to the valley church. On our approach to the church we could hear the congregation singing and it grew louder as we came nearer. I will never forget walking through the front opening of the church and stepping into this forceful blast of beautiful music. There were several hundred people there, all singing at the top of their lungs, in four part or even 5 or 6 part harmonies. No need for an organ or piano (which they didn't have). It was all a cappella with all the frills and accompaniment done by many as they filled in the gaps with their voices.

We were ushered to a bench, with no back rest, to sit together as a family on the women's side and I tried to join in. They were singing their version of an old hymn that I had learned in church as a boy, but no one ever sang it like this before. *"Step by step, step by step, I will follow Jesus"*. I couldn't sing, I was overcome with emotion; I literally broke down and cried. My first thought was, *"What in the world am I doing here? These people already have a vibrant life in Christ!"* Immediately on the heels of that thought came the realization that *people at home must hear this*! They have no idea what a church in the Congo sounds like when they sing praises to the Lord. This is the fruit of many: all their sacrificial financial giving, all their sacrificial sending of their young, married and single, of sons and daughters and all their sacrifice of prayers for the missionaries and the church leaders. Many missionaries died to bring the church in the Congo to a vibrant, praising bride of Christ and here I was almost 100 years later, a rooky missionary, experiencing live and vibrant fruit (just one local village church body) all around me. Again, I thought, what in the world am I doing here??? Yet God seemed to whisper, *"Don't worry, I have something special for you."* Little did I know or could even imagine the things that God had in store for us.

That "whisper" reminded me of the scripture that God gave us in Kitimat, which we memorized as a family and which was to come back to me many times through the years of our working in Africa. God definitely knows how to motivate us and how to prepare us for what lies ahead! He did that after our first church service experience through these verses that we memorized.

Servants for Jesus' Sake

My first night in the forest area was frightening to say the least. There was a generator (diesel motor) that was fired up at 6 pm and shut down at 9 pm. It was almost like Bible College again. Get all your work done before 9 because lights out at 9 p.m. sharp. All the "girls" were teachers at the large school complex on the station, except Trudy, who was the local professional nurse and ran the Medical Clinic and Maternity Ward on the station.

When the lights wen out, there was a littl warning of several minute and then blackness! If y

This is the ministry of the new agreement which God in his mercy has given us and nothing can daunt us. We use no hocus-pocus, no clever tricks, no dishonest manipulation of the Word of God. We speak the plain truth and so commend ourselves to every man's conscience in the sight of God. If our Gospel is "veiled", the veil must be in the minds of those who are spiritually dying. The spirit of this world has blinded the minds of those who do not believe, and prevents the light of the glorious Gospel of Christ, the image of God, from shining on them. For it is Christ Jesus the Lord whom we preach, not ourselves; we are your servants for his sake. God, who first ordered 'light to shine in darkness', has flooded our hearts with his light. We now can enlighten men only because we can give them knowledge of the glory of God, as we see it in the face of Jesus Christ.

"Ours is a straightforward ministry bringing light into darkness" 2 Corinthians 4:1-6 J.B. Phillips New Testament

"Johnny-on-the-spot" with lantern and matches, you were engulfed in pitch black heavy darkness! I've never seen it or felt it so black! Now I've walked under stars in the bush before, back in my hunting and camping days or even in the logging camps, but somehow it was never this dark! That first night, I couldn't even see my white fingers in front of my face. As we hit the sack, fumbling our way to the bed with damp covers from the humidity, I began to hear cries and wailing in the distance and then drums announcing the death of a family member. I had goose bumps all over. All of a sudden there was a shrill, piercing shriek of a wail just outside our house. I went straight up several inches and came down with my heart in my mouth! What now! Apparently, a family member had just heard the news of the death in a nearby village and needed to let everyone know her sadness of heart and crossed the mission station, not far from our house, with her weeping and wailing. That was culture shock! It shocked me right out of my skin. But the shock didn't last long, for we soon understood their expression of grief.

Not long after we had settled in, after we had just purchased our little hatchback Fiat, there came a loud knock on our door, in the middle of the night… perhaps midnight or 2 a.m. I was awake immediately. It was pitch dark and I wasn't about to get out of bed, not knowing what might be on the floor.

Actually, I was quite surprised at the great accommodations we had. I expected a one room mud hut with a dirt floor and grass roof, but instead the houses that the missionaries occupied had been built some years earlier of mud-clay brick, baked hard in a fiery furnace. The same bricks were used for the inside walls. The house had two bed rooms, two offices, a large living room area with the same brick type fireplace, a smooth cement floor and a tin corrugated roof! Even though the house was far above my expectations, I wasn't about to get up and step on a snake or a cockroach, a scorpion or a spider as big as your hand or driver ants. No sir, not me! These creatures can get in anywhere!

When we first got there and talked about the station we were warned by the girls that if we were invaded by driver ants (sometimes called Army ants), we should just get out of the house quickly with the children and leave all else behind. When food supplies become short, these ants will leave their ant hill and form marching columns of up to 50,000,000 strong. Though considered a menace to people, they can easily be avoided as a column can only travel about 20 meters in an hour. However, their presence can be beneficial to certain housing communities as they perform a "Pest Prevention Service" consuming most pests, from insects to large rats.

Driver Ants

They literally give your house a good cleaning of all insects and their eggs, but make sure the children and babies are taken away. Their bite is severely painful with each soldier ant leaving two puncture wounds when removed. And, removal is difficult as their jaws are extremely strong. One can pull

a soldier ant in two without it releasing its hold. Large numbers of ants can kill small animals or at least immobilize them and eat their flesh. In my bare feet, I wasn't about to step into some driver ants preparing to take over the house. My mind was going crazy!

Now the knock came again, this time more insistent and then a voice, "Ko-ko-ko!" (that's knocking with your voice). Did I say it was dark and there were always insects, snakes and cockroaches around? I did mention that, right? I did what any red-blooded husband from the Western world would do in a situation like that, I elbowed my wife (Gramma) and said, "Dawn, there's somebody at the door!" Being the brave and dutiful wife, she got up, lit a lantern and went to see what the knocking was all about. Apparently, there was an emergency at the clinic and a woman needed to get to the hospital, a good 45 minutes' drive away, down a jungle road--including log bridges with a few boards put over top as runners and some with just logs. The question was, could I take this "mama" and get her to the hospital at Kinkonzi as soon as possible? I always wanted to drive in a car rally, so here was a good reason for me to see what I could do. Little did they know who they were asking! This was a great challenge for me, at night, in the deep African forest with a moaning lady in the back seat and at least one or two relatives with her. Yes, I would do it and I was happy that I was in fact useful in at least doing something that I knew how to do.

The event went well, but it didn't take us long to understand that it might be wise to have a small petrol lamp burning during the night in case we needed to get up for the kids

Our "jungle" road between Kinkonzi and Maduda

or for people who came knocking, not to mention if mother nature would happen to call. So the next time, a few days later, when there came a knock on the door in the middle of the night, I gave Gramma the elbow again and then mentioned that it would be alright as there was a glimmer of light in the front room. She came back to the bedroom telling me it was the same kind of emergency and that I was needed to drive a woman who was having a breech birth to the hospital as quickly as possible. Gramma trimmed the lamp and I got up immediately, gingerly stepping where I could see that there was nothing underneath my feet. We raced over the jungle road and made it with only minutes to spare. By this time, I was getting to know the road fairly well and the villagers were getting to know my car for we also went to Kinkonzi from time to time on a weekend to visit fellow missionaries. Although when family and missionary colleagues were in the car, I drove a lot slower.

By the third or fourth time this knocking happened, I began wondering what they did before I got there. Surely there must be another way. I mean, I was happy to help in an emergency, but there was no compensation for my gas and my loss of sleep. Perhaps there was another person who could help. Actually, there was no one else. Well, there were the girls, but they took much longer to get to the destination point, with cars that might break down and besides they had too much work to do the next morning--always having a full load of classes to teach. Then my Father seemed to whisper, "You are My servant for Jesus' sake."

"OK, I Get It."

At first, I was happy to be useful, but by the fifth or sixth time this happened, always in the middle of the night, this new "taxi driver" had many questions! By now I had enough nerve to get up myself, get dressed and meet the person who was knocking with keys in hand. But my mind was saying, "Why always in the middle of the night?" and

From L to R: Emily (our Jon-Marc's "keeper"), Muanda (our cook), Loralee, Jon-Marc with Poba, our laundry helper, Gramma with Roddy and Grandpa and our little hatch back Fiat with a homemade roof rack that worked well when we all needed to get away on an outing or a vacation.

again, "What did they do before I came with my taxi service?" ...and "How come it is always me that has to use my car and gas—there is wear and tear on my car you know? Who's going to think of that?!" and "Who is going to buy me new tires?" I was beginning to have a few flats because of the sharp rocks on the edges of the road and I had a couple of bent in rims. For me, when I finally got over the complaining, I was happy with the fact that it now took less than 40 minutes. I had shaved at least 15 minutes off the time and knew the road like the back of my hand. I could drive that road in the dead of night and still make good time. It was especially fun just after a heavy rain where I could slither through the mud and splash down through the water holes. I'm sure some women thought they might not even get to the hospital alive!

In my quiet moments, I couldn't believe that I had come all this way (as a missionary) just to be a taxi-man! But in my complaining, and the complaints always wanted to be there after numerous trips, the Lord kept on bringing this scripture to mind, *"It is Christ Jesus as Lord whom we preach, not ourselves. We are your servants for Jesus' sake!"* I was on the road called "beginning-to-learn-what-it-means-to-be-a-servant", in another culture, for Jesus' sake. Outside I was pleasant; inside I was often kicking and complaining.

One day I was visited by the acting president of the church, Rev. Tama Tsasa, also the pastor of the 500 strong church at Maduda. He had a few people with him who spoke for him and they asked if I would be able to take the "Vice-President" to see the actual president who was very sick and dying in a village about 80 kilometers away—perhaps a couple of hours by car. It would be a ride further away from any large center and further into the Mayombe forest. I felt flattered that the president would ask this little missionary and said immediately that I would. I was thinking that we would be able converse on the way and this would be my opportunity to get to know him, perhaps even become friends with the "acting president" of the CMA church in the Congo, which at the time was about 60,000 members strong.

On the given day, his secretary, a fine Christian man who spoke French, told me that he was not able to go and that I would have to take pastor Tama on his own. Right, but who would interpret for me. He suggested we would get by and we did, but not as I anticipated. I started the conversation in French and the acting president smiled and said in Kikongo that he didn't really speak French. And the rest of the way we sat in silence--so much for getting to know this fine, dynamic man of God! Getting closer to our destination he motioned for me to turn and gave me directions with hand signals. He knew I didn't know Kikongo. We made it to the president's house, where I thought I would go in with him and meet this man of God who all knew was dying, but he motioned for me to wait for him in the car. Ooh-kay, I thought, at least they will come out and invite me in for something to eat before we leave. It was now already around noon and I had learned by this time to love Congolese food so was anticipating a good Congolese feast. But no invitation was given and no food!

I waited for several hours. I think one person from the village came and talked to me for a short time. Other than that, I was left alone. It finally dawned on me that this wasn't meant to be a social trip or a friendship trip. I was *purely* transportation, nothing less or nothing more. *Simply* put, my car was the taxi and I was meant to be the taxi-man. I may have been acting right, but I wasn't "pure" by any means and the complaints began arising one after the other. At least I thought, this being "church" business, I would get paid for the gas. Where did

The view of the Maduda Mission Station from our front veranda.

that thought come from?? Not a chance! I was the missionary-servant and this was my mission!

Finally, Pastor Tama returned with a big smile and motioned for us to turn around and go home. It was early evening by the time we reached the outskirts of the Maduda village and the pastor motioned for me to stop. I pulled over; he got out, said some sort of brief thanks, shut the door and was on his way to his house not far from the main road. That's it? No fanfare, no offer to pay my gas, no cheering for making good time there and back, no ceremonial offering of thanks. Just "good bye" and not even a prayer of blessing! I came home deflated and hungry. All that I was good for was being a taxi-man! ...and the Lord whispered, *"I put My word in your heart before you left that you would be **My servant**. Now you are learning to be just that!"*

On Being a Hearse

An experience that really capped off "being a servant" with great punctuation was when a man and wife approached the house with a little child on her shoulder, covered with a white shawl due to the hot sun. She stayed back a little and he came to the front door and knocked. We were having lunch on the veranda and I saw them through the screen coming up the wide walkway. Our house was at one end of the mission station and the church/chapel for the students was 130 meters straight across on the other end of the property. On either side of this

30-foot-wide thoroughfare were the other homes and the class rooms. I could easily see the couple coming and had already made up my mind.

I got up, went to the screen door and greeted the man. He asked if I could help him. He needed to go to his village and he needed a ride for his wife and child. "I knew it!" I said to myself and before he could explain or say anything more I exploded with "No, I don't think so!" In my mind I was saying, "Oh, this guy thinks this taxi man is an easy catch, a push over for helping people, so I'll just ask him to take me to my village some 50 klicks away." I reiterated my thoughts aloud, "I don't think I can do that today ...no, absolutely not!" I'm thinking again, "Pretty soon everybody and their dog will want a ride somewhere or other!" But before I could close the door and go back to my seat he finished his explanation.

"Oh," he said in faltering French, "you see, the baby that my wife is carrying just died at the clinic and I have no other way to get to my village to bury her. If we walk, it would take a long time to make it that far and the body would be decaying due to the hot sun." I was stunned by the grief that this couple must been going through, yet so calm. And yes, he was right. By the time he and his wife walked to the village the little baby's body would be decomposing and stinking. Then came his words again, "Would you please help us?"

Immediately I felt like an idiot for refusing so fast and being so hard. I regrouped and then responded with a, "Yes!" I told Gramma the story, which she pretty much knew already as the screen door was the only barrier between her and the man, some 20 feet away. She agreed that I should take them. I quickly put some gas in the car from a jerrycan in the garage and we were off... the man in front with me and the wife holding the corpse of her precious baby in the back. Again, I was thinking of the brighter side of the trip. Once we get to the village, people will receive us in true to Congolese fashion and hospitality. They will respect me for my service to this young couple and possibly even give me a meal for my good efforts and then I'll be on my way home. Funny how we often tend to think that we will be rewarded when we do some good deed, or at least hope we will! However, I learned, a true servant never expects any payment or reward for he is just doing his job—that of being a servant.

We made a few turns off the main road and then the road became narrower and narrower as we went further and deeper into the forest. The forest was thick and pressing in. I noticed as we passed a few villages there was a stirring, it seemed the word had gotten out, but no one had said a thing. As we passed close to the last village before the road narrowed completely and ended, I sensed there was some kind of commotion and noise, but how would anybody know what was happening. There were no phones to phone ahead and say, "Our baby died and we are coming home with the body." No, but there were jungle drums and I heard some of them off in the distance. By the time we got to the end of the road there was already a delegation to meet the couple. Suddenly, as we came into view, there was great weeping and wailing. Loud wails! Unrelenting and unnerving wails and loud crying! The likes of which I have never heard before, so close and in my face!

Well, forget about the missionary! They were showing their grief together with the young couple as they were ushered out of the car and down the trail to their village, I presumed some distance away. And again, there I was left standing… all alone! No "thank you", no food and no one to show me the way back. All the people that were there to meet the young family followed the couple and I could hear them crying and wailing in the distance as they continued, deeper into the forest.

I managed to turn around in that single lane, two-tire track, grassy road and headed for home. I was thankful for the small Fiat. It was great, but I had no music in the car for company, only the wind and the forest noises. I went home thinking of the loss and grief the couple must have felt and although the wailing was unnerving to me, it must have been a great comfort to the couple who I would never see again. And my Father whispered, *"You are my servant for Jesus' sake!"* I was finally beginning to understand and it was a good thing too for I would be a "taxi-man" in many and varied situations in the Congo for the rest of my time in Africa.

A Trek through the "Jungle"

Not too long after our arrival, I had the urge to see other villages and get to know the forest area first hand. Our cook was brought up in a village just over the next high hill (coming from BC I wouldn't call them mountains) and through the valley. Finally, one day he said that he would take me there on the trail that the old missionaries used to take to get to his village. There was a road that almost reached his village, but that was the long route. If I wanted to walk with him, he would take me to his village through the forest. I agreed to trek there with him, but asked if it would be all right if someone would come to pick us up after our hiking expedition. That was fine and Gramma agreed to pick me up at around 2 pm and we all would drive home. She would have a local gal with her who knew the way.

We started off after breakfast (we always ate at 7:30 am and the kids were up at least an hour before, if not two) and made our way through the jungle to the base of the "mountain" and then on up. It was

a fairly stiff climb for this white boy who thought he was in pretty good shape. Mid-way up we met a very old woman walking down with a strong stick for support. She was alone going somewhere, we didn't know where, but she was from our cook Muanda's village. He knew who she was and they quickly made the connections, in the Mayombe language, and then he explained that I was a missionary from Maduda going to visit her village. She immediately got down on her knees and began to thank me for coming. She said she hadn't seen a missionary trek through the forest to come to her village for many years (over 40 years), since she was a young woman. She was so grateful that she knelt in humbleness of heart, gratitude and respect for me, but more so I think for the former missionaries who had trekked through the forest to bring her (and her village) the gospel. She asked for a blessing. I was taken aback. Now I felt humbled and almost embarrassed, but there in the thick forest on the steep side of the mountain, I prayed God's blessing on her and her family. She was jubilant and again began her struggle down the hill. We, in turn bade her "good route" and began our struggle on the way to the top then down to the valley and the village below.

I think God allowed this encounter more for me than for her. This was possibly her last climb through the forest, but it was my first and the encounter would again instill in me a heart of gratitude for the missionaries who had gone before me, plowing the "field", sowing the seed and also reaping a harvest that prepared the "land" for other sowers and reapers.

By the time we got to the village it was around noon, the sun was high overhead as we emerged from the forest onto a wider dirt and grassy path into the village. They somehow knew that we were coming and many in the village were there to greet us. We were immediately taken to a house of one our cook's relatives and given water to drink. I can assure you I was thirsty and drank my fill with thankfulness. They then set a table before us and we were given some great Congolese food to eat. After a couple of hours, the ceremonies and the "banquet" were over. Abruptly, someone came running in to say that there was a car about a kilometer away with a "Mundele" in it. It was at the end of the road and I knew that it was Gramma. With a great "escort" of many, especially children, we made the final kilometer trek for the day, got to the car, said our good-byes and drove home.

A Bout with Hepatitis

Before we left, I was given an invitation to come again in two weeks to preach on a Sunday, but this time I said I would come with the car. In the meantime, I was preparing my school lessons and teaching classes, but for some reason my physical strength was failing. The Friday before I was to go back to the village, I walked from our house past the chapel to my last class for the day (about 200 meters in all). By the time I got there, I was completely exhausted, I had to sit down and rest before teaching. I knew the sun was hot, but something wasn't right. This wasn't like me. Sunday came, I got up early, gathered my Bible and notes and together with Muanda we made another trip to his village, only this time with our little Fiat Hatchback. We walked the last kilometer and I preached in French, with an interpreter, my first sermon in the Congo! Whether it touched hearts or not I do not remember, but after the meal of gratitude for my coming, I felt I had to go home. I wasn't feeling at all well and barely made it back to the car. By the time I made it home I was extremely fatigued, I had a high fever, I was nauseous and vomiting. My muscles and joints ached so badly that I went straight to bed—and there I stayed for the next six weeks. The doctor from Kinkonzi was summoned and after several visits finally decided that I had hepatitis, which I knew beforehand due to all the symptoms: I was jaundiced, my stools were white and my urine was dark brown (almost black) and I had lost my appetite. It was presumed that it came from the water that I so lustily drank the first time I visited Muanda's village. It was a dark time.

Doctor Stewart ordered complete bed rest with jello and powdered milk as my only diet. Fortunately, we had brought jello along in our barrels and so did the girls. I really don't care for the stuff, but there was plenty of it for the first few weeks until I could get down more substantial soft foods, like Quaker Oats. I was so weak it was a chore to raise my hand and I needed help getting to the bathroom. As hepatitis can be contagious, no one was to touch me or get close to me, so my kids were off limits and of course so was Dawn. I was alone in a dark bedroom. However, through the weeks the time in bed turned out to be a precious time with my Lord. Flat on my back, the only way I could look was up. I prayed much, listened to a series of tapes on the authority of the believer, which really encouraged my heart, received many student visitors and continued to practice my French in speaking with them.

This time was most difficult for Gramma who now had one of my classes on top of hers, 3 little kids to mother and now a 4th one, an invalid, who need to be taken care of. Of course, the kids were all over me in the beginning, climbing in bed with me and trying to console me until we found out that they could catch it too if they ate off my plate or drank from my cup etc. So, Gramma graciously tried to have them keep their distance from their Daddy. During this time Gramma was reading in Psalm 91 and was encouraged by these verses:

...*9For you have made the LORD, your refuge, Even the Most High, your dwelling place. 10No evil will befall you, nor will any plague come near your tent. 11For He will give His angels charge concerning you, to guard you in all your ways.*[20]

Then one day, Gramma noticed that Roddy was becoming quite lethargic. He wouldn't eat and then observed that his urine was dark and his stool was light. This wasn't right! She, by herself in the front room, stood in the middle of the room, lifted her Bible, open to Psalm 91, to the ceiling and shouted to God, "You promised that none of these plagues shall come nigh thy dwelling [King James Version]! I consider

---

[20] *Psalm 91:9-16 New American Standard Bible (NASB)*

more than one case of Hepatitis a plague. In the Name of Jesus, I rebuke it! Amen." The next day Roddy was running around like his normal self with no trace of symptoms.

After six weeks, I started to feel stronger and began to do light chores. I even began teaching again. Maybe I was doing too much, too soon, for I landed smack dab in bed again.

I felt the first time was permitted of God and He brought me a lot closer to Him. I gained back that relationship I had lost in France. But this time, I had a sense that this was not of God, but of the enemy. The next few days were not good and I didn't even have the strength to get up to take in the Bible study and prayer time that we had with the "girls" on Sunday evenings. But, while they were singing and praying I felt the Lord asked me to call them, "the elders", and have them pray over me.

However, much to my chagrin, I was too much of a chauvinist in those early days, thinking that men could only be "elders" or spiritual leaders, not understanding that these lady missionaries were all of that and more. It was a real struggle for me as I thought I was to be the "man" the "spiritual leader" of the group. Here I was flat on my back being nudged of God, my Father, to call the "girls" to come and anoint me and pray over me. The meeting was over, but I wouldn't give in to the Spirit's prompting. The "girls" were already out the door when I finally ate humble pie, again, and feebly called out to Dawn to have them come back in and pray for me. They were gracious enough to do just that and then went on their way again. It was a prayer of faith and of authority. The next day I was up and never looked back. God answered the prayers of his "elders" and from that day on I looked on single women missionaries in a much different light—through the eyes of the Holy Spirit.

My buddy and colleague, Ray Downey, also contracted Hepatitis A at about the same time around the end

Both Ray and I were recovering from Hepatitis

of October. By Christmas we were both well enough to drive to Muanda on the West Coast to spend our Christmas vacation on the seaside at a mission house in an area called "Vista". It was great to get together as families. I can still see Ray and me sitting on chairs trying to roast wieners. We felt like we just came out of a concentration camp. It felt a lot easier to sit than to stand at that point. I remember that it was also pineapple season and we bought loads of them. We ate them every day until our mouths broke out in blisters from all the acid.

Jon-Marc, Rodney and Loralee after fishing!

At Muanda, we were great fishermen. Our method was simple. We would go down to the beach early in the morning and watch the fishermen come in with their catch. We would bargain with them for the best they had and come home with Barracuda, Perch and Capitaine[21]—the greatest eating fish you can buy anywhere!

By the end of our stay there, about 10 days, we were ready to get back into the harness and face whatever would come our way. How could we know what God had in store for us?!

Jungle Breaks

After Christmas we went back to Maduda and got ready for the next school semester. I taught physical education to the 5th and 6th year (grades 11 and 12 in Canada) boys and religious studies.

We got to really enjoy our time in the deep forest. Every once in a while, we would take a break and trek to a water hole with a water fall and do some swimming and diving. We explored other sites and even got to swim in slow moving good-sized stream that seemed very safe for the whole family. There were vines hanging down so I profited from the Tarzan movies I had seen as a kid and started swinging down making ape like noises and then flopping un-ceremonial like into the stream to the glee and laughter of the kids—and the dubious wonder of

---

[21] *derived from the French for Captain, sometimes called Hogfish, an edible marine fish found in the western Atlantic*

my wife-- specially when I came up without my wedding ring! I had lost so much weight when sick with Hep A my fingers were too skinny to keep the

Rod, Loralee and Jon-Marc swimming in the Kinkonzi River

wedding ring on and with the pressure of the fall in the water it came off in the splash down—gone forever.

The Crippled Man

Not long after my bout with hepatitis, we were again sitting around the table on the veranda when saw a man with very crippled legs drag himself on the ground with his arms right up to our front screen door. He knocked and when I answered he asked for some money. I immediately thought of the story of Peter and John going to the temple to pray[22]. I remembered how they said that they had no money, but what they had they would give him. Peter said, *"I have no silver and gold, but what I do have I give to you. In the name of Jesus Christ of Nazareth, rise up and walk!"* Then they took him by the hand and raised him up. Immediately his legs and ankles straightened and he began walking and leaping and praising God.

There was a great inner urging to do that exact same thing. But my thoughts began to wander, "What if nothing happens and he doesn't get up and walk, then you will really look stupid!" …and, "What if he does rise up and walk, then I will have every invalid from miles around at my doorstep wanting to be prayed for and healed!" And then, "I'm just a rookie missionary, am I ready for this, how could I handle this?" Too many questions flooded my mind and although I didn't have a lot of "silver and gold" I had a little and gave him some money and he went on his way.

I agonized in my spirit over that visit. I confessed to not having obeyed the Holy Spirit and told the Lord that if I ever had an occasion

---

[22] *Acts 3:1-10*

like this again and He prompted me to speak on His behalf, as did Peter, I would not shrink back, no matter what the case. From that point on, there began the questioning in my spirit when a similar situation would arise, "Lord, what would You have me do in this situation?" and whatever HE said, whatever I felt the prompting of the spirit to do, I followed. It wasn't the easy way, but it was what I promised and it became the most encouraging way to me. God always showed up. However, I must say that I never had another experience just like that again during my whole time in Africa.

Enemy Attack

One day towards the end of the school year, I was called to the "girls" house for a very important matter. Gramma was busy with her classes, but I had a free afternoon and so went over immediately to see what the crucial issue was. I saw a young girl sitting in the front room with the missionaries all around. When the girl looked at me, I knew there was trouble, or should I say, "I knew she was troubled!"

I learned that the year before about the same time as this, when the seniors (the 6th year students or grade twelve) were getting ready to study hard for the government exams, a very odd and incomprehensible wave of hysteria occurred. It started first with the 6th year girls, in the dorms and then spread to the 6th year boys. It seemed that none of the students were in their right minds. It was so bad that none of the 6th year students could study and all were sent home to preserve the school from great calamity. No final exams were written.

Now, the Maduda Christian (or Mission) School had one of the best reputations in the area. It's students often gained the highest marks in the area (except at times for a friendly rival catholic school), so having to close its doors to the senior students without them being able to write the finals was a complete disgrace. It was a total catastrophe and the devil was happy.

This same catastrophe was about to be repeated. Some of the girls came to the missionaries saying that they had bad headaches and that some had already begun to flee into the forest. The girl sitting before us was one of the high school leaders. She said that she felt she was "going off her head" as the saying goes in French or Kikongo and that she was having bad dreams and horrible visions in the night that were scaring the whole dorm. The hysteria was again beginning. She came for help and the missionary "girls" called me as they had heard that we had had some dealing with the enemy and understood the authority that the believer has in Jesus.

I had called the chaplain, a pastor from Angola, to come with me, but he wasn't sure what to do. I felt we had to deal with the source, the devil and his evil spirits who would really like to bring down our Christian School for the second time. I began to recite some scriptures, we also read some key passages from the Bible and then we prayed claiming our authority in Jesus. Saying out loud that all authority is given to HIM and all principalities and powers are under His feet. We claimed out loud that we are seated in heavenly places with Christ Jesus in His eternal plan and therefore all these powers are also under our feet. We claimed the presence of Jesus and His Holy Spirit and stood against all the powers of darkness that would want to disturb this school year and the students from finishing well. We commanded Satan to leave the school alone and not to send any evil reinforcements, in the mighty Name of Jesus.

During this time the girl was very fidgety and uneasy. We turned our attention to her. I told the girl that I wasn't going to speak to her personally, but was going to test to see if there were any spirits present. I took a positive approach and demanded in the Name of Jesus for the evil spirit who was causing all this ruckus and confusion to reveal his name to us. Immediately she gave the name Satan. I didn't believe it, so I addressed the spirit that responded, told him that I felt he was lying and that I wanted his real name, in the authority of the Name of Jesus. Then she voiced the name "legion".

This we could believe because of the massive disturbance that was already beginning. In our immediate praying, we bound "Legion" together with all his cohort evil spirits and we cast them out of and away from this girl and the whole school. We commanded "Legion" to leave, to go to the pit and to take all his underlings with him—in the powerful Name of Jesus. We loosed her in His name to be free to study and pass her exams and we loosed the whole school from the grips of Satan in the powerful Name of Jesus Christ to do the same thing. Then we talked to Luzolo and tested to see if there were any more evil spirits that were tormenting her. Nothing showed up and she testified to the fact that she felt much better, that her head was clear and that she had no more fear.

Well that stopped the enemy in his tracks. The girls who fled came back to their rooms in the dorms. Both the girl's and the boy's dorms, were quiet. Everyone studied hard and passed with very high marks which was an example of God's grace, power and mercy to the whole school and to all schools that were in the surrounding area.

Director Klein's Visit

Not long after this the C&MA director for Africa came to Maduda for a visit. As we chatted, I asked what he thought the next steps for us would be. Our French was improving, not perfect by any means, but improving. Should we stay another year in Maduda and begin learning Kikongo? He was grateful that our French was better and that we were willing to stay in the Bas-Congo area, but the CMA church in the Congo had been requesting for a long time at least one missionary family to come and help the ministry in Kinshasa. He wanted us to go there. There was another missionary family there, Bud and Jean Hotalen, but they had been mainly dorm parents, looking after the missionary kids who went to The American School Of Kinshasa. Seeing that there were very few kids at this time in the mission, they were being called to Bouake, Cote d'Ivoire, to the missionary kids' school there. They had not been involved that much in the local church's ministry as they had been too occupied with the children. Now they would be moving on and he would like us to take their place.

Not that we had much choice in the matter, but we said we would pray about it and talk to him about it the next day. We were quite astonished that we would be asked to go to Kinshasa where there would be no other CMA missionaries and no one to show us the ropes. And yes, we did say we would go as we believed God had given us the green light. (Being the loner, I was glad that we would be breaking ground for the CMA in Kinshasa.) But, when we asked the Director what he thought we should do, he simply said, "Learn the language!" That's all he said. We found out immediately that the language was Lingala and no one in the mission knew that language. And also, there were no books in the mission's possession that would help us learn the language. Well, that was an encouraging note, as we would not have a language committee looking over our shoulders expecting certain results threatening to send us home if we didn't make the mark! No one (no other missionary) would know if we knew the language or not! We would set our own markers (I was cool with that). I was always fine with that! This Maverick was broadly smiling on the inside.

"But," I asked, "What are we to do once we learn the language?"

He threw it out again, "Learn the language," and said nothing else.

I came back with, "I understand that you want us to learn the language. I get it, but what else would be expected of us in Kinshasa?"

"Learn the language!" was his brisk reply.

"OOOOHHKAAY, I get it." was my reply, "but surely you must have something else in mind once we've LEARNED THE LANGUAGE."

One more time he looked me square in the eyes and said, "LEARN THE LANGUAGE!"

I got it! I was cheesed off that he couldn't say anything else, but he certainly got my adrenalin going and his responses had the desired effect in me. I said to myself, "OK buster, I will learn the language and do nothing else. I will learn the language so fast and so well your head will be spinning, MR. DIRECTOR!"

That interview got my adrenalin going so pumped that my memory flashed clear back to Mrs. Kincheloe's phonetics class at CBC where she got out the mirror and made us do such contortions with our mouths and tongues that we almost died laughing right in class. I remember she would almost climb down our throats just to see if we were making the right configurations with our tongues, teeth and lips. In short, she really prepped us for understanding that to learn another language well, we needed to lose all our inhibitions and familiar mouth formations!

Not only that, I remembered going through an elective phonetics class at UBC, doing almost the same thing. And then I remembered how we had the grueling task of learning "Pigeon English" in our month of Institute of Linguistics in Toronto just before leaving for France. It all came back to me in a flash and I knew that this was going to be no easy task. But at the same time, I was sure that I wasn't going to let brother Klein down!

Until this day, this is pretty much all that I remember about Mr. Kline, our USA CMA Africa director. That, and his answer to Gramma when she wrote him a letter from France telling him that she was pregnant and apologizing for the fact that she didn't know it before we left Canada and was sorry now for the fact that before getting to Africa we were going to have 3 kids—instead of just two. We were over the limits[23] that the CMA had set down for sending out missionaries, at that

---

[23] CMA USA stipulated that for them to send out missionary families they should not be over the age of 30 and they should not have more than 2 children. If they couldn't come in line with these two criteria they would not be sent.

time. He kindly wrote back and said, "Well, now that you are there, it will just save the board from having an extra meeting for your approval!" Just before we left for France, I turned 31 and just during our language school we had our 3rd child... this "Maverick" just slipped under the wire, AGAIN!

Gramma's Prayer Letters from Maduda

Gramma always wrote letters home to those who supported us in prayer. They were called prayer letters. For many years she sent them to her sister auntie Ruth and she in turn sent them to a long list of people who desired to receive them. I am convinced now that because of the prayers of the people in America (USA and Canada), we experienced answers to prayer and saw God intervene on our behalf many times during our ministry in Africa.

There were many times during our missionary career that I had prayed. "Lord lay it on the hearts of the people at home to pray." And, there were times,

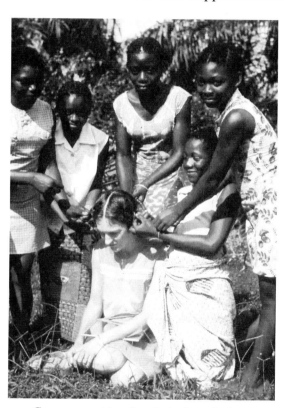

Gramma getting her hair done by her Maduda Jr. High School students!

not too infrequently, that we sensed that prayer support. We wrote these circular letters not only to show our appreciation to all who were praying but also to report on our family life and ministry to those who supported us financially.

B.P. 46 MADUDA par TSHELA, BAS-ZAIRE, REPUBLIQUE DU ZAIRE, AFRICA
Author's Note: Tshela is the nearest town of about 35,000 people, about 45 minutes away from Maduda on a dirt forest road. Written August 1973.
Dear Ones at Home:

All summer long Loralee was asking, "can we go home?" Well, now we're <u>home</u>, and it feels just great! After Sept. 4, Maduda will also be home for about 300 students, so there will be no end of things to do. Although "youth meetings" as such have been banned by the government, 2 eager young men who will be in their final year of high school, assured us that there would be nothing to stop us from giving an open invitation to anyone who wanted to come to our house for a discussion of the Bible and a time of prayer (every Monday evening). Only the very fortunate and bright ones ever have a chance to complete their studies at this high school, after which they are qualified to teach primary school. There are 1,100 who write the school's entrance exams, and only 60 who are accepted to enter the first year of high school--most of whom are 14 to 16 years old. Our main responsibilities are first of all to perfect our French by a proposed 6 hours of study per day; teach 1 hour per day, and just be here when the students need us. Seeing that Jim is the only man missionary on the station, and seeing that the great majority of the students are fellows, I have a feeling that the latter assignment will be the most time consuming (but probably the most rewarding also). Maybe you could pray that somehow our days could stretch.

When we first arrived in Kinshasa and were entertained in the homes of different missionaries, it seemed to be rather pretentious to ring a bell and have someone promptly come to clean all the dishes off the table, and set about to wash them. Our ideas were changed a bit when we found out how coveted the job of a "houseboy" really is. I had fuzzy ideas of a "boy" doing dishes and other odd jobs around the house. That isn't it at all. Our "boy" is the father of five, has the respected job description of "cook," and is one of the best paid men in his village (17 Zaire or $34.00 per month). He is a Christian, has a beautiful smile, is well trained and sings harmony whenever we strike up a tune! His French isn't fantastic, but with a few gestures we make out just fine.

To explain our situation here a bit, Maduda is a village of somewhere near 500 people--actually it is the largest village in all of Bas-Zaire. The mission houses and high school buildings are sort of together in a centralized area up on a hill. The closest city is Boma, about a 3 hour drive if everything goes fine. (Our first trip up, we had to wait ½ hour while they cut up a tree that had been felled across the road. We're in Africa! What's the rush?) The church here at Maduda has been indigenous ever since 1931 and is pastored by a wonderful Godly man who is the vice-president of the C&MA here in Zaire. We were amused by a translation of part of our introduction to the church people which of course was given in kikongo. The pastor explained why we had left our country and had come to help the Zairois church in a teaching ministry. Then he explained the fact that we were "REAL" missionaries because we had brought our three children with us. The 4 single girls informed us that the Zairois always did think that they were a strange breed of people, and the 2 missionary couples that had been here previously couldn't have any children. There haven't been any white children on this station for quite a few years so ours are still quite a novelty to the other children. One of the most important things in life to the Zairois is to have lots of children, so our having 3 in rather rapid succession has told them very realistically that we are just like they are. (I just hope we don't have to keep on proving it!) Other than having their hair tousled, the children have really had no upsets while playing with the national children. Loralee has singled out as a special friend, Pobe, the son of the village thief. Don't get upset, grandmas! He's a lovely gentle boy and is just thrilled with Loralee's attention. He has always been discriminated against in school because of his father, so now he's enjoying his new position of prestige. Anybody who can play on the missionary's porch, read books, play with a toy dog that walks, and eat cheese curls has got to be "in."

Another item that bears mentioning is the fact that the government has made it an offense to receive dollar cheques through the mails. We wouldn't want to land up in jail because of your generosity! We have had to open another account in Canada so as to be able to write cheques on our allowance. However, we will receive any money marked "Sawatsky Car" or otherwise, which is sent to our New York headquarters, 260 W 44th Street, New York, N.Y. 10036.

The next big item on our list is the receiving of our barrels. Duty charges can range from nothing to 100%! Seeing that we are commissioned by the King, we'll shoot for the bottom, i.e. the "nothing." Please pray that the officials whims will be favorable.

By the way, if you have any "good used clothing," there is no end of need here and many an odd job around the station could be paid for with a nice T shirt etc. I'm sure even "bad used clothing" would be better than what most have, but it is too expensive to send. It gets fairly chilly here in the cool season, so clothes are not only luxury items to these people. Most parcels have been getting through without being stolen of late as our food doesn't interest them and they are no longer allowed to wear European clothing--part of the government's new "Authenticity" program.

In case you're wondering about the food we eat, we haven't gone native yet--our stomachs aren't quite ready for that. They eat some very bland root vegetables and rice, which they spice up with hot peppers, so we buy our supplies at Boma, a port city which also caters to European taste buds. We were invited out to dinner to the high school director's home and for every bite of food, we had 2 swallows of water (that was warm too!). Being in the city might have some advantages, like being closer to food supplies etc. but being in the "bush" has others. The lush tropical growth is much denser here and it is much cooler--which is something we feel very thankful for. This is now our winter, the cool dry season. The hot rainy season begins October 15th. You might smile like we did, but they said, "just wait, the rains will come maybe one day early or one day late, but October 15th it is." Remember it is the wind that influences our unpredictable weather in the northern Hemisphere--there are no winds here!

Again, I intended this to be more brief and there are still oodles of things I didn't mention--next time. We appreciate any and all communications of your thoughts, and praise Jesus continually for people who care enough to pray.

Yours
at home in Africa
because of Jesus

Jim and Dawn Sawatsky and "clan"

P.S. There aren't even as many mosquitoes and flies here as there are in Kitimat B.C. (there are a few more lizards and cockroaches though).

Dear Ones at Home,

Well even the most predictable thing in Zaire (the commencement of the rainy season)
we found to be unpredictable!! It came a whole month late and consequently the bean
crop was ruined. We had some "showers" but were informed that that was not yet
"real" rain. Although we had never experienced the "real" rain, we had no trouble
recognizing it when it came, and we celebrated by just sitting and listening as our
whole house vibrated with its roar. It came just in time to save the peanut crop!

The Lord is also doing some unpredictable things in our lives. However, with the
discovery that His ways are always perfect, there is a new sense of security which
is based not on continually fluctuating circumstances, but on the reputation of
God Himself. What a marvellous thing to realize that Jesus had our circumstances
in mind when He said, "In everything give thanks for this is the will of God in
Christ Jesus concerning you." To be perfectly honest, it wasn't even too difficult
for Jim to say, "Thank you Jesus for hepatitis!" His schedule was getting so
hectic, it didn't take too much discernment to realize some of the purposes God
might have for his time in bed. French studies, Bible studies, Kikongo studies,
classes, weekend preaching assignments all came to an abrupt end on Nov. 11. No
doctor had to tell Jim to stay in bed, he just couldn't get up! Then came the
diagnosis--hepatitis with a possible four to six weeks in bed and a six month recovery period. (Hepatitis is a disease which damages the liver and is usually
contracted through impure water.)

The African custom when a friend is sick is to come and "sit" with that person.
Being of western culture, we feel a little bit strained just sitting without
"words," however, during these times of "sitting" Jim has formed some friendships
with students and pastors that may have taken many months during well and busy days.
Also during this time, the Lord communicated some real special promises to Jim
regarding our future ministry "in the city." We heard that we would be moved to
Kinshasa, the third largest city in all of Africa, sometime this summer (your summer). Although we love "the bush" just knowing that the Lord is going before us to
the city is good enough. There are advantages too, like running hot and cold water,
electricity all day long, an electric range in lieu of a wood stove (that makes the
kitchen like a blast furnace) and other things like fellowship in an English-speak-
ing international church!

Have you ever thought about how much the way you communicate, the way you express
yourself, is really you? All of a sudden it is a real shock to the personality to
realize that we can no longer relate to people in the manner in which we have become
accustomed. We can't use our own little pet expressions, or even ask the same kind
of questions in establishing relationships. In short, we've been feeling like we've
been going through a major personality change. In one sense, we feel like split per-
sonalities--one personality while speaking English and a different one emerging in
French. We are learning to daily commit this to the Lord and it is tremendously
rewarding to see Jesus use our feeble attempts to share His love with students. The
very morning we were leaving for our Christmas vacation, the drum at our Secondary
School was being beaten for an unusually long time. As we were sitting around our
breakfast table on our open veranda one could easily see that something unusual had
taken place. Our houseboy, Moanda, who has a reputation in the village for being up
on all the local news, informed us that a student in first year (Grade Seven) had
died that morning. I discovered that it was Mbumba, a boy from the very class I had
to teach that morning. We hear the death drums from various neighboring villages
almost once a week--death is an ever-present reality with our people. The Holy Spirit
used this death of their classmate to remind seven students of the need to be sure of
their personal salvation. Because there was no time to prepare a lesson to fit the

occasion, this was my first experience at really having to trust God to fill my mouth with the right words in French. After those seven students indicated their desire to follow Jesus, and after having prayed and counselled with them, on the way back to our house, I was left with the distinct impression that I had just been standing in the right place at the right time. Pray that these students will learn the disciplines necessary to becoming effective disciples of Jesus. They are the future teachers in our schools.

Another note of praise in answer to your specific "asking"...our barrels came through customs with a record low customs bill! First term missionaries used to receive exemption, but that is no longer the case. We won't complain at having to pay about $200.00 as the last two families have had to pay $600. and $1000. Anyone would have a hard time convincing us that prayer is a waste of time.

Tomorrow is the last day of our Christmas vacation. We have spent two wonderful weeks with our friends from Bible College days, Ray and Viola Downey, and their three girls, at "Vista," our mission house on the Atlantic coast. Here again we were reminded that our Father is a millionaire. Where else could we enjoy beaches--Hawaii style--perfectly private for forty cents a day? Although we love the snow, exchanging it for white surf and sand wasn't too difficult. We had a lovely Christmas and it was helped along by a few goodies that were included in our barrels. (Mom even slipped in a couple homemade Christmas puddings. Money just cannot buy things like that in this part of the world!) Thank you so much for all your Christmas greetings. I wish there was the time to acknowledge them all in a more personal way.

Our children are adapting to our new way of life with the kind of ease which is peculiar to the very young. Jean-Marc rides a back like a true African. There's a knack to it! If the child is too old when he starts, his legs just dangle instead of curling around the waist. We have all but given up trying to keep shoes on Loralee and Rod. This business of conforming to the group begins long before teen-age--how's two years old for starters? For an afternoon snack Loralee goes down to the river to catch little fish. Then she goes with Viviane, our baby sitter, to her house to cook time in palm oil, after which she eats them with great relish--heads and all! In some areas I'm adapting a bit slower. When the flour is wormy, I still pick the worms out of the bread--if they're visible. Jim doesn't bother. He says that a little extra protein never hurt anyone. And besides, they're cooked!

As usual I'm having a hard time knowing where to stop, but we do want to express our deepest gratitude for the communication of your love and prayers. It is the awareness of that concern that makes our home here in Africa feel safe and secure.

Praising Jesus at Maduda,

Jim & Dawn Sawatsky and family

P.S. I have permission from the editor in chief to add this footnote. I just want to praise Jesus with all of you who were praying for me in my recent illness. He has answered prayer and given me remarkable recovery strength so that even the doctor was surprised at my progress. Pounds are being added daily and I am now able to resume teaching and language studies, although I still need my "augmented" siesta each day.

Jim

Chapter Fourteen: Kinshasa 1974

Avenue de l'Eglise

The large house in Kinshasa had been used for a CMA kid's hostel and was an amalgamation of two full houses that were constructed as a duplex. Each side had three good sized bedrooms, one bath room and one large living dining room combined with a small kitchen in the back room. It was built on "Church" Avenue or "Avenue de l'Eglise" which had a slight incline, at the bottom of which was a bit of a marsh with no other housing in the immediate area except for our neighbors up the road and across the street down to the marsh. Our side was open, beside us and behind us. The house had a chain link 2-meter-high fence around it with barbed wire on top and two partly screened heavy duty metal

Loralee age 4 climbing to the top of our driveway gate—CMA house Kinshasa

gates, at least 3 meters wide and 2 meters high with spikes on top. The two gates were single gates side by side separated and anchored by a heavy duty 4-foot-wide rock column, each opening for its own side of the duplex. The house was basically one long large house with two gates, two parking driveways and two garages, built in flush with the outside of the houses. The lower end of the house had a smooth cement slab of about 40 x40 feet with a basketball hoop at the back end. It was a great yard for the kids to play in, ride their bikes and later shoot lizards off the fence with their pellet guns or catch all kinds of bugs and butterflies. The surface was so smooth on the cement slab that when it rained the kids would go out and slide around on their bare feet or even tummies as the heavy rains made for a great slippery surface.

The Sr. Hotalens had four children of their own, but the CMA missionaries' kids had been depleted to virtually none. When we began our move to Kinshasa, the Hotalens were in the process of moving to Cote d'Ivoire. They took basically everything in the house except for an old settee, a dining room table and chairs and a few kids' beds and the air conditioner in the master bedroom which we bought. It was best investment I had made up to that point (without realizing it). That bedroom became our haven, our prayer room, counselling room and Gramma's office. The first day we moved in we were expected to be hosts to several returning missionaries. I had to meet them at the airport and bring them to the mission house. Gramma had to have beds ready for them and feed them three meals a day until they could get down country. We were frantic for we had no bed linens and no food, but we did have the mission 18 passenger mini bus to transport everyone. I'll let Gramma explain this part:

"I remember that I had to feed 16 people (including our family) and had to prepare beds for most of them. I felt total panic as all our things were sitting in a truck in Boma waiting for a full load of other stuff to bring it to Kinshasa. I asked someone who had been there for a while where I could find a phone so that I could phone to Boma to check on the status of all our belongings, including food stuffs, furniture, bedding and kitchen utensils. I was informed that the only phone that seemed to function was at the Assembly of God mission headquarters down town Kinshasa. So, we went there immediately. It was a large house with extra living quarters on the property, but being downtown it was close to the central post office that was also the national telephone company and had good access to a telephone line that worked. An AOG missionary by the name of Sylvia Turner, just "happened" to be there at the same time. When she learned of our dilemma, she said, "Oh, I just received boxes of food stuffs from our ladies' prayer groups at home. I have packages of cake mixes, jellos, popcorn, Nesquick and preserves all done up in cans for long term storage. I have more than I can ever use in four years, so you can take all that you need and you don't have to pay me back. Furthermore, I have a friend who is a wife of a doctor and know that she would be happy to loan you all the linens and pillows you need to make up the beds for all your guests."

Well, we didn't even need to make that phone call. In one trip everything was taken care of, unheard of in Kinshasa. On my way back home, the Lord rebuked me by saying, "Before you pray, I will answer. You didn't even pray, you just panicked!"

I was very grateful for all the help and did thank God for his faithfulness in supplying all our needs."

The "National" Language

Before we left Maduda we had a visit with our Africa Area Director, Mr. Klein and his main theme was "learn the language!"

We really didn't know where to start, but found a work book that former missionaries to the Equator Province had written. Lingala was the principle language in that large area of the Congo, from here President Mobutu Sese Seko came. He soon tried to make Lingala into the "national language" of the then named Republic of Zaire. By the time we arrived in Kinshasa, Mobutu was well entrenched in the presidency of the country. He was also called Mobutu Sese Seko Koko Ngbendu Wa Za Banga ("The all-powerful warrior who, because of his endurance and inflexible will to win, will go from conquest to conquest, leaving fire in his wake").

His original name was Joseph (Désiré) Mobutu, born to common villagers October 14, 1930, in Lisala, Belgian Congo, now The Democratic Republic of the Congo. He came to be president of the country, that he later renamed the Republic of Zaire, after seizing power in a 1965 coup and ruling for some 32 years before being ousted in a rebellion in 1997. I've personally heard it said by government officials that after Mobutu became president he made a pact with the devil so that he would remain in power and in control of the whole country. He would seal the pact by renaming the people and the land (Zairians of Zaire), by renaming the central water system (the Zaire River) and by changing monetary system (the money to be called the "Zaire") and the devil would give him complete power and authority over all the country. But this would also mean he sold himself, his people and the land to the devil. With these new names Mobutu also laid claim to all the riches of the country and the people. He   controlled the water supply of the country (the Congo or Zaire River and the Inga Dam which could supply enough electricity to help all of Africa) and laid claim to the money of the people. That worked for a while, but I digress. Let me get back to Kinshasa and learning the language.

Language Study

So, Gramma and I were introduced to a young MK from the region of upper Zaire by the name John Tucker and asked him if he would help us learn the Lingala language. He agreed and after three months I gave my first sermon in church. It wasn't the greatest, but the people were kind and accepted it.[24] John was from the Bangala region of the northeast of the country, so we started learning the old Lingala or "Bangala" which later came in very handy to me when trying to understand the root meanings of the more technical terms and the Biblical or theological terms. Studies with John didn't last long for when he saw me on my way, by attending the message that I gave that Sunday, he felt he had done enough and began to lose interest.

Not long after I preached my first message in Lingala, I began to think that I would get by OK. The language would come on its own. That's when I ran into a startling scene. I was up town doing some bulk buying for missionaries down country. The warehouse was full of people buying large quantities of produce and groceries—it was the way it was done in those days as the local grocery stores had almost nothing in them—when all of a sudden, I heard a man hollering at the top of his voice, reaming out a black man. He was white and he scolded this Congolese with a tongue lashing that made me embarrassed! …and he did it in Lingala! I looked around; others were embarrassed too and felt very uncomfortable still I could see that they thought that it was the right thing to do. Obviously, this Congolese had made a grave error. But right then, the Lord seemed to whisper in my heart, "If this white man can express hatred and anger so fluently in Lingala, how much more fluently should you be able to express My love."

I said, "You're on." I went home that day with this scene etched in my mind and went straight to the books.

Congolese Pastoral Duties

We were excited about what God was doing in Kinshasa. Shortly

---

[24] Several years later, I found the message in my desk drawer and really couldn't make out what I was trying to say. But I had to start somewhere!

after we arrived the Congolese church required me to be the pastor of two churches. This wasn't my idea of what a missionary should do, not the CMA's either for that matter, but because I thought it the better part of wisdom to comply for a short time with the Congolese pastors this maverick said OK. There I was pastoring two churches and not really speaking Lingala well enough to pray fluently—just now barely able to do that in French. I certainly felt more comfortable in French, but most of my parishioners either knew Lingala well, or Kikongo, but not so much French! So, I learned while pastoring (one good way of learning a new language)! One of my churches doubled as a grade school class room and had a blackboard behind the pulpit. It was great, for in my speaking on Sunday morning or Wednesday night prayer time, if I didn't get the word in Lingala that I wanted, I would say it in French and ask who could give me the Lingala word (or words). Then I would write it (them) on the blackboard behind me. When I needed the word again, I would look back and give them that word in the sentence I was using and most of the time we would all say it together. After having used the new phrase a couple of times and having written it on the blackboard, I never forgot it. While visiting the parishioners, I generally went with a deacon from one of my churches, so he could interpret for me when I couldn't understand. We would pray with men and women in the home and I would learn key phrases in Lingala and soon I could put all those phrases together into a meaningful prayer conversation with God and with those for whom I was praying.

About six months after our arrival in Kinshasa there was a Lingala course being taught by a Congolese and the director of the Bible Society of Zaire. The American director sponsored the program and did some teaching, but Mr. Kabongo, our trainer, did most of it and he did an excellent job. I learned a lot. So much so that early in the new year of 1975 the Bible Society invited me to head up the translation team that would translate the Old Testament into modern day Lingala. There are several versions of Lingala; some might call them dialects, which were floating around in those days. There was Upper River Lingala, or Bangala or old Lingala (the language we started on) which many in Kinshasa found it difficult to understand. There was Catholic Lingala, Protestant Lingala and then the emerging modern-day Kinshasa Lingala. We were translating the OT into modern day Kinshasa Lingala. Later that year the Bible Society was asked by new missionaries to teach the course again, but the director didn't have time and Mr. Kabongo would not do it on his own. So, we teamed up, using the same exercise book. It was a lot of fun. One year I was a student and the next year I was the teacher, but Kabongo helped me a great deal.

During the first 3 years I was in Kinshasa ('74 to '77), I worked hard with the Congolese District Superintendent to establish or plant new churches and new prayer cells. Most of the churches sprouted from vibrant prayer cells meeting throughout the week. CMA pastors had been in Kinshasa for 10 years by the time we got there and had planted 9 churches—a great beginning for the CMA in Kinshasa. The District Superintendent, Pastor Mabiala Mavungu, was a go-getter and could see great opportunities to establish a witness for Christ in an "unchurched" area. He pastored one of the largest churches (of 500 to 600 members) for the CMA in Kinshasa. The church building also housed a large elementary and secondary school operating in two shifts. He was a busy man, but also had great vision. So much so that the missionary (myself) and the national pastor (Mabiala) working together created such synergetic energy that during those three years (including my learning the Lingala language, pastoring two churches and working with the Bible Society) we had encouraged the planting of 24 new CMA churches. Now, in total, in Kinshasa, before leaving in 1977 for home assignment, we had 33 vibrant churches meeting every Sunday morning (and many more prayer cells).

It was also in those years that Pastor Mavungu envisioned a Bible School at Kikimi which we worked hard to establish. Almost 40 years later I sent this note to the President of the CEAC (the Alliance Church of the Congo) after having been to Kinshasa and meeting the new director of the Kikimi Ministries.[25]

---

[25] ...*Just a little history: Gramma has supported Kikimi since she was there teaching in the 1990's. From time to time friends have sent funds to us for the purpose of supporting this ministry. This funding had never quit. So, with a little from us, and more from friends, especially one family, up till just recently, money came in for students in Kikimi Bible school every month.*

It was in 1976-77 that Pastor Mabiala Mavungu and I walked around a large plot of land near a small village called Kikimi. We had no money, but God had born in us a vision to have a plot of land where we could build a campus or Center, for young people to study the Bible, just as there was in Kinkonzi in Bas-Zaire.

We got there on a sand/dirt road that went directly past his church at Rifflart, past the village of Lemba Ebu and finally on to the village of Kikimi. We went directly to the chief of the village and the ensuing area to pay him a visit and then to solicit a few hectares. He received us graciously and then he showed us a wide field. We walked around the number of hectares (a dozen acres) he showed us, all the while praying over them and claiming the fields

The International Community of Kinshasa

The first thing that we were told when our CMA missionaries heard that we were going to Kinshasa was, "There is a big international community there, but don't get involved with them as they will keep you from your work with the national community and the national church." Well it turned out that it was the international community that actually helped us get established—some were missionaries and some were former missionaries who had come back in different roles, some were embassy personnel and other were business people. We were very glad for their help and they gave us good tips for living in Kinshasa. None of our C&MA missionaries were there, so we took encouragement from the international community.

In the "bush" our kids were in the village a lot of the time. They went there with Vivian, a girl who was hired to look after our kids while we were teaching. Jon-Marc would be on her back and the other two would follow her down the hill to explore the creek near the village with the other preschool kids in Maduda. Rod and Loralee were often not hungry at supper time. We figured out why by the yellow ring around their mouths that they had been eating saka-madeso (beans and

---

for a Bible School for the CEAZ in Kinshasa. We especially thought of the evangelists; those who were just starting to work on the plateau and who had very little or no Bible School training. Pastor Maurice was a visionary. I had a vehicle. And together we asked authorities for many plots of land in many neighborhoods of the vastly spread out city of about 3 to 4 million at that time. We always indicated that we were asking on behalf of the CEAZ Church and the land would be used for the construction of schools and churches for the CEAZ, but ultimately for the glory of God the Father.

Over many years following that first prayer walk, we had contributed to and encourage the construction of the Institute and participated in numerous graduation ceremonies. But as my ministry began to change, it was Mama Dawn, who took up the torch of Kikimi for the two of us. She started teaching at Kikimi the end of the ' 80s s and soon, born of God in her, there was a great desire to help feed the students who were coming to study each day with empty stomachs. She wasn't sure how to help until one day in the CEAZ Church at city Mama Mobutu God told her to feed students herself. We didn't have much money to spare, but we started to give the little we had and God began to provide for them in incredible ways. Each week, money would come in so that she had enough to buy food for the students. All this came to a crisis when the looting broke out in '91. One morning Mama Dawn thought she would buy rice and fish near Kikimi with Mama Deborah rather than in the city as was their habit and then bring it to the students. But unfortunately, she was arrested by the soldiers that morning, the Peugeot Pickup was confiscated and the women were left on the side of the road. Fortunately, we had a friend who ran a paint factory just a couple hundred meters away, so the ladies walked to his place for security. As all transportation was at a standstill, due to the looting and the rebelling soldiers, it took Mama Deborah a long time to get home. She finally arrived two days later, at home, with the $200 intact... more on this story in another section.

finely ground cassava leaves cooked in palm oil) in the village. We heard that they had also been trapping minnows (baby fish) in the creek and popping them in their mouths as did the village children. They began speaking Kiyombe and Rod even spoke to me at one point in Kiyombe after being reprimanded. I didn't know what he said, but I said, "Rod, you don't speak to me like that and in that tone of voice." I found out later that he told me to take off, repeating exactly what he had heard other kids say in the village when they weren't happy with someone or someone's actions toward them.

The kids were feeling quite at home in Maduda, but when we got to Kinshasa it was a completely different matter. There was no "village", it was city life. There were no village kids to play with and no one spoke Kiyombe, it was all French or Lingala. There were paved streets, mostly, and lots of cars where we lived. We finally found a new girl to help us with the children, but she turned out to be a prostitute, teaching our kids just the opposite moral ethics than what we were teaching and living. This was not good! That was when the Lord told Dawn that her first responsibility was for her kids and not to shove them off on someone we didn't know just to learn a new language. Jon-Marc was just over one year old, Rod was 2, almost 3 and Loralee was 4 years old when we arrived in Kinshasa. Dawn heard correctly and began pouring herself into her kids. There would be no more "girls" to whom we could pawn them off.

At first, we all went to the Zairian churches as we were expected to do on a Sunday, but that didn't turn out well. The church services lasted up to 3 hours, way too long for children, especially ours who didn't understand the new language and who had no friends at the church. Many of the Zairian children would come and pinch our kids just to see what their skin was like and/or pull their hair. Our kids now were beginning to extremely dislike going to the national churches. They began having bad impressions of what "church" was like—too long, too boring, no understanding of what was being said and too much fighting against the kids who always pestered them—we didn't want that. Therefore, seeing we were the only missionaries from our mission in Kinshasa and seeing that our children were starting to balk at going to Zairian churches and seeing that they had no Zairian friends in any of them, we made an executive decision that Dawn should go to the international church of Kinshasa with the children and I would continue going to the national churches.

Had we stayed in Maduda things would have been different. The children had begun to recognize other kids in church, they were starting to understand the language and had children their age or even older that they could communicate with and enjoy. In Kinshasa, in our neighborhood with high walls and fences, far from any Zairian church, there were no children they knew, no one to play with and no language used that was recognizable which resulted in them getting totally frustrated with life in Kinshasa. Jon-Marc shut up completely and didn't speak at all, only grunted! He was quite a bit over two before he began mouthing English words. Rod and Loralee were also unsettled.

However, that all changed when they began going to IPCK (the International Protestant Church of Kinshasa). They had mom with them all the time now (no long shoved off on some girl they didn't know or particularly like), they could enjoy Sunday School with children that spoke the same language (no more pinching and fingers in the hair), they could sing the songs in English and learn new "church" songs (the old hymns of the church and worship songs), they enjoyed children's church and it wasn't nearly as long. Soon good friendships were made which carried on into primary school, first in a British run school and then in the American School of Kinshasa.

It didn't take long for Dawn to be completely involved at IPCK for that became her home church. We also went there on Sunday evenings as a family and took in a short evening service. We really enjoyed the fellowship of other missionary families on a Sunday evening. I soon was asked to lead worship on those evening meetings and that pretty much lasted throughout the time we all lived in Kinshasa. Most often, Sylvia Turner (Aunt Sylvia) would play the piano (she could play anything, in any key) and I would lead worship with about 100 or so expats. We would sing the familiar hymns, but also would bring in some new worship songs brought to us from friends in America.

International Bible Study

Bud and Jean Hotalen passed on to us a Bible study that they had started with Dave and Dot, an American couple (from the embassy) and Bob and Prim, an African American pharmacist and his wife—we were all about the same age. They both had just come to know Jesus and were eager to study the Bible. Bud and Jean introduced us to each other just before they left and there we were in an instant Bible study with two other couples—brand new Christians. Dave and Dot lived just down the street from us in a palatial home and the other couple lived not that far away.

We always met at Dave and Dot's place. As they were close by, we showed our night guard where we were. We would put the kids to sleep, tell the night guard to keep an eye on them through an open window—with screen and antitheft bars—and to come and get us if there was a problem, then we walked up the road about half a block to have our study. Several in the group still smoked, a few drank, we all sat there with our Bibles open on our laps, trying to see each other through the smoke.

With a drink (alcohol) in one hand, a cigarette in the other they would ask good questions about Jesus and how to live the Christian life. We had good studies, but often wondered what we smelled like to the night guard ("sentinel" as he was always called in French and Lingala) as we came home. Little by little the Lord revealed himself to those couples, as He always does so intimately when we come to Him. The smoking went, the drinking in excess also went and new couples began coming to the study. We picked a book from the Bible and then began reading it together, stopping to give personal experience, to ask questions about it or to just marvel at the truth. Over the years, the study grew to become our "home church" fellowship. Eventually, there were two other neighborhood couples that joined us and we would have a good group of at least a dozen and sometimes more.

Sharon and Marty, up the street, came to know the Lord and grew in Him through the influence of that study. I remember Marty saying at a study, "that makes so much sense; I knew my church didn't have it right. We need to accept Jesus and change our meeting place on Sunday to the International Protestant Church of Kinshasa." And as Marty did, his family followed! I had the privilege of praying with Marty; Dawn had the privilege of praying with Sharon. After we got to know them well, Sharon was always at our place. She had no other place to go and was bored at home. After many visits and talking about the Lord and the Christian life and what that meant, Sharon said she wanted that personal relationship with God through His son Jesus as Gramma had explained it and as she saw it being lived in her friend Dawn. After that she became Dawn's right hand "man" in mission duties. At first, Gramma had great challenges in spending so much time with her when children and language study duties were calling, but it paid off in great dividends when Sharon gave her life to Jesus. The

Lord told Gramma that He loved white people too and that He brought some of them from around the world just to meet Him in Kinshasa. Together we had many opportunities to "disciple" internationals in Kinshasa—adults and young people from many nations, but all spoke English. Gramma was a great teacher and a compassionate disciple maker.

During our Bible Study, Dave gave up drinking and Dot gave up smoking! Although it was some time before Prim did, but that is another story. We never mentioned anything about it to them, but as we studied the scriptures the Holy Spirit began to work in their hearts. They began to understand that their bodies were temples of the Holy Spirit and belonged to God.

Dave told us one night at Bible study about what actually happened, for we knew that something had changed and there was no more booze at the study. He said that he couldn't sleep one night and finally he heard the Lord saying to him to get up and pour all his "booze" down the toilet. This was a hard thing for him to do as he had acquired a lot of it, a whole wall full. But to get the peace of God in his life he collected it all, poured it down the drain and went to bed. He still couldn't sleep and the Lord reminded him of a decanter that was in the corner that he had not emptied. He immediately got up, poured the last bit down the toilet, went to bed and slept like a baby. The next morning, he got up and went to work without having a drink in his hand as was his custom. Dave praised God for his deliverance and said, "I haven't touched the stuff since!" The Lord did tell him he could serve wine with guests at dinner, but for him it was forbidden. I think God saved him from actually becoming a serious alcoholic! We praised God with him.

The International Community

Ministry with the Zairian church was great! I enjoyed every minute of it. I even enjoyed learning the new language, so much so that my French almost slipped right out the window. It was Lingala that I lived and breathed and enjoyed communicating in. But the IPCK Sunday evenings and the mid-week Bible studies with our neighbors and others that came from different areas of the city became my church, my encouragement, my go to people for help and prayer. Both Gramma and I never regretted taking an active part in the international community and, in my opinion, it never interfered with or came before the reason for which we were sent to Zaire, not only by the mission but by Our Father Himself. As I look back on it now, being active in the international community was the best thing for Gramma and the kids at that time (I believe it kept our kids from rebellion against God as some MK's do) and it was also good for me!

Our Home Assignment was to be Missionary-In-Residence at Canadian Bible College and Canadian Theological College in Regina. From 33 degrees above zero Celsius to 33 degrees below zero Fahrenheit! God certainly has a sense of humor!

The Terrific Traffic Policeman of Kinshasa

Before we read more of Gramma's take on life I'd like to tell you a really encouraging story about a traffic cop.

The first thing we noticed in going down town Kinshasa was the little square platform (1 meter by 1 meter) about 1 meter off the pavement with a little 2-meter-high pointed roof over it. It was a police station for directing traffic. The policeman had a whistle and if he did his job correctly he could be very concise in giving directions… sometimes quite animated. But I learned very quickly never to look him in the eye. If you did, you were guilty of something and mostly likely you would get pulled over. There was always a 2nd policeman on the ground waiting for you to do something wrong. If your eyes met, you were in trouble. I learned this the hard way shortly after we landed in Kinshasa. I had made numerous trips already to the city center for I needed to arrange for tickets, buy spare automotive and generator parts etc. for the missionaries down country. In short, I was the "purchaser" for the missionaries, among the other duties I had. Later on, I gave this job over to Dawn and our neighbor Sharon Macfarlane who had just received Jesus into her life as mentioned earlier. Sharon and Marty and kids had become very good friends with our family.

While I was still doing the "purchasing" job, I happened go to town quite early this particular morning and finishing my errands in good time I was approaching a busy intersection from a side street, on my way home. It was coming into 30 June (the main drag) at a bit of an angle so I wasn't sure if I needed to wait for the policeman to change directions to give me the go ahead or if he would just motion me to go ahead after most of the traffic cleared the 4-way intersection.

So, I looked hard at the traffic cop to see if he would let me slip in. That was the first mistake of the morning. Our eyes met, and the guy on the ground came running over. I was the target! The white man with money!

"Mbote tata," I greeted him in Lingala. "How are you today?"

I didn't make much headway in softening him up. He quickly and rather roughly asked for my license and insurance papers. I handed them to him and asked him what was wrong. He told me that I had gone too far before stopping. I should have stopped a little distance farther back. I would have to go to the office with him and pay a fine for not stopping at the intersection.

"Well," I said. "There is no stop sign and no line indicating where I should stop."

"Oh yes," said he. "There is a line and you didn't stop behind it!"

Knowing that I wasn't going to get anywhere just arguing with him, I asked him to show me the line. I got out of the car and he pointed under the back part of the car and said, "Right here is the line." But there was no line there and I told him so!

"Yes," he postulated profusely. "But it used to be there, right there!" As a consequence, he was taking me to the police headquarters.

He got in the car and as he did, he said that he was hungry (now wanting me to pay him off). I was too naïve to think of anything else but exactly what he said. He said that he was hungry.

I was concerned and asked him, "Haven't you had any breakfast this morning?"

"No!" he replied curtly.

I then asked him, "Can I buy you some breakfast?" He was certainly OK with that and we found a small restaurant, Zairian style, not far away. I bought him an omelet with fresh bread and tea. He was a happy camper!

Speaking to myself, under my breath of course, I said, "Hmmm, while I have you here I might as well share my testimony with you. What hindereth me?" So, I did!

Belly full and a good story under his belt made him a friend. He just wanted to go back to his station and forget the ticket. I was OK with that, but asked him if he wanted to do this same thing again another time. I said, "I am often down town and would be happy to buy you a coffee anytime, if you would be free… and we could talk some more about life and God." Well, he was all over that!

I mentioned that if I saw him I would honk and tip up my hand as if drinking a cup of coffee; that would be the signal that I had time and would like to take him to the same shop for a break. It happened several times like that: I would honk, tip my hand with fingers pressed together as if holding a cup, he would nod, I would stop, he would climb down, give his partner the charge, come over, climb in the car and away we would go. During every coffee time we had together, we talked about the Lord and His plan of salvation. He was intrigued.

Finally, he asked if I would come to his house and have a meal together and pray for his wife who was pregnant and for his little son who woke up in the middle of the night screaming at the top of his lungs. It was getting too much for him and his wife and for the neighbors as well. I agreed.

His wife had aborted and had numerous miscarriages because when she was pregnant she always saw her uncle coming to her in a dream as an evil man to do her harm.[26] She felt it so real and so dark and so scary that she would be almost paralyzed with fear. Consequently, she would have a miscarriage. He wanted me to pray over her. Could God quieten his son and keep his wife from aborting this time? I said He could and I would come and pray with them.

The day arrived, I picked him up after his shift and we drove to his place, near city center. It was a very crowded neighborhood and he lived in a very flimsy house. No wonder everyone heard his child's piercing cries at night. Every house was the same. No sound proofing materials here! That day, after a wonderful Zairian meal and before we prayed for his wife and child I explained the gospel again to them both and then asked him if he wanted to receive Jesus the Christ (Yesu Masiya) into his life. He said he wanted to and we prayed together. Confessing sin and asking Jesus to come into his life, he opened his body, soul and spirit to God and to Him alone. He was radiant!

Then I asked his wife if she wanted to pray too. She said no! I was a bit shocked and so was my police friend. He began to scold her, but I immediately made it quite clear that if she wasn't ready, we could

---

[26] *In Congolese tradition, the mother's brother or the uncle would be the one responsible for the children. This is called an "avuncular or avunculocal society" which often occurs in matrilineal societies. Often the uncle can be a wicked person and threaten the child with evil intent or hold a curse over the child for any number of reasons.*

not force her to pray and accept Jesus into her life. She had to want to. He coaxed her, but she was defiant. He was disheartened for he thought now I wouldn't be able to pray for his son or his wife because she did not make a decision to follow Jesus. I assured him that he, now being the spiritual head of the home, could pray together with me for his wife and his son and God would intervene. So, we prayed in the Name of Jesus, bound the devil out and away from that little house. We asked Jesus to cover the boy and all that was in the house with His precious blood. We then prayed over his wife in similar manner, she being right there with us, but not bowing her head, or heart!

I left him in good spirits, but the wife was still solemn and hard in spirit. I told him to continue to pray for his wife and son and to find a good church nearby. I thought that I would see him soon, but I didn't get downtown for a week or so after that. I looked for him, but he wasn't there at his usual post. I wanted to take him for coffee and find out how he was doing. I never did see the brother again at any of the traffic control stations in the city.

Several months later, Gramma and I had to go to the large market in the center of the city, "le Grand Marché," as we all called it, to buy a certain kind of fish. We went deep into the maze of little plots of wares spread on the ground, some with crudely fixed table displays of hardware or of fruits and vegetables to find the fish market area. In that fish market area, with sewage running under our feet and the smell almost unbearable, I almost ran into our police man. I didn't recognize him.

"Hello pastor," he said. I was astounded. Here was a handsome young man dressed in "civvies", no uniform and I hardly recognized him.

"Where have you been my brother?" I asked heartily, hardly able to believe my eyes. "I've been looking for you!" To meet up with him in such a place in the middle of a city of perhaps four million people was difficult to believe, to say the least.

"Oh, I got an honorable discharge from the military and took it a few days after we met. I too have been looking for you, but didn't know your church or your place of abode."

Kinshasa Fish

We talked a bit as we were both pressed for time, but I know that God, in his love and mercy, had us bump into one another in le Grand Marché that day. Our Father rejoiced with us as we happily shared the news that his boy never did wake up or holler in the middle of the night after our visit together. ...and his wife? Well he was now the proud father of a little baby girl. Did he get to a church? Oh yes, he was involved in a good church just down the road from his place. "Does your wife go with you now?"

"I'm sad to say," he replied, "she stays at home, but my boy goes with me. I continue to pray for my wife." He was a much happier man than the first day I saw him ...and so was I!

More of Gramma's Prayer Letters

Please note: when Gramma was writing these letters the current prices for the following items in Canada in 1973 where approximately as follows:
- a gallon of gas = $0.39
- a dozen eggs = $0.78
- a gallon of milk = $1.30

B.P. 4464
Kinshasa II
Republique du Zaire
September, 1974

Dear "Other World" Friends,

While you were enjoying
the nicest, warmest days
of your summer, we in the
southern hemisphere were
experiencing the dead of
winter. The thermometer
dipped down to an all-time
low of around 58 degrees,
so you can imagine how
much we've been suffering
from the cold. Here in
Kinshasa, we still haven't
even managed to get chilly
enough to put sweaters on. Our blood still has a lot of thinning out to
do. We've been in the big city (of 2 million) for seven weeks now, and
needless to say, our life style has been drastically altered from that in
the bush. With electricity all day long, (at Maduda we had four hours in
the evening), things have been simplified a bit. No more stoking up the
old wood stove, or refilling the kerosene frig after everything had thawed
out. No more warming up the coals for the big old cumbersome charcoal
iron, and no more being kept awake half the night by death wails in the
village.

Now we are sometimes awakened by the shrill sound of a night watchman's
whistle warning other night watchmen (each house has one) of thieves, or
potential thieves in the neighborhood. Kinshasa is famous for two things.
It is the city with the highest cost of living in the world, and it has
some of the cleverest thieves! A roving band of robbers, estimated at
somewhere around two hundred, had terrorized the whole area a few short
months ago, involving unmentionable atrocities. Things are much quieter
now because the police caught forty of them, with the aid of an informer.
After displaying them in the public square, the President ordered them
away to be shot. We wouldn't recommend these measures to our government at home, but it has proved an effective deterrent here. Every time
we go downtown and are obliged to leave the car, we remind the Lord that
it is His responsibility to care for, seeing that it is His property.
Thieves here don't seem at all hindered by locked doors. I know our
guardian angels have a full time job. We want to thank all of you who
shared in buying the car. It's all paid for and there was even enough
left over for a tire fund. So we really praise the Lord!

We've heard some of your food prices have gome up. I'll pass on a few of
ours so that you'll not feel too bad about yours: one roll of toilet
tissue--50¢; a gallon of ice cream--$9.00; one egg--20¢; a gallon of
gas--$2.00; a pound of hamburger--$2.40; a small can of corn--$1.20;
a small bottle of relish--$3.00; just to mention a few. Doesn't that
make you want to count your blessings ? Needless to say we don't in-
dulge in a whole lot of ice cream, but we still haven't found a substitute for the first item. Banana leaves tend to play havoc with the

plumbing!

Our children are something like a little chameleon friend we had in
Maduda. He just adjusted to any environment he found himself in. All
year we couldn't keep shoes on the children, now all of a sudden, they're
crying for them. Here in Kinshasa, there is no danger of jiggers (little bugs that burrow under the skin around the toes and deposit their
eggs), so I was thinking that going barefoot would be a practical and
economical idea. But now, with all the "other kids" wearing shoes....

Well, today was our first Lingala lesson! That is our present full time
assignment--learning another language. Lingala is a trade language which
ties together all the tribal language groups that would naturally gather
in a metropolis like Kinshasa. It is the official language of President
Mobutu, the military, and Kinshasa. While studying Lingala, Jim will be
having a weekly Bible study and prayer sharing time with our pastors and
elders (in French until he can switch), so he looks forward to this as
being a real learning experience. Because our national church here has
been waiting for a missionary couple to work with them for several years,
they've got all sorts of jobs lined up for us. Starting September 9,
they've got us involved in a week of seminars with all the Christian
workers of the eight churches. They who know Kikongo and then learn Lingala, find the second language fairly easy to learn. They can't figure
out why we need time to study it--they don't. "Just go out and speak!"
is the advice we often get. We're left with the overwhelming feeling
that they think we're a lot smarter than we are. At any rate, we have
lots of motivation to learn: scores of open hearts to minister to, and
with the promise that we can literally partake of the "mind of Christ"
we are optimistic about the months ahead!

One of President Mobutu's latest moves has been to strike Christmas off
the holiday calendar. His long range plan is also to make Sunday a market day and Thursday a rest day. Signs seem to indicate that the body
of Christ here may have some difficult times ahead. Because our people
lack the "world view" that you at home have, they don't interpret the
"gloom news" like we do. We see a clear message in all this old world's
troubles: Jesus is coming soon! One thing we know for sure, the Lord
led us to Kinshasa. So after He enables us to communicate effectively,
we know we can also trust Him for the message He has for the members of
His body here.

We cannot express how much we value your holding us up to Jesus. Jim's
bout with hepatitis has left him weakened and not able to take long hours
of involvement, so for this physical need, it is an hour by hour relying
on borrowed strength. How many times we've been able to prove His
strength in our weakness.

                              Rejoicing with our hand in His,
                              Jim and Dawn Sawatsky & tribe

P.S. If you're planning on coming to the big fight between Ali and
Foreman here in Kinshasa, do drop in. We even have a guest room. (In
case you're wondering, we're not going! The cheapest seats are ten
dollars.)

Chapter Fifteen: Home Assignment 1977-78

Dr. L. L. King

While still in our first term in Zaire, I was asked to translate for many people: preachers and teachers who came through Zaire for ministry. One day we were instructed that we would have to host Dr. LL King, our Vice-President and Director of all missionary activity for the CMA in the USA. There wasn't yet a separation in the CMA between Canada and the USA. Dr. King was our highest boss, here on earth. He generally stayed in hotels for his own rest and privacy, but this time Mobutu had commandeered all the hotel rooms for his own conference and not a room was available anywhere and this maverick began to shake in his boots. This meant that he was going to have to stay in our very modest guest house.

I didn't really need to shake that much for he was a kind and gentle man and we had a great time together. As I took him around to see the ministry of the CMA in Kinshasa, I had to translate for him, not just before friends and pastors but also before a few congregations—everyone wanted to hear from him and he was an excellent orator. He was so articulate that he would sometimes use 3 or 4 adjectives in each sentence as he presented his lively and most vivid message. The trouble is, in Lingala, it takes a lot longer to express all those vivid pictures and metaphors, so from time to time I took quite a bit longer than he anticipated it would take and he was constantly trying to interrupt my translation.

Finally, I had to stop and explain to him (in English, in front of everyone) that it took a bit longer to get his ideas across, even though I was giving a dynamic interpretation of what he was saying. Not only that, I had to keep on going back and then bringing the people up to date on what he was saying so that I wouldn't lose them. He was not a shallow speaker. To my relief, he understood. The people gobbled up his messages, but I was generally spent at the end of them.

The Phone Call in Kinshasa

I guess he must have been impressed rather than distressed at all my gibberish (at least to him it was) in Lingala for I found out later that he strongly suggested that I be the Missionary-In-Residence at CBC/CTS the following year of Home Assignment. Instead of going home and going on tour we were to live in Regina, Saskatchewan. It was an honor to be chosen for that position, but it meant we would be away again from family for almost the whole year of "furlough". Gramma Dawn did not want that and she wasn't confident that this was what God wanted for us or that I could do the job. Neither was I for that matter and we declined.

But at the same time, I felt that God was saying that this appointment was from Him, not from Headquarters. So, I wrote those thoughts down on a piece of paper and put it under the blotter on my desk—even though we had respectfully declined the appointment. However, I soon learned that not even a maverick says no to the highest authority in the CMA mission's department. I gave many excuses, but finally confided in Gramma that I thought God was leading us to accept, even though it would mean a strenuous year away from family and a hard year of studying to fulfill my teaching role.

One day while we were at Marty and Sharon's place, our US embassy friend's just up the road, their telephone rang. They had a family of four kids, we had three just a bit younger and we used to spend family nights together whenever it was possible. The MacFarlane kids always jumped at the chance to take our kids to the pool down the road and supervise them and they always did a superb job. Our kids played very well with them, even though they were 3 to 5 years older. We were watching a movie that night as Marten had brought home a projector from the Embassy and a very large reel. We were interrupted by the phone, the only phone that worked around there because of their embassy connections. We heard, "Yes …yes, they are here, who would you like to speak to?" I was called to the phone. It was my Africa director on the phone strongly suggesting, after the greetings, that I accept the invitation from CBC and that we plan to be there for the school year. I said that after much prayer, we also thought that we should go, but I guess he hadn't received our letter yet.

It was an amazing confirmation for who would know where we were at that time? How would they know to contact us at this family's home? …and how did they get their number? We never did find out, but we certainly knew that God was in it and He seemed to say, "I know exactly where you are, all the time!"

CBC/CTS—On and Off Campus

That year at Canadian Bible College/Canadian Theological Seminary proved to be a marvelous year. The college rented a furnished house for us and we were able to buy a car which had a good block heater to plug in at night so that the car wouldn't freeze solid and not start in the mornings. Who would have thought that we would go from extremely hot and humid to extremely dry and cold for our year of "furlough"? Our kids shouted with glee at the sight of the first sight of snow and the cold didn't seem to bother them a bit! In fact, we all enjoyed the change!

I will be the first to admit, I am not an academic and it doesn't take long for one to figure that out for him/herself, but God gave me creative ideas in teaching and I really enjoyed the studying myself. I didn't have a Doctorate degree like the missionary who held this post the year before, but I was able to call on help from my university studies in Cultural Anthropology to explain the lessons and illustrate all points with firsthand experiences (sometimes hilarious) that I had over the past 5 years.

We had a great time relating to the students and staff alike, but a couple of the amazing experiences of that year happened off campus. At one point I prayed and asked God if I couldn't have some outside ministry with non-believers instead of always being around Christians. It seemed that I was getting stagnant! I wasn't used to that kind of life.

God heard my prayer and the next week I was called to counsel and spend time with a young married man who had a bipolar dysfunction. His wife was working, but due to his problem he couldn't work, so he laid around the house all day which made things worse. I knew by his actions that he needed deliverance, but was hesitant to do it alone. Nevertheless, I found time to spend with him. He was quite sedated, but we had good coffees together. One day at his house I shared the gospel with him. He prayed and received the Lord into his life. In my prayer I bound the enemy out of and away from his life and he became a changed man. He didn't go off his meds, but his wife knew immediately that this wasn't the same husband she had left that morning. What an answer to prayer.

About the same time this was happening I got a call to give a missionary presentation at the CMA church in Regina. I knew I wanted to give them some good African drum sounds, but they had a very poor sound system, even though they were a relatively large church. Sound systems in churches across Canada made a drastic change for the better in the '80s.

Understanding that I needed speakers that would bring out the bass sounds of these drums, I went on a hunt for some good speakers. I didn't have any at home so now would be an appropriate time to purchase a couple of good ones for myself. At the same time, I would be able to set them up and use them in the church. I went to an audio warehouse in Regina and there I began talking to a "salesman"—very much a hippie and very much looking like a druggie, unshaven with long straggly black hair. He was the only one available and came up to me with his salutation. I wasn't too keen on his personal presentation, but went along with him as my salesperson. He took me into an isolated sound room. I told him what I wanted and what I was going to do with them, so they needed to have a good bass sound. When he got me alone in that soundproof room the conversation went something like this:

"Are you a missionary or somethin'?"

"As a matter of fact, I am."

"Do you ever talk to God?" he asked.

"Yes, I do. Do you?"

"Oh yeah," he replied. "I talk to him a lot and he talks to me too."

"OOhh, how so? Do you read the Bible?"

"Oh yeah, I'm into that all the time!" He shot back.

"Well, does He talk to you through the Bible?" was my next question.

"Sometimes, mostly I hear his voice... He tells me what I should and shouldn't do."

"How's that," I questioned? By now I wasn't so much interested in a speaker system as I was in his life!"

He thought for a moment and then said, "Well, it's like this. I used to read "body" auras.[27] Satan gave me these powers and then later he told me he would make me a very powerful man, if I would just give my life completely to him. I was about to do that very thing when I heard another voice and I knew it was God. He told me not to do that. He said Satan would destroy my life, but if I gave my life to Him He would give me the peace that I was looking for. I weighed the two and realized that I didn't want my life to be destroyed, so I said, 'OK God you're on!' I gave my life to God right then and there."

Thinking about this a bit, I brought another person into the equation. "Have you ever heard of God's son Jesus? What do you think of Him?

---

[27] *An energy field around the human body*

"Well I don't really know that much about Him, but I have heard of Him."

"Would you like to know more about Him?

"Sure!"

After some more discussion, I asked, "Would you like to study the Bible together?" Well, he was quite excited about that and mentioned that he had a group of friends that wanted to get together to do that very thing, but didn't know anyone who could lead it. They tried meeting in the Catholic Church, but the Priest was too busy to spend a lot of time with them. Well, I wondered if they would like me to lead them in a study of the Bible. He said that they would be excited about that. And the study began—guys on drugs, trying to go straight, some very new Christians, meeting with a protestant minister in a Catholic church and just enjoying the presence of God. How cool was that!

Their prayers were invigorating. "Well God, here we are, just wanting to chat with you a bit! You know my mom is going through a "H" of a time trying to get off alcohol. Would you help her get off this blankety-blank stuff, zap her if you can? Of course you can, but do whatever is right for her." …etc.

At one of the studies one of the guys piped up, "Hey I heard a really neat song the other day at a camp fire I was at. I was invited to this youth meeting around a camp fire and they sang, 'Give me oil in my lamp keep me burnin' and then the second was even more fun. 'Give me gas in my Ford, keep me truckin' for the Lord.' Can we sing that? Well it just so happened that I knew the chorus from when I went to some youth groups when I was a kid. These guys were in their late teens, early 20's, but they thought it was the coolest song!

One day I went to my friend's house (the salesman) and as he was walking across the room he said, "Satan, in the Name of Jesus I rebuke you!" I asked him what the problem was. Apparently after giving his life to God, occasionally he would feel these scratches going down his back as if something with sharp claws was scratching him. When he would say that phrase quoted above, he would get relief. It didn't take long to learn he wanted to get rid of these painful scratches once and for all, so we prayed. He confessed and prayed over every and any foothold that Satan might have been able to secure in his life, including drugs, sex and the reading of auras. In prayer we covered him under the blood of Jesus, we bound the evil one out and away from his life and said amen! We praised God for his deliverance and my buddy never experienced that again.

All the guys in that Bible study began looking for Christian youth groups and got connected as God led them to different evangelical churches in their neighborhoods. I will never forget how God answered my prayer for "outside" ministry. That little study carried on until we had to leave CBC and prepare again for going back to Kinshasa. Don't get me wrong, the College experience was great, I loved it. I even wanted to pursue a Master's degree in Anthropology after that, but the CMA said that as far as they were concerned it would be better for us to go back to Zaire. We prayed about it and felt that they were right in their thinking, so we prepared for another 4 years of ministry in Africa. Though it was hard on my parents, we felt this was where God was leading again. Little did we know that this would begin a phase of ministry which would include the most testing of times, but also the most enjoyable and the most rewarding!

Our little family in Regina, 1977-78

Part IV Back to Congo Kinshasa

Chapter Sixteen: An African Fable

The Goat and the Gazelle

There was once a villager who took time to carve out of the African rain forest a large plot of land for a garden. He grew many vegetables there, such as Cassava plants, eggplant, several types of bananas and a few fruit trees. One year when he came to harvest the leaves of the cassava plant, he noticed that most of the leaves had already been eaten by some animal or perhaps several animals. He didn't know  who it was, but if it truly was an animal he would have to set a trap, or maybe two traps just to make sure that he would catch the culprit. He set the traps and then went on his way home.

Early the next morning the two animals came to eat the cassava leaves. One was Mr. Gazelle and the other Mr. Goat. They had been meeting in the garden for some time taking just a little bit of the garden products each time so as to not alarm the owner. However, as greed became a part of their daily activities they began eating more and more each day! This morning Mr. Gazelle was first and began eating, as was his custom, very early and no one else was in sight. All of a sudden there was a big whoosh and a snap and Mr. Gazelle was in the air hanging by his neck from one of the shade trees that protected the garden. He struggled vigorously, lashing out with his legs, trying to reach the ground or some solid object, but it was all to no avail. At that instant Mr. Goat appeared.

"Oh, my friend, don't struggle so," said Mr. Goat trying his best to calm the "lofty" Mr. Gazelle. "This is a small problem. Just relax! If you stop kicking you will survive, but if you don't the noose will tighten even more and you will not be able to breath." But for Mr. Gazelle it was not a small problem. He was not used to having a rope around his neck and continued to wriggle, but soon his kicking stopped as the noose choked him completely.

"Poor Mr. Gazelle, if he had only listened to me, he would still be alive," thought Mr. Goat as he went about the garden on his own, looking for food. It wasn't long before there was another whoosh, a snap and Mr. Goat was in the air dangling from a vine with a noose around his neck. Mr. Goat let out a baaah, but he wasn't really worried.

 This was a "small problem" as he was accustomed to nooses around the neck. He remained still and began eating the leaves and twigs that were very close to him, right where he was dangling! Not long after all this happened the owner of the garden came to see if he had caught anything. "Ah ha!" he exclaimed, "My plan worked!"

He cut down Mr. Gazelle and slung him over his shoulders to take home for his wife to fix some delicious meat. He recognized the goat as his neighbors and he muttered, "So… it was you all along. I'm going to talk to your owner and we will see what he has to say about this!"

As soon as Mr. Goat was lowered to the ground he began eating again. No problem with the noose. He was used to nooses and followed along the trail as the garden-owner led him towards the village. Mr. Goat would stop now and again to catch a mouthful of more greens before the noose tightened and pulled him again in the direction of the village. All of this did not bother Mr. Goat for in his mind all of that just happened was only a small problem. He was not bothered at all, not even a bit because he was used to a noose around his neck.

However, when he saw the garden-owner and the neighbor come out of the house with a long knife, coming straight towards him, he began to bleat, but it was too late. The two men had decided to share the goat to pay for the misfortune of the other and they cut the goat's throat. Mr. Goat tried to resist but what he thought was a "small problem" actually contributed to his demise!

African Understanding

You might think that what is bothering you just a bit is a little problem only. Or, you may think that the sin or little habit that is around your neck is only a little thing, easy to handle. Perhaps you are sure that the little "bad" habits you have will not hurt you. But be careful, for the little problems or what you think are little problems from your perspective can easily turn around and bite you and be the cause of your complete failure or even death.

A Scriptural or Moral understanding

Matthew 15:19 states, "For out of the heart come evil thoughts, murder, adultery, sexual immorality, theft, false witness, slander." And John concurs,

1 John 1:8 "If we say we have no sin, we deceive ourselves, and the truth is not in us.

Everyone, including missionaries, has problem with sin. It may be one bad habit or it may be many little bad habits that need to be taken care of. E. Stanley Jones says,[28]

"It is not enough to hate our sin, nor even to pray against it. We must surrender it."

He goes on to say that there is generally a log jam and there is one central log and if it would be removed all other "logs" will be released. He is speaking of sin of course. Herod, in Mark's account, had one central sin and although he had many others it was one central "log" that he couldn't pull out. He had unlawfully and sinfully married his brother's wife. When John the Baptist put his finger on it, he touched a sore spot! If he could have pulled that "log" out, all else could have been released. He might have even listened to John and become a follower of Jesus.

I understand log jams. I have worked in logging camps and saw-mills long enough to understand that when you deal with the one central log and get it out of the way, generally the whole thing is cleared up. We often go around thinking that the little things don't matter, we can handle them, but forget to see that if we don't find the central problem all these little things will bring us down and rupture our relationship with our heavenly Father.

In a missionary's life, often jealousy is the central log and often it is seen as a "little problem" around the neck, especially by the person who has the problem.

Gossip is another noose and so is ambition (for personal achievements). The two of them often work hand in hand to pull another down in order to raise oneself up in the eyes of one's colleagues.

I was very ambitious in my first couple of years in Kinshasa. It didn't take long for my wife to zero in on that. After a meal one day she said, "You're quite ambitious, aren't you?" I took that as a

---

[28] *Victorious Living by E Stanley Jones*

complement and agreed whole heartedly. Then she floored me with, "There is no place in a Christian's heart for personal ambition!"

"What do you mean," I retorted. "Of course there is!"

However, as soon as she said those words, I knew it was from God and He was telling me that I needed to adjust my thinking. I could be "ambitious" for him in sharing the gospel, but being personally ambitious, ambitious for my own gain, that was out of the question. Right then and there I gave my "ambition" to God and said, "I will not push open any doors again. I will wait until you open them and then I will go through them with all the energy You give me."

I've seen these "petits problèmes" in missionaries' lives. I've borne the brunt of some of these "little problems" and I've been guilty of having these "little problems" in my own life. I've seen and heard prayers over these so called little problems and I've even sensed remorse over them, from others and from my own personal feelings. However, as Jones says, that is not enough. We must *surrender* these little problems, completely, to the Lord and *HE* will deal with them. When we did that in our Kinshasa missionary team, through prayer and worship—praying first for others and their burdens, then making it a priority to spend time in worship and testimony of God's goodness in our ministries—our team was made new. This happened especially in the 1990's.

1 John 1:9 is also applicable here. I learned the above fable from Pastor Dede. As the evangelist with Sango Malamu I heard him preach most often that as we continually yield or surrender these "little problems" to Jesus, He is able and willing to keep on cleansing us, forgiving—to make clean, wipe away—all things that are not right! I can still see and hear in my mind's eye our brother Dede using this story in presenting the Gospel and seeing many people, being gripped by it, coming for repentance and prayer.

Missionary E Stanley Jones also describes, in another book called, "Abundant Life", his experience on a spiritual retreat at a spiritual hermitage or a monastery in Indian religions called an Ashram. All the attendees had jobs to attend to during certain hours and his job was to pick up all the paper on the grounds. He noticed that when people saw him doing this they didn't throw away their papers as they had done before. Fewer and fewer were found as the retreat days were coming to a close. But he began to notice a peculiar happening. Some people would now not blatantly throw scraps away but would crumple them up and throw them into a bush, or behind it, trying to hide their presence.

He then uses this as an example of people dealing with sin in their lives. When others see it, the person seems to deal with it to please them, not necessarily the perpetrator himself. He writes, *"Do not let this matter of getting rid of sin end in a stalemate, a compromise; don't be content with a conscience that will hide sins, but will not get rid of sins. Go back into the hidden recesses where you have tucked sins away, to the margins of the subconscious, and bring them all out—all. They will plead, will excuse, will procrastinate, but be relentless— bring them all out—not a thing must be left behind."*[29]

I told this African fable once at the giving of a bride price ceremony. It was a large ceremony with many of both the bride's and groom's extended families and friends in attendance. It happened that I was the MC of the ceremony, also known as the go-between or the "avocat" (literally it means the lawyer) for the groom to be. We enjoyed the giving of the bride price, which was quite extensive in cash and kind. We had a lot of fun that night, spinning a lot of made up stories in order to capture the interest of all.

At the end of the ceremony I gave a little preachment in the form of the story above. I made a brief application and let the chips fall where they may (all in Lingala of course).

After the ceremony ended and most of the guests had left, the host—the father of the bride—came up to me and said, "Well pastor you won!"

"Won?" I said totally taken by surprise, "Won what?" He went on to say that he had purchased a lot of beer for his guests, but after the story I told hardly any of them took a drink and now "I have all the beer left over. What am I going to do with it all?"

I didn't say it, but thought, "It serves you right. You know that normally most Christians in Zaire do not drink any alcoholic beverages." That is a church law, for many good reasons, but at functions like this many would lay aside their church and even personal parameters and imbibe. Their thinking would be that it is a "petit problem". Well it didn't happen that night, not many drank any of the alcoholic beverages that were provided and so the host said, "You win!"

---

[29] *Abundant Life, E Stanley Jones, page 24*

Well, I think God won that night. The whole affair was a God honoring ceremony and that is exactly what Charles and Elise really wanted.

Elise Vuvu and Charles Yangu

An Aside:

It was in the early 90's that Charles Yangu came to live with us, contrary to the wishes of many colleagues on both sides, his and ours. I believed that God had given us Charles for many reasons. He lived with us, got married to Elise Vuvu while at our home and brought his wife home to live with us. They also had their first and only son Joshua while in our home. We had a large

enough house for that to happen and it gave us immense joy as well as insight into the Congolese culture, ethics, values and philosophies. He was our disciple, but we did the learning. He was our pastor, but also our "son". Without him as chaplain of Studios Sango Malamu, SSM would not have had such a fruitful ministry. Charles and Elsie opened the door to many opportunities that would not have otherwise come our way. It was an invaluable experience for us. We loved them dearly.

Chapter Sixteen: Surprised by God

The Re-entry Surprise

Back to Kinshasa! It hadn't changed much in a year, but our place of lodging had. The mission house was to be occupied for another year before it would be free for us. So, the CMA Kinshasa missionaries secured a rental for us not far from the mission house.

The house on Ring Road was something else. In 1978, the house was situated in an area that was still a very low and swampy area of the city, very humid. Five years previous, just before we arrived at the mission property (on the other side of the swamp) the night guards had killed a 20-foot-long python which was hiding there. They cut it up and took it home for supper. On the east side of the swamp was our rented plot, on the road that was built around it; hence Ring Road! Our CMA missionaries had rented this place for us probably because of its proximity to the mission house. It had 3 bedrooms, a very low pitched flat tin roof which absorbed the heat very well. It had an 80 x120 foot back yard which gave space for a double carport and 3 small rooms on one side in a long rectangular structure; a cement patio about 30 feet wide behind the house, in front of the carport; a small banana grove and an uncultivated yard (50'x70') with debris and weeds.

The story goes that a group of military personnel lived there after it was first constructed, but they didn't take care of the place and were evicted. However, not before they stole the lighting fixtures and anything else that could be transported. It seemed that this house marked the beginning of another career— that of landscaping, cabinet making, plumbing and electrical

Gramma on motor bike at the Avenue du Ring

contracting. It seemed that every house from this point on we were to be Mr. fix-it in all of the above areas. Because my dad was first a farmer, a carpenter and then a building contractor while I was growing up, I had been given the opportunity to put my "nose" into all these areas, including car mechanics. While going to High School I also worked for a cabinet maker and ceramic tile contractor. During my time between CBC and University I also worked in several gas stations, doing lube jobs, oil changes, fixing tires, and tubes. I even worked on motors and transmissions. So, when I got to Africa, it wasn't much of a surprise to find out why God had given me these experiences. Dabbling in all these areas, in some measure, prepared me to exercise these limited gifts throughout my missionary career. Only He knew how much this experience would come in handy. I was to dig deep into this treasure chest in occupying this house.

The toilet was constantly plugged, the bathroom and kitchen sink leaked, and new lighting fixtures had to be put in. The house had a low ceiling, so the heat became stifling, especially in the bedrooms and especially where some of the ceiling asbestos squares were missing (which we repaired as soon as possible). We could open the windows in the main front room with a big set of French doors and in the dining area, so that the light breezes could pass through, but the bedrooms were very humid and "warm". We had one air conditioner which we kept from the other house, so I banged a hole in the cement brick wall of our bedroom and cemented in the air conditioner above the window.

After what little furniture we had was moved in and everything was fixed (except the toilet which kept on plugging up no matter what we did), which took us at least the first couple of weeks of occupancy, I turned my attention to the back yard. It was an absolute mess! I built a gazebo in one corner, not far from the house against the north wall, with a cute straw/grass roof for covering; put bricks around the driveway which curved around behind the house and gave way to a large cement patio area in front of the side building and carport. That large cemented area served to turn cars around and drive out instead of backing up all the way around the house to the front gate.

I hauled in some dirt, dug up a good part of the existing terrain by hand and spread new dirt within this large enclosure--with the high brick fence all around the yard. I then spread some manure around the banana trees and levelled it all by pulling a large beam that I found somewhere back and forth over the new dirt until all was flat. I didn't worry about patting it down for the rains would do that and I didn't worry about seeding grass as grass and weeds would grow on their own. I was sure the dirt was full of seeds… whether grass or weeds it didn't matter, when you cut it short it all looks like green lawn. I lost 20 lbs. that first month and was now ready for ministry.

But, the way the house seemed to break down all the time and the way the toilet was always plugged, we thought there must be a spiritual side to this problem. We prayed over the house, seriously! One Sunday morning when I had already left to preach in a church in the "Cité" (as neighborhood sections of the city were called), Gramma especially prayed for God to fix the toilet. It was the only toilet in the house and it was in a bad state. During her prayer, God gave her an idea to boil a pot of water, raise the boiling water over her head and pour it into the toilet (Gramma would never ever have thought of that on her own). She did just that and suddenly there was a gurgling and a back firing and then all went down the drain. It never plugged once after that. Not only that, nothing else leaked and the electricity always worked! We praised God for that, but we had other surprises...

The Gestetner Surprise

I had come to know a young man who was handicapped to the point that he needed crutches to get around and wore steel braces on his legs. John Mukhandi was a good typist and knew French well. He was a fine Christian young man who had just finished a course in typing. I asked him if he would translate and type some TEE[30] materials for us as we needed at least the basic course in Lingala to get started. He agreed and he did a great job, but it took him almost a year. That was fine because we really had not started anything as yet in the TEE program in Kinshasa--as they had in Lower Zaire in the Kikongo language. After 4 or 5 months of work and corrections, he had finally translated and typed out all one hundred pages on stencils for the Gestetner printing machine. Stencils were the only thing we could find or afford in those days. BUT we didn't have a Gestetner. I was sure we could find one somewhere in all of Kinshasa, but to my dismay not one mission organization had one that we could use. I prayed earnestly that the Lord would provide something for us. After all John had completed a monumental task.

In between my times of prayer, I would ask different contacts about a used printing machine that I could borrow or buy. Someone told me that IPCK (International Protestant Church of Kinshasa) had one at one time but it wasn't working anymore, maybe they still had it.

---

[30] *Theological education by Extension*

I immediately went to ask them. Long story short: they still had it and gave it to me because it didn't work. If I could repair it somehow and get parts for it somewhere, "God bless you!" was their response.

I brought the machine home, set it up in one of the back rooms by the carport and found to my surprise it was electric. It wasn't an American Gestetner, it was British made, but it looked like it would work with the American stencils that we had used. I plugged it in, turned it on and it seemed like it was going to run. I had gotten ink from them and a few stencils and tried it out. But it wouldn't turn. I began taking it apart, but couldn't figure out why it wouldn't turn over—it seemed like all the parts were there and nothing was broken, but it just wouldn't run.

That night, after praying about this again and asking the Lord for a solution, I went to sleep in our AC cooled bedroom. What a relief to get a good night's rest. But in the middle of the night, God gave me a dream and in that dream, He showed me exactly how the printing machine was to run, how to put each part together—in short, how to fix it. In my slumber, I could hardly wait until morning to go and fix the machine. I got up with the sun, went to the little room behind the house and started working on the machine, putting it together just like I saw it in my dream. To my delight and astonishment, the Gestetner turned over. I plugged it in and pressed the button, it ran like a well-oiled clock.

We already had the paper set aside and we had purchased the ink, so I put on a stencil and cranked out 100 copies of the 1st stencil. We needed 100 copies of 100 pages to complete the entire book. We found a more durable stiff paper, designed a cover for it and had a stencil made for it. We were ready to go. By this time, we had made acquaintances with the Tsasa brothers and they had come over to sing, but I also asked them if they would help put all the pages in piles. We worked hard that day and ran off 100 copies of 100 pages and put them in 100 piles—in the 3 rooms that were attached to the carport of which one room served as my office. Before the day was done we had assembled a few books, starting with the cover, then going to 2nd pile, page one, and working our way around from room to room to page 100. It was going to work… I was totally excited! God had answered prayer and given us the translator/typist, the printing machine, the instructions in a dream as to how to fix it, the funds to purchase all the paper, including the cover paper and everything else we needed to make that first book in Lingala. We were excited! The next day we would finish the job and have 100 books.

Case of the Missing Pages

Eager to get the books done, we started early. We collate all the pages… until we got to the last 25 or so. Another Surprise! We had only compiled around 74 complete books when many piles ran out of pages. From page 75 on some piles ran out of pages, some had 10 pages left, some 15 some 7 some 2 or 3. I couldn't believe it. I even ran more than 100 copies for each pile to make sure that we would have enough. We were all completely disappointed and bewildered. The only answer was that someone had come in and taken a bunch of pages from at least 25 piles. I was devastated! We needed all 100 copies. I prayed with Joseph and in my prayer, I did something that I had never done before. I asked the Lord to reveal the thief to us by making him sick. That would be the sign and I wouldn't have to suspect anyone. We all called it quits early and I went into the house to lick my wounds—mental and emotional wounds! I was discouraged to say the least. Later that day, in the evening, the night watchman came to the house, about 6 pm, to begin looking after the place during the night. The neighborhood was notorious for thieves, so we hired a night guard to keep watch over our "flock" by night. He knocked on the door and complained that he had a terrible ear ache all day. He had not had anything like that since he was a child. He asked if I had any medicine that I could give him to relieve the pain and heal his ear.

I looked at him square in the eye and said, "You are the one that stole all those pages!"

He was completely astonished and blurted out, "OH, no patron, I wouldn't do a thing like that! I'm a pastor's kid, I wouldn't steal pages!" He wasn't a young man, middle aged, but thought if he told me he was the son of a pastor then I would drop the accusation.

I didn't let it go. I firmly stated, "I prayed and asked the Lord to give me a sign and to make sick the one who stole the pages. That way

I would not have to suspect everyone who was in the yard yesterday. And now you're sick. YOU stole the pages!"

"Oh no patron, I would never steal. No, I didn't do it!" He was adamant.

"Yes, you did," I countered just as adamantly, "and I can forgive you for it, if you repent. But if you don't ask forgiveness you will have to meet your maker with this sin on your heart. It's up to you."

"No patron, I didn't do it!"

"Okay," I said, and mentioned the fact that I had no medicine handy to give him.

About 15-20 minutes later there was another knock at the back door. It was Fulani, the "sentinel" ("sentinel" is the word in French that these night watchmen were commonly called).

"Yes?"

"Patron," he said softly with his head down. "I stole the pages. I didn't think anyone would notice as there were so many pages in piles and I just went ahead and took some. Will you forgive me?"

"Yes, Fulani, I will. Thank you for owning up to it, but why? What would you do with all those papers? They had no value for you, did they?"

"Patron, I took them and sold them in the market for a penny a page, so that the women who sold peanuts would have something to wrap them in. They all wanted some pages for wrapping paper!"

Well, in my amazement and discouragement, I prayed with him as he asked God for forgiveness and then I prayed for our Lord to heal his ear problem, in Jesus Name. God must have done it because he never complained again of an earache. ...and he never stole again, but he had a bad habit of sleeping on the job. The gazebo was made especially for him. He could light a fire on the ground for warmth and he could be protected by the grass roof from rain. From there he could see the front gate and driveway and also the whole back yard with the carport and offices.

Surprised by Thieves

One dark night we went to bed in the middle of a huge thunderstorm with heavy duty rain—the only kind of rain one gets in the tropics. And on a tin roof it makes a terrible roaring noise (churches just sing during this time if it happens on a Sunday morning). It was still quite muggy, so I put on the AC and we went to sleep. In the middle of the storm a few hours later I was awakened with a start. The rain was still pouring on the tin roof, the AC was rattling, but I heard another noise. I quickly got up and went to the front room. There I saw a group of thieves ready to break through the front room French doors. They had them already partly open. I believe the Lord put it in my heart to whistle.

Now, when I was a little guy about 8 or 9 years old, my brother and I sat in the front room of our house, in Chilliwack, one Saturday morning determined to learn how to whistle like grandpa. We tried all morning. First my older brother Alf began to get the hang of it and then a while later I did too. We went outside and whistled as hard as we could and we never forgot how to do it. Later on, whenever I needed to call my kids and they were a long way away, I just whistled really hard. They would hear that shrill high-pitched sound and would come running. So, did our dog! And so did our mechanic/chauffeur as he would be driving out of the gates. He would stop and back up for last minute instructions. The whistle came in handy on many and varied occasions!

I had no other weapon, so I whistled as loud and as long as I could. It caught the thieves off guard they scattered like mice, over the wall and gone! Now, I had to contend with the night guard, who was sleeping in my car in the carport. Fulani had heard the whistling and came rushing out of his hibernation in a quandary. I was cheesed off. He was supposed to be on the lookout, not sleeping in my car! I told him what had happened, but that the thieves were gone now. But I added that he needed to stay awake for they might come back. Feeling a little guilty, I guess, he insisted that he walk around the yard. It was still raining and I thought it wasn't necessary. But he insisted, even though he would get drenched! As he did so, he slipped in a muddy section and fell smack on his rear. Not only did he get soaking wet but muddy as well! He stripped down, washed all his clothes, hung them up on a line in the carport, wrapped himself in an old sheet that he had for covering and promptly went to sleep again in the back of my car.

The thieves did come back. They stole his clothes and made some noise. He woke up saw that all his clothes were gone and came out of the carport hollering blue murder! I heard his voice in the bedroom and thought he was literally being murdered. I jumped up, my heart in my mouth now for the second time, ran to the front room and threw open the window. There he was wrapped in a sheet like a huge diaper, dancing around in the rain crying, "They stole my clothes, they stole my clothes!" When I finally got him calmed down enough he told me the story of falling in the mud, washing his clothes, crawling back into the back seat of the car and being awakened suddenly by the thieves who stole all his clothes.

By this time, I wasn't very happy or compassionate, sad to say. When he asked me for some clothes, I said I had nothing that would fit him (which was true) and that he would have to go home in his sheet. Which he did, about 5:30 am while I was still asleep--after all the interruptions during the night I needed a few more hours. Seeing him hollering and dancing around in the rain like he was on the war path with just his diaper on was actually a hilarious sight. I think I chuckled myself back to sleep.

Surprised by Neighbors

The next day the neighbors, whom we had not yet met due to the high walls that fenced in our yards, came over and asked what all the commotion was about the previous night. They were a young Zairian couple, just married and very sharp. Actually, they were strikingly beautiful and handsome. We invited them into the house and shared stories of "voleurs" (thieves) as they had had some stuff stolen from their yard too, despite all the high cement brick walls. During conversation, they asked us what we did, why were we in Kinshasa? We told them that we were missionaries. The immediate reply was, "Oh, those are the people we detest the most!" Another surprise, which caught us completely off guard!

"Well here we are, the people you detest the most, how can we help you?" I replied. We laughed and talked a bit more and found out that they had had very bad experiences with missionaries in the past (both brought up in parochial schools—one protestant and one catholic).[31] They finally said, "But you aren't anything like them."

---

[31] *both had been children of mixed race marriages and for that reason had to do penance everyday of their stay in the religious schools which left a very bad taste in their mouths. Most*

"Praise God for that!" I thought.

We became good friends. Miriam would come over once in a while during the day when she had free time and just play with the children. André was in business, but also wanted to be a professional basketball player. I actually went and saw him play a couple of times. He was good!

Gramma writes the following:

"Miriam and her husband had not been able to have children, so one afternoon she came over and asked if our children could go over to her place and play. She so loved children and just wanted to "hang out" with them (she had no other relatives in the city). They were fairly well-to-do and had a good-sized house next door, actually bigger than ours. After spending all afternoon over there Miriam brought them back home. She commented, 'I could tell by the way they treated one another and communicated together that whatever you've taught them works.' (Both Miriam and André had learned a fair amount of English.)

Another day she came over and asked me to come to her home and pray for her. I went and prayed that the Lord would heal whatever it was that was hindering her from having a child. A few days later Miriam came over again and informed me that she didn't know if God had healed her body, but He had healed her heart. The fear and anxiety that had taken hold of her was gone. Shortly after that she and André were transferred back to the Kivu province in the far east of Zaire where Miriam's parents lived."

To our dismay and regret we never saw or heard from them again.

Surprised by the Cook

Before I leave this chapter on surprised by God, I have one more surprise that God allowed to come our way. This one was perhaps the most devastating of all.

Sunday mornings I usually took a vehicle and headed out to a local Zairian Church to preach. I was invited most of the time to any one of the 30 plus churches that the CEAZ had in Kinshasa at that time. Two weeks earlier, as I was preparing a message, the District Superintendent came by with a large sack of money. My question was, "What do you want to me to do with it?" He said that he had no place to keep it and asked if I would hide it in our house somewhere. I was obliged to do

---

of the good schools were started by missionaries, in the early days of missions, but this couple's experiences were not positive--hence the detestation of missionaries!

it, so I counted it all, with the pastor, and then took it into my bedroom and hid it behind the sliding doors of a metal cabinet that we had put there. Although we had nothing with a lock on it, no one went into our bedroom except our own kids. I felt it would be safe there for a short time. The money, constituting a lot of "bricks"[32], had come from all the schools run by the national church at that time and the value was considerably high—enough to buy a good vehicle, about $4000.00US.

In Africa, generally, nothing moves very fast. What was expected to be a couple of days, turned out to be a couple of weeks! After two weeks, I decided that I should count the money again just to make sure no one had slipped into our bedroom while we were gone and helped himself—as did our famous "sentinel" with the pages. As I was counting it in the bedroom our cook knocked on the door and then opened it, broom in hand. Feigning being startled, he saw all the money on my bed. He excused himself saying that he was going to sweep the floors. I wasn't very happy and said that the next time he could wait until I opened the door or called him in. From that point on I was nervous. I told the DS to come immediately and pick up the money, but he replied that he wasn't ready yet.

The next day, Saturday, our cook, Pierre, asked Gramma if he could prepare our Sunday dinner and work for us that day instead of having a day off. He said he really needed the extra money. Having a heart of compassion, she agreed and felt that she could then even invite some friends over for a Sunday dinner after church at IPCK. Knowing that Dawn would be home when I got there after our service, about 2 o'clock or later, I didn't bring a bunch of keys with me. I was up and out of the house early; Dawn was picked up with the kids for church by friends later on, after Pierre had arrived. We both would be gone for the complete morning.

Pierre never prepared the food, but he did sizzle off with the money. He and another cook from the mission house collaborated on a plan they had connived including their plotted get-a-way. When Gramma returned, she too had left her keys in the house as we both thought that Pierre was completely trustworthy. He would be there ready to serve dinner when she got back. The house was completely locked up solid and no keys were to be found. She was completely

---

[32] *The Zaires were often packaged in large packets of low denominations which we called "bricks" (the size of a small brick). This made for a lot of bricks to make any amount of significant value.*

dumb founded, but the family with her, who had brought her home turned the tables and invited her and the kids to have lunch with them. She had no choice really but to accept. She presumed that Pierre had finished early and didn't think he needed to stay. Or perhaps there was a problem at home and he was needed immediately and made sure the house was locked before he left. She also thought that when I came home I would open the house and put the food away. After all we did have a fridge and the food wouldn't go bad in a couple of hours.

However, not having keys myself, when I got home I was locked out. No one was there, and the house was locked up solid. I had no way of knowing where Gramma was, where the kids were or what happened to the cook. It was now around 3 p.m. I was totally drenched in sweat after preaching my heart out and eating hot, very hot, Zairian food which I dearly loved. But I had to get into the house. I finally lifted some of the roofing tins, slipped through the opening. It was so hot and humid between the ceiling and the tins of the roof in that 2-foot space that I almost "stufficated"![33] I finally managed to crawl to a place where I knew there was a loose square tile in the ceiling, remove the tile and let myself down—completely soaked in sweat, very dusty and very dirty. I didn't know it could get so hot between the ceiling tile and the tin roof! By this time, I wasn't a happy camper, but I did find my keys and opened the back door. This whole experience was too out of the ordinary; too many things didn't add up and then it hit me, "Was the money still there?" I ran to the bedroom and opened the sliding doors. EMPTY! Nothing there! All the money was gone, all of it!

I knew it! It all came to me just as Gramma and the kids came home, happy about their dinner/lunch adventure. I was literally sick. By this time, it was close to 5 p.m. (it took me a good while to get into the house without the proper tools etc.) and we soon needed to head to the International church where I was to lead the service and the worship time. Pierre never did want to cook! He just wanted the time alone, when everyone would be gone, to steal the money and have enough time not only to get away from the house, but also to leave the country. Which he did! We soon found out that he never returned to his place of residence. He and his colleague were seen walking up the street carrying large satchels, but after that were never seen again. We did

---

[33] "the word "stufficated" is my concoction of a word meaning "the area being so stuffy and hot that I almost suffocated and passed out!"

find out that Pierre was Angolan, not Zairian, and that most likely he skipped off to Angola to set up his own business.

The Government Detective Agency

I soon had my first introduction to the Zairian police and the government detective agency. It wasn't a pleasant experience. They were loath to do anything, but take my car and drive around to suspected areas in which the thief might be hiding, given the revelation of his nationality. Well, I drove them here and there with all leads ending up as dead ends. They of course wanted me to pay for their time. I couldn't believe it. I really had had enough, so just walked away. The church's District Superintendent did not keep his end of the bargain in coming back (a few days later), I was innocently the victim of robbery, I used my car and gas to run around town to chase dead-end leads and on top of all that I was to pay the detectives to find the man who they would never find because we already knew he had skipped town and country. I felt awful, but had to leave it all in the hands of the church leaders.

We lived on "Ring Road" (or "Avenue du Ring" in French) for a year and then the other missionary couple who had come to Kinshasa, left for Home Assignment. We were happy to move back into the mission house which we had considered our "home".

A brick of the Zaire currency of the Republic of Zaire. At the height of the devaluation of the currency a large brick of Zaires like this might buy you a sack of rice!

Chapter Seventeen: 2nd Term Ministry 1978-82

CEAC Center of Evangelism

While at CBC/CTS as "Missionary-In-Residence" I was asked to speak at a "mish" meeting (Friday night was always mission's night at CBC). It happened that I was also seeking to raise substantial funds (around $10,000) to help purchase a strategic church property—which would eventually lead to the growth of strong French and Lingala Congregations in large new church buildings. I remember doing a mime and then a monolog on stage, coming in with my pretend motorbike--making bike sounds and all--describing the church property and dreaming in Lingala (translated into English at the same time) of how this special property could be so effectively used to reach many with the Good News (Sango Malamu) in the heart of the city. Somehow, through my feeble attempts at acting and speaking, the Holy Spirit touched the hearts of the students and teachers and the full amount above was raised. The Church property at Focobel with existing buildings was purchased. This was a very exciting time for the CEAZ in Kinshasa. Although I wasn't their pastor any longer, I was still very much emotionally attached and had the privilege of handing over funds raised to help complete the purchase of that large compound--on which the Focobel Lingalaphone church was already meeting. The funds which were raised outside of the Congo did not purchase the whole of it, but it did give them the final "straw" to break the hold that the owner of the property had upon them. They were now "free to fly" on their own turf!

Not long after that, the CEAZ (Communauté Evangélique de l'Alliance au Zaire) church in Kinshasa looked to acquire another large plot of land for a "Center Of Evangelism" across the alley from the Focobel church. It was during that time that I was accused of trading dollars on the black market, keeping the difference and giving the church the dollar amount that the bank would give—which was considerably lower. This of course was completely false.

It all started when the church absolutely wanted to purchase that property for a Center of Evangelism from a wealthy businessman who was a great friend of the CEAZ church in Kinshasa. He was going to give the CMA and/or the CEAZ churches in Kinshasa a great deal as he needed cash. His business was beginning to decline and he wanted to sell immediately. It was prize property on a main street of Kinshasa, in a well-known "quartier" of the city--a very good, centrally, located area called Kimbangu. The first installment on this property was paid

for by Samaritan's Purse. Franklin Graham had come through to investigate the possibility of helping the CMA in the medical ministry that they had at Kinkonzi. Franklin and Dr. Furman had been our guests while in Kinshasa. In fact, Dawn met them at the airport as I was out of town and she flew with

With the band Degarmo and Key

them to Kimpese (where another large mission hospital was located) and then on to Bas-Zaire and Kinkonzi, our mission hospital. Before they left for home, Franklin wanted to see some of the projects we had in the city. I told him about the vision of a CEAZ Center of Evangelism and Youth Center. He then visited the place pictured here with Sango Malamu and the group DeGarmo and Key during a concert in front of the elaborate house on the same property that the CEAC desperately wanted to buy. God touched Franklin's heart and he raised funds for the project and gave around $20,000 to make the first down payment in purchase of this prized property.

That made it our own property, but there still was a bundle left to pay. The CEAZ made a few payments, but that didn't amount to too much and didn't make the owners happy. By this time the businessman who owned the property had passed away and we were now dealing with the family who felt a sense of urgency to obtain all the funds needed for us to purchase the property. They came to us with an ultimatum. Either we get all the money in a few days or they would sell the property to someone else who was interested in it—another buyer.

That couldn't be possible, yet it was their threat. It was true that we really had not yet come through with the final payment, but we were doing our best to the raise the money. They couldn't sell the property under our noses! But then, anything can happen, if you give the right people the right amount of money under the table. We were desperate, but the CMA in Nyack, New York, would not be intimidated. They would not send us any money for this project.

I devised a plan! One of several churches in Kinshasa already received a 2/3rds money grant to put a roof on the church and then to finish the church. The grant stipulated that the church that received the grant would pay a third of the funds they had received back into a revolving fund, so that other churches could use those funds to put on roofs and finish their churches (complete with benches). This was the arrangement made between the CMA and the national CEAZ church.[34]   My idea was that if this particular large church that I had in mind was in agreement instead of using the final third of the funds granted to finish their church construction project, the congregation would immediately pay back the 1/3rd which they hadn't yet used, into the revolving fund. That was if the pastor and his board voted for it, along with the whole council of the Kinshasa CEAZ

Paul, Jim, and Joseph singing at the Center

churches (pastors and a few prominent lay people). Then the council of the CEAZ churches in Kinshasa could decide how to use those funds. This was a large church and they already had the roof put on, so they decided that they would finish the church building on their own, pay back immediately into the revolving account the c. $30,000 that was left for them to finish the church and allow the Kinshasa churches the use of those funds as they saw fit. Naturally, all the council agreed that those funds then would be used to make the final payment due on this property which would be the Kimbangu "Centre d'Evangelisation". It was done. As I look back on it now, it was a "maverick" move. It was

---

[34] *The agreement stipulated that if a local church could complete 1/3rd of the church construction on their own—up to being ready to put on the roof—then the CMA in the USA would supply the other 2/3rds for its completion: 1/3rd for the roof and 1/3rd to help completely finish the church outside and in, with benches etc. This final third though needed to be paid back into a revolving fund. The plan actually never worked well as none of the churches really paid back any significant amount into the revolving fund. The plan was based on western philosophy not on the eastern way of thinking. Eastern philosophy dictates that once I have something given to me, it is mine and I really don't have to pay anything back. What is more, if you give me something that will break down then it will be your responsibility to fix it. So the logic extends to the idea if I can't pay back the money given to me, then you will do it for me as this was your idea and you gave me the funds in the first place. Missionaries (and mission organizations) often got trapped between Western and Eastern ways of thinking.*

all above board, nothing illegal, the CEAZ churches made the decision, but it wasn't quite according to the agreed upon procedure. It was outside of the proverbial box. BUT, the churches of Kinshasa were excited to have their own center which would be for all the churches in Kinshasa--their own "Center of Evangelism" and their own youth center and book store.

Backlash – "High and Dry"

After some time, when this large congregation (especially some key businessmen in the church) fully realized what they had done, that they had actually given back the one third of "their" 2/3rds building fund money to the central treasury and that they would receive no more funds to finish the church, there was a great uproar. The pastor, instead of explaining the situation correctly, put the blame on me, suggesting that I had traded funds at the black-market rate, had given the church the bank rate and now they were out of money. What happened with the amount that was gained by trading at the black-market rate? Well, you guessed it. The pastor accused me of keeping those funds and went straight to the CMA national church president with this story. This, of course, was an absolute lie as the whole council of pastors and laymen in Kinshasa and especially the D.S. knew the whole true story. It was the council of pastors and laymen and the pastor of this large church who made the final decision, I had only put forward a plan that I thought might work to get the needed funds. But due to the fact that the pastor of this sizeable church was son of the CEAZ President at that time, he was believed.

The Visit from Nyack

The CMA mission area rep. for Africa came from Nyack for a visit to Zaire shortly after this occurred. I explained what had taken place, but after he had visited the CEAC headquarters in Boma, he came back to Kinshasa, sided with the President and his son and stripped me of all responsibilities and ministries (perhaps he didn't like my devised plan either). He gave me no explanation, no reason why and no opportunity to talk about it even though I had been the person responsible for all CMA mission work in Kinshasa. When I asked what I should then do, he said, "Oh, knowing you, you'll find something, I'm sure." …And what about the leadership of the Mission in Kinshasa? Oh, he said he was bringing in a missionary from the Lower Zaire area to do that—

with all due respect, someone who didn't know the city culture, didn't know the city churches or the language of the city, nor the vision of the city pastors? I couldn't believe it nor could I understand this seemingly impulsive move without hearing my explanation of things. The CMA Africa Director left me "high and dry" with no position or ministry and not one word of explanation as to why he had already made that decision. I found out later the "why" of all this (as intimated above) as a few Africans began to give me pieces of the puzzle and one or two missionaries as well.

At the time, I thought that everything was above board. I had given the church all the funds due them and their roof was on—a large steel structured solid roof. The church's pastor and council agreed that they could pay back the funds right away and finish the rest of the church building on their own—which they did. The money was put back in the revolving account and then deployed as the CEAC saw fit, which was in the agreement. AND, the CEAZ had their Center of Evangelism which was greatly used and a real gem for the Community. In looking back, I can see that this may not have been the best idea for acquiring the center, but there was no hanky-panky going on, no hocus-pocus and certainly no black-market sleight of hand. The funds were all there and put to good use.

Jesus is the great Redeemer and I can see now that He with His Father is always in control. For me this was a traumatic humbling experience, but He saw that He needed to chisel a few more "edges" off my character and continue forming me into the person HE wanted me to be. With His help I withstood the blow. The redeeming factors were that **Theo van Barneveld** came to Kinshasa and had an excellent ministry to the church and even to the people of the plateau. I was liberated to do TEE and then be intricately involved in what I would call Worship Evangelism with the Tsasa brothers. I'm sure this incident was another one of the "all things" that God's worked together for our good.

Persecution

Persecution comes in all forms. Sad to say it seems more often than not to come from Christian brothers and sisters rather than from the non-Christians. I read somewhere about a Christian leader who was going through serious problems of false accusations. In a state of emotional suffering and seeking God, he looked out the window and saw a dog playing ferociously with a rag that it had found. The dog would grab the rag in its teeth and then shake it violently and then lay it down. It would then pick the rag up again and repeat the procedure until the rag was demolished, torn apart. Then the writer said that God whispered to his heart that this is what He was allowing to happen to his reputation. The writer heard, "Be patient, I know what I'm doing!"

It was a serious lesson and I remember reading that and thinking, "Oh God, I hope I don't have to go through that experience!" But I think, in retrospect, that anyone living on the edge with God, taking chances and pushing forward with God, not being happy with the status quo, will most likely experience serous criticism which God allows and uses to mold and shape them into the people He wants them to be. And that was my experience--more than once! Perhaps this maverick is a slow learner.

The Bible talks quite plainly about this and I suppose a good title for that subject could be, "DON'T WORRY ABOUT YOUR REPUTATION." Jesus said in Mat 5:11, "Blessed are you when people insult you, persecute you and falsely say all kinds of evil against you because of me." We also read in 1 Cor. 4:12-13, "When we are cursed, we bless: when we are persecuted, we endure it; when we are slandered, we answer kindly. Up to this moment we have become the scum of the earth, the refuse of the world."

One might be tempted to say, as I was, "if I don't say anything to defend myself what will become of my reputation. I must look after it! (N'est-ce pas?)[35] I was encouraged of late in reading E. Stanley Jones on this subject. What he had to say on this subject was so similar to what I thought I heard God say to me that I thought I would include it here. I think that Jones' words just prove the consistency of God's message to us, His children. I quote,

> *"One who is living victoriously has gained victory over nervous concern about reputation. Look after your character and your reputation can look after itself. Be the kind of person about whom people won't believe things."*

In other words, don't be afraid of your reputation if they call you Beelzebub; the truth will emerge in the end. You can wait.

---

[35] *This expression in French is often used to convey the idea that what is being expressed must be right, right? More literally "is it not so?"*

When John Wesley's wife accused him of a certain sin, he exclaimed, 'There! The record is complete now; I've been accused of every sin in the catalog.' But his wife only succeeded in burying herself beneath her own slander." (ref: E. Stanly Jones)[36]

My first experience of this was in Kitimat. When we had only a very few families in our church, but during my first year in ministry it came to my attention that there were lies and gossip beginning to circulate about me as a pastor. The church board knew better, they did not believe it and told me to ignore it, but it was disconcerting to say the least to this young pastor. In my pursuit of God on this issue, it seemed that God was saying that all the gossip was purely enemy stuff and that I would never track it down. Don't even try! However, I did find out that I had inadvertently offended a family. I went to that family specifically to apologize for something that I had not intentionally done nor had any idea of what it was that had really offended them. I asked for forgiveness for offending them; I was forgiven, God was glorified, and the church began to grow. This family remained friends for many years after we left Kitimat and was the only family who consistently continued to keep in personal correspondence with us, even in Kinshasa, for many years.

In the three years that we were in Kitimat we came face to face with the enemy of our souls a number of times. We realized that we could never outsmart, out speak or outthink the enemy, only God could do that. We also learned where our authority lay--not in ourselves but in Jesus Christ alone. We learned on the road called "difficult challenges" how to walk in His authority and not our own. It certainly prepared us for all kinds of attacks that came our way in Africa.

Now, in the eyes of the African church leaders, and the African congregations, I was deemed "guilty as charged", for I had received correction and "punishment" from the President and the Mission. It was a very big "pill" to swallow. This was a very hard time for me and I was ready to go home. For the second time in my short missionary experience in Africa I asked myself the question, "What in the world am I doing here?" Many friends, Congolese and white, told me to stick up for my rights and to clear myself from the lies that had been circulating. But God had another plan. What the enemy meant for evil, God meant for good!

---

[36] From the devotional book by E Stanley Jones *"Victorious Living"*

The picture I got from my heavenly Father was very cute—in some sense. I definitely got the message that I should be quiet and that He would exonerate me, for he said vengeance is mine, I will repay. But the picture I got was something like, "Be quiet or I'll nail your other foot to the floor!" So, I was silent and asked the Lord what HE wanted me to do.

We read in Luke 9:51-56 that the Samaritans refused to receive Jesus and his disciples. The disciples were not happy and wanted to retaliate! Call down fire! But Jesus rebuked them and indicated that they should just go on to another village. I gleaned from this story (and began to understand) that if you are blocked in one area, pass on to the next "village". That "village" may also be nearer your goal, the reason for which God has called you to be his servant!

Theological Education by Extension

My next "village" was "TEE" in Kinshasa. He led me to begin a "TEE" or Theological Education by Extension program for the CEAZ in Kinshasa--which became one of the most exciting ministries that I was to be involved in over my 30 plus years of ministry in Africa.

We just got our feet wet in TEE in 1979 by printing those Lingala books. Many of the courses were in French, but the basic ones needed to be translated in Lingala for many elders of the churches and others involved in leadership in the local churches could not understand French well enough to do the study and homework that was required. I had already attended some meetings about TEE and the style of teaching and we already had one book printed. Yes, we could re-use the stencils of the pages that were stolen and complete that first book. Curiously, after that first printing the Gestetner that was repaired never did operate that good again, no matter what I tried, so we had to scrap it. But God in his mercy laid it on the heart of a business man in Chilliwack, my home town, to supply funds for a new printing machine and a new transposing machine so we could create pictures and good covers. He also supplied us with enough paper to print many books in Lingala and French. We were able order in other books and soon had a good number of courses in French and Lingala.

During my second term of ministry in Kinshasa, I had graduated from a moped (a low-power, lightweight motorized bicycle) to a 125 cc Yamaha Trail motorbike[37] and it was just the thing to get me into some hard spots that a car would be very difficult to drive into, if it could make it at all. Kinshasa is built on the banks of the huge Congo River, with some high hills, but also with a belt of sand about 50 to 60 kilometers wide snaking along with it (much of the Kinshasa low-lands is sandy soil, sometimes 20 to 30 feet deep).

We started with one class at the Focobel church, but it didn't take long for other churches to request these classes. Soon other churches became centers for Theological Education. Along with Focobel, churches in Kisenzo, Rifflart, Binza Delevo, Masina, Kingasani and even as far as Maluku (about 80 Kilometers from Kinshasa) became centers for TEE classes. Some of these areas were in pure sand, so the motorbike was the only way to get to these churches.

We had around 100 students and I was teaching a 2 hour class almost every day of the week, sometimes two a day. Soon some keen students who were also graduates of our Bible School in Kinkonzi could also teach, for

Riding my 175 cc. to a TEE class with a pack sack on my back full of materials.

this kind of teaching was more a calling of the students together to hear their reports and to discuss and answer their questions, conferring with them as well on their homework of past and present lessons. In brief, the leader is more of a facilitator, giving direction to the homework of the students, mainly moderating the vitally important discussions and personal applications of the lessons; there were lesson books for student and teacher. There were basic courses in Prayer, Christian Doctrine, Mission or "on being Servants" and the like, but oh so

[37] *Later on, we rode a 175 cc—Gramma and I both rode that one--and then I had a 650 cc to get into the difficult sandy areas of the city. I also often rode a 250 cc and a 375 cc, but those were friends' bikes.*

powerful! One course would often bring about significant changes in a student's life.

I remember two stories in particular:

Prayer for Healing

A young man in our group at Focobel lifted his hand and said that he had a report (testimony) to give. We always started with the possibility of student reports, so after opening prayer, this young father wanted the floor. "OK, brother you have the floor." This was his narrative, as I can now remember it.

He said, "I went home after our class last Saturday to find my daughter not feeling well. We thought that she would be better in the morning, so we put her to bed early. We had no medicine to give her, but we prayed over her. In the morning, she was in bad shape and we didn't know what to do. I remembered what we had learned in class about God being our healer (of all our diseases and sickness), so I said to my wife that we would not go to the shaman (witchdoctor), but go first to the pastor and then to the clinic. Let us pray first with the pastor over her and then maybe we can find some money to take her to the clinic. I told my wife what I had learned in class, so we went in faith to the pastor and we prayed over her and she was instantly healed. One minute the child was crying and feverish and the next she was calm and cool. We never got to the clinic, so we don't know what she had, but God intervened and healed her! I'm so glad I learned about Jesus bearing our sins and sicknesses on the cross and that God the Father is also our healer. We experienced that last week and I just want to praise God before you all and say that what we are learning is real and effective if we just put it into practice and trust our heavenly Father.

Prayer for a son—fighting the Enemy

A family man in Kingasani whose son would wake up screaming every night at midnight came to class and told us this story. He started with a song ("I have decided to follow Jesus") and then he said, "We had been learning about the power in the name of Jesus last week and how we need not run to the diviner or the fetish doctor or the witchdoctor for help. Well, my son has been waking up every night around midnight and screaming so loudly that it would wake up our whole household; not only ours, but all our neighbors around us (in the neighborhoods the houses/huts would be built very close together, some made of sticks and mud and others of sand and cement bricks-- with tin roofs). My neighbors asked me to do something about it. 'You must take him to the fetish man' they said, 'so he can give you a fetish to ward off the spirits that are making him cry and scream.'

I said that I would pray and God would take care of it. But I didn't pray right away. I was hoping that all would be quiet. But it wasn't. The neighbors said that they would take him to the witchdoctor, but I refused. Then my father-in-law, who was staying with us, said that he would give me the money to take him to the witchdoctor for something to keep our son quiet at night or he would take him himself. But I said, 'No!' I told my neighbors and all my family that I would pray to God in the Name of Jesus and that He would take care of this problem. So one night this last week I went out in the darkness and looked up at the stars and prayed in the Name of Jesus that He would give my son a good sleep, take away the fear and give him peace so that my father-in-law and all my neighbors would know that my God is real and more powerful and any fetish or witchdoctor."

"That night my son was quiet and slept through the night—and has done so until today! Many people, including my father-in-law asked what kind of fetish I gave him, but I told them straight, that I prayed to God the Father through His son Jesus to give peace to my son and He did – and then I added that he could do the same for them! All were amazed at God's intervention. I'm so glad that we have this class to learn about God's love and desire to help us.

Vindication

Two years after all the kafuffle and shake up in my life (the accusations and disciplinary action), after the initial shock wore off, while I was actively engaged in growing the TEE ministry, the Lord began giving me a series of messages on the characteristics of the early church (from the beginning chapters of Acts). I prepared them, not having the faintest idea as to where they would or should be delivered. Then I received a message from the CMA national church president asking me to come and be the guest speaker at the conference for all the 400 pastors plus delegates who would be coming to the annual conference in the Lower Zaire area. Although bewildered at the invitation, after having been so severely treated, I knew then why God had given me these messages. I accepted. I spoke in French and Lingala for 4 sessions—a series of 4 messages. The last day of the conference, the Sunday morning with perhaps a thousand people or more present, at the large Kinkonzi church, the host pastor got up after I had delivered the last message and said, among other closing remarks, "Pastor Sawatsky, we believe you are a man sent from God!" I guess it was his way of saying, on behalf of the church, "We have seen God's blessing on your life and we were wrong about you and the discipline you received, please forgive us. I don't know, but I took it as that. At least I heard God whisper in my heart, "You have just been justified and exonerated!" I knew then that God had followed through on His promise to vindicate, and I thanked HIM for this added blessing!

The Center

The Center of Evangelism then became the focal point of many rallies and evangelism for at least the next 10 years (until 1989 or so). We started a great book store that was thriving in its time and SSM held many evangelistic rallies at the center, including one with *Degarmo and Key*, a Christian rock group who came to visit Missionary Aviation Fellowship (MAF), who in turn asked us to show them around. We travelled a little with them and did several concerts with them. It was a lot of fun, and they went back to raise funds for MAF to fly us around to many parts of Zaire. Many CMA conferences were held there at the center and gatherings of all CMA churches in Kinshasa took place for special services. But as times were changing so was the church. A French Church, that had started in the plot of land across the alley, grew and began expanding into quite a large congregation. The local churches, Lingalaphone and Francophone began building a large church structure on the original Focobel site. That being done the French congregation raised funds, moved to the Center for Evangelism site, built another large structure, demolishing the original fantasy house with all its curlicues. That area is now headquarters for all the CMA churches in Kinshasa, hosting a large and completed building, used for many ministries. At one time the Center was even used for TEE classes and classes for the deaf. It certainly was a great multipurpose Center of Evangelism for the CEAZ in Kinshasa, at the time serving some 60 or more neighborhood churches.

Our Prayer Times

During this time of personal crisis ('78 – '80), I would ask the Lord during our noon prayer times what He wanted us/me to do. One day it became very clear. As I knelt beside the bed (Gramma would lay down and I would kneel—that's just the way we felt most comfortable talking to God), I sensed the Lord calling me personally into a ministry of evangelism. I immediately said in my heart, "Oh no Lord, you must be mistaken, I am not an evangelist." Yet there was no other call but that one! I then said, haltingly, "...Uhhh, OK Lord, if you supply the evangelist!" I sensed a nod of agreement from my heavenly Father; His call was confirmed in my heart! At the same time, He gave me a picture of an organization that I was to be a part of—an organization that would lead many to Jesus. In my wondering what this was all about, I asked the Lord, "Well, who would be the founder or leader of this organization?" ...and He replied immediately, "YOU!"

"Oh no, I couldn't accept that!" ...but God doesn't make mistakes. We do (make mistakes), in trying to understand Him on our own, sometimes, but He is perfect in all His ways! I didn't tell anyone about this for many years, as I thought it too pretentious. I just kept all these things in my heart and "meditated on them."

Well, it wasn't long before we were involved in evangelism campaigns! We started out by using the Alliance Youth Corps (AYC) students to be involved in evangelism, but after a few weeks they always left for home. After this conversation with God and His call to evangelism, I began to think, "Why shouldn't we, the Congolese, instead of just the AYC students, be able to do that same kind of singing and preaching—leading many to Jesus. This was the seed thought to the birth and conception of the Trio Sango Malamu.

It was during those AYC students' visits that we formed a singing group and went as far as Tshela, deep in the Mayombe area, to do a ministry of evangelism with a guest evangelist. We were a mixed group of young Alliance Youth Corps university/college students (guys and gals) and some young Congolese. It was during this outing that I was given a special experience of encouragement. We sang together, played our guitars, and prayed with people at the end of the meeting. While we were all praying, a middle-aged woman came to me for a prayer of healing. Her right arm had gone limp, she couldn't move it enough to do the work in the family fields.

She told me her story: Her husband was wanting to divorce her because she could no longer do the women's work around the house and in the gardens (in the forest). She was very sad that she couldn't work anymore and completely depressed that her husband would send her away. Where would she go and what would she do with only one arm. She couldn't hoe the fields, she couldn't reap the harvest, she couldn't gather wood for cooking and she couldn't carry her loads back to the village. She was destitute and came for prayer for healing.

Well, I immediately prayed for her and in my praying, I felt I should take authority over the enemy Satan and his evil spirits, so I did! I bound the enemy out and away from her life (she was a believer, I had determined), I asked the Lord to cover her under the blood of Jesus because we read that the accuser of the brethren (sisters too) is overcome by the blood of the lamb.[38] While I was praying I felt a quick crack as if she were cracking her knuckles, but because there were a lot of other people wanting prayer, I had to move on and pray with others. However, I was sure that the Lord did something in her arm for why would I feel that crack (very lightly) if He hadn't done anything. Possibly I would never know.

I just "happened" to be in Tshela about two weeks later on another assignment and stopped to greet the pastor of the church there. While I was there, I saw the man who was an elder of that little church that we were ministering in two weeks earlier. I recognized him for he was instrumental in leading our small group while we were there. As he was crossing the church campus I called out to him.

"Hey brother, greetings! What's new? Are you well?" ("Mbote ndeko, boni? Sango nini? Oza malamu?") After the greeting and as he was coming closer I asked if he knew the woman I had prayed for two weeks earlier. Before I had even finished asking the question he replied, "I know exactly who you are talking about. I've seen her several times and she told me to tell you, if I ever saw you again, that the Lord healed her arm, she is out working in the field gardens and her husband is pleased with her and will not divorce her. As a matter of fact he is even coming to church with her now. She is praising God for his great mercy and grace to her." What great news! What an encouragement that was to me.

---

[38] Revelation 12:9-11: [9] And the great dragon was cast out, that old serpent, called the Devil, and Satan, which deceiveth the whole world: he was cast out into the earth, and his angels were cast out with him. [10] And I heard a loud voice saying in heaven, Now is come salvation, and strength, and the kingdom of our God, and the power of his Christ: for the accuser of our brethren is cast down, which accused them before our God day and night. [11] And they overcame him by the blood of the Lamb, and by the word of their testimony; and they loved not their lives unto the death.

The Miracle of the Snake

It was during the last year of the AYC visits, while a crew of five were staying at our home, that we decided to round up a few MKs (college age) who had some motor bikes and with the one I had and one I could borrow, we all went on a little motor bike outing to the Congo River, not far outside of the city. There were about 8 or 9 of us riding out to the sand bars for a little swim and fun on the beach. It wasn't that hot as it was the dry season and the river was low with plenty of good sand bars to speed along with our motor bikes, do wheelies and donuts and a few other fun tricks to show off our expertise. There were around 4 or 5 bikes and most all had passengers—mainly girls, our foster daughter Kathy was also there with us.

After the bike shenanigans were over we all thought of going for a cool dip in a little eddy of the river. We wouldn't go too deep in the river for many had been caught by the current and swept away. We were told to be careful.[39] Thinking that I wouldn't go in, it was cool season after all, about 72 degrees F, so I suggested they do the swimming. But they insisted that I go in and I insisted that I would not! It soon became a friendly struggle and all the guys piled on me and threw me in. That began the splashing around in the eddy and a lot of laughter and dunking with everyone taking part.

While this was happening, I walked to the edge of the river and stood there watching the show, with my ankles almost covered in the cool water. There was a story that a missionary had introduced a water hyacinth into the Congo River and it grew so prolifically that there were now lots of clumps of flower, stems and debris (weeds) from the plant always floating down river. Usually you pay no attention to it. And on this day, with water covering my toes, I felt some of this water plant attach itself to my ankles. My immediate response was to kick it in the air, catch the weed before it landed and throw it away. I had done it many times before. As I was about to do this, I heard a still small voice deep inside me say, "Be still, don't move!"

With the commotion that was going on in the water, I forgot the weeds and began laughing, just standing there amused at the pranks

---

[39] *Later we experienced that hazard full on as one of our associates had a college age son who, with another group of college kids visiting their parents, went for a swim in the river. One of the gals went too far and began struggling to swim for shore and without hesitation this young man dove in to help. He was a good swimmer and he got her to quiet water, but in the process, he got caught by the current and his body was never found.*

being carried on in the water. When I came to feel the "weeds" again around my feet, I was going to kick them off, in the air, catch them and throw them away. Again, I heard, "Be still, don't move!" And again, I got distracted by the hubbub in the water.

The third time I felt the "weeds", I thought, "Okay, this time I am going to make these weeds a football, kick them high in the air, catch them on the way down and throw them aside." But again, I heard, "Be still, don't move!" Now I am really wondering what this voice is all about, so I finally looked down to my ankles and what I saw was a snake warming itself around my feet, curling itself around my ankles. When I finally looked down and saw it, I was calm and didn't move until I soon saw it slither off and up the sand bank.

I hollered to the kids in the river, "Hey you guys there is a snake here!" At the word snake, all movement stopped, immediately. They looked up and saw it on the bank and then the snake fearing danger, made a direct beeline for the middle of the crowd in the water. The kids separated as fast as they could, some even tried to walk on water, and then they watched as the poisonous black viper cut through them like a

'KISS OF DEATH'

■ The African black mamba is widely regarded as the deadliest snake on the planet, killing tens of thousands every year.
■ It can deliver up to 12 repeated bites, injecting enough venom to kill 25 men.
■ Its bite is called 'the kiss of death', as without anti-venom, the mortality rate is 100 per cent – the highest among venomous snakes.
■ Its venom causes rapid paralysis and can kill in as little as 30 minutes. Enzymes in the snake's saliva start to digest the prey instantly.
■ It is one of the fastest snakes in

Predator: The black mamba

the world, slithering at speeds of up to 12.5mph.
■ It gets its name not from its skin colour, which tends to be olive to gray, but from the blue-black hue of the inside of its mouth.

saw, without touching anyone on either side.[40] One of the MKs had a sling shot, but by the time he reached it, the snake was way out in the middle of the river and gone! They can slither on the water a lot faster than we could even run full out! I didn't know what kind of snake it was, but some of the MKs did and said that if it would have bitten me, I would have had a mere few minutes to take my final breaths. **How grateful I was that I listened to that still small voice.** Thank you

---

[40]*http://www.lobshots.com/wp-content/uploads/2011/12/the-black-mamba-kiss-of-death.jpg*

Lord for saving my life! But curiously enough, at the time I saw the snake around my ankles, I wasn't even afraid. I was calm as a cucumber. Any other time, I would have been shaking in my boots. I don't like snakes!

The Miracle Washing Machine

When we came home and told the story to Dawn and the kids, we found that Gramma had her own story to tell. As you can imagine, with all this company and our three little kids, she had a lot of washing to do. Due to very low water pressure during the day, Dawn had gotten up very early that morning to do the washing while the pressure was good. She had a big load and the machine was full of water and clothes when suddenly it made a terrible noise and with a clunk it stopped. Gramma was beside herself and had no idea what to do, it was after all, about 16 years old. So she prayed, and asked the Lord to heal it. And left it alone until the morning, not knowing if it would ever run again. When she went back again to do the wash, during our bike ride to the river, she prayed again, asking the Lord to please keep it running until we could find someone to fix it. She started it and it ran well. It ran so well that we used it for the next 10 years. When we finally found someone who we thought could fix it, the machine actually died on us. Bert was with us 10 years later and was a great handyman. He looked at the washing machine and said that there was no way to fix it and it actually should not have been running at all. He saw the problem and said that it was only a miracle that the washing machine lasted this long. With the problem as he saw it, the washing machine should not have been able to operate! It was truly a miracle.

Gulf Oil was finishing up an offshore drilling platform and had a heavy-duty Maytag available. They said they would give it to us for a favor that I had done for them, since our machine was now irreparable. The catch was that it was a 110-volt machine and we used 220 volts in Africa. No matter, Bert knew how to make the conversion and we had a relatively new heavy duty washing machine for free (we knew it was God's provision). Not only did God keep the old one going, He kept it going until He found a replacement for it!!!

The Suburban

It was the 2nd year of our 2nd term that we heard about the present from 10th Avenue Alliance Church—the church in which Gramma and

I met and were married. One Wednesday evening before we left for our 2nd term in Africa, we had had the privilege of addressing those who came out for prayer meeting. Out of about 5 or 6 hundred that comprised the congregation at that time, perhaps 80 were out that night. I really wanted to address the whole church, but this was as far as I got and pastor Brooks wasn't even there, as I recall. Nevertheless, I was grateful for this opportunity to share our ministry and to unburden my heart before the people. One of the biggest burdens on my heart was the need for a large 4-wheel drive vehicle—with AC! We had a Chevrolet Suburban in mind, but that was over 10 grand and it would take a lot of people pulling together to help us get that. There weren't that many at the prayer meeting that night, but the challenge did not go unnoticed. "J'ai livré mon âme" as they say in French (literally, I delivered my soul or gave them the whole burden on my heart), yet there seemed to be no significant outcome that evening. We went back to the Congo thinking that we would try to make do with whatever 2nd hand car we could find—which we did for a year or so.

It was towards the end of that first year of our 2nd term, before we moved back into the mission house from our Ring Road abode that Gramma was stopped in her house work by God when he indicated very forcefully that she should read John 1:50b. She dropped everything, plopped up on the bed full of washing and read, *"Do you believe this just because I told you I had seen you under the fig tree? **You will see greater things than this."***

To Gramma it meant, *"You ain't seen nothin' yet!"* It was the next day that we received a most wonderful and amazing letter from 10th Avenue Alliance church, and a confirmation from headquarters, that the 10th Ave. Sunday School had raised over 10 grand to not only buy the Suburban (with AC), but also pay for all the shipping to our Port of Matadi! We couldn't believe it! But it was true! Apparently, Johnny Friesen, the Sunday School Superintendent, together with a great fund raiser, my brother-in-law George Schroeder, had rallied the troops and presented this burden to the whole of the 10th Avenue Alliance Church through the Sunday School and challenged them to raise the funds that were needed. And they did just that! It was a real shock to us, but what an answer to prayer! We would finally have the vehicle that was needed for church planting, TEE (Theological Education by Extension) and Evangelism. I was ecstatic with joy and praise to the Lord for again taking my feeble efforts and transferring the burden on to someone else who could run with it for a time. I had not shared this burden with any other church group for I felt the Lord wanted me to share it only with the 10th Avenue Alliance Church—our home church for many years. Johnny and George caught the burden and ran with it and saw it right to the end. We were and still are deeply grateful for the Sunday School, of all ages, at 10th Avenue for showering us with such generosity and compassion.

It didn't take long before we had that long, shiny, new, sky blue Suburban in our yard and ready for action. We used that to carry a dozen or more pastors and/or AYC students from Kinshasa to bas-Zaire and back, to carry all our evangelism gear for many years and to bring students and teachers to our TEE  classes, not to mention the many trips up town for purchases great and small. We felt secure in it and when we got to our destination after a long ride we were still fresh because the truck was equipped with AC. How we praised the Lord for that!

The Incubation Period

All through this, I still had a great desire to be involved in somehow forming a group of musicians. As this dream and vision was developing, it seemed that God was giving me two burdens as cause for the ministry of a music group. The first burden of this ministry was to let our people at home (in North America) know how their giving of time, money, energy and the giving of their children had borne fruit in the Congo—the first "mission field" of the CMA in North America. We couldn't bring all of North America to see what was happening and what had happened with the spread of the gospel in Zaire, but perhaps we could bring a few Zairians to give representation of that fruit to the people of North America—and even share the gospel with them at the same time in testimony and music. That was the dream and passion of mine from that first day we set foot in our first church service in Maduda.

The other one, due to His calling me into "evangelism" through that vision in prayer, was to share this saving grace of God, the Gospel of Jesus Christ, whenever we could, wherever He would send us, and as a result see many come to a knowledge of His grace through the power of worship and music, congregational singing and participation, as well as testimony and preaching. Along with this activity, we had a great desire to see these new converts "discipled" by the local Christian leaders in the churches where they would be worshipping.

It is important to make this part of my story a separate section as it represents some of the best years of my life, the most enjoyable, the most interesting and perhaps the most spiritually productive ministry of my life. During this time, I used to say to Gramma, "I can't believe that we are getting paid to do this!" Albeit the "pay" wasn't that grand or glorious; nevertheless, we never went without, we were never in dire financial straits.

There were very few times during our 30 plus years that the C&MA (both in Canada and the USA), due to the national budget not being met, had to cut back on our allowance (just a bit). For the most part, we always received what they had promised. The Christian and Missionary Alliance, as a missionary society, has always been very accommodating, very gentle with this maverick and very understanding in allowing us and the Sango Malamu ministry to push the boundaries of personal ministry and mission policy! We were blessed to work with and under the supervision of very understanding leaders of both USA and Canada. As I look back on our ministry, as I see it now, I believe they made exceptions along the way for two reasons;

1. Because of their holy passion to do all they could to be good "caretakers" of all their missionaries and ministries, us included, and

2. Because they were open to experiencing new and innovative ways of proclaiming the gospel.

God sees their hearts and blesses them!

SECTION TWO

PART V - The Birth and Ministry of "Trio Sango Malamu"

Chapter Eighteen - The Birth of a Vision

Through that first visit to the church in Maduda, the vision of bringing a group of singers or Congolese music to our western churches was born in my spirit. Truly, people at home needed to hear this. They needed to hear firsthand what their sacrifice had accomplished. I tried to start a singing group in Maduda, but soon realized I did not understand Congolese music and needed much more experience, so I set about praying for a group that I could work with. In the meantime, God had so much for me to learn, including the language, the culture, the operation of the church and just plain living in another culture.

Six years of Praying

After I had been praying for six years, often enquiring out loud of the Lord if in some way I could form a music group, two young men stood up to sing in the Focobel church in Kinshasa—where I had been the pastor for a short time. They were both sons of one of my elders (deacons), Papa Tsasa, and they sang very well. It seemed to me that God whispered in my heart, "Start with them." And He gave me permission to approach these young men to see if we could try singing together. I sensed this could be the start of what I had been praying for, if they agreed. Perhaps we could begin singing together… and playing for they both played guitars.

In retrospect, I see how our Father had arranged this and had even brought me earlier to an empty house in which I found a brand-new upright bass fiddle. A rich businessman—the one who was showing me around his large, empty house, that would eventually become the CEAZ Center of Evangelism—had brought a whole band of instruments from France for his kids, but no one knew what to do with this instrument, so there it sat. I told him, "I know what to do with it!" He allowed me to take it. I put strings and a bridge on it and I began playing it in my home. It was shortly after this that I met Joe and Paul Tsasa and heard them sing for the first time.

After my message that Sunday morning, I went over to them, thanked them for their good music and asked if we could try something together. I mentioned that I had found a bass fiddle and it would be fun

193

to try a song or two together. They were kind and agreed that we could have a trial practice one day the coming week! They would come over to my place and bring their guitars.

Trio Sango Malamu

First photo of the Trio Sango Malamu in 1979

And so it was that Paul and Joseph Tsasa actually came to my place to sing, accompanying themselves with their guitars. I tried to join them with my voice and the bass fiddle. There was one big problem, they knew no English songs and I knew no Kikongo songs. The only song that we could really jell on was "Yesu Azali Awa". They of course knew this popular song in Lingala and it happened that I did too. We sang and played that song together and it went well, it clicked! …and that was the beginning of a whole new and exciting ministry for us. The *Trio Sango Malamu*[41] was born in 1979, during the latter part of that year and the song, "Yesu Azali Awa" (Jesus Is Here) became our signature song, sung all over North America, Africa and Europe—always encouraging the audience, no matter where we were, to raise

---

[41] *"Sango Malamu" meaning "Good News" or the Good New Trio. In North America we were known as "The Kinshasa Trio" and later on as "The Kinshasa Band" but in Africa we were always "Sango Malamu" or "Trio Sango Malamu".*

their hands and sing along with us, singing "Alleluia to Jesus!" This vision conceived in my heart the very first day in I set foot in an African church, was now in the birthing canal getting ready to pop out.

We began practicing and I soon learned songs in Kikongo, French and Lingala. Joseph Tsasa, the elder brother, was the lead singer, the lead guitar player and the main song writer. He had a gift that was rarely seen in the Congo, for he knew how to harmonize, sing and arrange not only Congolese style but also western style.

Our group was a hybrid between American and Congolese styles. And perhaps that was the reason the Congolese began to gobble up our music. I only realized that our style was neither purely Congolese nor purely American after we had sung for several years. It was a blend of both. Paul Tsasa sang harmony well and played rhythm guitar to accompany his older brother. They both understood western chord progressions, but certainly had the Zairian rhythms—it was all very natural for them. The style of music was unique—trying to identify it, many listeners had remarked that it sounded something like Hawaiian, but we had never been there nor listened much to their music. It was our unique blend.

Trio Sango Malamu, just gone electric 1981-82

Chapter Nineteen: Trio Sango Malamu & Evangelism

The Letter from CMA HQ

Now, due to that prayer time "vision", I knew we were to be involved in evangelism. I began challenging the young men of the trio to think in that regard. So, we set up a few out-door campaigns. I would arrange with the pastors a time and place where we could sing and play and preach in a series of meetings, in the open air, to help the planting of a new prayer cell or church. We had very little to set up when we first started as all our instruments were acoustic, but in those first meetings, I was responsible for it all--the setup, the songs we would sing, the preaching and the praying with people who responded. It didn't take long for the "guys" to understand the significance of what we were doing and to join in on all the activities. All the while I was praying for an evangelist to come and join us.

About this same time, that we began singing in a few churches, just getting our "feet wet" in ministry, I received a letter from the CMA in the USA asking if I could put together a group that would come to sing and minister in North America. Would I??? What a question! They wanted a group to come and promote church planting in Zaire, namely Kinshasa. Churches were growing rapidly and needed places to meet, the African churches were asking for help from the CMA USA. The CMA vision was to bring a group over to do a tour, sing and promote the ministry in Zaire, ask the people to release some of their personal funds to help put badly needed roofs on churches in this country of Zaire.

The Tsasa brothers and I had come together sometime in late '79. The invitation was for March of 1980 for 6 weeks of travel across the North America—the US and Canada, eh? It was suggested that I put together a singing group for this special ministry and of course I thought of my first vision of bringing the Zairian church to Canada. My vision was different, but could the two marry effectively? I thought so. In any case, it seemed that God was confirming this to me. I had given my vision to HIM, He was now giving the vision back to me! That is what I believed, and I immediately responded affirmatively asking how many singers I could bring to America. I suggested a male choir of 20 to 30 men, but CMA replied immediately with the cautious answer that they thought 20 would be too large a group.

The male choirs in the Congo are absolutely fantastic, with full 4 part harmonies, but this was not yet to be. I then suggested 8 to 12 men, but that still was too large a group. I was confused, how was I going to help accomplish this goal of the CMA. They finally came back with the response, "we understand that you are singing with two young men, perhaps we could bring the three of you to do a tour." How could we give the people at home the full meal deal with just three guys (and one of them being white)? ...and they said, "We would like you to come in March of 1980." We had just started, how was this possible?

Serious Preparations

By this time, we had moved into the mission house again and it was getting close to Christmas. The three of us talked it over and agreed that we could do this as we felt that God was in it. We began to do some hard practicing. We just made time for it and it turned out that we really enjoyed singing and playing together. We not only needed to practice, but we needed to feel like a group, know everything by memory and understand the capabilities of each other. This was a tall order in the three months that we had to get ready before leaving. For those three months we practiced 5 to 6 hours a day, almost every day, and then we scheduled "evangelistic" meetings in growing churches almost every evening. We were completely acoustic, but we managed to sing before small crowds so that they could hear us in the open air. I would prepare the way with the pastor, sing with the guys, preach a message of salvation and then pray with those who wanted to pray and ask the Lord Jesus into their lives. It was a heavy schedule, but by the time three months were over, we knew all our songs inside and out. We knew each other's singing habits, musical patterns, so that we could concentrate on one thing only, worship Jesus and bring Him to the people. Our instruments became so much a part of us that we shared/preached the Good News with our singing and playing in a manner that was personal. We forgot about trying to harmonize or getting the right rhythms or playing the right notes. We were at the point where we could uniquely concentrate on the message and sing it under the unction of the Holy Spirit. **Ours wasn't performance based, we weren't professional musicians. We were simply sharing the gifts that God had given us, helping others to see the light of Jesus as we desired to reflect Him to those who would listen.**

The Kinshasa Story

In March of 1980 we left for the metropolis of New York and the Nyack Missionary College. Only God knew how exciting and exacting this ministry in USA and Canada would be. We came straight from the great "village" of Kinshasa to the skyscrapers of New York with a stopover in Belgium. We all were naïve about the weather conditions in Europe and America. We wore only our light African shirts as it was nice and "warm" in Kinshasa when we left around 11 o'clock in the evening. We almost froze to death in the Belgium airport. None of us had the forethought to bring along a jacket or at least a sweater.

It was only March and the transfer area of the Belgium airport was partially in the open air with no heating whatsoever. We were shivering, all of us, waiting for several hours to catch our next plane. However, we arrived safely in New York with our large African drum (over a meter high and 25 cm in diameter). The hollow inside made for a great compartment to put all the mail that friends sent along with us, all stamped with USA stamps. Mail went in and out of the Congo so sporadically in those days that if anyone was leaving, the whole expatriate community came to give them their letters and cards to mail once the shores of America were reached.

The Congolese drum full of mail.

Once the drum and the "mail" cleared customs (without too much of a hitch), we were met by CMA representatives who were going to travel with us and off we went to Nyack Missionary College where we would sleep in the dorms until the preliminaries were taken care of and all were ready for our "tour". I well remember the first morning we woke up in Nyack, it was snowing! I thought how cool for the Tsasa brothers to see it snowing having never seen snow before.

I'm sure there were plenty of new experiences which presented a good amount of culture shock, but they never let it show. Yes, we were still singing, but in New York—of all places. There were so many different venues that it almost made our heads spin. The audience was predominantly white, our music was different, in a different language and it seemed no one was really happy, for no one moved to the rhythm. Even the students didn't move a muscle and the crowd was hard to read! We couldn't tell if they were with us or against us. However, as we began to lose ourselves in the singing of the songs we knew so well, the Holy Spirit anointed our efforts.

Though the audience didn't move as Zairians did during the church service, they did surround us with love and congratulations after the service. They certainly let us know that they loved our music (that was a relief)! Many gave enough funds to make this whole endeavor worthwhile. The Project and The Presentation was called "The Kinshasa Story" and the purpose was to raise funds to help congregations put on roofs of their unfinished churches in Kinshasa. It seemed that this venture actually was God's vision, for reasons we may never understand this side of heaven—and He chose to bless this motley crew from the 3rd world in the process. Oh, we all had music in us, but we weren't by any means trained musicians. It was a real-life example of how God uses the week, the untrained and the simple to present his most precious message and then blesses it to bear fruit-- as only He can.

We travelled to CMA strategic areas, across the New England states, then down to Florida and many places in between ministering to all ages and finally across Canada (Toronto to Vancouver). The children were excited about our music and so were the retired folk. The ones in between were touched by the dedication of the young African's abilities, their humility and their desire for ministry.

Tom White prepared a multi-media presentation of the many churches that were in need of help. Other speakers came along to help motivate the audiences and God blessed all of our efforts. A good sum of money was raised for the project "Roofs for Churches" in Zaire. Tom even won an award with his audio-visual presentation at the

International Film Festival of New York with our Trio Sango Malamu as the background music. He was kind enough to give us the award that he had won.

We ministered in the USA first and then when this tour was

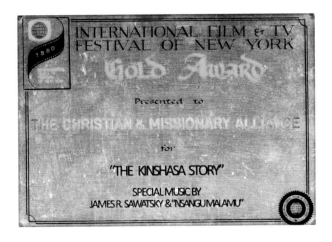

over, true to maverick form and his dreams, I requested that we prolong the tour in order give our presentation to more churches in Canada. After all I was a Canadian missionary and it would be good for the CMA in Canada to take in this ministry as well. I felt we could do it well on our own and with some persuasion, the CMA leaders gave us their blessing. I never looked back for this was the beginning of the vision of bringing a small part of African missions to Canada.

I was soon telephoning pastors and churches in Canada to see if they had a spot where this "motley crew" could minister to their people. I had great faith in the abilities of the Zairian brothers and knew the people would love them and would want to hear them. Therefore, with that positive attitude, although I've never been known to be "pushy" (tongue in cheek), we were "invited" to minister in some of the key churches in Canada from the east to the west. We took an offering each night and the people gave generously to the project. We paid our own expenses from the offerings, as did the US tour, but we also contributed to the overall Kinshasa Story project. It was the first time Joe and Paul had seen so much flat land (across the central prairies of Manitoba, Saskatchewan and Alberta) and witnessed daylight until 9 o'clock in those early spring evenings.

We were near the end of our two months of touring when we received a call from CMA headquarters in New York. They wanted us to minister/sing at the USA council in May at Hartford, Connecticut before the brothers went back to Zaire. They would fly us from Vancouver to Harford and then fly the brothers back to the Congo. It was a wonderful plan. We really enjoyed ministering there. Jokingly the president of the CMA at the time, Dr. Rambo I believe, called us Jim Sawatsky and the Inkspots!

The CMA, wanting to surprise me after two months plus of being away from my wife and family, made arrangements to bring Dawn to Council, unbeknownst to me. When I saw her, it was a complete and total surprise! I couldn't believe it, although the way I controlled the greeting, Dr. Rambo said it seemed like I was greeting my grandmother. However, in the hotel room it was a different story! I talked so much that night that Gramma fell asleep listening to me. The only time that ever happened in our lives! But, I must admit, I have fallen asleep while she was talking, more than once, I think! We had a wonderful time at Council and even were allowed vacation time back in the Vancouver area after the brothers flew back to Zaire. Then we flew back to meet our kids at the airport in Kinshasa who were being so well looked after by Dr. and Mrs. Green, our CMA missionary colleagues.

As a group, we were often asked about our most unique experience or what we noticed the most about life in North America. Finally, one day in a small meeting, Joe got up the courage to say that Americans were more concerned about their stomachs than anything else. To back that up he mentioned that at every church function there had to be food and that he was surprised at the number of "fat" Americans they saw (even in the early 1980's). Well, they wanted to know! Joe was never one to be overly diplomatic, at least not in another language. Curiously enough I don't recall us being asked that question again.

I think that first morning in the cafeteria at Nyack College had something to do with this response. I can remember going through the line to get our food. Not really knowing all the different foods, the guys were very modest in their helpings and made sure their plates were not overloaded. We found place to sit down at a table very near the exit of the food line. It was the first table we found empty and took it. We were not yet ready to do a lot of socializing in this strange environment.

After we prayed over our meal, we looked around and all of us saw a gal exit the food line, she was fairly plump with a good amount of food on her plate. It was a contrast to what we generally saw as we all were pretty slim in those days. Then we noticed the next gal, even heavier, with more food on her plate, exiting the food line. We had not even taken a bite of our own food yet when we noticed a very plump gal, heavier than the other two, plate bulging with food. We looked at each other amazed at the progression. But before we could get to eating, another person, a guy this time, almost bigger that all the gals put together coming off the line, walking with difficulty and carrying a platter heaped to over flowing with food. We couldn't believe it. We all looked at each other while Joe uttered silently the word, "Tubby!" (in French, too-bee) and we all burst out laughing. Fortunately, no one knew us, or knew what we were laughing at. It would have been quite rude, but we couldn't hold it in. It was so opposite to the norm in Zaire that it seemed hilarious, especially because he looked just like the comic book character which was circulating in Zaire at the time, with the same name!

Culture shock was relieved when we got to Raleigh, NC where a large community of Zairians lived. Their warm embraces and recognizable food encouraged the guys to continue to the end of the tour. We travelled by commercial plane, by car or van and by private small plane to our destinations. The ministry was exciting, exacting and blessed. I thought, "This was just the beginning of the fulfillment of the vision."

The Death of the Vision

The attack of the enemy often happens when a ministry experiences the blessing of God and our "Kinshasa Trio" did not prove to be the exception. We arrived back in Kinshasa at different times as Gramma and I had several weeks' vacation in Canada before departing for Kinshasa. Our time with family was special.

Back in Kinshasa a Zairian pastor made much to do about our trip and had the brothers on national TV with their family singing and playing as if the whole family went on this tour. They then began singing as a team of brothers and sisters. For this to happen without any explanation, and after what I thought was a highly-blessed tour in Canada and the USA, really left me flat, emotionally. Coming back to Kinshasa to find this out was a shock. So much so that I felt that Sango Malamu had died. It felt like we had been usurped by the "enemy" and our ministry was finished! This seemed so definite that I even began telling a few people that our group had broken up. I prayed, "I guess You, Lord, had just a short tour in mind for us, so I give this ministry back to you. Thank you for the brief time we had together and the blessing you showered upon us. It's all Yours!"

After having prayed and given "Sango Malamu" its right to die, I came out of my office and told Gramma that Sango Malamu had died and it was all over. She wasn't sure, but I couldn't see how it could continue when the brothers were doing stuff on their own and singing as a family now.

The Sowing Principle

Again, God had some lessons to teach me. He accepted my giving the ministry to Him and then he showed me the "Sowing Principle." The Bible clearly says that unless a grain of wheat falls into the ground and DIES, it cannot bear fruit.

It wasn't long after having told Gramma that Sango Malamu had died, the Tsasa brothers came to my office and said they wanted to talk. I was happy to see them, but was ready for them to say that this was the end of our ministry (although I had a hard time reconciling this with the "call" I received to be involved in evangelism). To my great surprise they wanted to apologize for what happened, for leaving me out of the picture and really wanted us to continue again. I mentioned that I thought Sango Malamu had died, but they didn't agree. They weren't in agreement with what the Pastor had done. It is hard as young Congolese to go against a senior pastor. They still desired to minister together. Sango malamu having "died" (in my mind), the Lord miraculously raised it up to an even greater ministry. Actually, this is when the full ministry of the Sango Malamu Trio began in earnest, reaching out to the Congolese and the rest of Africa—and the Lord even brought us an evangelist!

As we were candidly sharing, Paul and Joe mentioned something that lay heavy on their hearts. They confessed that in having to practice all the time and in doing that for the better part of most days, but getting no remuneration for it, they were having a hard time making ends meet! There was no time to look for an outside job to at least pay for all their transportation. I immediately understood and kicked myself in the proverbial behind for not seeing this myself and broaching the subject first. I was getting support from the CMA, but they weren't! I said that I would look around for funds to help them gain some "bus fare". I looked at the going wages and then tried to raise funds accordingly. God was gracious enough to bring along friends who desired to help in our ministry and with some extra funds from a CMA special ministry fund, from that point on, we could give a monthly stipend to Paul and Joe and even helped Paul finish his Auto-electric technical course.

CMA had a policy of not giving national pastors support, but technically these young men were musician/evangelists, from whose ministry many churches in Kinshasa received help in their outreach programs. So, it seemed that God had His stamp of blessing on us. Though I am sad to say they didn't get a great amount, it was enough for them to take a little home to their family and to keep them in bus and taxi fare. I always wished I could have given them more.

When we first started, we never thought much of doing anything outside of Kinshasa. That was our "field" of ministry. All we had to do was to bring our acoustic instruments and sing. But as we began holding evangelistic meetings outdoors, we needed "wattage-power" for our voices and instruments as listeners several rows back couldn't hear us very well. We began looking for electric guitars and amplifiers—more than the little equipment we brought back with us from the tour in the USA and Canada. We had very little funding, but we were able to buy very reasonably some sound equipment locally (amplifiers, mikes, chords etc.) which we felt God brought our way. We gradually increased our equipment until a few years down the road we had about some 1000 watts of power pouring out of heavy duty speakers. It all was blessing from God, Himself!

Growing and Bearing Fruit

As the founder of the group, I felt a certain responsibility to lead it. As mentioned, I did the preaching and the setup of all the equipment (mikes, speakers, amplifiers and putting all the chords in the right spots) as these young men did not have much experience doing that. Joe was about age 22 and Paul was about 18 during this time.

However, it didn't take long and Paul became responsible for all the sound set up, while Joseph became our "chef d'orchestre" taking care of all the music, what we sang, when and how. The vision I had to bring African worship and music to North America by now was now starting to take shape—but in a different form than I expected.

Almost immediately after our tour in North America, God brought along a great evangelist by the name of Kibutu Ngimbi. I always called him "Brother Kibutu." He was a rather tall, handsome young man with a heart for God and the spiritual gift of prophesy—especially that of telling forth the Gospel of Christ. He came from the Mayombe area, the same as the Tsasa family, where we started our ministry in Africa. As a matter of fact, he was at the Maduda School when we started teaching there. He was in the 5th year (grade 11), so we didn't really get to know him then. But the year after we left, there was a Holy Spirit revival among the students at that school and that is when Brother Kibutu had a personal encounter with Jesus Christ.

The HQ of the CMA and the CEAZ was in Boma, a major city of

Trio Sango Malamu with Gramma and our evangelist
brother Kibutu in Bouake, Côte d'Ivoire

the Lower Zaire province, so we were all of the same tribal family. Kibutu was God's appointed evangelist for us. During the next four years we did a lot of travelling as we ministered together. Kibutu was actually a staff member of Campus Crusade for Christ in Kinshasa and had many invitations to go into post-secondary schools and to the University campuses of Kinshasa. We also went to many high schools and mission stations with Mission controlled schools—tailoring and/or sewing schools, nursing schools—some Catholic, but mostly Protestant. Many young people accepted the Lord. I still get comments to this day from people who accepted the Lord and had a life changing experiences in Christ when they were in high school, university or even in grade school.

We sang at a lot of special church meetings on our own, without our evangelist, but when we were invited, often by other communities, to hold evangelism campaigns, we always made sure that brother Kibutu could be with us. Often, Brother Kibutu would invite us to come along with him in accepting invitations to speak at schools and universities in Kinshasa. At such times we were we known as the "group Sango Malamu from Campus Crusade." On the other hand, when we were involved in ministry for the CEAZ, whether in Kinshasa or in Bas-Zaire, we would be known as the CEAZ group Sango Malamu. It was common knowledge that Kibutu grew up in the Mayombe area and that made him CEAZ (in the church's thinking).

It seemed that my being a part of the group as a white person, not feeling the need to declare any "colors" (tribal, denominational or racial lines), we were often just known as an interdenominational group. Perhaps that is why we were often busier outside of the CEAZ than inside our own church affiliation. It was like God called us to be evangelists in our own Jerusalem (that's where we started), but also in Samaria (other parts the Congo) and even to the "uttermost" parts of the world (other areas in Africa, Europe and North America). Although we didn't know it at the time, this is what was going to happen.

Our Children

Up to this point in our ministry our children stayed and played at home and went to school in Kinshasa. First, they started at the British School, thinking that we Canadians had ties with Britain and it would be a good fit for them. Wrong again. They were not used to the rough and tumble tactics of the European mentality. Both Rod and Loralee were sensitive kids and would not fight back when bullied, which seemed to happen there. It didn't take long for us to switch to the American School of Kinshasa where all three of our children fit in very well to the American culture and education system. We gratefully enjoyed having our children at home and they did well at school. We even had Kristy Downey live with us for a transition year. The mission was okay with having all our kids educated at TASOK even though it cost was a bit heavy, financially.

Nevertheless, in 1984 both Gramma and I sensed that the Lord was leading us to send them to a great missionary kid's school in Cote d'Ivoire called Ivory Coast Academy or simply ICA. We saw some signs in our kid's social relationships that lead us to understand that there needed to be a change. At this time, both Rod and Loralee were in middle school and were forming life changing relationship and habits, desperately wanting to have at least one intimate friend who really loved Jesus. They grew up loving him, but didn't see that in a many of their peers. I asked Rod one day if he would like to go to a school where he would have strong Christian friends his age. His reply was that he would like nothing more. Loralee felt the same way. Jon-

Marc being younger was doing quite well, but would want to go along with his older siblings. Because of their desires, in 1984 when Loralee was 14, Rod 13 and J-M 11, they left with one of us at the beginning of the school year for ICA. They were to leave home, never to return for any full year again, or so I thought!

After they left, I cried uncontrollably, like a baby. I knew that this was the last stage of our time as a complete family together. They would only come home for a few months and then be off to school again (and soon it would be post-secondary in Canada—even further away). We missed out on their singing in groups, their sports event and their plays. But they gained good Christian friends and were in an environment that upheld Christian morals and honored God and His Word. Some of the rules may have been a bit strict, but I saw that as good opportunity for teaching our kids discipline and respect for authority. Despite the strict rules, according to them, they loved being there and felt it was a God opportunity for them. Not everything went as smooth as glass, but it was much better, I think, than the alternative. God is good. Today all three of them love God, they all have taken their hand at leading in worship, in very different settings, but all want to praise Him with their lives and their children's lives. For that I am truly grateful.

Loralee, Jon-Marc and Rod off to International Christian Academy, Bouake, Cote d'Ivoire

Chapter Twenty: The Life and times of Sango Malamu, Part 1

Diverse Venues

The initial vision and dream, in fact, took us to many areas in West Africa, Europe, Canada and the USA, but we spent more time in Canada than anywhere else outside of the Congo. We ministered in almost all the larger churches in Canada, travelling across the country

a couple of times. We ministered in many of the Eastern, Central and Southern United states. We sang at the Billy Graham congress on evangelism in Amsterdam in '86 and later on with the 2nd generation of Sango Malamu we toured Holland.

We sang in beautiful hotels, in fancy TV studios and on the radio. We slept in great and sometimes even swanky accommodations, but also we bunked in with the poorest of the poor, on cement or even dirt floors. I experienced rats running over my head while sleeping on a dirt floor in a Community office on the fetish infested Bateke plateau and then got kicked out early in the morning by the local officials.

We made several trips by dugout canoe and by native river boats up the Congo River ministering all along that river to isolated villages, paddling as far as 200 kilometers up river. Our goal was always to open up as many villages as possible along the way to the Good News of Jesus Christ.

One of our theme songs was, "We are the soldiers of the Army of Salvation... we will not tire but give testimony to the whole world, seeking people for the sake of Jesus Christ." We sang that in English as well as in Lingala and shouted the "WE ARE..." part.

During this time, we recorded around 10 cassette albums and ministered to perhaps hundreds of thousands of people. In one year alone (I only kept track of one year), I remember around 100,000 people heard the message of salvation through our ministry and approximately 10,000 made decisions to follow Jesus as their personal Savior and Messiah. It was consistently around 10% of those who came to the meetings who would respond to an invitation to receive Jesus as their Lord and Savior.

Photo taken in on the CMA mission station in Bobo Dioulasso, BF.

We travelled by Suburban 4x4 and by pickup truck, by MAF air planes, by large commercial planes, by dugout canoes and by small outboards. We always brought all our own equipment and sometimes had to personally carry it a loong distant to get to the meeting place for lack of roads. We must have set up and taken down our equipment, whether inside a building or outdoors, hundreds of times (I would say 90% of our ministry was outside of a church building), but I can remember only once being rained out—and that meeting had pretty well already ended by the time we had to throw everything into the vehicles. If it looked like rain, we prayed and God always "held the rain" for us until after our outdoor meeting was over!

In our travels by motor vehicle, we sometimes got stuck in sand or mud holes; we barely made it across some bridges and carried home gifts given from grateful receivers of the gospel in the form of chickens and goats in and on top of the vehicles. We ministered in areas where the temperature went up to 43 degrees C (in West Africa) and down to as low as -25 degrees C (in Canada).

We sang and preached on many mission stations, including Catholic and protestant, in small secluded villages and some large ones on the main roads—sometimes for weeks of meetings, sometimes only one-night stands. We ministered and sang in French, Kikongo, Lingala and English for the Tsasa brothers knew all four languages (a few times in Swahili) as we ministered to the people who spoke those languages. I only knew three of the languages plus enough Kikongo to understand what I was singing about, to pray a short prayer and to greet the people.

We have ridden on motor bikes, horses, donkeys and even a camel, on tractors and ski mobiles, crowded taxis and taxi busses where the colloquial expression is to "sardinez-vous" or "sardine yourselves" so that more people can cram in, but thank God most of the time we had our pickup and suburban to take us to our meetings.

In our travels, we have eaten monkey meat, forest rat, antelope, numerous kinds of fish, certain types of grass and leaves, palm oil, peanuts, fermented cassava root, termites and caterpillars. We've drunk all colors of water from clear to brown; we've drunk indigenous teas and coffees and God gave us good health through it all. We've preached openly to diamond smugglers, marijuana growers, prostitutes, doctors, lawyers and high ranking political figures, villagers, regional and tribal chiefs and never once been kidnapped, shot at (as a group) or speared because of sharing the gospel of Jesus. We have sung to fetish worshippers, those who believed in divination and those who believed Satan was their god, but we never once got beat up, **thank the Lord**!

When we felt attacked by the enemy, we fasted and prayed, and God protected us. When many things seemed to go completely wrong before we left for an evangelism tour, whether inside or out of the country, we began to fast and pray. As a result, there were no more problems before we left!

When we would come home to find our loved ones seriously ill and to find that other mishaps had taken place, we fasted and prayed "en route" and came home to peace. God saw our hearts, He heard our prayers and He answered us by His grace. We never went hungry or thirsty, although at times there was very little for us in the way of food and/or water. We just trusted God to provide.

One time in a distant village each day we were rationed to a cup of water

Trio Sango Malamu in front of an MAF plane in the late 1980's

with which to wash, shave and brush our teeth. We did just great! Sometimes we would travel all day without a bite of food, but we survived! The original Sango Malamu Trio, which gradually morphed into the "Groupe Sango Malamu" in Zaire and the "Kinshasa Band" in North America, had 10 wonderful years of ministry together.

We worked with many and various evangelists but there were primarily two evangelists we felt were our own, brother Kibutu Ngimbi (now Dr. Kibutu pastor of the largest evangelical church in Belgium) and the Rev. Dede Kikavuanga Dongo (now pastor of the church called, "The Corner Stone," which is a branch off the church now called "Le Rocher" at cité Mama Mobutu).

We loved "our" evangelists and we enjoyed travelling with them. We slept with them, ate with them and marveled at the gift God had given them and how He honored that gift. We ministered together for about 3-4 years with brother Kibutu, while God in his mercy was preparing brother Dede to be with us the rest of the time. Dede and brother Jean Tsakala were with us almost five years as the group developed to become an Evangelistic Organization in the Congo. We never really called ourselves an organization, but that is what it was— or perhaps a smooth running "organism". Often Dede, our evangelist, and Jean, our director for evangelism (also our discipleship leader), would go on ahead of us into an area, prepare the leaders of the churches for follow up ministries and sometimes even stay behind to make sure all went well after we left. We had at least seven young men in the group ministering in the Congo, with a lot of equipment. When we drove to an area, we often had to take two vehicles, our Suburban and our pickup truck. When we flew with MAF we needed their largest turbo prop plane, the Cessna Caravan.

After several years with just the three of us (Joe on lead guitar, Paul on accompaniment guitar or rhythm guitar and me on the upright bass first, then the electric bass as seen in the pictures), we saw that Paul and Joe's younger brother David, could play bass for us. Although I had learned a lot in playing African rhythms, David far surpassed me and our group became more Zairian, in color and in genre of music. Although David rarely sang, his bass really helped bring out the solid African rhythms. I was glad he came along as I had reached my maximum potential in bass playing and then he carried on from there.

I felt I couldn't just stand there and sing—I had to play something—so I grabbed an electronic keyboard from somewhere that had a rhythm and drum section on it and began pushing buttons to bring in the drums and began playing a few background chords to fill in for a more complete sound. A year or so later we were able to acquire a much more capable drum set and keyboards and although we used the electronic drum from the synthesizer, we were able to augment the

The Sango Malamu Evangelistic Team – Sometimes Gramma would come with us.

drum sound with a special drum pad that gave us great drum sounds. Tito, the Tsasas' cousin was a great equipment guy and helped us immensely in putting all the sound equipment together, including the loading and unloading of it all. He also became the one playing the drum pad on some of the songs.

We also occasionally invited Edo Bumba to join us, especially if we were in Matadi, where he lived. We would always drop in to see him if we were going through town and enjoyed his friendship and fellowship immensely. At one point when I couldn't go to bas Zaire with the group I suggested that they go on their own and take Edo with them to Maduda and a few other places, which they did. I heard that they had a great ministry. I was working myself out of a job and was quite pleased with that, but I wouldn't yet give in completely. Edo was called to Sweden to study classical guitar, so we bade him farewell and continued as we were for several more years.

In 1982, two years after our tour in North America for the "Kinshasa Story", and in 1988-89, through the aid of a Christian business man, Daryl Brooks (son of the pastor who married us), and with the approval of the CMA in Canada, we travelled extensively in the Western Canadian provinces and in Washington State. The Peace Portal Alliance Church called Gramma and I to be missionaries in residence the summer of 1982.[42] The church was also happy to receive Trio Sango Malamu and provided lodging for the brothers on the church campus. We sang in many of the CMA churches in the Fraser Valley area and then with a beautiful camping Van that Daryl allowed us to use, we travelled fall, winter and spring throughout BC, Alberta, Saskatchewan, Manitoba, Ontario and Quebec. We put quite a few miles on the Van and were so very grateful for this provision. We couldn't have done what we did without it.

Everywhere we went, we brought worship Zairian style to the congregations and even had them stand up and join us by learning the song, "Yesu Azali Awa". We even had the audiences raising their hands in praise as the Zairians did. Some who said beforehand, "You'll never get me to raise my hand," found themselves entering in with joy! And we left many with a high-quality cassette tape of most of the songs we sang—for a small donation.

At one point we were introduced again to Bob Brooks of Little Mountain Sound. Gramma and I had water skied with him on lake Shawinigan on Vancouver Island with Gramma's parents before we were married. Now, 22 years later, we were reintroduced, but this time because of our African/Western music. After some brief conversations, he offered to record our music, free of charge. What a gift! They did an excellent job and Bob Brooks even played keys with us on a few songs. He also found us a drummer. Everyone donated their time and talents. We recorded when the studio had down time so as not to infringe on any other group that had booked and paid for their time at Little Mountain Sound. Bob was the head of the recording studio and

---

[42] *We asked them what they meant by "Missionary In Residence" and what we were to do. They said that it was more about them than us. They wanted to have a ministry to us more than what we were expected to do. They rented and furnished a great place for us to live (a 3 bedroom home, not far from the beach). They stocked the shelves, gave our whole family some winter clothes and generally were there for us. It was a tremendous ministry to us. In turn we were active in the church; leading in worship, helping with the youth and women's ministries.*

he oversaw the project. We were so grateful for his kind heart and interest in our ministry. It certainly was a God "thing" for us. We could never have recorded in Canada on our own.

In order for us to give these cassettes away and raise money for ministry in Zaire, we needed to start our own non-profit organization. So in 1983, I approached a group of men to see if they would be willing to serve on the board of an organization called "Good News International Ministries." They were willing and with their help we received accreditation from the Canadian and BC Governments to begin a non-profit society that would support ministry of spreading the Good News in Africa by every means possible, including the dissemination of Christian tapes and literature. This began the 30-year ministry of GNI ministries through which we raised thousands of support dollars for ministry and equipment in Zaire.

Through donations and the "gifts"[43] from the tapes we were able to raise enough funds to support our ministry in Canada for that year. In 1983, we were able to buy and send a couple of good 125 cc motor bikes back to Kinshasa with the Tsasa brothers for their ministry and transportation. We were truly grateful.

Ketchikan, Alaska

We did a lot of travelling in B.C. while in Canada that year and also in 1987-88. In these last years, we even got as far as Kitimat and Terrace, where Gramma and I started out in pastoral ministry, and then on to Prince Rupert and Ketchikan, Alaska. We didn't have a CMA church in Prince Rupert, but people who knew people who knew us,

---

[43] *We didn't sell tapes, but gave them away as gifts. Those who requested and received them gave us a donation for our ministry and travelling expenses.*

heard that we were in the area and asked us to come. We did have a CMA church in Ketchikan and when they heard that we were in Prince Rupert, they invited us to take a ferry ride up to Ketchikan.

We had a marvelous time there and they even raised enough funds to bring Joe's wife Arlette and little Jim to Canada. Because we had no upfront money, we always stipulated that the inviting church would have to give us "food and lodging" and allow us to take an offering. God blessed our ministry and with the food and lodging taken care of, the offerings and the "gifts" from our tapes we were again able to pay

PRINCE RUPERT, B.C., FRIDAY, MAY 27, 1988

The Daily News entertainm

Rockin'

African melodies were perform-ed by the Kinshasa Band from Zaire at the Bethel First Baptist Church last night. Pictured with their instruments inside the church are Lutete Tsasa (left,) Lukanga Tsasa, Jim Sawatzky (missionary in Zaire for 13 years,) and Tama Tsasa. The Tsasa brothers and Sawatzky are part of the Christian and Missionary Alliance of Canada. The men go to Ketchikan after their stay in Prince Rupert and then travel back to Canada for other stops in the West. Zaire, formerly Belgium Congo, is located in the centre of Africa and has a population of 35 million. Sawatzky said the Kin-shasa Band were musical mis-sionaries in that country.

(D'Angelo photo)

Newspaper clippings of the Kinshasa Band in Prince Rupert BC. We had no church affiliation there, but the people heard we were coming through their city on our way to Alaska and insisted that we hold a concert the night before we left on the ferry. A reporter heard about our coming and wrote up an article on us and took pictures after the concert.

for all our travelling expenses, including air fare from Kinshasa and back. We never had a lot left over, but we could help all the guys with some financial assistance. These young men did not do this for the money, but they did do it to please the Lord and bless the people of Canada.

God returned blessing to them in later years.

Degarmo and Key

One day, MAF[44] came to us with the news that they were hosting a group called Degarmo and Key. They told us this was a Christian Rock group, who were coming to observe the ministry of MAF to promote it in their concerts. They also wanted to make a video—somewhere outside the city of Kinshasa. MAF came to us because they didn't know exactly how to receive and entertain the group. They said, "You guys are musicians whom they could probably identify with, could you show them around and hang out with them?" We didn't know who they were, but were happy to help. We had a great time.

We found out that this group was in the forefront of Christian Rock in the USA. They said, "We're doing in the USA what you guys are doing here in Zaire. You guys don't play much in churches, but hold meetings outside the church buildings and call people to Christ. We do the same. You sing the gospel and we do too. You minister a lot to youth and so do  we." And that was the truth of it, but that is as far as the analogy went. However, there was one more similarity. Their music was the vanguard of what became known as Christian Rock. Not many had begun sharing the gospel in that format. Our group was the first of its kind on the Christian scene in the Zaire which many began to copy. The difference

---

[44] *Missionary Aviation Fellowship*

was that our music, our style, and our target cultures were totally different!

Before they left, we planned a concert in the open air, in front of a fancy large house with a big court yard that would hold well over a hundred people, the CEAZ Center of Evangelism. We opened for them with a few songs and then they did their "thing". Their music was twice a loud, twice as hard, twice as fast as ours and taxed our equipment to the fullest, but we had a great time. The enclosed picture is with all of us after the concert. God blessed their ministry and they raised a lot of funds to help MAF in their ministry and also help them fly us around the Congo to share the gospel of Jesus in many other remote places to which we could not have otherwise gone.

The Kajiji Excursions

We ministered in many areas of the Congo—from Lower Congo to the Equator province and all places in between. At one point, we were invited to Kajiji, a Mennonite mission station and educational center with a hospital nursing school that had begun in 1955. The hospital had 144 beds and a large maternity ward. More recently a tuberculosis treatment center moved to the site, and a nutritional center enhanced both programs. They also had a primary school complex, a large secondary school and a large school for sewing, tailoring, and technical training of various disciplines. It was a big station and village center with a lot of students of varying degrees of interest in their pursuit of education all primarily run by the Mennonite Brethren Church Community.

Although it was primarily a Mission Station, there were many family members present from outside the area who needed to prepare food for the hospital patients. Unfortunately, there were also diamond smugglers in the area. The diamonds came from Angola as the border between Angola and Zaire was just a few kilometers south of the station. There were forests, grass lands, and savanna along the borders of each country, with very little border patrol protection, which made it easy for people to pick up diamonds in the south, cross into the Congo and make their way to Kinshasa in order to sell their "stash" in the underground market. Or, they would simply take it to Belgium. All these people were woven into the tapestry to which we were called to share the gospel. We didn't know all of this at the time of the invitation, but we knew there were a variety of people from all different backgrounds who frequented the mission.

The first time we arrived there was by plane. Missionary Aviation Fellowship was willing to make their Cessna 208B Grand Caravan single engine turbo-prop and a pilot available to us, but at a cost of $2000.00US. We couldn't believe it would cost that much, but when we analyzed it and broke it down the cost to charter the plane and pilot was only $500 each way. That meant to drop us off and fly back was $1000. Then to fly in to pick us up and fly us back would be another thousand bucks (it would be at least a 3-hour round trip). We prayed as a team about this and we felt that God was directing us there. Kajiji would look after us once we got there, but we would have to get there by our own means, mainly MAF. If this was God's open door for us, He would provide!

I shared our desire to respond affirmatively to this invitation from the Kajiji mission station with both the International Protestant Church of Kinshasa and MAF. I believed God moved them and they both pledged 500 dollars towards this project. MAF had some funds in an evangelism account and IPCK would raise the funds from their members. OK, great! We can get there now, but how do we get back. The CMA mission through various donors committed another $500. We were missing only one, one-way trip for the plane, but in faith we said that we would go and God would provide the final $500 bucks. MAF agreed!

The day came, and we loaded seven guys, our small packs and the 1000 lbs. of gear (everything we had) and took off from the city airport. We were surprised that this Cessna Caravan could in fact get us all in, including all our personal gear, our instruments and sound equipment. But it was a good trip of just around an hour and a half. Now I knew that Joe and Paul sometimes would get sick while flying in small planes (Gramma does too), so I offered them "bags".

I found this out while we were flying from Edmonton to Grand Prairie during a Canadian tour we were doing. The Grand Prairie and Beaverlodge churches had invited us for meetings and were paying the small Cessna plane and pilot to bring us there. The plane was a brand new, beautiful four-seater Cessna, donated by a Christian dentist for the purpose of getting us to that Peace River area. There were low lying clouds, so the pilot requested to fly at an altitude of 2000 ft., just below the clouds all the way there. It was a very bumpy ride, but I could see the ground well and had no problem with the turbulence.

Half way there, I looked behind me and saw the brothers already pretty "pale". I think it was just a little over one hour of flight time. Further on, I was getting uneasy as I saw their faces change from "pale" to "green!"[45] I mentioned to Joe to get a bag ready and he had one in his hand, but thought he could make it as now we were almost at our destination. Suddenly there was a mighty explosion in the back seat. Joe couldn't get the bag open fast enough and the vomit went all over the back-seat area of this brand-new Cessna. I felt bad for Joe; I felt bad for the pilot, but I really felt bad for the dentist and the new plane. What to do?

We got out of the plane as soon as we could as the smell was not pleasant. When we taxied up to a hangar, the young man who received us there took one look at the situation and told us not to worry. He could clean that up in a "jiffy" as he had the right kind of product to do it. He showed us the spray can and smiled. We left it with him and got into the car that was waiting for us, saying good bye and good luck to the pilot that offered his services. But that was when I knew these guys had a hard time in small planes.

In the Caravan with all of us squished in, I was wondering how the guys would fare in this plane. It was a little bit larger than a four-seater, but still not a large commercial airline. Well, you guessed it, by the time we landed in Kajiji, both Paul and Joe were "deathly" ill. They didn't throw up, but flopped prostrate under the plane for shade and didn't move for about thirty minutes or more. Meanwhile the choirs which were there to meet and greet us, having to stand their distance from the airplane, just continued singing their welcome songs. However, with their repertoire depleting and no movement under the plane, they finished their songs, waved and shouted words of welcome and left. Little by little the crowd dissipated as they saw we weren't going to move until all of us could walk together from the airport to the station and our accommodations. Generally, the crowd would walk us to the station with singing and the waving of palm fronds to honor our arrival. But this time it didn't work. The Tsasa brothers were flat out under the plane... and still green.

---

[45] I'm sure the guys will forgive me, but flying with my brothers was the only time I saw "green" Africans.

Finally, the pilot said that he had to get back as there were other flights to make that day. He had waited long enough and was ready to move the plane around for takeoff.

We finally got the guys out from

In front of MAF Caravan at Kajiji-Joe, Tito, Jean, Dede, Jim, Paul & David

under the plane and were about to wave the pilot good bye when two men, well dressed, came running in a frenzy from the direction of the mission station, shouting for the pilot to wait. He had already started the motor and was about to taxi out to make the take off. We also shouted and waved frantically, but the plane was already running and getting ready to move. We all finally caught the pilot's eye and he shut off the engine, opened the door and jumped out to see what the problem was. He thought maybe there was an emergency. It turned out to be no emergency, just a couple of "diamond smugglers" that badly needed a ride to Kinshasa.

The pilot made it very clear this was not a commercial airplane and that he wasn't allowed to sell tickets to the public. They could charter the plane if they wanted, but that would cost them $500. You guessed it! That was the remaining 500 bucks that was needed to come to the total of $2000 for the whole project of our use of the plane. Amazingly they agreed! They paid the pilot the $500 right there, they got in the plane and took off leaving us standing there with our mouths open.

I prayed a prayer of thanksgiving in my spirit as the plane flew into the distance, "Thank you, Lord! Thank you for even using diamond smugglers to complete Your/our mission!" Then I realized that had the brothers been in good health and in good spirits we would have walked away a lot sooner, the plane would have taken off and we would not have had that last $500 to complete the costs of the flights. God even used motion sickness—making the pilot wait in compassion for the sick guys under the plane just long enough for news to get to the traffickers so they could get ready, run to the airport, pay the fee, and fly out. God is amazing and has a sense of humor for sure!

A Side Trip at Kajiji

After that we made several trips into that area. I can only say that God directed us there and He gave us very a fruitful ministry at Kajiji. We travelled by truck and by plane to different villages along the way and sometimes by motor bike to scout out areas that were less travelled by a mundele.

One of those trips we made was with Jim Smith and crew from his mission station, Nkara Awa. Jim and Nancy had come to the Congo to take over the ministry that had been started much earlier by his father who was a missionary dentist, but who was heavily involved in evangelism. Jim had grown up in the Congo and knew the Bandundu language of Kituba very well. He had an old German four-wheel drive seven ton Army truck, called by the Africans a "silauka" (pronounced "Seela-ooka") and we travelled the rough, bumpy, rutty and sometimes muddy roads from Kikwit to Kajiji. We had taken some motor bikes along, but I didn't have mine. Jim Smith and John Rouster had their bikes and wanted to go out scouting around while it was day and there was no ministry going on... ministry always started around 4 p.m. (setting up at least) and went until no one was left hanging around with whom to talk or pray—sometimes until 11 p.m.

There was game in the country and lions, but during the day they are pretty quiet. The men managed to secure a 125-cc motor bike for me from the chief so that I could accompany them. Then at the last minute a gal from the Mennonite Central Committee wanted to come along, so John decided to take her on the back of his bike. Mine looked new, a Yamaha 125cc trail bike, but actually it had been already driven into the ground and had little power left. Nevertheless, I was used to riding that kind of bike so I kept up quite well.

The problem was, as we got deeper into sand and ruts, John was not an experienced enough rider and almost dumped the bike with his passenger several times. Seeing I was the more experienced rider of the three of us, I was elected to take the passenger on my bike. This wasn't a good idea, but we were too far now to turn back and still accomplish our goal. We wanted to drive as far as we could to get to the plateau mountain which rose out of the adjacent valley several hundred meters. It could be seen for miles around and we heard that there were human sacrifices made on the top. It was totally flat on top. Although it looked near, it turned out to be quiet a distance by road. By the time we got to the base (we found our way by asking at various villages along the road), as far as the road and trail would take us, it was mid-afternoon.

Nevertheless, we climbed up that mountain. The little black sweat flies were as thick as a swarm of bees. They were in our mouths, our noses, our eyes and hair, but we persevered. The tall elephant grass was well over 6 feet tall in places and no one knew what kind of snake or poisonous critter could be awaiting us as we couldn't see more than a foot, if that, in front of us. A wall of thick grass surrounded us. Yet, we could see up and we found where we could climb the face of the mountain and get to the top. We made it above the grass land, above the flies, above the tree line and up to the flat top. The top was a big as a couple of football fields joined together. It was covered with boulders, some as big as a Congolese village house, but there was no evidence of an altar and no remains of animal and or human bones.

After taking a few pictures of the beautiful view, we powered down to our bikes which were absolutely covered with black flies. We couldn't even see the handlebars for the flies… again we dove into the swarm, got our bikes started and took off down the trail as fast as we could. Going downhill I made pretty good time and was right there in the lead, even with the extra person, but going on the straight, through serious sand and mud holes my bike just didn't have the guts to keep up. The motor on my bike had very little compression left so it bogged down easily.

As you can imagine, by now it was getting close to 6 p.m. which meant night was falling. Darkness doesn't hesitate when it begins to fall in the Congo. There is very little twilight. The other guys in their haste had left us behind. I didn't worry too much for I could still hear their motors echoing back their noises as they pushed on ahead. Yet suddenly, we were now surrounded by pitch black darkness and with only the head lamp to show us about 30 feet ahead. Of course, we had to slow down now for we couldn't anticipate the bumps and sand as we could during the daylight hours.

And then it happened! I ran out of gas! My bike sputtered to a stop, the light went dead and the silence was a deafening contrast to our buzzing along. We couldn't see each other and neither of us had a flash light. We were in the middle of lion country without light, gas or communication of any kind and we were on a lonely road no one would be travelling at night; not anywhere near a village.

My first thought was of those lousy "friends" who left me alone with this single gal whom they wanted to bring along but made me carry as a passenger on the slowest, most useless motorbike …and they were not to be heard of anywhere in the distance. Then, I thought of the headlines in the Alliance news or papers at home:

"Missionary husband and father of 3 young children has been found dead!

…presumably eaten by lions along with a young single woman supposedly doing missionary work in the same area. Apparently, they were both riding the motorbike that was found without gas and abandoned not far from the scene."

We couldn't see our own hands let alone each other as the darkness had fully descended. We could hear the noises of the savanna with a light sprinkling of trees which housed owls and other sorts of critters. We decided not to walk, but to wait by the bike until the others were aware that we were no longer following them and hopefully come back to see what was happening. It seemed like a long time before we could hear the faint roar of a motorbike, but it probably was only about 20 minutes. John came back and found us, but instead of waiting with us with the light he had, he immediately turned around and took off down the road to tell the truck which was now in search of us where we were and to bring us some gas. After another 20 minutes of so the "silauka" did finally arrive with a barrel of gas. We loaded up and I said the young MCC missionary that she could now go with the truck, but by this time we were so fed up with them leaving us so far behind and making us wait so long for help that she decided she would finish the course with me and get home at least a little faster than the truck.

When we left in the morning it was T-shirt weather with the sun out in full force. We never anticipated being out at night and it became cold. It was well over 30 degrees Celsius at mid-day, but now it wasn't much more than 15 degrees with a lot of humidity and we were almost frozen in the wind with just the T shirt on. But we managed to get home after the evening meeting was already over. It was a good thing they didn't wait for us before they started. They had a good meeting and we learned our lessons. I would never do that again, although I must admit it was a great adventure!

Villages, Schools, and Refugee Camps

On many occasions during our time together we travelled to bas-Zaire to hold days of meetings with the CEAZ students at Inga, (the

large dam site), Maduda, Kwimba, Tshela, and Boma schools. We even went as far west as the CEAZ Muanda school on the Coast. At each area, we would spend three to five days holding evangelistic meetings (playing, singing, and preaching). We would often stop on the way to have meetings of one to three days with the villages and towns we would pass through—like Seke, Banza, Kimpese, Matadi, Inkisi, and Mbanza Ngungu. In the schools, as in the villages, many would come to Jesus and accept Him as their Lord and Savior. We often counselled and prayed with students and villagers into the night after the meeting. We generally conducted our meetings in the late afternoon and early evenings, yet even during the day individuals would seek one or several of us out for counsel and prayer. The CMA budgeted a ministry fund for us so we could always pay our own travelling expenses, but the people always looked after us well once we got to our destination. The Lord always provided for us.

On one occasion, we were invited to minister in the Angolan refugee camps that were set up in the Bas-Zaire area. The Angolan civil war lasted for 27 years, beginning in 1975 and continuing, with some interludes, until 2002. Being that parts of the Bas-Zaire province is on the Angolan border, there were a lot of refugee settlements which grew up in that area. On this trip, I think we hit all the major refugee villages and were gone for several weeks. Missionary David Jones and Pastor

Sergio Pinto from Brazil came for that length of time and we all descended on the Portuguese speaking Angolan camps. David Jones and Pastor Pinto gave testimony and preached in Portuguese. We sang

in Kikongo, Lingala and French (all languages mostly understood by the villagers) and even learned a song in Portuguese. So, many heard the gospel sung and preached in their mother tongue and in other languages that they grew up speaking. They well understood the claims of Christ and many responded positively to what they heard. [46] Around the table we added English. So, we used 5 languages for friendly conversation and towards the end of our time together we even sang at least one song in all the 5 languages.

These were exciting times! We were used to sleeping and eating as the villagers, drinking their water, using their "toilets" (outside holes in the ground mostly), showering in the cool morning with a bucket of cool water (sometimes heated for the guests) and enjoying their homemade teas and bread. For me, the food was always good, but the best part was that many of the villagers, far away from any kind of civilization, heard the good news, danced to the happy rhythms of the music, and gave their lives to Jesus. In these types of meetings and travels, sometimes many miles from home or any doctor, we never got ill on the road. The Lord always took good care of us.[47]

The Sad News

It was during this time, in November of 1986 that I received some very jolting news. I had no way of knowing what was going on with

---

[46] *Many received the Lord into their lives on that trip and some are in ministry today. Some 30 years later, Marta Heleno Carvalho said this on Facebook to David Jones (translated from Portuguese), "My life has never been the same since that trip. I clearly heard God talking to me to serve him. I was 12 to 13 years old at the time."*

[47] *David Jones did get seriously ill with malaria after we arrived home and was in a clinic for a few days with quinine dripping into his veins. We prayed hard for him as he was in bad shape, but thank the Lord he revived well enough to be on his way home in a few days.*

friends and family in Canada, or even at home in Kinshasa for that matter, as there was no communication at all with outside world once we were in the camps. On our way home, we stopped at Boma and someone relayed a radio message that my mom (your great grandmother) was in the hospital, but it was an old message and I figured that she would be well and out of the hospital by the time I received that message.

Not so! I got home a few days later and found no one home but our cook, Papa Jean. I asked him how things were and he replied, "Oh, everything is fine, **but they just buried your mother yesterday!**"

I said, "WHAT?"

"Yes," he replied. "They had the funeral and buried your mother yesterday."

That was a shock! How did he know? Where were Dawn and the kids? I sat down and realized I had just paid a dear price for being a missionary in Africa. It was two years or more since I last saw my mom, and now, I will never see her again this side of heaven. I will not be there to console my father or my brothers and sisters. I suffered a great loss that day. But the verse the Lord gave me as we were first leaving for Africa came immediately to mind. It was from Mark chapter 10:28-30:

> [28]*Peter began to say to Him, "Behold, we have left everything and followed You." [29]Jesus said, "Truly I say to you, there is no one who has left house or brothers or sisters* ***or mother or father*** *or children or farms, for My sake and for the gospel's sake, [30]but that he will receive a hundred times as much now in the present age, houses and brothers and sisters* ***and mothers*** *and children and farms, along with persecutions; and in the age to come, eternal life.*[48]

I half-way expected something like this would happen when I first read this verse (many years before) and now it was the only comfort I had. God knew it all along. It was some time before Gramma got home to relay the few details that she had. It didn't matter; God had taken my mom home to be with Him, she was in a better land. I too would join her one day, but I would grieve. There was no money for me to fly home for the funeral, but that didn't matter now as it was already too late for that! That entire week (while I was gone) Gramma felt that Great Gramma Sawatsky (Martha) was just looking over her shoulder

---

[48] *Mark 10:28-30 New American Standard Bible (NASB)*

as she was walking around the house and she often said, "See mom, this is where we live, this is how the children look and these people are the ones with whom we minister. This is our place, our home."

Martha Sawatsky was the sweetest most humble, gentle and loving person you could meet anywhere. She was known for her hospitality and has a legacy in her granddaughter, Auntie Loralee.[49]

Loralee's Miracle

During one of our meetings that we were having in the area of Kinshasa, I came home pretty late. Wanting to just flop in bed, I didn't hesitate to make for the bedroom after I got home with all the equipment well secured, put in place and locked up. When I walked through the door of our bedroom, I saw in the dim light of the night, two bumps on the bed—one was Gramma and the other was Loralee. She must have been about five years old at the time—a little old for sleeping with mom. I soon found out that they weren't sleeping even though it was late. I probed for the problem.

Gramma quickly explained that Loralee had a very high fever and a fierce headache. For a young child to have something like that I thought something was seriously the matter. I immediately said let's pray. But Gramma said, "Well, we have already prayed!" I wasn't to be dissuaded or deterred from what I felt I should do.

I said, "OK then, let's pray again!" Loralee was writhing in our bed, not knowing how to cope with such a bad headache. I immediately thought of cerebral malaria or at the very least a strong case of malaria—with such a high fever. As I began to pray, I sensed that I was moved to do something that I had never done before. I even felt a little embarrassed for praying as I was about to pray in front of Gramma and Loralee, but before I could shrink back to think that I shouldn't pray this way.

I blurted out, "You fever, I rebuke you! I command you to leave, in Jesus' Name! You have no right here. And you, headache, I command you in the Name of Jesus to leave!" The prayer was very short and to the point. I had never addressed an illness before as "you".

---

[49] At 83 years of age, my mom did her best to live until we came home again. We were to come only six months later, but she didn't make it. Interestingly, my dad died at 87 four years to the day after my mother passed away—six months before we were evacuated back to Canada. At almost 50 I felt orphaned.

I surprised myself, but in looking back I realize that the Holy Spirit directed me.

Then I said, "Now let us praise the Lord for we know that the enemy can't stand the praises of Jesus. Let's all sing!

Loralee uttered, "Oh daddy, I can't sing, I just can't sing with this headache."

"Oh yes you can," I returned. "You know the song,

'Praise him (Jesus), praise Him, praise him in the morning, Praise Him in the noontime Praise Him, praise Him, Praise Him when the sun goes down.'"

We all began to sing, haltingly at first for Loralee, but then we sang in full voice. But before we could finish the final line of the song, Loralee burst out with, "Daddy, daddy, my headaches gone!" I felt her forehead and her fever was gone as well.

The next morning, she said that when she was in her own bed, she was visiting with angels who appeared to her and she had a good chat with them.

My thoughts were turned to when I was in Bible College and how God intervened and healed my planter's wart on the bottom of my foot. I was in my 2nd year at CBC and was in agony. I could hardly walk (only on the side of my foot). I asked the nurse to have a look at it and she diagnosed it as an ingrown plantar wart and the only way to get rid of that was to see a doctor and have him dig it out. That was not good news. It was then that I thought that I really needed to experience healing for myself. If not, how could I pray for healing for others.

In the middle of the day, I went to my dorm room, knelt beside my bed, and earnestly prayed in Jesus Name for Him to bring healing to my foot. I quickly took off my shoe and sock to see if it had already disappeared. To my discouragement it was still there.

The same time the next day, after class, I got alone with God and earnestly sought Him and asked Him to heal my foot. Immediately I took off my shoe and sock and behold, it was still there—more painful than ever. The third day I did the same routine. I didn't take off my shoe—I could feel it. No result. But the fourth day, after classes, I realized that I wasn't limping.

I ran to my dorm room, threw off my shoe, tore off my sock and looked for the plantar wart (or at least a scar). Nothing!! Maybe I forgot which foot it was, I threw off the other shoe and sock. Nothing! Both feet, not a scar or trace of anything and the plantar wart was big, ugly and hurtful, growing deep into the bottom of my foot! I looked at both feet again. The skin was smooth with no trace of anything, not even a small lump. It was then that I knew the Lord had healed me through persevering prayer. His healing wasn't in my time, immediately at my disposal, but He did heal me in His way, in His time. I was healed beautifully and from that time on I knew that I would have faith to pray for healing for I had experienced His healing touch!

Was this just a prayer for healing for Loralee or was it a definite "fight" against the enemy who always wants to destroy us? Praise God that I listened to the voice of the Holy Spirit prompting me to pray the way that I did and thank you Lord that "in all these things, we are more than conquerors through Him who loved us." (Romans 8:37)

The Plateau of the Bateke

We often went out on the Bateke Plateau, an area starting about 80 kilometers east of Kinshasa. The plateau was a vast expense of land, home for the primarily animistic Bateke tribes. There were no stronger fetishes than the ones procured from the Bateke. I remember flying into some of the areas with a MAF helicopter scouting out villages where we could preach the gospel. Many were resistant to the good news of Jesus.

Flying over the villages in the little bubble of a helicopter was a thrilling experience. It was like an extended ride at the mid-way, but we were on a mission and we made good contacts. We touched down in one village and were met by the local warlock, medicine man or witch doctor. He was Satan's man and he was proud of it, scantily dressed smeared with white powder of some sort all over his face and body. He would not come to shake our hands for he wanted to have no part of the missionary or the Christian message.

However, there were a few who understood why we came and after a short meeting with the elders of the village they agreed that the evangelist who was with us could come and share the good news of Jesus with them, but the witch doctor's behavior was most indicative of the hold that Satan had over this area. I mentioned to someone that it was very rude for a man not to greet a visitor who had come a long way to visit the village. The word must have gotten to him as the man finally came and reached out his hand in welcome as we were on our way out.

Miracle at Kingankati

Another incident on the Bateke Plateau was a little more intense. The whole group arrived at the village of Kingankati about the middle to late afternoon. We had travelled by convoy of pickup trucks from early morning, got stuck in the sand and generally had a rough ride. We were glad we had enough time to set up before it got dark. The few contacts we had in the village were not as ready for us as we might have thought. No matter, we asked for a place to set up for our meeting. The only place that was good for us and the place we were asked to use was in front of the local bar, the only store type building in the village. It had a few tables outside under a grass roof and a sort of cemented area in front of that, perhaps for dancing. There was a good clearing in front of the store so we setup mike stands and speaker stands on the flat dance area facing toward the open court in front of the bar.

After our set up and mike check, we turned off the generator motor until it was time to start. It starts to get dark in the Congo around 6 p.m. We general start playing and singing around 5 or 5:30 just while there is still some daylight. We were going to do the same here, but the bar opened and started their music. We were a little confused, but we soon realized that when we would start no one would hear the bar music. Our music would drown it out immediately. And that is exactly what happened.

We started to play, couldn't hear the bar music, and the people started to come and see what was going on. Our music was louder and it was live, not a cassette player! We had quite a crowd that night, but not a lot of people stayed to pray to receive Jesus into their lives. Not long after we got there we heard a rumor that this place was known as the lying and thieving capital of the Bateke. Some missionaries had come to settle in the village, but they were run out by the villagers steeling them blind. They came to set up a mission station and left within the year with absolutely nothing. Whatever they brought with them, including a tractor and other farming equipment was all stolen.

Then the comment was made, "Make sure that you keep close tabs on all your stuff or it will get stolen."

After a short prayer time, I can't remember praying with anyone in that village, the contacts that we had there invited us to have a meal with them. During the meal we were reminded to guard our equipment well. So after eating we went outside threw our heavy tarps over the trucks and all the equipment and then backed the trucks up to the walls of the house we were sleeping in. There was nothing that could be taken out of the trucks without moving them--or at least without making a big noise. We were in the house and would keep eyes and ears open.

Morning came and I was the first one up. I moved my truck to have a look-see. It all seemed to be there, but then I saw a big gaping hole where the generator/motor should be. Somebody had stolen our generator (and it wasn't even ours; we had borrowed it from a fellow missionary with the Assembly of God mission as ours was being repaired). We were devastated! How could this have happened? There was no way anyone could have stolen it and a jerry can which they thought was full of gas. The Jerry can was actually full of drinking water, which caused the thieves to just throw it in away in the tall grass. But the generator motor that ran all our equipment was gone.

I was standing by our truck, dumbfounded, trying to think of what we could do, when a group of singers filed by chanting something innocuous, for me at least. But they stopped, and the leader said, "We believe in divination. Just pay us some money and through consulting the spirits we will get your motor back."

"Hmmm," I thought. "It sure doesn't take long for news to get around in this village!"

Jean had just come to stand beside me and immediately came up with, "Oh NO! We will pray, we will ask God and He will give us our motor back!"

"Amen!" was all that I could say.

Still in shock, we decided to go into the small house where we had some tea and bread for breakfast and pray. We called in our contact man and a few others with our team and explained the situation (as if they didn't know already) and told them that we would pray, asking God for the motor to be brought back. We were about to start when our contact man in the back row of chairs said he had something to say.

"I know a féticheur (a shaman)," He announced. "He's just down the road and would consult his fetishes if we paid him some money.

He would be able to get that motor back for you." (Hmmm, it wasn't for "us," now it was for "you.") I was astounded and speechless. Our contact man who was supposed to be a Christian said that?

Our director Jean jumped in again and gave his announcement in a strong voice, **"NO! We will pray now and God will give us back the motor!"** What faith in the midst of Satanic attacks! All I could say was a hearty "Amen!" But now God was really on the line. We came preaching the good news of Jesus. God the Father was our solid rock, our help in time of need, our provider. Jesus was our Redeemer, the Holy Spirit our guide. Would the Trinity jump in and really help in time of need?

After we finished praying our prayer of faith we went out on to the dirt road in front and wondered where and how God would direct us. As we were deliberating, a man, dressed differently, came sauntering up to us. With a scoffing laugh he said, "You believe in God? I believe in Satan! He is my god. I talk to him, I ask him my questions and he tells me everything I need to know!" He ended with another scoffing laugh as his exclamation mark and then added "Just give me some money and I'll ask him (Satan) where the motor is and he'll tell me where it is and I'll get it for you." What to do in the face of such opposition?

Our evangelist Dede was right there beside me and spoke up immediately, "Oh no! We won't give you any money. We have prayed, and God will give us back that motor because **greater is He that is in us than he that is in you**!" The man stopped scoffing, stopped talking, turned around and left.

I suggested that we drive my little car about 15 miles back to the main drag where I saw some policemen hanging out. I thought they might have a bead on things (in case someone came through there with a generator). To be sure, it was a bit heavy and conspicuous. So that is what we did. But when we got there and explained to some people and the police what had happened, bedlam broke out and we got so much advice that it started to make our heads swim.

I said to Jean, "This is too much. Let's go back. I believe that God has already given us back our motor!"

On the way back, we stopped to let a young boy through a large mud puddle/water hole (a small lake actually). As he came through and passed the window of the car he calmly said, "Mundele (white man) they have found your motor!" I guess everyone knew for miles around already that the white man lost his motor at Kingankati. But sure enough, when we got back to the village the news was that the motor was found and the group had taken the truck and all the equipment on to the next village another 20 kilometers or so down the road. We made a right angle left turn and followed their tracks getting to the next village about the same time as they did.

"What happened?" was my first question. Apparently, the "man of Satan" began trembling and went and got the motor after we left and brought it to the group (we had already found the jerry can). He then had the gall to ask for some money because he "found" it. The group said that we had prayed and it was God who directed him to give back the motor. No money would be given. And besides they all didn't have any. None of us really carried any amount of money with us on these trips. We carried with us all that we needed--gas, some snack food, water, and a set of fresh clothing. God provided the rest.

We did hear later, through CEAZ evangelists that travelled in the area preaching the gospel, that Satan's power was broken in that village and a church was constructed with many coming to know Jesus and worshipping there. Praise God for His unfailing power and grace towards us and towards them.

Freedom for Two Old Women

On the same trip, in the next village, God had prepared another very stimulating and encouraging experience for us. Two older women came to me after our meeting and asked for prayer. Curiously enough, they came each on their own (that is at separate times), but expressed the same problem. The problem that they expressed, after praying to receive Jesus into their lives, was the problem of evil spirit visitors in the night. These evil spirits had been bothering them, sexually, every night since they were young teenagers. They had not had a good night's sleep since that time due to these nightly visitors. They asked me if Jesus could help them. My answer, in brief, was, "Oh yes, He can! Would you like us to pray together over this problem?"

And of course, they really wanted to pray about this. I prayed over them individually, but claimed the same thing—that they belonged to Jesus, that they had been bought with the precious blood of Christ and that they were no long bound to Satan. We proclaimed freedom from all those visits in the Name of Jesus, we declared ourselves to be covered by the blood of Jesus and we told Satan and all his evil spirits that they had no right to enter again into their houses.

The barrier to these visits and the freedom from any more disturbing presence was and is always the blood of Jesus. For we know that the accuser of our brothers and sisters in Christ (the accuser working day and night) is certainly overcome by the blood of the Lamb—the blood of Jesus—and their testimony.[50]

The next day before we left, as we were packing up everything and making sure all the equipment was with us (nothing stolen), these women visited me, again at separate times, but they both had the same message. "Thank you so much for coming. God bless you! I had the best sleep that I have ever had since I was a young girl!" They went away "walking and leaping and praising God" as the kid's chorus goes. Well, not literally, but I could certainly see a joy on their faces, new Light in their eyes and a spring in their step.

We often have sung in churches or have sung in a "hymn sing" the gospel hymn, "There's Power in The Blood." Due to many experiences in ministry over the years, I have increasingly come to appreciate the truth of that song. However, I think that the many who have sung this song have not really experienced or fully comprehended how wonderfully powerful the blood of Jesus actually is. This song was written by L. E. Jones (Lewis Edgar Jones,1865-1936) and is the song for which he is best known (of all his 400 plus songs). He graduated from Moody Bible Institute, in Chicago, in the same class as famed evangelist Billy Sunday. Jones became actively involved in the YMCA, holding various positions in that organization over the years.[51] His hymn writing (of both words and music) was a sideline, but I am personally convinced that he had personal experience of the power of the blood of Jesus in his life for no one could write a song such as this without firsthand knowledge of the efficacy of the blood of Jesus on many fronts and on many levels.

The Miracle of the Fish and Five Cassava Roots

While we were moving slowly up river, having meetings in many of the larger villages along the river banks we came to a small village which had a unique story to tell us. We had finished our afternoon and

---

[50] Revelation 12:10-11Good News Translation (GNT)

[51] https://wordwisehymns.com/2010/02/08/today-in-1865-lewis-jones-born/

evening meeting and all had gone well. We were now invited to sit down around a camp fire and have something to eat. So far, we had eaten caterpillars and monkey meat. It wasn't a surprise to us now what might be on the menu. Of course, as visitors, village food was the only source of nourishment we received. We never brought food with us as we were always invited to come and hold meetings and anticipating that we would be cared for by those who invited us. On these up-river village trips we were always guided by evangelist Lisagola. Lisagola was pioneering the work along the river for the CEAZ with the people known as the Bangala (People of the river). He was a fiery evangelist, with only one good eye, but had great vision for reaching the Bateke and the river people with the gospel. It was at his invitation that we would travel a couple hundred kilometers up river, first by paddling our own dugout canoe, then by two 20-foot dugouts chained together with a 12-horse outboard on the end of one and later by a small 50-foot-long and 8 feet wide river cargo boat powered by a 25-horse outboard motor.

By now brother Dede Kikavuanga Dongo was our only evangelist. He was affirmed in his faith by our ministry and when I heard him give his testimony of how he came to faith in Jesus, at one of our meetings at the CEAZ Center of Evangelism in Kinshasa, God seemed to indicate to me that He could be our next evangelist as

Some 20 years later, Jim with evangelist, now pastor, Rev. Dede Kikavuanga Dongo

brother Kibutu had already left for studies in Europe. I approached him one day shortly after that and asked if he ever thought of being an evangelist. He mentioned that he would love to be one, he would love to preach, and he felt that God had called him to do that, but didn't know how.

Even though he had never preached before, I sensed that Dede had a gift of evangelism and prophecy on him—speaking forth the word of God. Not that I was a great preacher, but I told him that I would be his coach and teacher, although I knew that God Himself would do the honing. At some smaller meetings he was given the opportunity to exercise his gift and did well. I gave him a few constructive criticisms and words of instruction and encouragement and he was off to the races (figuratively).

With very little instruction, he studied hard and spoke well. Gramma and I then sent him to an evangelism course held at the Campus Crusade office in Kinshasa. This was very helpful for him. He was very fluent in both Lingala and French, but Lingala seemed to roll off his tongue like water off a duck's back. He was a natural. He was with us on this river trip. So when our contact man stood up to give thanks for the food, he mentioned that the fish we were about to eat was God given. We all nodded in agreement and he prayed.

After the prayer and while we were eating, the man who asked Dede to pray, wasn't satisfied with just a nod of agreement. He felt that we had to know the whole story.

He said, "I want you to understand that this fish that we are eating tonight was provided by God Himself." After a brief pause he continued, "I left last night, in the middle of the night, from the village where we had our last meeting and paddled up river so I could get to this village early in the morning before the villagers went off to their gardens. I wanted to let them know that they had visitors coming and that they should bring back extra food. Although I tried to get here as fast as I could, by the time I arrived they had all left for their fields. The only people I saw were two young boys in their small canoe on the river. Everyone else was gone.

"I didn't know what to do, so I went into my house to pray and spent time asking the Lord to provide food for our visitors who are coming to share the gospel of Jesus. As I was praying there was a knock on the door. When I went to see who it was, here were the two young boys at my door holding up a big fish. I asked them where they got the fish and they told me this story.

'We were paddling on the river when we saw a piece of broken paddle floating down river which we decided to pick up out of the water. When we reached the oar, we found a fishing line attached to it. Curious about the line, we began to pull in the line and then we felt a tug. As we pulled harder, we found a fish on the end of the line, already spent but fresh. We pulled the fish into the boat and came to your house to let you know what we found. We weren't sure what to do with it.'

"I told them that I was just praying for God to provide food for the visitors that were coming, and He did just that! We all knew it was from God and we thanked Him for it. So quite literally, you are eating what God has provided and we praise Him for His provision!"

It reminded me immediately of the story of the disciples catching a fish with a coin in its mouth in Matthew chapter 24.[52] Now, we were all excited and gave thanks to God again, for His provision.

The Geba/Yowa Trip

At one point, we were challenged and invited by a fellow missionary to go to an area just north of the Angolan boarder that was referred to as the Geba/Yowa area (two larger villages in that desolate area). We travelled from Kinshasa to Inkisi and then straight south towards the Angolan border. These are very small villages, not even on the map, but somehow God directed us there. On the way we saw a number of young people in different smaller villages all smeared in grease and white powder. We knew we were in a strong fetish and witchcraft area. But we knew the villages were expecting us, so we charged on, almost getting stuck a few times in the sandy roads. The only transportation in there was the big heavy 7-ton trucks (often old German Army 4-wheel drive vehicles refurbished and sent to Africa). Ruts were deep and wide, sometimes not easily driven over by our smaller vehicles.

We made it to our destination in one day, perhaps 150-170 kilometers. It took us the whole day to get there, get lodged and get our bearings. We were all settled into one house which was made available for us… not far from the local "bank". The bank, as we called it, was the communal outhouse, except there was no house, it was just "out" with a few waist high sticks and straw around a hole in the ground. The hole was covered over generally with a few small tree trunks with a smaller hole available for you to do your "business". You needed to know well how to squat in the right spot and how to balance on the small logs so not to fall in. If the surrounding "fence" had a lot of see-through gaps in it, we called it a modern bank with lots of windows and air-conditioning. If the "bank" was well surrounded with good protection, then it was a regular bank with good service. When a person had to make the walk, he was almost always asked if he had his check book with him. The "check book" was the roll of toilet paper we always carried with us on a trip like this. And, after he returned, most often he was asked (especially if he was one of the first ones to use the

---

[52] *Matt 24: 26 "…go to the lake and throw out your line. Take the first fish you catch; open its mouth and you will find a four-drachma coin. Take it and give it to them for my tax and yours."*

bank), "Were you well received? Was it busy, did you have to stand in line and wait? Was it a modern bank or just the regular kind? Were you able to do your business well, without interruptions or complications?" What got the most giggles and laughter was the question, "Did you make a deposit or a withdrawal this time?" All questions had underlying meanings that you can probably figure out. It was a way of having some extra fun! There were serious times, of course, but we also had a lot of laughs on those trips.

Village 1- "They had never heard..."

The next day we were at village 1. It took us a while to get there but we arrived in midafternoon, at about 3 or 4 o'clock, and immediately started to set up in a clearing at the center of the village. I asked some of the locals who had come with us from our base village if these people had ever heard the gospel message or heard about Jesus before. They said, "No! We don't think they know about Jesus or know who He is."

I never thought I would have the privilege of bringing the "Good News" to people who had never heard of Jesus before. This day of ministry suddenly took on new meaning and excitement, at least for me. I think the whole village was present that night. At first there were just a few hanging around watching us set up, but when we started to play and sing our songs of praise and testimony it didn't take long for the whole village to come out. By the time we finished singing and playing, including them in some of the songs as well, it was already dark, but the few lights that we had from the generator were good enough to keep the people seeing what was going on. We probably sang for an hour or so, then we showed the Jesus film (in a language they could understand) for two hours and then our evangelist preached after that for almost an hour. By the time we were through, we were all tired, but well fed (spiritually)!

The announcement was given, "We are all through now, no more playing or speaking. If you understood the message and the film and you want to stay and pray with us and receive this message, to receive Jesus into your life, we will pray with you. The rest of you can go to your homes."

We started to play our instruments again, just softly, to send off the people with a little bit of music, but nobody moved. You would think after four hours that they had had enough, but they all just sat there. Well, we said it again, "We are all done now, no more music. You see that the guys are unplugging the mics and packing up their instruments. You all can go home now. We give you the road.[53] Only those who want to stay and pray with us, you may stay where you are and we will come and pray with you."

So, in packing up, I looked up and saw that nobody had moved. The evangelist then told them one more time that we were all done and only those who wanted to pray with us to receive this Jesus that we were singing and talking about should stay and we would pray with them. When nobody moved again, it finally hit us. The evangelist said, "Do you all receive this message and do you all want to pray and received Jesus into your lives?" There was a resounding "Yes!"

What an exhilarating experience, to pray with the whole group and then deep into the night with many on a one to one basis. The whole village accepted the gospel message and received Jesus into their lives that night. Sins were confessed and forgiven, angels were rejoicing in heaven and we came home very late to our base—very late, very tired, but very happy! What an experience to share the good news of Jesus with those who had never really heard "His-story" before and then for them to accept that message as an entire village! We certainly made "history" that night. A night we will never forget!

Village 2 – The Village Demoniac

The next evening, we were in village number two. This village was much larger and quite a distance away. The road took us across into Angola and then back into the Congo in order to arrive at our destination. There were a few key church leaders who came along with us as they had a burden for some time to reach this village with the gospel. No one really announced that we were coming, we just showed up. Perhaps a runner was sent across the grass lands and through the forest earlier that day to let them know that we were coming, but it seemed to me that as we drove through the village (about a kilometer long) that our arrival was fresh news. We told the chief why we had come and asked where we could set up. It seemed that in this village as well, very few had heard the gospel message.

We set up at the end of the village we had just driven through and began playing and singing. It didn't take long for the crowd to come

---

[53] To "give someone the road" is to say, "You are free to leave now." Often, unless you say this to your Congolese visitors, they will not leave. They wait until you give them the road.

around and start dancing and swaying to the music. At one point, one man came forward, unkempt and dressed in rags (literally), and started to dance. His dancing was much more pronounced than the rest of the group and then became quite lewd. We stopped playing and said, "In the name of Jesus be calm!" The man immediately stopped his acting out and we continued to play and sing, then we showed the Jesus film and preached, just as we had done the previous night.

However, this night the evangelist was moved to ask people to come forward for prayer if they wanted to receive this Jesus that we were talking about. It wasn't surprising to me to see this same man be the first to come forward. While we were singing, even during the showing of the Jesus film and while the evangelist was preaching he was encircling the whole group of listeners with a great longing in his eyes. I could see clearly that he wanted to have what we had. But as he stood there with the many who came to the front, all of a sudden it was as if some of the young men had come with great force and grabbed him, threw him down and started beating and kicking him. Yet, all I could see was this man forcefully falling and writhing on the ground. No one else was around him.

I thought, "Oh no, it is just like the enemy to create such a fuss, so that all the seekers would get spooked and run away." But the crowd did not move, they just watched his writhing. I instantly said again, "In the Name of Jesus, stop, be still, be calm." He stopped immediately and some of the team went to help him up and took him a few meters away to begin praying with him. At this period in our ministry, I did a lot of clean up while the others on the team did a lot of praying and counselling. I was happy with that. Although I missed the privilege of leading many to the Lord on a personal basis, I was happy that my Congolese colleagues were now doing that. After all, even though I knew the language fairly well, I would never know it as well as these guys did and understand the problems of the people as they understood them for I was born in another color, another culture and another continent! And yet, it was because we were together as a team that we all had this privilege of sharing the good news just as we were doing.

After I had done most of the packing up, I went over to see how the team was doing with the man who had been acting out. I still didn't realize that he was the village demoniac. The villagers were used to his antics and that is why they did not disperse immediately while he was writhing on the ground. It was scary to me, but they had seen this often before. As I came up to the group I heard this man say, "I'm OK now on the inside, but they are still bothering me on the outside!" He was flinching as if he was being pinched all over. One of the group asked if he had any fetishes in his house, any sort of emblems which were used for witchcraft. He acknowledged that he did, so we all jumped on one of the trucks and went some 500 meters to the end of the village where he had a small hut.

A small group went into the house and brought out everything he had showed them--all kinds of ugly stuff.[54] We poured some kerosene on it all, threw it in a large garbage pit in front of his hut and set fire to everything. While everything was burning we began to sing "Yesu azali awa" or "Jesus is here with us, Halleluiah to Jesus!" At first, he was barely singing, but when we got to the chorus, singing halleluiah to Jesus, we lifted our hands in praise to Him (as we generally did in singing that song), he began to sing louder and also raise his hands. By the time we finished singing, he too was singing with us in full voice, in freedom and in joy. He was completely delivered.

We finally had to leave, but invited him and others to come to the church service at our base village, the Yowa village center, the next morning, even though it was about a 10-kilometer hike across the grass lands (as the crow flies) to get there.

The next morning, he was the first one in church, but he was also followed by a group of young men from his village. We found out later that they had come so see him completely disrupt this church with his lewd acts and foolish gesticulations. However, he was not so dirty now, cleaned up considerably wearing better clothes and he sat peacefully taking in the whole church service as if he were watching an amazing circus. At the end of the service, when people were called forward to pray, he was the first one there. However, this time, he came forward to seal the deal! He just wanted us to pray for him. He needed to have our blessing in the new life he found in Jesus and the new freedom he had found in Him. We did that and he went on his way rejoicing.

We also prayed with the other men who had accompanied him (they though for amusement) because they saw what a transformation had taken place in his life and they too wanted to have a personal relationship with this powerful God. They told us that many had tried to help him, witch doctors of all sorts etc., but none could help him. Now that they saw the change made in him by the God we served, they

---

[54] *Generally, bits of soiled cloth, hair, animal parts, trinkets, amulets, shells and the like.*

wanted to have that same kind of freedom and relationship with Him. So, we prayed with them all to receive Jesus as their personal savior.

What an exciting trip this was, not to mention the many others that received Jesus into their lives in our base village.

Ten years later a young pastor came to our house to see Gramma as she was teaching with him in a Bible school in a village just on the outskirts of Kinshasa. It was called the Kikimi Bible School. When I saw him, it brought back many memories of our Ngeba/Yowa excursion. He was a teenager at the time we were there and he had followed us around having a hunger in his heart for God. During one of the meetings that he was at, God called him to be a pastor and to come back to these villages, to plant churches and to pastor them. He did just that! He became their pastor, acting as one during his vacation times between his years of study and then fulltime pastor after he graduated from the Kinkonzi Bible School.

Just before he was to chat with Gramma, I asked him, "Say, do you remember that man…?" And before I could finish the sentence, he said, "I know just who you are referring to and yes, I do remember him well. In fact, every time I see him he asks me to greet you for him and say thank you for coming and sharing the good news about Jesus with him. His life was completely changed."

"So, what happened to him? I thought that with no one there to really disciple him he might have fallen back into Satan's traps."

"Oh no," said pastor Nzuzi. "He was completely changed. He cleaned up his life in every way, and his house! He got married and has children and is an elder in the church I planted there. I don't get back there that often now, but

Joseph Tsasa (or Big Joe), Paul Tsasa (or Pajot) and Jim (or Tata Jim) in 1987

every time I see him, he tells me to greet you and bless you for coming!"

Chapter Twenty-One: The Life and Times of Sango Malamu, Part 2

West Africa with Howard Jones

In Kinshasa, the Sango Malamu Team, held services in many schools and Universities, indoors and outdoors but mostly in the open air. The open air was our main venue in the Congo and then in other parts of West and Central Africa. We travelled to Gabon, Burkina Faso, Mali and Cote d'Ivoire with evangelists such as Kibutu Ngimbi, Isaac Kieta and the Billy Graham Evangelistic Association (BGEA)

 evangelist, Rev. Howard O. Jones.[55] Howard was the first black associate evangelist of the BGEA and traveled the world with Graham, handling much of the groundwork for the evangelist's African crusade in 1960. He was also the principal speaker for BGEA's "Hour of Freedom" radio broadcast for 35 years and became the first African American to be inducted into the National Religious Broadcasters Hall of Fame in 1995. It was a real delight for us to minister with him and his wife Wanda in the Congo and across West Africa where the CMA was involved in mission activities.

The usual format was that we would start singing and often engage the audience in our music in some way. The music though was always a build up to the verbal presentation of the gospel. We then would sing at the end, often during the invitation for people to come forward and accept Jesus as Lord into their hearts and lives. At one of our meetings with Howard in the Hotel Ivoire, in Abidjan, we sang quite a bit longer than normal. We shared our testimonies and sang in French (all were

---

[55] *Dr. Howard O. Jones, a former Christian and Missionary Alliance pastor, passed away on November 14, 2010, at the age of 89. A onetime jazz musician, he accepted Jesus as Lord and Savior at an Alliance church in Oberlin, OH and later enrolled at then Nyack Missionary Training Institute [of the CMA] to fulfill his dream of becoming a preacher of the gospel. He and his wife, Wanda, who predeceased Dr. Jones in 2001, were both Nyack alumni who lived in West Africa doing missionary work from 1959 to 1964.*

Dr. Jones is widely known for breaking the color barrier in 1958, when he became the first African American who was invited by Billy Graham to be a part of the internationally renowned evangelist's crusade team. He served with the Billy Graham Evangelistic Association (BGEA) for 35 years. http://www.nyack.edu/blog/NyackNews/753

French speakers), we also sang in Lingala, Kikongo and English. We must have carried on for almost an hour. The venue was beautiful, just the three of us on stage, and the people kept on asking for more—they wouldn't let us quit. All the while Howard was chafing at the bit wanting to preach. We were billed as the Sango Malamu Trio from Kinshasa, Zaire, and that drew the crowd. Everyone wanted to hear Zairian music; the place was packed.

Not to be outdone, Howard Jones got up and gave a great message and he also spoke for an hour (with an interpreter of cou〔 〕c). It was a good thing we were in Africa as meetings are generally open ended. No need for time

restraints. Even at that, the audience was a little restless towards the end. Nevertheless, there were a number who came forward to receive Christ as their Savior and Lord that day.

A few days later we were singing in Bouake in a large open-air stadium, just like we had done in Gabon. Then we were off to Mali and Burkina Faso. In Mali, it was so hot that we had trouble sleeping at night. I remember the last night we were there. The mission had the use of a beautiful large house with many rooms and bath rooms, all air conditioned, but they only put Howard and Wanda in the house. For 3 or 4 days the three of us, Joe, Paul and myself, were given a sun baked 100 degree (plus) small bedroom to sleep in, just large enough for three beds. The fan on the ceiling had only helicopter speed which almost blew our sheets off when we turned it on; otherwise we could hardly breathe in the stifling heat. The sun baked brick walls kept the room "nice and hot". The trouble was, after a joyful meal of couscous and shrimp at a Vietnamese restaurant (a final thank-you gift from the CMA mission), I got food poisoning and got incredibly sick.

I was on the toilet all night with a bowl on my knees. Everything came out of both ends so fast it was impossible to control either. On top of that it was so hot that there seemed no relief even for the few hours I could lie down. As we all left the next morning, the Joneses indicated that we all could have slept in their house as there was plenty of room. Too late! However, I did let the mission director know that when you invite a group for ministry and they are pretty much ministering all afternoon and evening, the only polite thing to do would be to give them the best and most relaxing accommodations that you have. "Remember," I said, trying to be somewhat polite, "We are not at home, but are travelling to many countries and need good rest and care." I suppose the mission director thought that good "rest and care" only applied to the speaker, not the musician evangelists. I got over it.

Trio Sango Malamu together with Howard and Wanda Jones and Isaac

Ministering with Dr. Isaac Keita and Dr. Kibutu Ngimbi

It certainly was a treat to be on the road with these powerful men of God as well. On one tour Isaac translated for Howard Jones and then we carried on after Howard left with Isaac. At the time he was a young man, but already a powerful and eloquent speaker. We greatly enjoyed his fellowship. And as with brother Kibutu, many people came to receive Jesus into their lives and become new "creations" in Him through his preaching. All the countries in which we ministered retained French as their official language, so it was easy for us as a team to sing, testify in the meetings and pray with many who came forward. We were all fluent in French.

At one point while we were in Mali, we set up an outdoor campaign meeting with a portable stage. In the wide expansive clearing we set up a string of lights and a loud speaker system powered by a generator. Gramma came along on this West Africa tour to join us and our evangelist was the now Dr. Kibutu Ngimbi. At the time, he was a young, strong and handsome man, as were all the guys on the team. I was the short white guy with very little color!

The late Dr. Isaac Keita

We were at a spot, in the middle of a predominantly Muslim town when something very strange happened. We didn't notice anything unusual except that we had great freedom in

Dr. Kibutu Ngimbi.

praising God and many were moving to the rhythm of the songs and joining us praising Him, listening carefully to the messages that were being sung. What actually was happening while we were singing and praising God, we were unaware of until many years later. The story came to us through a student who went to a Theological Seminary in the Central African Republic. He came from the CEAZ in Boma, Bas-Zaire, where Sango Malamu was well known at the time. This student left Boma for studies in the CAR (in French, *République Centrafricaine*) where he was put together with a roommate from Mali. As they started to get to know each other, the Malian understood that his roommate came from Zaire and immediately asked about news from Sango Malamu. The Zairian student was greatly surprised at this question, for he knew about our ministry and had often heard us, but didn't realize that anyone from Mali would know us. The Zairian told him what he had recently heard about the group and then asked the Malian roommate how he had come to know us (Sango Malamu).

The Zairian brother related the following message to me. He said that his Malian roommate used to be a Muslim, but despite that came to the fringes of one of our meetings in his town just to see what was going on. He really enjoyed the music, but what really caught his eye was a young man who was very sick. While Sango Malamu was singing and praising God, he saw that this man was healed before his very eyes. He realized that the God who we were singing about and who we were praising must be real; the most powerful God of all—for how else could a sick man like this be healed while people were honoring His Name. The Malian then said that that night, he was one of the many who received Jesus into his life. His life was immediately changed and he felt a call from God to go into the ministry and become a pastor. Now here he was finishing his theological studies with a roommate from the same country as Sango Malamu and wanted to know how we were doing. Were we still singing together and praising God? The young man from Boma assured him that we were. When he got back from the CAR many years later, the Zairian brother told me this story.

How amazing God is! We are just anointed to be faithful to do what he has called us to do and not to know everything about how the Holy Trinity does their work behind the scenes. Praise God for that! Had we known about that earlier, we could have thought that we were great channels of His grace and power. Perhaps our focus could have changed from being on the Lord to how great we were. But no, our Father always made sure that we knew how dependent on Him we needed to be and occasionally sent us stories like this just for our encouragement—a long time after the fact!

Gramma joins the Sango Malamu Team

In 1984, on one of our West African tours, Gramma came along with us. She even played the electronic drums, that is, she pushed the right buttons at the right time. She was good at it and it was a delight for me to have her along. It was at the time when we were asking God whether we should send our children away to missionary kids' school in Bouake, Cote d'Ivoire, or not. We were praying much about it and have included a letter in the next few pages where she explains how we felt with this venture after we did a praise concert (Sango Malamu) at ICA on a Sunday Evening. It was great fun.

This tour was before Burkina Faso had changed its name and for that reason Gramma refers to the country in the old name of Upper Volta. We did this tour in March and then only four months later August 4, 1984, the name was changed to Burkina Faso. It was two years earlier that we did the tour with Howard Jones. It was at that time that we were caught up in a change in government.

After Howard and Wanda had left, we carried on with our brother

Isaac Keita. A coup took place while we were in Bobo Dioulasso and were not able to have any public meetings nor move around the country or even leave the missionary compound for a whole week. This was in, as Gramma says, "The backside of the desert!"

0Below is the edited version of a four-page letter she wrote to her sister Auntie Ruth while we were in Libreville, Gabon, on our way home.

Just before leaving for Libreville on one of our West African tours. (mid 1980's)

Live on TV in Abidjan, Côte d'Ivoire

Gramma and Grandpa at age 40 around the time the pictures above were taken, before the West African tour with Howard Jones.

March 12, 1984

Dear Norm, Ruth, Darla & Paul:

Well, we're on the last leg of our journey - it's been 5 weeks since we've seen our kids so I'm starting to really kinda miss 'em! Although this is just practice for some longer stints coming up.

I can't remember if I mentioned anything before about being in the process of deciding whether or not to send them to the Ivory Coast Academy at Bouake, Ivory Coast, but this has been in the balance for the last couple of months.

Strangely enough, although no one was pushing the idea at all, we both started sensing that was what the Lord wanted us to do. We approached the subject when Dave Kennedy, our Africa Area Director, was in Kin, and he said that really, they would like all the Zaire missionaries to send their kids there. Our mothers in Kinshasa have a real struggle trying to balance home & family, and ministry - that would certainly help solve that problem.

But apart from that, we were starting to see that our kids really need Christian friends. There isn't one boy Rod's age who really loves the Lord and wants to walk with Him. All the boys in Rod's class want to talk about is the latest X-rated videos that they watched when their parents were out. I think he feels a bit like Lot in Sodom. Laralee isn't much better off...

... We started talking positively about I.C.A. to the kids and they got quite excited about the possibility of making Christian friends. I praise the Lord for the opportunity of seeing I.C.A. What a confirmation of the peace that the

Celui qui boira de l'eau que je lui donnerai n'aura jamais soif...Jean 4:14

Lord was giving us that we were making the right decision even before seeing the place. On Sunday night we put on

249

a Praise Concert and so many of the kids that came up to talk to us were just our kids' age. I guess being away from parents engenders a certain kind of maturity & independance but what a beautiful bunch of kids! We also saw the dorms where they would be staying, and they were really homey & neat. The dorm parents, Bud & Jean Hotelan, where Loralee will be staying, were missionaries in Zaire and we lived together for a month, just before they left for Ivory Coast when we first moved to Kinshasa. Jean has to be one of the most beautiful, warm, Spirit-filled women that I've ever been priviledged to know. I couldn't think of anyone who I'd rather my daughter live with (if it had to be away from me.) And the couple that run our boys dorm are just super too - Evan & Jewel Evans. Evan is Gene Evans son, so he grew up in the Dalat School & knows all about the advantages & disadvantages of dorm life from the inside. Everyone says they love the kids entrusted to their care and the sentiment is completely mutual. Sometimes (since filling out the forms & leaving the cheque) I have thought, "I must be nuts to send my kids away when I don't have to," but you know what, we both have such a peace that this is God's will I can't believe it. All the kids we talked to absolutely love it there. The rules are really quite strict, but you never saw such a happy bunch of kids walking around a school campus. So different from schools where everyone is "doing their own thing." The Our kids might have some misgivings at first, but I'm really excited for them, I know they're going to love it and be incredibly enriched.

We're going to have to tell them ahead of time not to feel guilty that they don't miss us very much :°) !

Right now we're in Libreville Gabon, on the last

of an evangelistic tour. We left Kin. with Paul, Joseph, Jim + I + Kibutu, our very gifted young evangelist friend. We landed in Abidjan, Ivory Coast + spent 10 days there involved in an evangelistic thrust - working together with Campus Crusade in a "Here's Life Abidjan" Crusade. Then we went on to paint north, Yamossokoro, Bouake then up to Upper Volta. I'll tell you, that's the back side of the dessert if I ever saw it! I have never been so hot in my life. It would go up to 110°F in our room, and everything was hot to your touch, the walls, the shampoo, your pen - everything, because it was hotter than your body temperature. Once we woke up at night, we could hardly breathe. So we took a shower, got our towels wet, laid them on top of us with a fan blowing on us. That's what you call "home-made air conditioning"! Electricity is too expensive there so none of the missionaries have air conditioning!! Boy, I'm going back to Kinshasa with a whole new list of things to praise the Lord for: trees, grass, rain, air conditioning in our bedrooms!!

One thing that really touched me while there in Bobo-Dioulasso, Upper Volta. I thought, "no wonder the world has an impossible time trying to figure out "the will of God." They're convinced that God is going to make them do something that they're just going to hate doing. Well, it was quite something seeing those missionaries in Upper Volta functioning in the full joy of the Lord. They wouldn't rather be any other place in the world - the Lord had called them there - yet it isn't natural enjoying eating red dust for 8 months

Goûtez et voyez combien l'Eternel est bon! Psaume 34:8

251

out of the year on the back side of the desert! That has to be a miracle of grace!

During these 18 meetings we saw around 600 people pray to receive Christ. The Bible School students there at Maranatha Bible School (CMA) had their hands full with all the counselling & follow-up responsabilities. All together we've worked with 3 different evangelists - all Africans. One Yiranow had been at C.B.C. for 2 years the other young fellow, a converted Muslim who also evidenced the real annointing of the Lord. Jim says that even though he enjoyed working with Howard Jones, working with Africans who know the heart and mentality of their own people is so much more effective.

I'm sure there will be a letter from you waiting in Kin, but I think I'll just mail this at the airport here, or else send it with someone going to the States from here - I may meet someone tomorrow as I'm speaking at an International Bible Study.

I know some had mentioned they received the prayer letter just before we left, so I'm sure I'll return to a pile of mail. I got all caught up with my letter answering in Upper Volta - so I sure feel good about that.

Well, it's bed time - not nearly so hot here - only about 80°F (10 P.M.) so with a fan it's comfortable.

Trust everything is fine "chez-nous". We love you loads and are very-happy that you're related to us! Friends can always fade in & out of your life. Relatives can't!!!

LUV xox Jim & Dawn.

Fufu, Caterpillars and The Chief

We got up early on that morning. It was around 5 a.m. We had decided to meet our connecting party on the river, some 100 kilometers out of the city. We had loaded all our sound equipment and instruments in the Suburban the night before. I'm not sure if the whole musical team slept at our place or if they arrived by taxi, but we all took off very early. The last stretch, a few kilometers, became increasingly difficult to navigate. The Suburban had 4 wheel-drive at one point, but now only the back two wheels gave us the power we needed to get around the deep crevices and ruts the rains had made in the seldom used road down to the river. It seemed we weren't going to make it, but I learned early on in my junior high school days to never say die until you can't breathe! We bumped and lurched until all the passengers had to get out and we finally made it close to the river where our contacts were waiting with the 30-foot-long dugout canoe.

We loaded all our stuff in the canoe, parked the vehicle the best we could, prayed God's protection over it and left, paddling up river with our two guides. The paddling is done with long oars, standing up, one in front and one at the back. As we were guests we were to rest safely in the canoe, making sure that we had good balance (however we took turns helping with the third oar that was available). Lisagola was our evangelist guide. He had an urgent desire to take the message of the gospel to the villages up our side of the river[56] and so arranged for us to accompany him with our generator motor for electricity and all our electric guitars, speakers, mics, stands and the lot. As we were paddling up river around midday,

---

[56] *Our side was the Zairian side, what used to be the Belgian Congo. The other side of the river, several hundred meters away, was the other Congo, the French Congo—two different countries.*

The Congo River (also known as the Zaire River) is the second largest river in the world by discharge (after the Amazon), and the world's deepest river with measured depths in excess of 220 m (720 ft). The Congo river has an overall length of 4,700 km (2,920 mi), which makes it the [world's] ninth longest river. It crosses the equator twice. The Congo Basin has a total area of about 4 million km², or 13% of the entire African landmass.-From Wikipedia, the free encyclopedia.

trying to reach our first village before nightfall, we noticed a storm brewing in the direction the river was taking us.

The Rain Storm

Generally, a rain storm in the Congo, will last 20 minutes and then it lets up enough for everyone to continue their normal activity. But this storm was a douser! The wind started to whip up the waves of the river so that we could no longer make headway. We beached the large canoe, found a tarp amidst all our stuff and used it to cover all six of us. We all hunkered down and were pretty much dry, but the rain pelted our equipment and started to fill up the canoe. It lasted for almost an hour and then it settled into a drizzle. We decided to move on as now we would soon be paddling up river in the dark. We bailed the water out of the canoe, covered up the equipment which was already soaking wet with the tarp and headed, in the drizzle, back up river. Fortunately, the wind had died down and we could paddle without a struggle.

It didn't take long for the night to close in. As we were sticking pretty close to shore to minimize the strength of the current, sometimes we would be hitting some of the low-lying branches of nearby trees. It was my fear that a snake or other poisonous critters would be lurking in the branches for us, but we encountered only leaves as we slithered our way in the dark, up the river to our destination.

Our destination was the village of our two Christian guides. They were solid young men and we learned to love them dearly. They knew the river like the back of their hands as they had "grown up" on it, but we were all totally drenched when we finally got to our destination. It was about 1 o'clock in the morning when we arrived and the village began to stir. They first took us into a small house where I was to sleep. It had two rooms of about 2 meters square separated by a doorway and a curtain. There was nothing in the first room, but a dirt floor. We sat on some low stools which were brought in and someone built a fire in the middle of the room. That fire was surely a blessing as we now needed the warmth from the cool of the night, with all our clothing completely wet. As we began to warm ourselves, other young men from the village brought all our stuff from the canoe and stored it somewhere to their liking. Some women brought us a couple of pots of food. It wasn't much, but we were hungry and any little bit would stave off the pangs—we hadn't eaten all day as we couldn't find a MacDonald's anywhere on the river bank!

"Fufu" is the staple food in that area. It is cassava root ground up into flour, then mixed with hot water and stirred until it becomes a big ball of dough. It is this dough that they call fufu and it settles like a ball in the stomach

and makes one feel full. It has very little food value, if any at all. But

I can handle it, if there would be some gravy or sauce from a local kill or fish. Well, there was a little gravy. It came from the pot in which the "binzo" had been cooking. Binzo means caterpillars that have been dried and fried. Some food value, but not that appetizing. It's a bit like chewing on leather. Nevertheless, this was the food offered to us and we ate it with gratitude. No cutlery of course, a handful of fufu and then a handful of binzo. It was quite a picture—six bedraggled guys, still soaking wet, huddling around a small fire in the middle of that small room, scraping balls of "glue" from their fingers and then popping in handfuls of caterpillars. At times like this I often said to myself, "Boy, if people at home could see me now!"

Our Equipment

I slipped my way over to the next room which was just big enough for a bed and space for me to put the small bag of the few extra clothes I had brought along. I hung up the wet stuff, on sticks that were sticking out of the mud and stick house, used my flashlight from my bag to see if any creepy crawlies were on or in the bed and promptly flopped down to sleep. Before going to sleep I must have found something that was mostly dry and slipped it on. The bed must have had a sheet on it and that was all that I needed to keep me warm.

The next morning the sun was up bright and early! When we finally got all the equipment rounded up, we unpacked it and spread it all out in the hot sun for an hour or so. We weren't going anywhere that day anyhow. All the speakers, the guitars and cases, all the cables and mics, the mixing board and generator motor, everything, had to be dried out by the heat of the midday sun! After an hour or a little more, we assembled everything, wiped off the sand and dirt and set it all up to see if we had electricity and if the mixer, speakers, mics and instruments all worked—without shorting out! We prayed and fired up the generator, then turned on the switch. No smoke, not short-outs, it all worked perfectly, "thank you Lord!"

Seeing we were testing all the instruments and mics we thought we might as well have a meeting, so we began to sing. Well, it didn't take long for the whole village to come out. Most of them stayed at home that day and the few that had gone to the fields were on their way home. It was mid-afternoon, and the sun was hot, but we were glad for it after the experience of the previous day. We played and sang for about an hour, praising the Lord for the fact that He had kept all our equipment from breaking down. After the music, we decided to hear a message from God's word. I think I spoke that day and a few villagers expressed their desire to receive Jesus into their lives including the assistant chief.

After we had prayed with the people the acting chief of the area invited us into his home. It was about the same size as the one I had slept in, but his bed was right in the first room. He sat on his bed as we all stood around him and began reaching under the bed for various and sundry boxes—some locally made, about the size of a jewelry box and others a little smaller. In these boxes were all sorts of ugly objects— parts of a finger nail, bits of hair (human and animal), a part of a hoof of some local game, some strips of oily cloth, a piece of rusty iron of some kind etc. Each box contained its sordid contents. They were all fetishes.

As he brought them out, he began speaking to these fetishes. He would say, "You, fetish of hunting, I don't need you anymore. Jesus has come into my life and He will provide me with the meat that I need." Then he would pull out another box, a round container, and say, "You, fetish of money, I renounce you and tell you I don't need you anymore. I have accepted Jesus into my life and He will provide for me. He will provide all that I need."

As he did this with many small containers, he exposed all the contents. As he spoke to the fetishes of hunting, money, sex, authority and power, he also denounced them all, drew a line on the dirt floor and put them across the line, one by one, speaking directly to each one indicating that they didn't belong to him anymore. It is interesting to

note here that he didn't speak about them; he spoke directly to these fetishes addressing them as he would a person. To me it looked like a pile of garbage, but to him it all had real significance, it was spiritually living "stuff" and he publicly, in a loud voice, denounced it all. Nobody told him to do this or told him what to do; he knew it in his heart and in so doing gave a powerful testimony to God's amazing grace and his new life in Christ. The Holy Spirit moved him to do it all, so we definitely witnessed the Holy Trinity at work that day!

We finally took all the "garbage" (fetishes) and paddled out into the river and sank the complete package all wrapped up in an old piece of cloth, all the while raising our hands and singing "Yesu azali awa…" or "Jesus is here with us, halleluiah to Jesus." What a struggle to get there, but what a reward at the end of the struggle. All the water our equipment had taken in should have completely destroyed it, **but God…** We were to get to the village much earlier and go on to the next village early that morning, but God… We weren't going to have a meeting in that village as the two young men, our guides, had done a lot of preaching there already, but God…

That whole trip up and down the river yielded a great harvest of people who had not heard much of the gospel, if any at all. It seemed like we were the first group of evangelists to share the gospel with these river people (at least in a long, long time) as most of villages along the river bank, on that almost 200-kilometer trip, had no witness of Jesus much less a church in which to worship. Many were touched with the love of God, the witness of Jesus and the power of the Holy Spirit as we gave personal testimonies, preached to small congregations, and sat around small fires, listening to their stories and sharing our own.

We made not a few such excursions up river, first by paddling our own dugout canoe, then with two canoes chained together, propelled by a small 20 horse outboard motor, and then by larger river boats (in French, *Baleinière*) of perhaps 40 feet long all propelled slowly up the river by a small 20 or 25 horse outboard engine. We never got rained out again.

We ate a lot of food which we ordinarily wouldn't eat (local game like monkey, small antelope, forest rat and other forest meat as well as local fish which no one knew the name of (in my language at least). We had close encounters with snakes, scorpions and spiders as big as your hand and slept in all kinds of beds and conditions. One early morning I woke up in the bed provided for me in a mud hut to see a very large spider (it looked like it was the size of my hand and fingers) with harry legs in the sapling rafters, right above my head. I said to myself, "If that thing falls it will fall right on top of my face!" So I rolled over on my side to let it fall behind me and promptly went back to sleep for another hour or so. When I got up this time the spider was nowhere to be seen!

Another time, after a long meeting, I was shown to my sleeping accommodations in the blackness of night. It was a small office-room in the local community center building (a small house) with no furniture and a dirt floor. I didn't have a blanket, so I just put on my hoody and promptly threw down a sponge mattress which I generally carried with me (just in case there wasn't a bed available), flopped down in the pitch blackness and went to sleep. I woke up in the middle of the night when I felt a rat (I'm sure it was) running across my head. In my semi-conscious state, I grabbed the hood part of my hoody, pulled it over my head, drew the strings tight and promptly went back to sleep. Early the next morning I was almost booted out by some official that wasn't happy with several of us taking up lodging in the community official "office"! The others had already scrambled out of there, so I was left to my own sense of direction to find the trucks and the rest of the group who had been scattered throughout the village.

On one occasion, coming down river, in a couple of canoes chained together, we were very close to capsizing during another wind storm. I forgot all about our equipment and was looking at how I was going to swim to shore, yet God protected us all--including the equipment. God always brought us home safely, without illness or serious accident. The cool thing about all these excursions was that we also prayed with a lot of people to receive Jesus. Later, as other missionaries went up river with high powered boats to bring discipleship lessons to the believers up and down the river, many churches were established. God knew what He was up to! When He sent us, He was just paving the way for many to become believers, then later to grow as disciples and do church together—worship together in their own villages.

The Best Equipment

The first or second year of our ministry in Kinshasa, I was at a wake of a rich man who had just recently passed away. He was a well-known business man who had one foot in the church and the other in all kinds of secular endeavors. He gave much to the CEAZ church but also was very much involved in all kinds of business dealings which had nothing to do with the church or could have even been opposed to Christian principles. At the wake there were those who wanted to remember him as a church man, but also there were those who represented the darker side. The church leaders had a few lanterns for light, a program to follow and were going to use a megaphone for amplification—that is all they had to announce the events, to sing into and to preach into.

There were hundreds of people who crammed into this large courtyard. But the secular group, with their message, had brought strings of lights, big speakers, heavy duty amplifiers with lots of instruments and a well-known music group to announce their program and do their singing. An argument ensued as to who would start the wake "festivities". The church leaders said they would, the secular group said emphatically that they would start and do their thing and then in the middle of the night sometime the church could do whatever they wanted. The church leaders refused that idea and a heated exchange took place. After awhile, the secular group said, "OK! You do your thing and we'll do ours! Let's see who will be listened too!"

Well the church had to take a back seat because all they had was a megaphone and the other group had powerful wattage behind them.

Although I wasn't in on the discussion I knew what was going on and went away discouraged not able to meet the eyes of those who felt superior since they were much better equipped. They had the lesser important message, but they had the most superior equipment to announce it.

Not long after that incident, as I was walking down a very busy section of the city one day, I heard all this music blaring from one boutique after another. Then I heard a really loud group of speakers belting out the popular music of the day so loud that there was complete distortion (of course Zairians don't mind that, but I didn't know it then). It hit me that this music was all about glorifying secular thought and/or sensual love. Nothing was playing that would glorify the Father or His Son Jesus, representing real love and pure philosophy. Right there on the spot I asked the Lord, "Why is it that the enemy of our souls has the worst message (morally) and always has the best equipment to herald it and we who have the best message have nothing but a megaphone, at best, to announce it to the masses?" At least that is how it appeared to me to be in Kinshasa (and the rest of Africa for that matter).

...the best equipment to proclaim the best message!

It was a rhetorical question of course and I didn't wait for an answer, but followed it up with, "Lord, if you give us the best equipment (or really good equipment) I will proclaim the best message, loud and clear!" My thought was to proclaim the best message with the best equipment. That was well before Sango Malamu was born. However, a seed was planted!

When Trio Sango Malamu started, we began with acoustic instruments only. And then, since people could not hear us in the open-air meetings, our Father began giving us better instruments and more powerful equipment. Eventually our equipment was good enough to herald the "Best News" to massive crowds if necessary. When we sang with our daughter Loralee (I love you Jesus) at the Centennial services for the CMA in Boma (Bas-Zaire) a few years later. An estimated 25,000 people were well able to hear us as well as all who spoke at the gathering, using our God given equipment. When all is said and done, during the last years of Sango Malamu's ministry in Africa, I believe we had about 1000 watts of power or more (and that was a lot in those days).

When we powered up for the glory of God, we were heard. We announced loud and clear the BEST message. We often sang an opening song in French that said, "We announce to you (we proclaim to you) the Love, the Peace, the Joy of Jesus." What a thrill that was! People heard us a long way off and often came quickly to see what was going on. They heard the Good News loud and clear. Thank You, Lord!

We recorded some ten albums and mostly sang our own music. I had written a few songs but most of our songs were written by "big Joe" (Joseph Tsasa). Joe would come with a song and we would put our ideas together to make our own arrangements. We sang in good harmony, played our own instruments at the same time and operated our own sound. The first album that we put out was recorded in a makeshift garage on just a stereo cassette deck--which meant that every time someone made a mistake or the sound wasn't well balanced we had to make the adjustments and record the song all over again—the whole song.

We were so meticulous in our recording that when someone from the government radio station heard the tape, he thought that we had recorded it in a professional studio (in Europe or in Brazzaville—across the river). He was so surprised to hear we did it in our own garage that he came all the way from the national station to see our little, humble studio and still couldn't believe it. God provided us with the best of equipment in guitars, amplifiers and speakers and microphones. He gave us just what we needed and later He would provide us with a complete professional audio studio, a three-camera video recording studio and a well-furnished radio station with a transmitter and high antenna tower that would reach the cities of Kinshasa and Brazzaville, around 12 million people.

The Best Message

It is my opinion that no one in Africa needs to be told that God exists. Africa has been aware of the spirit world for centuries if not millennia. Everyone believes there is a God! At least that has been our experience. What most of our audience didn't know was that this God who they believed was there, somewhere, is a benevolent Father of Light and that we as humans can in fact have a personal relationship, a loving intimate relationship, with Him through His Son Jesus. Our message was that simple. God, our heavenly Father, sent His Son Jesus, the Messiah, to earth **to redeem us**, **to give us hope** in this life and to give us **a future with Him** here on earth and in heaven—for all eternity![57] As mentioned above, we would often start our meetings with the song, « Nous vous annonçons la paix, la joie, l'amour en Jésus. »![58] The Peace of Jesus, His joy He gives people and His love and hope is all seen in the redemption factor! Let me unpack that a bit.

This verb "redeem" or the noun "redemption" contains both a negative and a positive connotation. The negative aspect has to do with the fact that there needs to be compensation **for the faults or bad aspects** of something or someone. Or, there needs to be a price paid to regain possession of something (or someone) that was **lost or stolen**! The culpabilities of people or their bad actions or even people (or things) who are "lost" or "stolen" declare the negative side of redemption—it begs for one to rectify or "redeem" the situation. Concurring with this is the Bible which says, "we have all gone astray" [59] and we have gone our own way (meaning lost). The writer of the Proverbs says (14:12) there is a way which seems right to a person, but the end of that way is certain destruction. I experienced that in my youth, so I understand this negative aspect of redemption! If there wasn't this side to "redemption" the word would have no meaning at all.

Allow me to go just a little bit deeper into this negative aspect of redemption. There is a current flowing deep and wide underneath African life and culture. That current is the realm of the spirit world. When anything goes wrong, it is most often explained away as "ndoki" or witchcraft—something went wrong in the spirit world, someone must pay! No one would say that this is a good thing. It is very scary to many, but very real. Ndoki or Kindoki (or witchcraft as we would call it) is often what is considered the cause of a death or of serious problems, but witchcraft is also considered the place to go to find a

---

[57] *Jeremiah 29:11 For I know the plans I have for you," declares the LORD, "plans to prosper you and not to harm you, plans to give you hope and a future.*

[58] *"We announce to you (we proclaim to you) the Peace, the Joy, the Love of Jesus."*

[59] *1 Peter 2:25 For you were straying like sheep, but have now returned to the Shepherd and Overseer of your souls.*

Isa 53:6 We all, like sheep, have gone astray, each of us has turned to our own way; and the LORD has laid on him the iniquity of us all.

remedy or a solution for these problems in life. That is, often there is the desire to seek out greater spiritual power (add in sorcery) to overcome the lesser power that may be the cause of the calamity. When one does this the end result is pitting Satan against himself—that is the lesser darkness is to be overcome by the stronger or the greater darkness. When you analyze this, it is the dark side pitted against the darker side which only leads to utter darkness. There is no hope here, no peace but fear and turmoil.

I have seen this terrible darkness, this fear and despair in many lives, in many villages and many communities. The only solution for this is Light and Love! Light dispels darkness and Love takes away fear and hate. And the only Light that could ever shine into this darkness is the Light of the world which is Jesus Himself! The only Love that could ever dispel fear and hate is the Love of God himself—for He is Love![60]

And here comes the positive side of "redemption". When we (the group Sango Malamu) would come into an area, set up our equipment and begin to play and sing praises to our Lord the Redeemer, Light would begin to shine. It is not exactly like turning on a switch and then instantly the whole area is flooded with light! No, it is more like lighting candles one at a time until the place is flooded with light and the tide of darkness is stemmed. Announcing or declaring the peace, the joy and the love of Jesus to be present is the beginning of the battle. It is the beginning of replacing darkness with the Light, the beginning of putting darkness to flight. You see, when we would sing praises to our God or sing a message of the love of God, the peace of Jesus or present a message declaring the presence of the Holy Spirit, so many things would be happening in the spirit world. Things not necessarily seen with the naked eye, but still recognizable to a Christian having at least a partial understanding of how God works. When we would begin to sing and give honor to the King of Kings, Praise the Lord, testify and preach, even in the darkest of areas, we would sense and recognize (by being alert to the working of the Holy Spirit) the following:

1. God's special presence would descend and envelope the place of our meeting, whether outside (where most of our meeting were) or inside.
2. The darkness of the evil one would begin to disappear (in some places this was more of a battle than in others).

---

[60] *John 4:18*

3. People would be loosed of their chains, the chains of sin and witchcraft the enemy had put around them.
4. The Holy Spirit would be present in such a way that the audience would be given liberty to enter into the worship time (for where the spirit of the Lord is there is freedom)[61] and
5. Their minds would be free from clutter and confusion from the dark side and begin to understand the real meaning of the words spoken and/or sung.

There would be freedom to respond to the Good News that we were bringing in music and in the preaching of God's word. Some would just cry in His presence and others would be healed.

There would be freedom to bring personal fetishes (inanimate objects of worship considered to be inhabited by evil spirits), to be burned.

We would sense freedom in the many who would stay behind to ask Jesus into their lives where before some of them were opposed to us, to God and the Bible.

Now that is the positive side of redemption: men and women, young people and children being redeemed, not by using money or things of this world, but being bought by the precious blood of Jesus.[62]

When the people prayed and received Jesus into their hearts (their lives), Jesus became their Redeemer for they then understood that He had already paid the price for their freedom, their joy and their hope. They were lost in darkness, but He regained possession of them and brought them to Light and a new life in Him. Jesus is the (and became their) blessed Redeemer and that is very positive. Redeeming Love was our message and still is! This blessed Redeemer brought and eternal life to many; He brought them His love and His peace. We were His vessels to bring Africa (and America) the best message we could ever bring. I couldn't believe I got paid for doing it!

Uncle Rod, put a great piece of graphic art together which encapsulates what is said above and I just recently came across it. It is pictured here on the next page.

---

[61] *2 Corinthians 3:17*

[62] *1 Peter 1:18-19 For you know that it was not with perishable things such as silver or gold that you were redeemed from the empty way of life handed down to you from your ancestors, [19] but with the precious blood of Christ, a lamb without blemish or defect.*

This art and graphic lettering was done by our son, Graphic Designer Rod Sawatsky and the quote is from Martin Luther King Jr.

He writes, *"I am picturing a generation of young Africans taking up this message of vulnerable love that changes our hearts and minds. It is their indomitable spirit and willingness to love in spite of suffering that inspires me...more than cynicism or frustration with consumerism ever could. I'm thinking of my orphan friends in the Philippines and African villages from my youth when I post this."*

Lessons Learned

Paul and Joe taught me a lot about the African way of life. We spent a lot of time in villages, learning their ways and also a good block of time working with Christian leaders and Pastors, understanding ministry from their points of view. But my major lessons came from these young guys that worked with me for ten years, including Jean and Dede. If we didn't have any special functions to sing at, we had our own evangelistic outdoor meetings. There were no lack of invitations and we spent a lot of time together!

It was early on in our ministry when I parked one day in a busy intersection, another market place outside of city center, waiting for Paul and Joseph. We were to meet there at an appointed time as we had a meeting to play at. I had the Suburban packed with all our equipment and got there on time. Normally waiting for a few minutes in the hot sun was not a big deal, but in that area, teaming with people, looking in the truck, calling me a "Mundele" or white man (although that didn't bother me that much, I never did really get used to liking the appellation) and generally swarming the vehicle, I didn't want to wait too long. But a few minutes turned into 20 then 40, then almost an hour before they finally showed up. I was plenty hot, both under the collar and throughout my whole body. I couldn't have the windows wide open for fear of some thievery, which could easily have happened. It was stuffy in the vehicle and I was dripping with sweat. They got in and indicated they were ready to go with no immediate apology or explanation. Soooo, on the way I ranted and raged for a while and then shut up. After some time of silence, they apologized and said that their neighbor had just passed away and the family came over to let them know just as they were leaving. The walk from their house to where I was had to be at least 20 minutes, but they had to spend some time with the neighbors. They couldn't leave just like that, so they created time. In their minds, they wouldn't be late as the death and their neighbors (or more simply put "relationships") were much more important than getting somewhere at an appointed time. They knew I would wait. But as a "white man" I was fuming!

I must say that I felt not a little foolish when I heard their story. I apologized for not understanding and shooting off at the mouth. After that, I learned that I needed first to wait for an explanation, if there was one, before I even commented on anything. And I learned how important relationships and family are in the Congolese and/or African culture.

I also began to understand that slow was good, especially if you wanted to last a long time in Africa (not that I gained **a whole lot** of patience, that was hard for me). When we walked, it was slow. When we packed up and put our equipment away it was at slow speed. When we arrived (generally by motor vehicle(s) of some kind) we slowly got out of the vehicle and slowly went to meet the pastor. In the beginning, I was always the first one in line, the first one to get out and meet the pastor, the first to put things away and the first one to react. But as I studied my colleagues, I began to learn how to slow down. It was useless anyhow to be the first in anything as I would always have to wait for the others to catch up. I decided that I would wait until one of the team made the first move, whether to sit down, to stand up, to go and meet the pastor who invited us or to begin setting up. I learned from Paul and Joe to s-l-o-w d-o-w-n. I forced myself to wait, to allow my colleagues to take the lead. I learned so well that when Gramma and I would go anywhere, we were almost always late, and she was always two or three paces ahead of me. Life doesn't race by you so fast at the speed of a snail.

In Canada, when we would arrive at a church, we would sit in the Van, thank the Lord for getting us to this next meeting place safely and then just sit for a while. Sometimes we wouldn't move for a good 5 minutes, while the pastor was waiting for us at the door, not sure if he should interrupt us or just wait. No, we were just taking our time getting out of the vehicle. Normally I would have been out the door almost before the vehicle had stopped, but I learned to slow down, take time, collect my thoughts, and then nonchalantly meander over to where the pastor was, with the rest of the group, and heartily greet him.

It's good not to be in a hurry… as the motto for Bobby Schuler's church says, "I'm not what I do, I'm not what I have, I'm not what people say about me, **I am the beloved of God**. It's who I am; no one can take it from me. I don't have to worry, **I don't have to hurry**, I can trust my friend Jesus and share His love with the world."

During our ministry in the open air and in many churches in America, in the years of 1980, 1982-1983, and again in 1988-89, we travelled from the State of Georgia to the province of Ontario; from the West coast of Vancouver Island across to the eastern coast of the Gaspe Peninsula in Quebec; from the west coast of Washington State up to Ketchikan, Alaska. What a treat to take "Congolese Worship" to all these places. We got visas to travel to the US quite easily as we had done that before without repercussion. On our way back into Canada one night rather late, the guys had to go into the border station to show their visas. When the agent found out what we did, he said to Paul and Joe, "Oh, so you guys are like missionaries to Canada, eh?" We agreed, and it was as if God let us know that this is who we were. Zairian or Congolese missionaries to Canada!

Although the Sango Malamu Trio has not now sung together on a regular basis for quite a few years, we are still good friends today even though our parting was not on the best of terms—the details of which are best to be kept among us. However, I can say that Joe was to go back and get things ready for our recording studio. Paul, having taken courses in audio engineering from a training school in Vancouver was finishing his year and was soon going to be the primary operator of our new studio. We had purchased all the equipment. It was ready to be shipped to Zaire—a semi-professional studio here, but in the Congo, it would be one of the best in the land.

The bass player, young David, needed to go home early. Joe too, with his family, was on his way home not long after his younger brother's departure, but when he got to Montreal, decided to use the rest of his ticket to go to North Carolina, where friends and relatives were already living. Paul was going to stay in Vancouver until his school year was over and then go back with us to Kinshasa to set up the studio. Although this was Paul's plan, it never worked out that way. He was persuaded by his brother and other friends in Raleigh to stay in the USA after his classes were finished. There was a sizable amount of cash donated for Paul to take home with him as a home coming present for himself and his family, but the morning I called to let him know what actually transpired and how we got that money for him, I found out that he had already left early for North Carolina and would in fact not be coming back with me. To put it mildly, it was discouraging and very disappointing. I tried to give the money back to the donor, but he refused saying that it was a gift to the ministry and if it didn't go to Paul then I should just simply put it towards preparing the new studio.

So there I was! A pro audio recording studio all packed and ready to take with us to Kinshasa and no one to set it up or run it. Fortunately, Daryl Brooks came to my aid again and sent his son-in-law-to-be, Rod Froehler, out to Kinshasa with us, to help us set up. Rod helped us immensely. God provided another in Paul's place, for Rod had gone through the same training as Paul. He was big Rod and our son was little Rod. Both Rods came back with us and provided expert assistance in setting up and running the audio recording studio.

What an answer to prayer that was!

Part VI SSM—Audio and Video; Radio and Television

Chapter Twenty–Two: The Audio Production Studio, SSM

A Personal Inventory

It seemed like every time during our years of home assignment, we would take stock of our "missionary call" and see if we were actually doing the right thing. Both Gramma and I would ask the Lord for a green light to go back—more specifically, a Word from Him who originally

sent us. When we received that assurance, we discussed what each of had received from the Lord and then acted whole heartedly on it.

When we came home for two years, it was a different story. We had several other opportunities to minister at home, which seemed sometimes more interesting than going back to Africa. What also was an alluring fact of staying in North America was that two of our kids would be out of school. They wouldn't be going back to Africa with us. Even though they thought they were ready for the "outside" world, we weren't so sure about that. Remember, they had spent most of their years in Africa, living in different culture, with different ethics and mores then in Canada. Their world view was different than most kids their age.

So, what were we to do? Our 2nd year of furlough I thought that I would have to work at an outside job, seeing we didn't get the Minister of Worship position at our home church, Peace Portal Alliance in White Rock (South Surrey). However, the CMA in Canada, suggested that they keep us on home assignment another year and requested that we go on a couple of missionary tours—speaking in many churches in eastern Canada as well as the in the west. I whole heartedly agreed. Yet during my times at home, as Missionary-in-Residence at PPAC, I led worship those two years and loved it. I even did a worship seminar for our church leaders and musicians.

When I was about to do the tour of the west, Alberta and BC, I had the idea of bringing my daughter (Auntie Loralee) along with me on the tour to provide music. I brought the keyboards with me and we sang together. She also sang many songs on her own with canned music. Up to this point I had always managed to have the Kinshasa Trio involved, but now I was alone. It was this year that the group had disbanded. So we loaded our van with what equipment we needed and left for a couple of months of Spring tour. I promised to help pay her next year's tuition at Bible College if she helped me on my home service tour. It worked out great!

It was during this time that I was asking God again what my future would hold. Should I go back to the Congo or should I stay with the kids in Canada? It was a big decision for me because I felt that if I was to go back, I couldn't go with the CMA. I thought what I wanted to do couldn't be done with the CMA in Canada or the USA.

Two things came out of that turbulence. One was an interesting conversation with the Lord: this conversation was not pinned on any special portion of scripture on which I could hang my missionary hat. I kept on asking, but He was silent. Then after a time, in the quietness of my personal study in the basement of the house we were living in, just two blocks east of the White Rock City border, I heard the Lord say to me, "What culture do you feel the most comfortable in?"

"Why, I guess, the Congolese culture." I murmured under my breath. I had already spent at least 16 of my best years there.

"What group of people do you feel most comfortable speaking to—in a church meeting or on an individual basis?" Was the next question.

"What? What do you mean?" was my taken-a-back response. "Why I, eh, I guess the Congolese!"

"And what language do you feel most comfortable preaching in?" He asked.

"Well I guess, Lingala. I have more fun speaking in that language and I get more of a response from the people as well"

And,

"What music do you enjoy the most?"

Without hesitation, my reply was, "Congolese music, of course!"

Then I felt His voice go silent. No more questions and no more comments, but when I added up all my replies, I realized that He was making a good point. All my answers were founded in my missionary experience in the Congo, nothing was given for Canada. It seemed to me that His silence said, "I rest my case. You now make up your own mind as to what you are going to do!"

At that point I knew that my call to the Congo was renewed and God would bless me there whether I went with the CMA, as an independent, or with another missionary organization.

The other point the Lord brought to my attention WAS a scripture that He pointed out to me in Luke 9:62,

Then Jesus declared, "No one who puts his hand to the plow and then looks back is fit for the kingdom of God."

It was very pointed. I felt the Lord was saying to me that if I reneged on His call, I wasn't worthy of working in His vineyard or fit for His kingdom. I immediately got the picture and responded positively. It was like I was being slapped on the hands for asking Him, again, what I should do! I never asked again after that. He made it very plain to me.

The Vision

The vision for a studio was constantly there during our ministry with the Kinshasa Trio. Having the matter confirmed with God, after two years of home service to see our older kids graduated from High School and then settled, we were ready to take Kinshasa by storm, with some twenty plus luggage bags (mostly hockey bags) which included our personal items and all the recording equipment. We prayed hard that we would be able to bring all the stuff back with us.

We knew more delicate and expensive items could be stolen, broken, or lost if they weren't packed just right and sent as our personal baggage. So, we included the mixing board, all the heavy tape recorders, all the effects modules, all the chords and cables, with all the reels of tape we could squeeze in as our personal baggage and asked the Lord to bless us and give us favor at the airport—which He did. We were able to bring everything with us right to Kinshasa without paying any extra baggage… UNHEARD OF, UNTHINKABLE, yet truc! Our Father is truly the "Way-Maker".

Even before we left for home assignment, I had told Gramma about the vision God had given me of starting a professional studio to get Christian music out into the market place so that believers all over the Congo could hear Christian praise music on their own ghetto blasters— it seemed like every family had at least one of those machines.

Whenever a choir or any special music was to be presented in church there would be a rush from the congregation. A crowd of people with their tape recorders would quickly push their way to the front in order to record the music. At best it would be very poor quality with a lot of extraneous noises—especially the clicking sounds of other tape recorders present and even some feedback noises at times, not to mention the coughs and chickens in the background.

After seeing this happen numerous times, it finally got through to my head and heart that our church people were hungry for good Christian music and there was virtually nothing available. Then came the next thought, "Why not make good quality Christian music available, of the many choirs, so that people wouldn't have to rush forward and record and be (what I thought was) a definite distraction from the music and the message?" Thus, the vision of setting up in the Congo a semi-pro or professional recording studio in order to make Christian cassettes as available as Bibles was born.

When I shared that vision with Gramma, there was a definite barrage of questions and obstacles presented. My visions scared her completely, but I knew that if I could get the vision passed her then I had a good indication it was from God! Her immediate questions were:

1. What do you know about recording studios?

2. What kind of training have you had to set up a professional recording studio?

3. Do you know it costs a lot of money to do that?

4. Where will you get the money?

5. How will you get all that equipment safely to Kinshasa?

6. Where will you set it all up?"

And there were a few more that I won't mention here.

My answers to these questions were pretty short at the time. They were, in the same order:

1. Not much!

2. No training!

3. Yes, I know it costs a lot of money!

4. I don't know!

5. I don't know and

6. I don't know!

"BUT if this is from God," I said, "Then He will provide! He will provide the knowhow, the building, and the funds. Don't forget that Paul Tsasa has already been sent to get professional sound engineer training and that was certainly a God thing. So God is, in fact, beginning to provide."

The Provision

Little Mountain Sound recorded our first album in Canada called "Soldiers of The Army" (of salvation) a couple of years before this and did it pro bono for the sake of helping our ministry in Canada and in the Congo. At that time, Little Mountain Sound was owned and managed by Bob Brooks (no relation to Daryl). A year or so later when they heard that our ministry had vision of setting up a Christian sound recording studio in Kinshasa, as part of the Sango Malamu ministry, they gave of their expertise freely in putting the whole studio together. Only God could have done that! They made out a list of everything we would need and gave us ideas of where we could buy the equipment. We were well on our way...

Gramma's auntie Blanche Palmer, for many years a missionary in the Philippines, due to her internment during WWII had received funds from the American Gov't as compensation for the suffering she had gone through (we almost lost her) and she had invested that in property. Now she was failing in health. She had sold her property and had moved to White Rock not far from us where she was living out her remaining days. Gramma approached her and asked her how she would like to leave a legacy with the funds she now had. Auntie Blanche indicated that she would like to help provide a studio in Kinshasa for Christian music and that she would like to help her ministry back in the Philippine Islands. Not long after that conversation Auntie passed away, but she had willed $35,000 to the establishment of a Christian recording studio in Kinshasa. Some other private donors gave $10,000 and we had enough to purchase and send all the equipment to Kinshasa. God was indeed opening doors that we had never thought of, nor could have. The Sango Malamu Studio in Kinshasa would become a reality and God was making it happen.

I reached out to Willys and Thelma Braun, former CMA missionaries who were building a new campus at that time with their ministry called Evangelism Resources, to see if they could provide studio space on the ER campus. Willys and Thelma, the founding couple and CEOs of this organization, had been building this wonderful campus for a school of evangelism—a training center for evangelists. To my delight and surprise Willys already had the desire to have a recording studio and had already committed a large room on the main floor of one of his two story buildings just for that purpose. The room was 40 feet by 40 feet, plus it had a good-sized room for a control room and sound booth. There would be plenty of room for a great recording studio. I proposed a plan to Willys. I said, "Willys, you have the room and I have the recording equipment and the ability to set it up and run it. Why don't we work together? I won't charge you for any recordings and you won't charge me for the room." He agreed and that worked out well for many years.

The Studio Setup

Our goal in Kinshasa was to get our studio up and running as quickly as possible, to record as many Christian groups as we could and to flood the market with Christian cassettes—music which would give praise and honor to our Lord. I felt the Lord had given us a mandate to do this in two years. The Bible Society had done a great job of importing Bibles in all four major languages of Zaire and one could buy a Bible at any book store or even at a news stand on the street. Our aim was to make available, to the whole city of Kinshasa, Christian music on cassette just as Bibles were available. We felt a

Studios Sango Malamu's control room for their sound recording ministry with the sound engineers and Sango Malamu 2, in c.1993

God given desire to make Christian cassettes just as available in all four languages as well and to do it in two years. Why in 2 years, I wasn't sure, but that was the innate desire and mandate I felt I had from the Lord.

Willys Braun was also a visionary and could see how we both could benefit from this agreement and correspondingly give progress to the gospel. We signed a non-profit working agreement together and so began our joint ministry. However, when we arrived in Kinshasa his studio was still under construction. So, we set up in our front room. We had just rented a spacious house which had a very large front room, from a military general. Poor Gramma! For 8 weeks (or more) we hosted all manner of artists coming into our front room to record and make music such as we had not yet heard! There were some excellent groups, but others were not so good! It didn't matter, all who came to record were given equal opportunity. If they were a Christian group and they could pay the small recording fee, they could record.

The very first day, after we were provisionally all set up in our house, using the dining room as a "control room" and the front room as the "recording theater", I began to think, "What if nobody comes to record?" I had never thought of that before, but it could be a reality! Was it possible that we had raised funds for all this equipment and brought all of it over to Kinshasa just to be a failure! Immediately I brushed those thoughts from my mind, knowing that God provided the personnel, the place for the studio and all the equipment in miraculous ways. It just couldn't be a failure!

The news of the studio in our home spread by word of mouth so quickly that by the time we finally moved into our new studios that Willys had so aptly prepared we were on the go almost 24/7. We didn't know exactly when we could move in, but a thunderstorm gave us the answer. A little over two months after we had started up there was a terrific thunder and lightning storm one evening. We had unplugged all the equipment in case of electrical surges which often occurred at such times and were in bed when we heard an enormously loud explosion. It was as if someone had dropped a bomb in the neighbor's yard behind us. Well, I wasn't far wrong in my guess as the lighting had hit a power station just behind our yard and the whole thing exploded taking out the power of our whole segment of the city. We had no electricity for two solid weeks.

The Move

During this time, I told the guys that the Lord had provided a break for us, so we might as well move, even though the other building wasn't yet quite finished. Now was the time. Big Rod had helped us set up perfectly in our house, but now I was the only operator and "technician" to set up everything in the new studio. Rod was a good teacher. It took us a week to move and set up everything in the new place and another week making sound proof walls in the control room, putting channels for cables in the cement floor, putting the right covering on them and then carpet over that. Creating a bass blead room off to one side and creating a separate sound proof isolation booth off to the side of the main control room had to be done as well. Getting the air conditioning in and setting up all the equipment with the right fuse capacity, the right phases of electricity and the right amount of circuit breakers in case of brown outs or spikes in the electricity was also a priority. With the humidity in Kinshasa, the equipment needed air AC, or it wouldn't last. There were no windows, no air ventilation in the entire studio so AC units needed to be installed for the control room as well as the equipment room and the recording theatre. Thank the Lord there was still pretty good electricity in those days in Kinshasa.

We asked the workers to put the high ceiling on a slight incline for better diffusion of sound and they tried. But their valiant efforts only made the ceiling perfectly level! I guess I should have just kept silent and all would have worked out OK. However, with what carpeting I could find and with other sound proofing materials I could scare up in the city, we made the large recording theater as good a recording area as possible. We even had a large double pane glass window which was slanted on both sides to give us good sound proofing and sound diffusion between the control room and the recording theater. It was shaping up to be one of the best studios in Kinshasa. We were "simple" people with not a lot of technical savvy, but God used us to build this ministry and He blessed it.[63] In His time He also brought the right people along to help us "get the job done."

---

[63]*This reminds me again of the scripture found in 1Corinthians 1:26-28(NIV):* <u>The Foolish to Shame the Wise</u>*...[26]For consider your calling, brethren, that there were not many wise according to the flesh, not many mighty, not many noble; [27]but God has chosen the foolish things of the world to shame the wise, and God has chosen the weak things of the world to shame the things which are strong, [28]and the base things of the world and the despised God has chosen, the things that are not, so that He may nullify the things that are,...*

After we got underway with the first Christian professional Protestant recording studio in Kinshasa (perhaps in all of the Congo), set up on the campus of the ER Center of Evangelism, the groups just kept on coming. The amazing thing, to me at least, was the fact that although the Sango Malamu Trio was the first Christian band of its kind in the Congo, other groups really got the vision.

After ten years of Sango Malamu ministry, there were so many new Christian groups wanting to record that we needed two shifts—one during the day and another at night to accommodate them all. For the next 5 years or so we would be recording over a hundred albums a year (103 to 105).

Studios Sango Malamu's control room for their sound recording ministry with sound engineer Joel Bumba and Jim in c.1994

One of the numerous recording artists who frequented our studios

Chapter Twenty–Three: Planting a New Church

Meeting with the African Director

During our two-year home assignment, as mentioned earlier, I was able to bring the Trio back for one more big tour across Canada. The vision of bringing the Congolese and their music to Canada was being fulfilled. We travelled to all the major cities and churches of the CMA in Canada sharing what missions had accomplished in the Congo. We thanked the people for sending their sons and daughters and their finances for building the body of Christ in the Congo. And we led them in worship, Congolese style! It was an exciting time.

During our travels, we were invited to the Canadian Assembly in Saskatoon—one of the first that CMA in Canada had organized. However, I was still under the leadership of David Kennedy, then the African director for the CMA in the USA. The complete transition had not yet happened. CMA in Canada was just fleshing out its independence.

David called me in for an interview and the first serious question he asked me as we were looking at future ministry was, "Jim, what do you want to do?" By this time, I knew that God was opening doors for the planting of a professional recording studio, but I also knew that the CMA was all about planting churches, not studios! My answer was simple and clear, or so I thought, "Well, Dave, what I want to do, I can't do with the Alliance."

To my surprise, he said, "Try me!"

Well, I poured out my heart for the vision of wanting to start a new ministry, a new non-profit organization, in Kinshasa, which would record Christian artists and make Christian music and cassettes as available as Bibles were available in Kinshasa. My goal was to flood the music market in Kinshasa, and why not all the Congo, with praise and worship music for the honor and glory of our King, Jesus.

I explained the details of the vision and added that I wasn't asking any CMA church for funding on this. This project was to be completely autonomous, a ministry completely independent of the CMA in Canada and the USA and the CMA in the Congo.

After my rather lengthy explanation he simply said, "I think we can do this."

I replied, "You must realize, David, that this ministry cannot be under the CMA in Canada, the USA or the Congo. This must be an independent ministry. If not, it won't succeed." I couldn't have any church leader trying to call the shots on this. I felt that I needed to set it up as a separate non-profit organization in the Congo for ministry to the Congo.

He replied, "I understand. I think we can do this. We will give you the liberty of starting this ministry, if you give us half your time to plant a new church, in a new neighborhood in the city of Kinshasa."

I thought I would have to leave the CMA and go out on my own, but here was the answer. I couldn't believe it. I responded with, "Are you serious? Are you sure?"

I repeated what I said earlier, just in case he didn't catch it, "This organization that I envision starting cannot be under the CMA in Canada, the USA nor the CMA in the Congo. This organization must be a separate entity, all on its own, and cannot be run by anyone else but the founder, which would be me. If other people are in charge, it will die. If any CMA national church wants to direct this organization, it will die."

I took a deep breath and asked him again, "Are you sure you are OK with this?"

He was quite sure and so the ministry of planting the recording studio SSM and the ministry of planting the Congolese CMA church at Cité Mama Mobutu began as soon as we hit the pavement of the airport in Kinshasa.

I was so pumped; jet lag wasn't even a factor. I was out immediately looking for transportation and a house. As I was doing this, I was approached by my colleague Bill Finnemore, who also had a burden to plant a church in that new neighborhood and we hooked up. The area for the founding of this new church was a unique large hill with a thousand or more newly built houses on all sides which only the middle class could afford. That meant that these people were mainly French speakers and they also had a good sense of decorum and order. They may have been born in the village, but they had good paying jobs and were well-educated people. The hundreds of lots and houses were not cheap, but were being bought up as quickly as the construction was completed by a government sponsored European construction company.

The New Church at Cité Mama Mobutu

Early in 1990, after some research, we were sure that this neighborhood was the right site for the new church and we scouted around for a place to begin. We found the greatest place to start. The land scape was such that the whole neighborhood was built in terraces on a large sloping hill on top of which was a beautifully built small  hotel, with restaurant, swimming pool and conference room (with a stage) that would comfortably hold up to 100 people. We saw this room as a wonderful place to start the church. It had good surroundings, was air-conditioned, had good seats (about 80 upholstered steel stacking chairs) and was available on Sunday mornings. We asked to rent the place for four evenings leading to the first Sunday and asked to rent it every Sunday morning, all morning for the next two years. We signed a contract, put some money upfront that the CMA had sent for just such a purpose and began visiting all the houses, as many as possible, advertising the showing of the Jesus film, starting in a week, from Wednesday to Saturday.

I called all the former Sango Malamu supporters and prayer partners to one spot, and shared our vision with them and asked if they would want to be part of this blitz of evangelism. They did. We then went out in pairs with tracts and a brochure we had printed up announcing the showing of the Jesus film and that we would be starting a new protestant church in the area (the only one among the thousands of homes in this new neighborhood). There was a Catholic church somewhere there already, but no other church at all. The anticipation of this neighborhood was that soon there would be 10,000 people residing there, in the first stage of this project. From Sunday to Wednesday we distributed tracts and invitations in the afternoon and evening and on Wednesday we started showing the film, in the conference room of the hotel. Each night we would sing a little, show one reel of the film (about one hour in length), then we would have an evangelist speak (those who were affiliated with the Sango Malamu Ministry before we had left in 1987). Our own evangelist Dede

Kikavuanga Dongo was among the speakers. There was always an invitation to accept Jesus after the reel and the preaching.

We did this for four nights and by the time Saturday night came, the place was bursting with people—so much so that we had to open all the windows and doors and side patio doors to allow the people from outside to watch. Many came to receive Jesus into their lives and then on Saturday evening we announced that there was going to be a church service at 10 am the next day, Sunday, for all who had just received Jesus into their lives that week and for anyone else who would care to join us.

Not everyone who prayed came the first Sunday to church, but we had about 70 to 80 people. I was surprised! Some of our smaller neighborhood churches that had been meeting for years only had that amount of people. That Sunday morning, I knew that how we would "do" church would set a precedent for how we would continue to conduct our worship services. Early that morning I asked the Lord what He wanted us to do (the same as I did Saturday night when I got home and knew there would be a church service to prepare for).

We had asked a good speaker, a former magistrate and one who knew French very well (was trained in theology in France), Pastor Babaka, and I had asked brother Dede to moderate and conduct the service. I also asked all the musicians from the new Studio Sango Malamu to come and help lead worship. We would practice a bit Saturday afternoon and then it would be one of the musician/singers that would lead our worship, but all would come and play: two guitars, bass, two keyboards, one with a rhythm section.

When I asked the Lord what kind of format he wanted and what we should do that first Sunday morning, I got just three things. I believe He said, "I want you to worship Me, to hear from Me (I took that to be good preaching) and to respond to Me."

Entrance to Cité Mama Mobutu

Okay... I understood the worship part. And I well understood the preaching part for that is why we asked pastor Babaka if he would be our preaching pastor (he had said yes after a little persuasion). But I wasn't too sure about the "respond to me" part, but I agreed! Consequently, after the preaching we always had an open "altar" for people to come and pray and respond to what they had just heard through the worship and preaching. We also opened it up for testimonies and prayer requests for a short time in the very beginning. But as the congregation grew it was getting harder and harder to control that part.

We met there every Sunday for the next year or so and the Lord blessed. We worshipped, we heard from God through His servant and then we responded to what He was saying to us. Our service would last perhaps 2 to 2 1/2 hours—40 to 45 minutes of worship and prayer, 40 to 45 minutes of preaching and up to 40 minutes of response time (offering was given on the way out the doors). We had a wonderful time. The advantage of this start up is that Studio Sango Malamu had the musicians, the instruments, and the sound system, which we brought every Sunday. That was a real plus.

We also had two experienced pastor/evangelists who gave of their time. All was volunteer work at the very beginning, but as money was coming in we would pay the preachers, but never the musicians. I guess they saw it as their privilege and duty for this was part of the ministry of SSM. It might have even been understood that if they didn't come they no longer worked at SSM. It was never put that way, but looking back on it now it may have been understood that way. All who participated in the beginning were only part time and voluntary and most all had their own regular jobs to go to during the week.

Bill Finnemore was busy with finding land, procuring it and getting a building program going for what we envisioned to be a large church. We had plans for a church which could accommodate 1000 or more people. Many miracles took place during this ministry which could even fill another book. I stayed on as a pastor, being the founding pastor, for many years and then when Pastor Mabiala Kenzo came to be our pastor (another miracle) it was time for me to resign and leave it completely in the very capable hands of the Congolese.

By this time (c.1995) SSM had become Studios Sango Malamu (with three or four different studios for different projects). We were also running our own radio station, video studios, post production studio, distributing house, music academy, and worship seminar ministry--seminars were being held around the city and in the bas-Congo area. So, I gently asked if I could be released from the pastoral staff of the church, which now had at least three full time pastors. The Finnemores never returned to the Congo after the pillaging and looting of 1991, the church building was already well constructed.

After several years, the church moved from the hotel to the lot of Pastor Babaka, who by this time had become the full-time pastor. We made too much noise for those who wanted to sleep in at the hotel on Sunday mornings and we were bursting at the seams, so we moved to a make shift tent covering in the open yard of the pastor. We lost some folks, but the new church building was not yet finished to the point where we could meet. When we came back in 1992 the church was almost ready to move into their new building. It soon became the permanent home of the CEAZ church at Cité Mama Mobutu. When all the missionaries left, the church still carried on. It didn't take long for the original worship team to develop, add members and lead with their own style of music and arrangements

After a couple of years, the church construction was finished to the point where we could now worship inside the building, even though construction was still carrying on. Pastor Babaka, after several years of great ministry, felt that he was being stretched too far (he was also the director of another ministry in the city) and submitted his resignation as lead pastor. I knew we needed a very good communicator, an educated man and one anointed by the Holy Spirit to fill his position or the church would cease to grow. Pastor Dede was still there, but couldn't handle the ministry on his own. It was now too big and he wasn't yet ordained, which means a lot in the Congolese culture.

I prayed about what we should do and felt I could do what missionaries are not supposed to do. I went to the president of the CMA in the Congo (the CEAC) and asked for the pastor I thought was the right one for the job—a young man by the name of Mabiala Kenzo. It was audacious of me, I know, but felt so strongly about getting the right man that I made this request at the risk of being branded once again a maverick! But I was ready to bear the brunt of storm that may arise within the CEAZ for such a move.

I thank God for wise President Kuvuna, who listened intently to my request in a private audience. He never revealed what we talked about, but did understand the importance of a good man at the Cité Mama Mobutu Alliance Church. It was only a few months later that Rev. Mabiala Kenzo was sent by the pastoral placement committee to Kinshasa and our newly established church. What an answer to prayer!

Under his ministry and the college of pastors, the church at Cité Mama Mobutu reached its zenith with almost 1000 parishioners meeting every Sunday and in many other church related meetings of prayer and teaching throughout the week.

It wasn't long before Pastor Mabiala Kenzo called Charles Yangu to be his associate. Charles, who was then living with us with us, together with Runo Moyo and Camille Ntoto, often led in worship and helped us understand the meaning and purpose of worship. It was only after Charles was hired on as a full-time pastor that I began to diminish my pastoral responsibilities at the church. SSM was taking increasingly more of my time and more full-time pastors were being ⌐ to the college which now seemed to indicate that my work there ₃ done. I submitted my resignation with the understanding that I ₌uld from time to time still do some worship seminars, but overall, I ₒuld not attend the pastoral meetings or be involved in the ongoing ₗeadership of the church.

Under the profound teaching of Pastor Mabiala the church began to grow exponentially. It is still going strong today with both Lingala and French services. When I went back in December of 2015, I was asked to preach there. To my amazement the church was celebrating their 25th anniversary. I was really taken aback when they honored me as their founding pastor. What an experience! That event was an exciting occasion for me, perhaps God ordained.

Entertaining Angels Unawares

It was under the unique style of preaching of our evangelist Pastor Dede Kikavuanga Dongo that this whole Idea of opening our home to strangers really began. The Bible does say very explicitly that we should show hospitality.[64] And in another passage the writer to the Hebrews gives very explicit instructions as we see here in the Amplified New Testament

(Hebrews 13:1-2)

Let love for your fellow believers continue and be a fixed practice with you [never let it fail]. ***2 Do not forget or neglect or refuse to extend hospitality to strangers** [in the brotherhood—being friendly,*

---

[64] *8Above all, love one another deeply, because love covers over a multitude of sins. **9Show hospitality to one another without complaining.** 10As good stewards of the manifold grace of God, each of you should use whatever gift he has received to serve one another. I Peter 4:8-10*

cordial, and gracious, sharing the comforts of your home and doing your part generously], for through **it some have entertained angels without knowing it.**

This was the text of Pastor Dede's message and God used it to really change my heart.

Just before this message Gramma came to me one day, after our children were no longer with us in the Congo, and said, "I think we should open our home to Congolese to come and have a place of retreat or a place to stay if they really need one."

"What?!" I almost shouted, taken completely by surprise. "Why would we want to do that? When I come home I want to be able to strip down and sit around with just a pair of shorts on, drink a coke and cool off (we had no air conditioning in the place). I'm with people all day, every day at the studio or at the Cité Mama Mobutu church and when I come home I need to relax, not be dressed and have to face people again." (If you haven't guessed by now, tests say that I am an introvert and lose energy when I am with people.)

I continued with, "Absolutely not! It ain't gunna happen!"

Gramma braved the storm and gently replied, "Well, I just think the Lord is speaking to me to do that. We have two extra rooms now that our kids are gone. Many Congolese have no place to go to be alone, to have a personal retreat. I think He is saying that we should open our home to them, to come a stay for a brief time."

"Do you know what you are saying?" I retorted. "Nobody else does this and I don't like it. How do we know who they might be or how long they might stay? We could take in some thieves and be robbed blind!" Actually, that had already happened without us opening our home to "strangers"! (But that is another story which I will have to tell you another time.)

"Well," she said. "Just think about it and talk to the Lord about it."

I didn't need to talk to the Lord about it for I knew (or at least I thought I knew) the consequences of all of this and for me, there was "no way".

It wasn't long after this "discussion" that we went to church and heard Pastor Dede give his message on "Entertaining Angels Unawares". It was a powerful message and one that may not have ever been given again to a Congolese congregation for the Congolese are the most hospitable people you can find anywhere. Maybe it was just for this white boy! I heard what the Lord was saying. I knew He was speaking to me through this message, but I didn't like it.

On the way home, Gramma said to me in kind of a soft and gentle manner, "Did the Lord say anything to you this morning through pastor Dede's message?"

I immediately replied, "Yes He did, …and I don't need to hear it again from you!"

We laugh at that statement now, but I was definitely sensing God speaking to me about this matter of opening our home, but at that moment I didn't want to discuss it any further. Being under this "conviction" I went to a men's retreat that was put on by the IPCK (International Protestant Church of Kinshasa) men. It was a two-day retreat at a large church not far from our place. There again, the Lord spoke to me about this matter as the main speaker of the retreat was challenging us to give up to God what things we held most closely for ourselves.

I came home at the end of the retreat with the resolve that I would in fact say something to Gramma about this. When we had time to chat, I said, "OK! If you find someone or a small group of people who really need a place to stay for a few days of quiet retreat, go ahead and open our home to them. I may be kicking and screaming about it, but don't pay attention to me as I know that the Lord is speaking to me about this and I think you are right in wanting to serve His people this way."

Not a few days later, I came home to find three young adult ladies, university age, in my home. I panicked! What are they doing here? What are we going to feed them? Too many questions were coming to mind. But Gramma soon calmed my fears by saying that they just wanted a place to spend time in fasting and prayer. All they needed to have was one room and to use the guest bathroom and shower. They would only be with us a couple of days.

Well, it happened that while I was in my bathroom, next to their room, that I overheard, in muffled tones, their prayer time. As I listened more intently I could hear them praying for the "white people" who had opened their home to them for this prayer retreat. By now they were not praying in quiet tones, but in loud voices praising God for this opportunity and then calling down blessing on us in so many ways that I was literally stunned. Immediately I was grateful that I had said yes to Gramma, and to God, and then thought, "If this is what is going to happen, we cannot afford to NOT do this! We need God's blessing and they are interceding on our behalf for it!"

From that moment on, our home became an unofficial guest home for the homeless, the sick in need of recovery, for business men and missionaries, black and white, pastors and presidents—not of the country, but of denominations and mission organizations, both in the country and from outside the country. At one point, while I was away, Gramma entertained and fed some 30 plus refugees who landed on our doorstep from Congo Brazzaville when they had to literally flee for their lives.[65]

This "open door" policy was not exactly according to mission regulations, but it wasn't exactly contrary to good missionary policy either, so we continued on with this "opening our home to strangers" throughout our stay in the Congo—and it carries on even until today. We received some criticism from both the missionaries and the Congolese leaders, but in the end, they came around—seeing what a great blessing it was to us and the people who stayed with us. Some were (and even now are) strangers, others were ones we knew about and some whom we knew personally—to a greater or lesser degree. Some were sick and in need of a quiet place to endure their sickness or a place to recuperate for a time. Some stayed for only a night, others stayed much longer. Charles stayed for just over three years.

We also made a sleeping room in a series of small rooms in a long lean-to off the garage. This was mainly used by one of our sound engineers at Studios SM. We also cleared a room in the back of the house off the back veranda which had a separate door. This was used as storage, but at one point we cleared it completely, sanitized it and use it as a hospital room which our neighbor, an excellent Congolese doctor, could use it from time to time to help patients recover from serious illnesses. The Azitas were a family who lived next door, but whose kids were almost always on our doorstep or in our home. Doctor

---

[65] In 1997 we had to flee to Congo Brazzaville, across the river, as Kabila and his rag-a-muffin army marched into Kinshasa. After peace was assured I flew in to Kinshasa with Gramma and then, a few days later I flew out with MAF to have a conference with the church president and leaders of the CMA in the Lower Congo region (then known as Bas-Zaire). While I was there in Boma, Congo-Brazzaville rebelled. There was a terrible uprising between tribal factions using automatic light and heavy artillery against each side. It was so bad that all expatriates, fearing for their lives, had to flee Brazzaville to the now peaceful Kinshasa. So, it was that some of our own missionaries and other expatriates ended on our doorstep, the only CMA missionaries still residing in Kinshasa after the rebel Kabila had taken over the city and the country.

Azita was travelling a lot for the government and Mama Azita was also working as a head nurse at the Kitambu hospital. It was after school and on weekends that the three or four younger children were often over just having fun with us as surrogate parents.

The hospital room was unofficial and was used once as an operating room for a serious operation. Although Doctor Azita was very accomplished (educated in France and conscripted by President Mobutu himself to be his personal doctor), sometimes operations can go awry. That happened this one time and the doctor almost lost his patient. We prayed hard, the bleeding was finally stopped, and the patient pulled through, but I said to Gramma (whose idea all of this was) that we could not afford to do this any longer. If that person had died while in our unofficial care, we could have been in deep… trouble! It never happened again.

We also opened our home to street kids who had nowhere to go or nothing to do during the day. Some had distant relatives with whom they could stay overnight, but most of them were completely orphaned. We tried to clean them up, Charles had Bible teaching sessions with them, we listened to their plight and tried to help them go to school, but as we weren't set up as an orphanage or a home for street kids, many of them did not follow through on their commitment to change. Some went to school, but only for a short time. One boy faked it for three or four years, until his senior year in high school and one day never showed his face again. That's when we found out, doing some research, that he also had not followed through on his commitment to have a good education. We had limited funds, but what we could afford we helped them. It certainly was an outreach and they certainly heard the Good News. We leave the results with the Lord!

The Studio staff came for cool water, cookies or a coke. They came for meetings, prayer and parties and sometimes for all nights of prayer and fasting. The door was revolving, but never once did we miss a thing. My fears of thievery were totally unfounded. If ever we had too many people or I needed a break, or a rest, I would simply go to my bedroom, shut the door and read or just sit in the easy chair and watch a little TV (in the latter years we did have a TV and could get one or two stations with a make shift antenna). I've learned many times over that if God opens the door for you to do what He has planned for you, he will protect what is His and take good care of you as you walk on through.

Chapter Twenty–Four: The "Pillage"

After SSM had been up and running for two years and we had achieved our goal of making Christian cassettes as available to the public as Bibles were available, we were notified by the CB radio, which squealed and crackled in our front room, that there was trouble in the city. In 1989, when we came back to establish the Sango Malamu Studio, we had come back with two of our children. Loralee was left at Canadian Bible College, Jon-Marc had flown on his own to Bouake, Ivory Coast, to finish his High School at ICA. And Rod came back with us to Kinshasa to help in setting up the studio. Even though he had just graduated from high school, he was quite proficient on the computer and was great at lettering and designing. His work was soon to be cut out for him.

In 1991 we had seen J-M graduate from Ivory Coast Academy and had flown back to Kinshasa with him where his brother was waiting to see him before he travelled back to Canada. All CMA missionary kids received one free round trip back to where they grew up to see that country for the last time, that is if they didn't end up there as missionaries themselves. Rod wanted to come back right away with us, so that was his trip back. Loralee was coming back that summer to be with us as Rod was already there and J-M had just come home from graduating at ICA. It was a perfect setup. All three of our kids would be home together, probably for the last time and we would take our vacation together at the beach in Muanda, at the CMA Mission House (at a little place called Vista).

Just before Loralee came home Gramma started having serious pains in her neck and down her arm. I took her to a French vertebrae specialist who was practicing in Kinshasa only to find out that she had a serious pinched nerve problem and needed to have spinal cord surgery as soon as possible or she would soon lose all feeling and mobility in her left arm. This was serious stuff and I immediately requested prayer for her from our missionaries and other friends in the IPCK fellowship. Apparently, when Gramma was in Junior High school she injured her neck by doing too many forward rolls on the gym hardwood floor. She was a good gymnast and became the junior women's champion for all British Columbia, but now she paid a dear price. I agonized in prayer over this, not only for her physical healing but also for the fact that if she had to leave she would miss being with our children for this summer vacation time—a last fling as it were together before they all flew the nest, to most probably be apart for the rest of our lives. This was NOT a good thing. I waited for His answer. He said, "Ask Me for anything in my Name and I will give it to you!" I was asking, confessing, and searching my heart for any obstacle that might hinder His working in our lives. But there was no healing. He said He would give us "anything we would ask for" if we would abide in Him. I was "abiding" but still no answer.

Meanwhile we were having to make arrangements to fly Gramma home. She was in serious pain and was already finding it difficult to use her left arm. It seemed that God was opening the doors for her to leave, in a somewhat miraculous way, but He did not bring about her healing—at least not at this time. She did fly to Canada where she was met by her sister and husband, Auntie Ruth and Uncle Norm Wylie (our double wedding partners). By miracle after miracle Gramma was given an operation on her neck to rectify the pinched nerve and the entire problem of pain and immobility within a two-week period. Unheard of, unthinkable, yet it happened.

This whole story is for Gramma herself to tell, but later on when she arrived to convalesce in B.C., for her neck was still very stiff, Uncle Gary prayed for her for total movement and healing. Gramma was instantly healed. She had full movement from that day until now. The specialist who performed the operation said that it would last her for about ten years. That was twenty-six years ago!

It was a tough time for us all who were left in Kinshasa. However, we did go on our vacation without her and shared the mission house with our colleagues, Stan and Connie Hotalen and family. We had a wonderful time there, but we surely missed Mom (Gramma). While we were there, towards the end of our time at the beach, Johnathan, Hotalen's little boy only 18 months old, suffered from a severe and unknown illness. One minute he was saying good night to us all and about an hour later I was driving him as fast as I could to an intensive care nurse who we knew, who was vacationing at the Gulf Oil compound in Muanda. I had never driven so fast over those hazardous roads, but we didn't make it there in time and he passed away in his daddy's arms. This was the saddest experience I ever had to go through.

After a long time of trying to revive the little boy, a doctor was called in and he pronounced the sweet little one dead. I carried him into a vacant house where we put the air conditioning up to full blast and in the morning, I was able to pick him up and put him in a small coffin that had already been purchased from a local coffin maker. The Hotalen's had connected with MAF and they were on their way to pick up the family and fly them back to Kinshasa where they would have the funeral and burial.

That summer was getting more difficult all the time. We tried to make it back for the funeral, driving our car and Stan's, but we couldn't get there fast enough. It was a long trip by vehicle and due to the rough roads, we had to take our time. Rod was driving Stan's jeep and happened to slip it onto its side in a mud hole, but thanks to local men it was quickly erected, and he and J-M were on his way home again. But there were a few dents in Stan's sleek blue jeep. No, it surely wasn't the best summer vacation we had ever had!

We made it home in time to take in a memorial service for Johnathan a few days later and join the grieving process with Stan and Connie. Loralee and I sang "Faithful One". It was a bit difficult to get through, but we made it through the tears without choking up.

Loralee and Rod flew home at separate times according to their tickets which they had secured on their own and Jon-Marc stayed with us until September. He would be leaving to spend a week or so with Auntie Ruth and Uncle Norm, see some good ICA friends just south of the border and then go to CBC for the fall registration. Gramma was now home, and J-M had just left a few weeks earlier when I heard the Citizen Band radio squeaking out, "Sky 5, sky 5, sky 5!" (Our CB code name.)

The Evacuation

I was at home with Gramma and Judy, a young visitor (from Canada) when the message came. Gramma was getting ready to be on her way to the Bible School where she taught every Monday. She drove with Judy and her Zairian friend, Mama Deborah, as well as a male student who was going to ride in the back of the pick-up as all their books and teaching aids were also going to be on the front seat with the three ladies. Gramma was the chauffeur.

We all prayed as we heard the message, but we had heard this before and generally on the ring road around the city there would be no problem. We had no indication from the Lord that they shouldn't go, but we also didn't know the severity of the problem. So, Gramma and the passengers decided to leave around 7:30 in the morning to get to the Bible School in time to teach their classes. Kikimi was in the suburbs about an hour's drive from our home, on the other side of the city.

As I wasn't needed at the Studio, I stayed at home to listen to the CB to see if there would be anymore chatter about the conditions in the city. Apparently, the army savagely mutinied because there was no money in the military treasury to pay them (the paymaster general seemed to have taken it all for himself and told the military leaders to go out and get their own pay). All military in Kinshasa rebelled and began looting and thieving, shooting anyone in their way and invading private houses as well as all the stores and factories. There were frequent updates, but by 10:00 a.m. I was hearing that we all needed to go to a central area for protection or we could be stripped, beaten, if not shot and royally ripped off. I had no idea now where Gramma was, but got hold of the other missionaries in the area on the CB and told them I was coming in my car to pick them up. They would need to bring a bag of things and follow me in their own cars. We would all drive together in a tight cavalcade.

We were in a grouping of three or four cars and drove as fast as we dare to the big Gulf Oil center—a large compound not far from where we lived (several kilometers) which was well guarded and well encased in high walls with razor wire on top. It was a fortified area in the middle of a section of the city which was very highly populated. There were many groups of people giving us the victory sign on the way, so we gave it right back to them, to make it known we were not against anyone—at least until we reached the compound. Whites seemed to be the target. Being white was synonymous with being wealthy. Soldiers with guns and rifles were everywhere shooting at random, often in the air just to intimidate people. Yet we found out later that there was indeed a lot of looting, pillaging, and raping going on. Kinshasa quickly became a very ugly scene.

We understood that other "whites", mainly Americans had already begun to gather at the Gulf compound. As we approached the heavy gates I tooted the horn as a sign that we were there for we knew that they were expecting us, but no one was quick to open the gates. We laid on the horns and this time someone looked through a sliding peep hole in the gate. When they saw that we were all white they finally opened up and ushered us in. "So, what was the hesitation," I asked. They told us this story…

A large group of soldiers had just banged on the gate and ordered them to open up. They had guns and were going to come in and rampage the compound. What the soldiers didn't know was that there were two former special ops guys on the compound, working now for the oil company--one was a former US marine and the other was a former soldier with the Belgian elite forces. The Marine had a 12-gauge double barrel shot gun in hand and the other had his automatic pistol. When the US Marine and the Belgian walked out with the shot gun and pistol in hand, the soldiers, a bit surprised, demanded that they open the gates and let them in or they would shoot them both. Their reply was that if that was the way they wanted it they would take 10 guys or more with them. They made sure the looting soldiers knew that they weren't bluffing! When the group saw that these two guys were serious, the picture changed drastically. The soldiers decided to move on. No Zairian soldier wanted to pay the price of death so that the others could get the loot.

No wonder they were hesitant in opening the big doors! We came there not more than five minutes after the rebel soldiers had been dispersed. We were thanking God we had not bumped into them. However, the Belgian still had his gun in hand and asked me if I would drive him to his home a few kilometers away. His dad was there, visiting him from Belgium and he really wanted to check and see if his household and everything at his place was still intact. I agreed to drive him there while he sat in the passenger seat with arm and gun displayed out the window. We found out that many civilians, generally good people of the neighborhood, were now getting into the military act, stealing all kinds of materials from the houses and yards of the people who had fled, generally expatriates. I even saw a man with a big air conditioner on his head, but when he saw us with the gun out the window, he ditched the AC and scrambled up over a wall and was gone. We met others and some military, but when they saw the Belgium in fatigues and his gun ready for action, they just looked and we passed by without incident. His dad and home were safe. They had not been disturbed. His whole compound had not been disturbed so we left to join the others at the Gulf property.

When we got back to the Gulf compound, some ten acres of beautiful houses and lawns with many vehicles, stock piles of materials and workshops, we began hearing stories of atrocities that the soldiers were committing as they were shooting up neighborhoods and menacing the people, including raping the women and young girls. The military was on a rampage and there was no stopping them. They were not just tearing up the city, looting and destroying big and small businesses alike, but they were also going into all the expatriate's homes pillaging and destroying them as well. One missionary was sitting at his desk when a bullet came through his roof and landed right on his desk in front of him. That is when he decided he should leave.

Meanwhile, Gramma had her own issues to deal with as she was on the road and had personally been confronted by the military. I had no idea what was happening with her. I thought that she was doing well, that she had escaped the city and was on the outskirts in that little suburban village called Kikimi, where the Bible School was located. Little did I know!

There were no phones like there are today. Now-a-days in the Congo it seems everyone has a phone, including high school students. At that time, we had no way of communicating to each other from where she was. All embassy reports were saying that the city was completely overrun by the military, all the embassies were on lockdown. There was no way to know if Dawn and our visitor, Judy, and Mama Deborah were okay. In the compound, all the men slept together in two separate houses as did all the women and children (there were a few empty houses which we could take over). It wasn't until the next day that I heard via the US embassy that two Canadian ladies and a Zairian woman had spent the night at the Israeli Ambassador's house and had walked over to the American Ambassador's residence that morning. They would be transferred to the Golf compound by American Marines as soon as they felt that the way would be clear. I was greatly relieved to hear this and knew that it must be Gramma and Judy, but was really anxious to see her and hear her story. And, where was our Peugeot pickup? To be sure, Gramma had a story to tell.

Gramma came the next day in the afternoon and we had a joyous reunion. I then asked about the pickup… and her story began.

In Gramma's Own Words

"Judy Oberg, my sister Joy's friend who was involved in the leadership of the children's ministry at the Langley Vineyard, arrived on our doorstep. She didn't even have our address or directions from the airport to our house, but within 3 hrs. by word of mouth, found us. After a day to combat jet lag, she headed down our dusty gravel road for a walk. By the time she came back, she had used the bit of French

she had learned in high school and had a whole entourage of kids following her.

"The next day was Monday, which was my day to drive out to the Bible Institute to teach for four hrs. I usually brought fish, beans and rice to help feed the students, but for some reason I had thought I would try to buy the food at a place that was much closer to the Bible Institute. From Kinshasa, over the less than smooth roads to Kikimi, it was about an hour's drive—around the edge of the city and into the countryside. We had heard some talk that morning over the CB radio that there may be some trouble brewing, but that was nothing new. Judy felt, when she asked the Lord about going, that He had said, 'You can go, and I'll be with you.' So, Mama Deborah, my Congolese friend who also taught at the B.I and a young man (student) who also needed a ride, together with Judy and I, set off for Kikimi. As I drove along the ring road, I turned a corner and was confronted by a whole platoon of solders, blocking the road. I had to stop or I would have run over several of them. The leaders came to the window and apologized for needing to commandeer my vehicle. Immediately many soldiers piled into the back of the pickup. So many jumped in the back that I knew I needed to drive very carefully or I would be fish-tailing it down the street. The leader signalled for me to take them to the smaller national airport at Ndolo, near the center of town. When the soldiers dismounted, another group of soldiers stopped me and asked if I would please take them to the center of the city. I politely refused and told them that I had already taken these other soldiers very much out of my way and that I was a bit late for teaching my classes at the Bible Institute.

"As I proceeded on my way, now in the industrial part of the city on the route Poids Lourds, I saw another line of soldiers who had taken up their position across the road. Again, I had to stop, but I could see that this group was different! I could even see from afar that there was darkness on them. As soon as I stopped, hands came through the windows. We didn't have air condition in the vehicle, so the windows were wide open. They grabbed at my ear rings, watch, ring and necklace. Judy wore a small pouch around her middle and that was grabbed. Their eyes told me, 'the lights are on, but nobody is home.' I just knew that this story would not have a good ending if I sat there and did nothing.

I remember hearing some other missionary stories, so I spoke out the window in a loud voice, 'In the Name of Jesus Christ, I command you to be calm.' I spoke in English because I know that spirits are multilingual. The soldiers immediately dropped their hands, together with their guns, and they just became ordinary, Lingala speaking soldiers. One of them came around and opened the door on the driver's side and gently lifted me out of the vehicle (after I had been ordered out and replied that I wouldn't leave the vehicle). I tried to hide my purse in the folds of my full skirt, but he saw it and we had a tug-of-war right in front of everyone. He got the purse, I was left with the handles! As soon as he set me on the ground, I saw the little gold star of David that had flown off my necklace. It was the only souvenir that I had bought in Israel when I had gone there with a friend and her 3 teenagers some years before. I picked it up unobtrusively and put it in my pocket. Right at that point I felt the Lord say to me, 'I will take care of every little detail.'

"I noticed that the soldier who had won the tug-o-war contest was trying to open my purse. He was tugging at the zipper, but it wouldn't open. At that point the soldier turned to me and said in Lingala, 'Hey lady, where is your money?' I was glad he asked where my money was because there were two zipper openings on that purse. One was for my money and the other for God's money. I had a big brick of Zaires in God's side (about 4 inches thick, worth about $200.00 US) for buying food for the students, but I opened the side which contained my money, easily, and presented my money to him. It amounted to about $12.00. At the same time, I showed him my credit card and driver's license and other pieces of important documents and explained to him that they wouldn't do him any good, but they were very important to me. I asked if I could keep them and he complied, letting me now have the purse. He didn't even notice the two zippers and the big brick of Zaires that was bulging out the one side of it. That side of the purse contained God's money (for food for the students) and He was looking after it.

The solders immediately filled the pickup, inside and out, and bumped along down the road in first gear. Apparently, no one had taken driver's ed. As they lurched and jerked along, Mama Deborah, scolded them for taking all our money, especially from a missionary woman who was here, thinking only of how she could bring help to his people and not leaving us with any taxi or bus fare to get home. The one who received the $12.00 felt so guilty that he threw it all back just as the vehicle slowly made its way to the downtown area.

"After they drove off, I noticed that we were only about 200 meters from the front gate of a Jewish friend of ours who had a paint factory business; the only person we knew in that part of the city.

There were roving bands of thieves at this point pillaging and looting and setting fires to large stores and factories in the area all around Abe's place. We were followed by other soldiers who seemed to have less than good intentions towards us as white women in a hostile area, but fortunately we made it to Abe's big iron door before they could display their desires. When we were let into his compound, we found many Israeli families already there preparing to go to the Ambassador's compound. Before we all left, Abe asked us to pray for the safety of his factory. It was about a year or so later that we were able to touch base with Abe again and found out that although all the businesses around him were ruined or burnt to the ground, his place was never touched!

"Under Abe's care we were able to escape the compound of the factory and travel in convoy to the home of the Israeli ambassador. There we spent the night under the protection of Israel. The next morning, we were ushered over to the American Ambassador's residence from where we were taken in another convoy to the Gulf Oil compound and reunited with grandpa."

The River Crossing

Truth be known, I wasn't that well physically and was on my way to see the doctor after the ladies left for the Bible School at Kikimi. It was only about an hour later that I decided not to leave due to the chatter on the CB radio. From the Gulf Oil compound, I could communicate with the Canadian Embassy and ask them what they were doing to get their people out of the city. Their response was that there wasn't a problem and that we should just stay where we were living and soon everything would blow over. The American Embassy, however, said that we were in a life-threatening situation and that we should leave as soon as possible. They would be doing everything they could to get us out across the Congo River, over to Brazzaville and then out on a flight home. As a few Canadians mixed in with many Americans, they would look after us and get us to Canada. The plan was to get us to Brazzaville, there we would be separated into various accommodations and then from there we would be able to leave for America.

Now that Gramma had already joined up with me, we were at ease to leave together with everyone at the Gulf Oil compound. We were taken in convoy down town to the Belgian Embassy in "centre ville" to be processed to cross the river in a large ferry to Brazzaville, Republic of Congo. This passenger ferry could take hundreds of people in one sailing. While we were waiting for certain formalities to be arranged I went for a little walk-about. It seemed like by this time the center of the city was well controlled by the Belgian Armed Forces who had parachuted in. Apparently, Mobutu had given Belgium a quick call for help and now there were Belgian armed forces everywhere in the City Center. While I was scouting around the now very quiet city, I heard several gun shots. Suddenly, the soldiers that were casually looking around were on high alert and had quickly run for cover behind cars and doors or cement structures. While I, not being trained as a soldier and having previously heard lots of gun fire around the city, remained out in the open still gawking around. I noticed that all the soldiers, who were all heavily armed, had disappeared and then heard one say, "get down you idiot, before you get shot!" It didn't take me long to find a doorway to duck into. Fortunately, there were no more gunshots and now it was time to load up and get to the ferry crossing. We each only had one small suitcase.[66]

When we got to the ferry terminal, the clamour was disheartening. There were hundreds of people wanting to go across. Fortunately, we had the American Embassy personnel to run interference for us which helped immensely. In the process of lining up for the ferry we were categorized into nationalities according to the passports that we were carrying. "All Canadians over here," someone shouted, and we joined in that line with many others. It seemed like there were a lot of Canadians, mostly of Pakistani or Indian descent, who were branching off into the Canadian line. When I asked the person next to me how he happened to get there he told me that the Canadian Embassy had come

---

[66] Gramma only had the clothes on her back (that she had been sleeping in for two days) when she finally arrived at the Gulf Oil compound, so we persuaded the Embassy authorities to allow us to go home for a few hours one afternoon while it was relatively quiet. Seeing we had come in our car, we took the chance of going back to our home. I had asked some guys from the studio to stay and look after the place and they did just that. When we arrived, they were there. They didn't open the doors right away either as some of the neighborhood people knew that we had left and were ready to pillage our place, but the guys dissuaded them. They told them in no uncertain terms that they were not about to let anyone in the yard. As a matter of fact, when we got in our house, we noticed that a lot of sound and computer equipment was missing. The guys quickly let us know that they had put it all up in the attic for fear of the neighbors trying to force themselves in, so all the important stuff was hidden. Gramma got a suitcase and filled it as quickly as she could and we left without a mishap. This time our chauffer, Poto Ntona, took us in our vehicle to the Gulf compound and bade us goodbye with crocodile tears as we stood with our arms around each other praying for one another's safety. We consoled him saying we would be back, so take care of the vehicle and the house (which he most assuredly did).

to pick him up and had brought him there with many others. …hmmm I guess they found out that it wasn't so safe after all and began taking care of their own. However, they never contacted us, before or after. That got me wondering a little just how effective they are in a crisis situation. I think I'll stick with the Americans. After all, we always celebrated July 4th with them in Kinshasa at TASOK (the American School of Kinshasa, where our kids had gone) and they gave us free hotdogs and ice cream.

The Reception

Once across the river, we were again segregated to a place of refuge for only Canadians. We were bussed to quite a large two-story building. It had a large patio outside and the grounds were quite elaborate. We soon found out that this used to be an Embassy building for some European country. However, I recognized the place immediately as Pastor Charles and I and an Assembly of God missionary, Sylvia Turner, had conducted a week-long seminar on worship in that building. It now belonged to the Assembly of God mission who had plans of turning the whole bottom (main) floor into class room space for a Bible School. We were ushered in on the main level floor, but we were one of the last ones there and the only room we had to sit down and even sleep was in the middle of a common room with many other Indo-Canadians, who all spoke their own Punjabi language. We had no sleeping bags, of course, so we thought we would just have to sleep on the floor. Judy was still with us.

As we were looking around, the host and hostess came down the stairs of this two-story monster building to see who their guests were and how many! There were a lot more there than they had anticipated. As soon as they saw us (the three of us) they were surprised and invited us to come upstairs and stay with them—they had plenty of room with their kids being away at school. We gratefully accepted their invitation as I was not feeling at all well. I didn't know what the problem was, but knew something was wrong.

The hostess had made two pots of couscous and a big pot of goulash to put over it. The pots contained enough to feed 40 people. She knew because she had done this before. When we looked at the number of people gathering we knew there was not enough. The hostess didn't know what to do, but asked that we pray with them that God would multiply the food. Judy who was with us mentioned earlier in her time with us that she had faith to believe that God would provide for the hungry. I was about to pray when Gramma elbowed Judy and asked her to pray reminding her that she had faith for God to provide. She accepted gladly and prayed that our Father would bless the food and multiply it so that all could be fed. There were plenty of paper plates and plastic forks and spoons on hand. In her prayer, she also asked that there be leftovers so that we could know that all were fed.

The food, plates and utensils were all taken down stairs and then we waited. They had made a small bit of extra food so that we all (five of us) could have some food as well. When the girls went down to collect the plates and plastics, as well as the pots the food was in, they saw, to their amazement, that there actually was food left over. When they counted the plates, there were 120 dirty plates! Thank you, Lord! You do have mercy on us and care for Canadians as well as Congolese. I would say that 97 percent of the people below were Indo-Canadians, mostly Muslim. God is no respecter of persons. He loves us all. By His answering our prayer we were encouraged in our faith, our love for others of different beliefs and could believe that He would provide for those whom we left behind in dire circumstances. Food in Kinshasa would now be hard to come by as the soldiers had ransacked the city.

The Flight Home

The next morning the hostess, who was also a nurse, thought I looked worse and decided that she should call her friend, who was the U.S. embassy doctor there in Brazzaville. The doctor came and made a house call to see this ailing Canadian. She looked worried and said that it could be appendicitis but thought that there was something else the matter as well. She gave me some heavy-duty antibiotics and said for me to start them right away. She asked for our passports and said that she would do what she could to get us out of the country as soon as possible.

Later that day, she came with two black embassy vehicles. Our passports in hand, she mounted the stairs and said, "OK, grab your stuff we're going to drive you to the airport and put you on a plane that will take you immediately to the US and from there the Canadians will take you to Montreal and Toronto." We were shocked. Just like that? We quickly grabbed onto one small suitcase each and followed her to the vehicles. This was riding in style. We had no sooner given our thanks to the host and hostess and said our good-byes, than we were driving out of the city to the international airport, up onto the tarmac and stopped right in front the stairs to the big Boeing 747 which was awaiting us. The doctor ushered us up the stairs into the awaiting plane and found that we were, in fact, the first persons to come aboard. The doctor then gave our passports to the Steward in charge and said, "First class for these people, please."

Now as we were getting out of the big black shiny vehicles with bullet proof doors and windows, we saw a bus waiting not far from us, also on the tarmac by the plane. As we were about to mount the stairs I looked up and saw a number of people we knew, waiting in the bus to get on the same plane. Their mouths were wide open! They were all Americans, many of them missionaries, from Kinshasa. I'm sure they were wondering how we managed to get such first-class treatment by the American Embassy. But all that they said was, "Sawatsky???"

I went to the nose of the 747 and thought that this was first class, but it turned out to be only business class. The steward came to me and said that I didn't have to stay there, I could go up to first class if I liked. I wasn't sure for I was comfortable where I was and by this time there were a few friends around. A little later I got up and asked the steward to show me to the first-class area and he took me up the stairs to the second story. It was first class indeed! Wide seats, your own screen for movies and lots of room to lean back and relax as well as sleep with your own pillow and blanket! I indicated I would stay if I could have my friends come up there with me. Before I knew it, a dozen or so friends who were with Gramma in the business section were climbing the stairs to join me. It seemed that I was the "patron" of that area and as I saw people getting on the plane from the upstairs window, I would send someone down to invite them up to join us. We were an elite group of older missionaries, all friends, from various missions or support employment and we had a ball! It took us some time before everyone was on board so while we were waiting there was a lot of laughter. There were without a doubt some good comedians in the group and we all could sing. As it was fairly quiet up there, we enjoyed ourselves thoroughly without having to shout. We got good food, watched a good movie and chatted until such time as we touched down in the Canary Islands. By that time, it was midnight and we all slept until early morning. We touched down at Andrews Airforce base in Washington and from there Canada picked us up and flew us to Toronto where we were met by a crowd of reporters, a few dignitaries and Gramma's sister—Auntie Ruth and Uncle Norm.

I thought the hullabaloo was finally over. It was Saturday evening when we finally were resting in their home and the phone rings. It was pastor Ken Opperman of the Bayview Glen Alliance Church asking us if we would speak and share our experiences on the Sunday morning. That would be the next morning and we were now preparing to get a good night's sleep. Of course, jet lag wasn't helping us, so in the middle of the night we prepared our messages and in the morning said that we would share something that God had placed on our hearts. God was gracious to us, gave us a compelling message where both of us spoke, complementing each other. At first, we said that we couldn't be able to speak, we were too frazzled, but the Lord gave us both a short message and we shared the pulpit that morning. We were glad we did!

It almost goes without saying that we were not dressed that well—nothing like the pastors. All we had were everyday clothes that we would wear in the heat of Kinshasa. We had no dress suits or pretty dresses and we were a bit cold (though Gramma did borrow a nice blouse and skirt from Auntie Ruth). It was in the fall of 1991. This didn't get unnoticed by especially one business man and his wife who found us after the morning service was over. They asked Dawn to come to their high-end ladies clothing warehouse where they gave her the run of the place to pick out whatever she needed (wanted). Now you know that Gramma is fairly conservative and when she said that she was finished, they looked at her little pile and decided to take her around again, piling on the expensive clothing. That year she was the most modern and chic looking missionary who ever came off the "field" (mission field, that is).

When we arrived in the greater Vancouver area, at our home church in White Rock. We were asked to house sit, beginning immediately, for a couple who was leaving their home for a three-month vacation. After that, another house opened up for four months and then we were asked by another couple to take over their home for another five months while they went back to Saskatchewan to help the family finish off the growing season and the harvesting.

It was during those last five months that Ray Downey and I went back to Kinshasa for two weeks to assess the situation in the Congo. Were we, as a mission, able to go back there? If so, were we to bring in other missionaries? One thing was sure, our missionary force would be permanently depleted.

It was also during those last five months, from April to August that we were able to have all our kids (your parents) live with us for the last time. While we were in this beautiful house, that so graciously was made available to us, your mom, or Auntie Loralee, got married to a wonderful man named Brian Thiessen. When he phoned to ask if he could come and see us, one fine Sunday, I knew immediately what he was going to say. I asked Gramma where my shotgun was, I wanted to greet him at the door with it. But not having one at hand we welcomed him in and were very happy to add him to the family when he asked us for our daughter's hand in marriage.

It was also during this time that we felt God again solidified His call to return to Kinshasa, to Studios Sango Malamu and the newly founded Alliance Church at Cité Mama Mobutu. It was a crossroads time, a time of crisis in our lives when we were actually asked to go to another area of CMA ministry—Malaysia. It was tempting, but that really wasn't for us. God still had many good things in store for us in Kinshasa, still called Zaire, but soon to be the DRC (Democratic Republic of Congo). These were exciting times!

Chapter Twenty–Five: The Aftermath

The Arial View

Coming back to Kinshasa for this exploratory trip in the cool season of 1992 (around May), I remember flying low over where the large General Motors Plant was, with its hundreds of newly fabricated cars (Opels) in their parking lot. It was a large acreage supporting a new car assembly plant and large repair shop (garage) with a separate section for a bodywork and paint shop. It had been a full out assembly plant with a large cafeteria for it's over a hundred workers and many luxurious offices. It was built of the local construction materials of cement brick with steel posts supporting the steel girders, rafters, and corrugated roofing tins. I had flown over it before and knew the area well, but this time had trouble spotting it. Making sure of my bearings, I looked at the exact spot, but found nothing—no plant, no garage, no paint shop, no offices and no cars! Apparently during the pillaging there were three waves of looters who picked it clean. All that remained of GM Zaire was a partial structural skeleton and the familiar blue GM logo. I could see a few steel posts that were bent over, which somehow had weathered the storm. Nothing was left standing on that acreage— no buildings, no bricks, no electrical or any construction materials whatsoever and no vehicles. It was unbelievable. From my perspective it seemed as if millions of driver ants had passed through and cleaned the place out! What were we in for?

It was the first wave of looters from a Zairian military unit based at the nearby airport who stole all the plant's vehicles. The second wave of rioters took all the assembly-line equipment and everything else that wasn't welded down. By this time there wasn't much left for the third wave of looting citizens, so they took the walls and the roof and everything else that might have been left.

Keith Richburg from the Washington post[67] saw the aftermath like this: "The devastated [GM] plant, part of a row of newly abandoned factories on the route into Kinshasa from the airport, stands as a compelling metaphor for the hollow shell that is now Zaire's economy. Potentially one of the richest countries in Africa -- a country with enough arable land and hydroelectric potential to feed and power the entire continent -- Zaire has been stripped bare and left to wither."

---

[67] *http://www.washingtonpost.com/wpsrv/inatl/longterm/congo/stories/033192.htm*

I was happy to be back, although I knew the task before me was quite daunting, but to see the collateral damage was like driving through a war zone. All the stores in the major downtown districts seemed like they had been shelled with heavy artillery and all that was left were gaping holes where there once were roofs, windows, doors and AC units. The markets and stores were now endless lines of vendors who displayed their wares on the sidewalks and streets of "Centre Ville." And much of it was what had been stolen.

The people seemed like sticks walking. The increase in malnutrition had taken its toll, particularly among children. They were not quite starving because they could fill up on widely  available cassava root, a starchy staple. It would fill their stomachs, but cassava has little nutritional value.

My colleague Ray Downey, director of the mission at the time, and I had flown into Kinshasa to do an assessment of the situation and to see if any missionaries could return. The day after our arrival he flew with MAF to Boma to take care of all the Bas-Zaire affairs and to meet with the leadership of the CEAZ church. I was left to deal with the scene in Kinshasa where four to five missionary families plus three single gals had been living. All their household items had to be packed, all the houses vacated, and the renting contracts had to be terminated. This was going to be a big job for one guy. I had a three-week period in which to get everything done (not to mention what needed to be done in my own house and with the ministry of SSM).

A Deep Hole of Depression

Not long after I arrived at our house, I heard from Pastor Babaka of the Cité Mama Mobutu neighborhood church. He came over to our place on Luyeye Street, General Eluki's place, to welcome me back. After a delightful greeting and reunion on the driveway inside the compound of our home, I found out that he was very sad and down hearted. I asked if he could come into the house and we would pray together.

He told me that his son-in-law, who got married to his oldest daughter and who had the reception in our home, had run off, never to be seen or heard of again. That was only part of the story. He had not only finally gotten his wife pregnant but also her younger sister—both at the same time. Apparently, he told the younger sister that her older sister couldn't conceive and convinced the younger sister to have sex with him, so she could give the family a child and grandchild. Well they both got pregnant at about the same time and the son-in-law took off. It was a heavy burden for the whole family, but as father and pastor it was especially hard on him.

We began to pray. I can't remember all that we said but I do remember that I asked the Lord to transfer his burden on to me. I would help carry it and lighten his load. I remember he went away with more of a spring in his step and with a heart of praise. His load was lightened. But my dark night of depression was approaching.

It was about five o'clock when he left and it didn't take long for the sun to set. As it did, I was alone in the house. The guys who had lived there had kept it in good condition, but there was no food left in the fridge (of course) and nothing in the freezer. We had told them to make themselves at home and to eat all that was in the fridge and freezer in case the electricity would be cut off during the revolt. We didn't want anything to go to waste. Consequently, there was no food in the house. I sat there in the dark, not having the ambition or courage to move. A deep cloud of despair seemed to engulf me and I had no hope!

I began to cry, I felt so alone, so discouraged that I couldn't see my way out. I could never accomplish what we had come to do; it was too ominous a task. How could I ever get it done!? I sat there with tears streaming down my face thinking I was a failure and didn't know how to explain my ineptness and darkness of soul. After many hours of this solitary darkness, I finally dragged myself to the light and the computer room (earlier I had put it on and it was still running) where I saw on the screen the words of a worship song. I read praises to God and turned to another song on the screen and began singing it, aloud. I kept this up for about fifteen minutes and it seemed the dark cloud had begun to lift and I felt I could go to sleep.

That night I relearned again the importance of worship and praise to our heavenly Father and His son Jesus which brings us into the presence of the Holy Spirit in a unique way. When I began to praise the Lord, the fear and gloom, darkness and despair began to leave. Peace came to my heart and to my whole body. The next morning, I was up early ready to get on the gigantic task that was before me which by the grace of God I was able to accomplish. If I had not had that experience of the deep darkness of depression, I would not have believed that people could get so low! Also, I soon realized that I had prayed to take on Pastor Babaka's burden. I think the Lord transferred it on to my "shoulders" (spiritually speaking) and the devil piggy backed on that transfer and made it all the worse. I thank God that I was directed to the computer and the songs of praise. The devil can't stand praises to the King of Kings and Lord of Lords... it torments him! ...and he took off!

The Mission Rented Properties

My job was to pack up all the houses that the missionaries had vacated, pay off all the owners of these rented properties and move all the furniture and personal belongings of all the houses to the mission property which was still intact. It was a humongous task and I only had a few weeks to take care of it all. What made it even more difficult was the fact that one of the missionary houses had been broken into, completely looted and gutted. Apparently in leaving, the family gave a spare house key to their chauffeur who had taken them to an evacuation spot. Before they parted, the missionary gave him explicit instructions as to what he should do with it. However, it appeared that the chauffeur never followed those instructions for "somehow" the key was used for a great looting spree.

When I came to their house not only was all their furniture gone but all the doors and door cases, all the windows and window frames, all the electrical fixtures and most of the plumbing (toilets and sinks) were gone. Fortunately, the roof was still there! It cost me a lot of haggling, a lot of sweat, a lot of work and a lot of money (over $10,000.00US of mission funds) to get everything right to the specs and appreciation of the owner. It took me all of the three weeks that I was there to finish this project.

It was during this time that I had to meet with two Generals of Mobutu's army to finalize payment of rents and to whom I had to turn over the keys after their final inspection of the houses. The single gals and another family had rented houses from General Bolozi (chief of security for Mobutu) and I had rented from General Eluki. On the day that I had to meet with general Bolozi, a man quite feared by most military and civilians alike, I had not yet taken down the CB radio from the house that we were to meet in. The house was virtually empty, but the CB was on the stand in the corner. I had given a CB to the SSM administration office so that while I was in the area, we could remain in contact in case of emergency at the studio. While I was talking to General Bolozi getting ready for an inspection of the houses (two of them), the CB blares our family code, "Sky 5, sky 5!"

I excused myself and went to answer. If I didn't, the studio would continue calling and make a lot of noise. I said, "Sky 5 here."

"Oh, bonjour mon maréchal," said the voice on the other side.

I quickly mentioned in soft tones that I was busy and would call back later. I didn't say that I was with General Bolozi so the voice on the other end came back with, "OK mon maréchal, plus tard."[68] (OK my marshal, later.) When I turned back to Bolozi, he had a smirk on his face and said, "So you too are a marshal, are you?" Of course, I knew he heard the short conversation as the CB was loud enough for all to hear.

"Yes," I said. "I am a marshal for Jesus." I didn't want him to come to any false conclusion. "It's just a nick name that they call me." But the nick name has stuck until today.[69]

The General and I finished our business without further interruptions. I was able to pack up all the houses using barrels, suitcases and crates and take them all over to the mission house which had a large warehouse on the property, once used as the Sango Malamu practice room and recording studio.

Les généraux ex-FAZ Bolozi, Baramoto, Eluki et Nzimbi

---

[68] *The nickname "maréchal" or marshal in English, came from an experience that I had with Edo Bumba. There was also a famous military general by the name of Bumba. So, one day I addressed Edo as Mon Général inferring he was General Bumba. He came back immediately with "Oui Mon Maréchal." (as in president, Maréchal Mobutu) And both names stuck!*

[69] *Photo from the internet: http://www.congoplanete.com/article.jsp?id=45261824*

Chapter Twenty-six: New Horizons

The Birthing of New Ministries

God put it on our hearts to get the studio up and running and well established in two years. That short-term goal became a high priority. I asked the Lord to bring us the right people and enough personnel so that if we had to leave or something happened to me, the studio could carry on without us. So, we established a non-profit organization as soon as we got into the permanent buildings on the campus of Evangelism Resources. In about a year we had all the necessary permits and paper work to legally operate in Kinshasa as a non-profit registered organization with a president, vice-president, secretary and treasurer. All the officers also constituted our General Assembly with possibly one to two others at the very beginning. We didn't get our "personnalité civile" (our country wide legal documents) until many years later, but we were able to function quite legally in Kinshasa.

Just as we were getting ready to hit our maximum strength in ministry, recording up to 100 albums in the second year, going almost 24/7 with one shift in the morning and another in the evening, the pillaging and looting of the soldiers took place over the whole city. It didn't take long for the "white community" to get targeted as well, for they were the rich. We were counselled by the leaders of our CEAZ church to leave and followed their advice. It was almost two years to the day that we had to leave from when we first opened the studio to begin Christian recordings. SSM was already in capable hands and they carried on without much of a break in their schedule. We prayed much, and the Lord guarded the studios and the whole campus. Nothing was pillaged or stolen. We were so grateful.

I did receive a phone call at home early one morning and it was from Kinshasa. It was Big Jon Mukhandi on the phone, our administrator. I was very apprehensive and thought that he was calling to let me know that the studio and the campus was pillaged, and all was gone. I braced myself for the news. After a brief greeting, it didn't take long for Big to say he had a problem! OOhh, here comes the news! I was expecting the worst.

"What's the problem, Big?" I said. We mostly called him Big, sometime Big Jon, hardly ever "Jean", his Christian name.

"We have run out of guitar strings and can't find any in the city! Do you think you could bring some when you come back!"

"Guitar Stings!" I said, "Is that all? You still have all the equipment? Nothing is stolen?"

"Oh no," he replied, "Nothing is stolen. Everything is intact and we are working very hard. But we have broken some guitar strings and can't find any in the city, please bring some with you when you come back. Can you do that?"

Well, of course I could and had planned on it anyhow, but what a relief to understand that God had really answered prayer and kept everyone and His SSM safe.

After we got back and well settled, which took some time as Ray and I came back on our own again to see where we would live and where we could find lodgings, we felt it was safe enough to call in other missionaries. However, all that this evacuation gave us a sense that it was used by God to help us pare down our missionary force. After all, the CMA mission by this time had been in the Congo/Zaire well over 100 years. The missionary force was drastically reduced and although the CEAZ church felt the lack, they jumped to the challenge themselves. It didn't take long for the CEAZ to take charge of the hospital, the seminary and other key ministries in the lower Congo area and have them running very well indeed.

The missionary force mainly stayed in Kinshasa from this point on. From there we could continue with some important ministries like the founding and ongoing ministries of larger churches and especially the nursing and evangelistic ministries out on the plateau Bateke.

I found a house for a very reasonable rate right behind the campus of ER—where our studios were located. It was a large house with plenty of space to have guests and offices for me as I continued being president of SSM. Of course, the landlords wanted an arm and a leg for the rent, but I reasoned with them and let them know that there were no expatriates coming back in the near future, only missionaries who could never afford the price they were asking ($2000 a month). I got them down to $550.00 a month and a promise to clean up the place and to make it beautiful—and keep it that way. God granted us favor with the owners (the whole family) and we moved in. The back wall of our garage was the perimeter wall of the ER Campus. I got permission from the owners of the house and ER to punch a hole through the wall and put in a heavy-duty gate that would be locked on our side, so as to allow us to walk through to the campus and to our studios. That saved us a lot of running around and a lot of gas.

From the time we got back in 1992 and for the next 5 years, the Lord seemed to give us greater vision for new ministries. Some were new, others seemed to be a natural outflow of existing ministries. Over the years, every time I received a vision, in my own heart and mind, I gave it back to God and asked Him to open doors if it was from him. I also shared the visions with Gramma and I knew if I could get it by her, it must be from God! She had so many tough questions that I knew if I could answer them with what God was giving me, she would agree, and we would have a green light.

The Reproduction Studio

Out of our audio recording studios came the first real-time reproduction studio with as many as 20 to 25 cassettes reproduced at one time, in about 1 hour (most tapes were an hour long). That meant that in an 8-hour day we could reproduce around 150-200 tapes (depending on how many tape machines were running). But each week we had the capacity to put out into the market place some 1000 tapes or 4000 a month. In less than 2 years, the market place was flooded with Christian tapes from $3.00 to $5.00 a cassette. The Christian Bible stores as well as the secular boutiques; the Catholics, the Protestants and the Kimbanguists (an indigenous faith); the National Radio station and the private TV stations were all looking for Christian music recorded by Studios Sango Malamu.

The Design Studio

Our son Rod began designing for print all the album covers, so we started the Sango Malamu Album Design and Printing ministry for Christian artists in Kinshasa, also the first of its kind. We took orders,

Rod would design all the covers and get them print ready on the computer and then we would farm out the printing to several print shops, always looking for the best deals, supervising the job to make sure it was well done.

The Distribution House

At the same time, with all these tapes accumulating, we began the Sango Malamu Distribution House, to get all these artists out into the population. We often made contracts with the Christian musicians to pay for their recordings and then recuperate the studio costs from the sale of their tapes at a certain percentage until the costs were covered. We began supplying all book stores, boutiques and Bible houses with ristian cassette tapes, well packaged and well reproduced and well corded. In two years, the word on the street came back to us saying nat no one was buying secular tapes anymore; all that the population wanted was the Christian cassettes produced and distributed by Studio Sango Malamu. In two years our goal had been accomplished.

The Music and Worship Academy

A year or so after our return on 1992, the Sango Malamu Academy of Music (and worship) was founded. We were able to speak into the lives of both budding musicians and those who had already recorded with us. We taught the meaning of worship, what happens when you worship the Lord and how the worship leader conducts himself or herself. We taught new musicians and even mature musicians how to read and write music and to arrange music and how to record. We even gave them supervised studio time to practice recording the groups that came. We also taught how to properly use a sound system and how to take care of instruments and equipment. It was the first Christian worship and music school ever established in Kinshasa and the Congo and out of this Academy came several nights of special music and worship productions that had far reaching effects into the Christian community of Kinshasa. These were mainly conceived and produced by one of Sango Malamu's best sound engineers and musicians, Joel Bumba.

The Video Studio

It didn't take long for artists to request to do music videos of their most popular songs. The vision for this was already there, but when groups began requesting this, I felt it was time to begin. It had already been hinted by a fellow missionary that a cousin videographer was willing to come and help set up a video studio if ever we should need one. That seed began to germinate.

It wasn't long after this that I contacted Mark Turner, a professional videographer, and told him of our desire to have a video studio in order to make professional videos of music groups, of conferences and special meetings for airing on TV stations or in private homes—another good way to share the Gospel. We had no budget for this, only a vision. I mentioned this to Mark, but on his side he had already began to run with this. I repeatedly mentioned to Mark that we had no money to give him or to the project, we had no place to install the studio, we had no video equipment yet (no cameras etc.) and we had no personnel to run the equipment if we could procure it. But Mark felt this was of God and on his end of things, he began to make arrangements to come to Kinshasa—with his whole family, wife and two teenagers. We didn't even have housing for him, but he felt he could stay with his cousin Wayne (and Sylvia) Turner—AOG missionaries.

Spurred on by his faith, I wrote to our mission headquarters in Colorado Springs and presented the vision to our director for Africa, Bob Fetherlin (who later became Dr. Robert Fetherlin vice-president for International Ministries for the CMA in the USA). It sometimes takes many weeks for mail to go and return, so it was about a month and a half later that I received a letter back from Bob saying that he and his African team didn't think that we should go into Video and Television at this time. He gave us a definite red light on the project.

Now this project was not a CMA project, but a SSM project. Nevertheless, I really needed the blessing of my leaders in this and had no desire to go against their directives, although that could have been done. At the same time, I received a short letter from Mark saying that everything was done on his side. That is, he had sold his house, had put all his stuff in storage and bought the tickets for Kinshasa. All four of them were in the process of getting their immunization shots and getting the visas for the Congo (Zaire).

When I heard from Bob, I was in a quandary as to how to handle the situation. When I heard from Mark, I really broke into a sweat! I got down on my knees and cried out to God to change the hearts of my leaders so that we could get a green light from them and their blessing.

I wrote another letter to Bob mentioning how disappointed we were at his news and described the fact that the vision was not a TV station, only a video studio (to feed the stations with good quality programming). I wrote Mark how pleased I was with his progress and that we would be in touch again once we landed in North America.

The letters from Mark and Bob came just a few weeks before we were scheduled to return to Canada for a very short time of home service (about 3 months). I came to Canada with a heavy burden on my shoulders. However, the first phone call that I received in the basement apartment of Uncle Gary and Auntie Joy's home in Langley was from Director Bob Fetherlin.

We had just arrived the night before and woke up to Auntie Joy calling from above that there was a phone call for me. It was Bob and he said, "I just wanted to let you know before you really start your home service that we have approved the project of starting a video studio and you have the green light to go ahead on the project." And then he added, "I thought this would be good news for you and wanted to get it to you right away!" Yes, it was good news!!! A burden was surely lifted, and I felt it was an answer to my prayers.

However, another burden quickly took its place. I now had the awesome responsibility of raising $50,000.00 to $60,000.00 American dollars to get this project off and running. At that moment, all we had was the vision, the professional to train us, but still had no money for equipment, no equipment, no personnel to run the studio and no place to put it. I began to pray the funds to come in and asked the Lord how I should approach people and what group of people I should speak to. I felt He indicated that I needed to contact only one person and the rest would fall in place. That was startling.

About that time, I was put in contact with a man in Holland who was a believer and who was also a videographer, who knew the equipment we needed and knew where to get it at a good price. We needed 240-volt equipment and PAL/SECAM for analogue broadcast television systems, European and Congolese standard. North America didn't have that standard, so we continued to explore the Dutch contingency.

That was good news! I also put Mark in touch with our Dutch contact so that they could discuss and prepare all the equipment that we needed, at least 50 thousand US dollars' worth. The rate of exchange was about the same as it is today—the Canadian dollar was worth about

73% of the US dollar, i.e. 1 Canadian dollar would get you only 73 cents US. This meant that I had to raise many more Canadian dollars to meet the 50 to 60 grand US that we needed.

Things were coming together on Mark's side and his research for the best equipment for us, but I still had no money! One day I was speaking to one of the pastors of Peace Portal Alliance Church about ministry and he asked a leading question as to what I was up to. I explained the video project to him and how much money I had to raise float the project. He said he knew a man who had written a book on how missionaries should go about raising funds. He immediately got my attention and I asked him if he could introduce me to that man. The pastor was most willing to do so. I certainly could use all the help available in knowing how to raise money for a project.

I was able to make an appointment to meet with him at a restaurant for lunch. As we talked, I was gleaning information from him, but also sharing our project with him. At one point he just stopped abruptly and asked me two questions. "How much do money you need to raise?" and "Where do think it will come from?" Interesting questions! I told him 50 grand US (at the minimum) and then felt I should share with him that God impressed upon my heart that the funds would come mainly from one man. I didn't know who he was, but wanted to be prepared to share the vision and the project in good fashion when the time came. That was why I was gleaning info from him.

In the middle of our conversation he took out his check book and wrote out a check for 60,000 Canadian dollars and said perhaps that would be a good start. I agreed that it would. I couldn't believe my eyes! Oh, I thanked him calmly for his generous gift, but when we finished our luncheon, I got into my little car and hollered at the top of my lungs, "Praise the LOOOORRRRD!" I couldn't believe it! I had heard God right! But I never suspected it would be this man from whom I just wanted to glean information.

Overall, during the few months that we were in Canada, the whole project came together and we raised around ninety thousand Canadian dollars through GNI Ministries, not sharing the project with any of the CMA churches. Although we had the green light from HQ to go ahead with the project it wasn't a CMA project. It was a Good News International Ministries project for Studios Sango Malamu. I didn't feel right trying to raise funds for this from our CMA churches.

On our return home to Kinshasa, Mark, our son Rod and I went on ahead to Holland to test and pick up all the equipment. We brought it all with us as our own luggage and as access baggage, got it to our home in Kinshasa safe and sound—nothing was broken, and nothing was lost! We bought the equipment, shipped it with us and set it all up in our sound production studio for exactly the amount we had raised. Not a penny was left over. We were given space on the second floor overlooking the recording theatre which would now double for our video stage. We never suspected that the upstairs room would be available, but God opened all the doors!

Mark and family taught us how to set up the stage area, how to set up and use the equipment and how to produce a video of high quality. Rod learned videoing and video editing very quickly. He had just graduated from design school and wanted more experience in the Congo, so came back to help us set up the video project. He taught the right guys video editing, using the new computers and software that we were able to purchase. God supplied the right personnel and the project was a remarkable success. We made many videos, filmed many conferences, and put many of our projects on the TV stations that were looking for religious broadcasting. This studio was the forerunner of the next vision—a radio and a TV station of our own!

The Seminar Ministry

There were two young men who were exceptional in their teaching and content. Rene Futi Luemba and Charles Yangu both became officially ordained down the road, but at this time Studios Sango Malamu was at its apex in ministry and these men were heavily involved with us. Brother Futi, our SSM general director, was our radio pastor, conference or seminar speaker even before started his own churches. He had a dynamic presence, a good sense of humor and a keen and spirit-led mind. He represented our ministry all over Kinshasa and even in some areas of the Lower-Congo.

Pastor Charles was our SSM chaplain, a pastor at the Cité Mama Mobutu church and a great spiritual leader. He greatly helped keep SSM on track and counselled with many of the people working at SSM. Both Charles and Elise were like our own children and we now miss them very much. Both passed away at too early an age even for the Congolese, but both are now celebrating together with their Savior.

Charles and Futi knew their authority in Jesus, knew how to combat the enemy and had hearts to worship God with all their being. We did many two to four-day seminars together on worship, sometimes all three of us taking turns, sometimes just two of us, but always God blessed in marvelous ways. Some who attended were set free from the chains of the enemy, some made more serious and deeper commitments to Christ. We could always sense when the Spirit of God was moving in hearts and lives of those who came. It was a most thrilling and rewarding experience for me. We travelled together out of the city as far west as Muanda, some 550 kilometers, on the coast including Boma and Kinkonzi and a few spots in between.

A Christian Radio Station

We had long envisioned a Christian Radio station, "to give the winds—*the air waves*—a mighty voice that Jesus Saves" as the song states. We wanted to air strong and sound doctrinal teaching, discipleship programs, children's programs, cultural programs and agricultural or rural programs along with all this good music that Studios Sango Malamu was producing.[70] But it would never work, President Mobutu would never allow another station to rival his national radio station… but this deserves a chapter of its own.

The Change in Mission Policy

When we returned in 1992 there was the agreement with the CMA mission that we would go for 2 years and then come on home assignment for several months. If it was desirable and safe for us to return, then we should go for another 2 years and after that be on home assignment again for another 3 to 4 months. This proved to be a valuable format for ministry for us. One, it helped us keep in close contact with an ongoing and growing ministry in the Congo. Our presence was still required, and we would not want to upset the flow with a change in administration for a year. Three months would be OK. And two, it helped us keep in fairly close contact with our supporters, our donors and the board and ministry of GNI Ministries.

---

[70] *We had already changed our name from "Studio" to "Studios" as so many studio rooms were being used: for production, post production, graphic design, distribution, Radio and Video. With all these "studios" being used, we felt we had to change the name from singular to plural. Thus, began the name "Studios Sango Malamu". The initials and our logo remained the same.*

The acquiring of Studio C-the scriptures on tape

At one point we began recording the New Testament in Lingala to be played on the radio for those who couldn't read or who didn't have a Bible. This was one of the programs that was most listened to on the radio. Then we got in touch with an organization that was founded for that purpose—putting the Bible on tape in many languages for all to hear, their slogan being "faith comes by hearing".

We partnered with Hosanna/Faith Comes By Hearing and developed another studio. We received equipment to do separate digital recordings of the scriptures using various voices. The reading would be done by a narrator, but all other scriptures would be read (animated) by other voices.

This was a great idea and opportunity for us, but due to many problems we couldn't follow through on our obligations. Agreeing with Hosanna, this studio was moved to Ghana where they were able to finish the project of the New Testament in an animated format.

The Jesus Film

Our studios were also adapted for Campus Crusade, for a certain time, to make various language sound tracks for the story of Jesus—commonly known as "The Jesus Film". This was a great opportunity to have even a wider ministry experience. This program went well and was finished in due time.

Over the course of time we showed the "Jesus Film" to thousands of people—in the cities and in the bush! In one year alone, we ministered to at least 100,000 people, mainly in remote areas. Through this film, our singing and our preaching, for we always gave a message after the film, we saw many people come to the give their lives to Jesus. It was an awesome experience.

It seemed like our singing and music drew the crowds and prepared them to hear the gospel. The Jesus Film gave the crowd the knowledge of who Jesus was and what he came to do for them (and all humanity). Our preaching and testimonies gave the people a personal understanding and a personal invitation to received Jesus into their lives. It didn't matter if our meetings were four hours long, most of the people always stayed to the very end.

The film was so vivid at times, especially during the crucifixion of Jesus, that the crowds would lament in loud groans and cries and pull at their hair and clothing in sympathy and desperation. A few times we had to stop the film and give the audience time to self-compose. At such times we just needed to reassure the people that this was a film, but it was exactly what Jesus did for us.

We travelled with the Jesus Film in French and in Lingala. We would show either one depending on the education of the people we were addressing. In village areas and in more remote areas we always used the Lingala film, but in the cities and around the schools or universities we used the French film. I must admit it was a bit odd at first to hear Jesus speak in French and more unique still to hear him speak in Lingala!

Interestingly enough, no matter where we were, it seemed that 10% of the hearers, on a regular basis, would respond to give their hearts to Jesus, asking Him into their lives. We generally stayed and prayed with individuals long after the meeting was over, sometimes into the late-night hours.

We were privileged, for a brief period of time, through our studios, to be part of putting new languages on the Jesus film and have an even

wider impact in sharing the Gospel.

Studios and offices of Radio and TV Sango Malamu. Headquarters of SSM Ministries. Below: The Presidents' office

Chapter Twenty-seven: Radio Sango Malamu

As I was having coffee and croissants with a business man, the owner of the expansive Okapi Hotel and restaurant, I was challenged by him with this remark, "You have all this music that you are recording, why don't you start a radio station so that you can play it and get it out there for all to hear?"

My response was, "Yes, you're right. That is the vision and we would like to do that, but President Mobutu would never allow that. He would never give us a license to broadcast."

"Oh, I think he would," was his retort. "I think you could do it!"

I most definitely disagreed with him, but after some discussion I rejoined, "Ok, would you help me get a broadcast license?"

ith that question there was a bit of hesitation on his part, but wh pressed him on it he said he would. We left that meeting with the ea that he would see what he could do and let me know. I was happy with that.

Shortly after that coffee time in 1991, the great "pillage" took place in Kinshasa—the pillaging and looting by the military and then by civilians that brought Kinshasa to its knees. We were evacuated, but after we came back in '92, I took a trip around Binza to have a look at the Okapi Hotel. To my amazement there was nothing there! Most of the buildings were totally demolished and what was left were only shells, part of a few buildings with which the pickers couldn't walk away. Everything was gone: not only all the hotel furniture and beds were gone but also all the roofing materials, all the electrical materials, all the windows and doors with frames, all the plumbing and most of the building materials such as bricks and wood used for rafters. I couldn't believe my eyes. Needless to say, I never saw the owner again as he lived clear across the Congo on the eastern side and never came back to rebuild. I heard that he did get some compensation from President Mobutu himself.

However, while I was home I made contact with a missionary who confirmed to me that he had a license to broadcast in one of the most eastern provinces of the Congo. I asked him about how we could get a license in Kinshasa and he suggested that set up a satellite radio station on his license. That would be good enough to get us started and we would call it Radio Sango Malamu, a satellite of his radio station. We both thought this a good idea.

A Humble Beginning[71]

We had duplicate copies of the license to broadcast from the mission in the east and took them to "La Voix du Zaire",[72] the national radio station. When they saw them, they said that there would be nothing to hinder us from starting to broadcast if we had the equipment.

During our time in Langley, B.C., before leaving for Zaire in 1992, I kept GNI Ministries abreast of our vision for a radio station. We started to raise funds for that and were able to raise funding for a 250-watt transmitter and a (whip) antenna. We managed to scrape together the 5 grand that it cost us at the time and purchased both through HCJB. I don't remember how it was sent to us, but I do remember that it fit well into a suitcase. Perhaps it was carried into the country by some missionary coming in or by a group coming in on a short-term mission's trip and could do us a favor by bringing the extra luggage.

SSM rented a room in a house that was situated on the top of the highest hill in Kinshasa. We set the antenna up on the roof of the house, supported with guide wires, scraped together a CD player, a cassette player, a mixer, a microphone and put it all together on a table in an otherwise bare room and connected it all to the transmitter. We were ready to broadcast.

I was able to recruit a few able voices who were interested and willing to talk on the radio, but I found in one person who worked with us in the studio, a person who had the technical ability to operate the radio equipment. He was a good French, Lingala and Swahili speaker and had a great personality. His name was Kool Matope, now known around the world as Léon Georges Matope. I gave him all the support I could, and he gravitated to the job for a short time. Other young men and women came along later and did a fantastic job of announcing, interviewing and/or being a regular disc jockey, but Kool gave us a great start. Many tuned in just to hear him. He never divulged his name, he just called himself "La Colombe" or The Dove. He worked incognito until finally family and friends recognized his voice and although he didn't give up his name on the air, many knew who he really was.

---

[71] *An Article was written for the Alliance Witness at that time about the humble beginnings of the Radio station called "Let the Earth Hear His Voice." April 1997. It will be attached at the end of the chapter.*
[72] *Translated means: "The Voice of Zaire"*

When I shared this photo with him some 23 years later, he posted it on Facebook with these words:

« LE 31 DÉC 1993 à 10h !!! 1ère EMISSION TEST de la RADIO SANGO MALAMU FM 104.5 MHz. Photo prise par papa Jim Sawatsky !!! ALLELLUIAAAAAA SOIS BÉNI MON SEIGNEUR JÉSUS-CHRIST pour ce jour-là car ma vie n'a plus jamais été la même !!! Merci de tout cœur papa Jim de m'avoir associé à ce projet qui a béni et bénit encore le peuple de DIEU !!! »[73]

Shut Down

Just as we were getting well known in the city, after broadcasting for three months, the government shut us down. It seemed that ·erywhere we went down town or into the markets, Radio Sango ːalamu was blaring over portable radios, presenting the good news of ˙esus. JUST LIKE I HAD DREAMED! Whether it was through music, through preaching, through discipleship courses, through agricultural tips or programs on family harmony or thorugh ministry to children, the whole Gospel was aired and passed on to all peoples in Kinshasa. The papers reported that over 60% of the population was listening to our Christian radio station. Of course, the government woke up! But still didn't know who we were. Few people did. After three months, they finally tracked us down and told us to shut down the radio or government soldiers would come in and confiscate all the equipment. What we thought was legal broadcasting, to them was illegal! We did not go through the proper channels.

We wanted to keep our equipment, so we shut down.

We went to see the Minister of Information and Press who shut us down. He granted us a hearing and said that someone representing us had already been there. It wasn't true, but it didn't take me long to find out that the Church of Christ in Zaire (ECZ) had gone to him and asked him to open it up, grant them an official license so that they could operate in our stead. ˙ That was denied! And when he found out who I was, the President of Studios Sango Malamu, including the Radio Sango Malamu, he was a little more tolerable. His answer was that I

---

[73] *Dec 31st, 1993 at 10 a.m.!!! The first transmission test of Radio Sango Malamu 104.5 Mhz. Photo taken by Jim Sawatsky!!! Alleluia!!! Be blessed my Savior Jesus Christ for that day, for my life was never again the same!!! I thank you with all my heart papa Jim for having associated me with this radio project that has blessed me and continues to bless many of God's people [in the Congo]..*

needed to have a license from his office to get back on the air and I needed to follow proper protocol. OK, that was good with me, "We'll gather all the official forms, fill them out and present them to you immediately," I said in compliance, for he absolutely refused to accept the documents we had from station in the Kivu province. I was most happy to register as our own Radio Sango Malamu station.

"But," he said, "even if you do that, I will never give you a license to operate here in Kinshasa. You will never get a license, no matter what you do!"

We were shut down on a Monday evening, after a day of broadcasting, without being able to notify our listening audience. The next morning the radio was silent!

An Impromptu Prayer Meeting

We didn't tell anybody, but that week I was giving a worship seminar to the students of the School of Evangelism. I was on campus, in the chapel, that very first morning of being shut down. I asked the students, about 50 or so were present (some outsiders came as well), after a good time of worship, "How many heard Radio Sango Malamu this morning?" It was about 11 a.m. in the morning, time enough for many to have heard our broadcasting which generally started at 6 a.m. No one lifted his hand and finally they began to murmur and say that it wasn't on this morning. I heard them and came back with, "You're right, it wasn't on this morning because the government shut us down!"

At that news, there was an immediate woeful and awful cry.

"They can't do this!" one said.

"This is our radio (meaning the Christians' radio). This isn't possible!" enjoined another.

Quickly though, without much ado, it seemed like everyone slid down on their knees to pray. It didn't take long for a prophetic voice to speak saying, "The Lord says, 'This is My radio and I will bring it back on the air!'" That was good to hear, but the message didn't really sink in until that message was repeated several times. People then stood up and spoke in tongues, giving a message in another language. I was going to ask for an interpretation (as the Bible says there should be), but before I could say anything each message in tongues was interpreted by another. It was an early church experience. The message was all the same with few variations. "'This is my radio,' says the Lord. 'I will bring it back on the air!'"

This all happened before I had an audience with the Minister of Information and Press. Having this confirmation under my belt I went to see the Minister with a spring in my step. Can you imagine how I felt when the Minister said that our Radio Sango Malamu would never get back on the air again, we would never get a license to broadcast. I couldn't believe what I was hearing.

A New Minister of Information and Press

I felt sick, but not daunted. As Paul writes, "Knocked down, but not knocked out!"[74] We received all the paper work, filled them all in with the accompanying documents, registered them with the office of the Minister and waited… in prayer!

The next thing we heard was that the Minister who shut us down had been replaced, so we immediately made application to see the new Minister. We were granted an audience very soon and I took with me the Vice-President of SSM and our Public Relations Officer. The elevator didn't work so we had to climb the 17 stories, in the pitch-black darkness of the stair well as there was no light available, none of the light bulbs had been replaced. Not only was it dark, but it was very hot and humid with no air flow whatsoever.

At one of our stops, to wipe the perspiration from our brows (it was freely flowing) and to catch our breath, I mentioned to the other two that I thought the Lord was saying to me that we should pray with the Minister before we did anything else. We all agreed that if this what the Lord was saying, then this is what we should do. We finally made it to the 17th floor and were accepted into the grand and spacious, air-conditioned office of the new Minister of Information and Press of the Republic of Zaire. He welcomed us to sit around his elaborated desk and was about to say something, but with courage I interrupted and said, "Excuse me Mister Minister, but before we do anything else we would like to pray with you. Could we do that?"

He looked at me with big eyes (and I thought he was going to demand that we leave immediately), he stood up before us, slapped his hands on the desk (OOhh, here it comes) and said, "OK, let's pray!"

I was shocked! Immediately I knew that this man had some Christian teaching in his background for no one says 'let's pray' without having some knowledge of prayer or of this Christian habit. I asked our Vice-President to pray as he had a gift of prayer, I believe,

---

[74] *2 Corinthians 4:9 J.B. Phillips New Testament*

and knew the French language very well. He began praying (all our conversation with the Minister would be in the French language). He prayed so hard, binding Satan our enemy, out of and away from that place (the physical office and the political office that he held) against all magic, clairvoyance, all evil spirits and witchcraft, and so long I thought we would get thrown out of there at any moment. But then he switched and began to pray blessing on the Minister, his office, his work and his family. This too went on for some time (and now I was feeling better with this, but was thinking he could finish anytime) until he was sure that he covered every area of this man's "Ministry" and then said, "In Jesus' Name, Amen!"

Well… we all said Amen after him and sat down. The Minister looked at all of us and then said with a chuckle of gladness and surprise, "Nobody has every prayed for me like that before! I have never been blessed like that, ever! And what is more, if you were not praying while you were denouncing all the evil and darkness in this office, I would have broken out in laugher because you were right on! That is exactly what has been happening in this office!"

We talked a little more and then he said, "If you keep on praying like this you will get your license, but I can't give it to you now. There is too much darkness against you. You are not fighting against people or the government, you are fighting against real witchcraft and darkness. Keep on praying!"

Again, we went away a bit sad (because we didn't get our license to broadcast), but we were encouraged to continue praying that God would defeat the darkness that was against us.

Radio Sango Malamu on the Air

It was only three weeks later that we requested another audience with the Minister. It was granted, but this time the elevators worked, and we walked into his office quite refreshed. The Minister in turn was glad to see us and not only welcomed us into his office as friends, but took us to an ante-room that was well furnished with sofas and easy chairs. When we all finally sat down, his first words were, "Before we do anything else, I suppose you would like to pray." This time we prayed a short prayer and got down to business.

"I believe you have been praying, haven't you?" was his beginning.

"Yes, we have," we acknowledged.

"Well, I thought so because I can give you your license today!" Whether he liked it or not, we all jumped for joy and praised the Lord. When we were finally calmed down he added, "But it will cost you $10,000.00 US." We were flabbergasted!

"Mr. Minister," I exclaimed. "Where in the world do you think we could get this amount of money? There is no way we can afford that amount of money. I guess that a broadcast license is way out of our reach." Without thinking about it, I was acting like a good Zairian would have acted and this began the open bargaining.

"Well now, just a minute!" he immediately countered. "How about 5000 US dollars. Yes, we'll cut it down to 5 grand."

"That is still too much for us, sir," I replied. "We could never afford that amount either! I just don't know where we could get that amount of money."

"Well, OK," he replied, without hesitation. Now the bargaining was becoming serious. "You've been on the air for three months already, so it isn't as if you are just beginning. How about we charge you $2000 and you can have your license immediately."

I agreed! I didn't know from where we would get the 2-grand, but it was attainable, I thought and shook hands with him on it. It didn't take long, and God did bring in the $2,000.00 for us. Within a week from that day we were back on the air with **Radio Sango Malamu, RSM 104.5 FM** broadcasting the Good News and we had a legitimate and legal license.[75]

We found out later that the minister had gone to a Campus Crusade Bible study with Futi (our General Director) at his brother's house and he actually understood the gospel message. His wife and mother were believers and they threatened him seriously if he didn't use his influence to put RSM back on the air! God has his ways…

Another Black Out

From that day to this Radio Sango Malamu has broadcasted almost 24/7 without a shut down. Except for a couple of really strenuous circumstances, nothing to do with our legal right to broadcast. One such time was when our transmitter (only 250 watts) burnt out from overheating, due to the fact that we had no air conditioning in the room and no fans. Our emotions were down. What to do? I was just about to

---

[75] *I believe it was sometime in May of 1994 that we got our permanent broadcasting license.*

set up a new and higher antenna tower that had been given to us from Gulf Oil. It was a great tower and we had everything in place, just waiting for a long crane to help us set it up. While figuring out how to fix the transmitter, we went ahead with setting up the antenna tower.

Early in the morning of the day that we were ready to do the job of raising it, the Lord gave me a surprising verse in my reading of the day.

12Now I want you to know, brothers and sisters, that what has happened to me has actually served to advance the gospel. (Philippians 1:12)

Now, what was going to happen? I shared this with Poto our chauffeur (another Congolese son). I said to Poto that I was sure that this was for us and this morning's activities, but what was going to happen. I gave him instructions that when he goes to help us that morning, he shouldn't park the vehicle anywhere near the spot where we were about to raise the antenna and tower. We all got there on time, even the crane and the operator were there on time. We had all the guide wires in place, the foundation was well set, the crane had his hook in and began to raise the tower. The crane raised the triangular constructed tower and we got the two legs set in place. We just needed to have the third one aligned, but when I looked up and saw the hook of the crane fall from its position and the whole antenna and tower began to fall I hollered, "HOLD IT, HOLD IT!"

I shouted to the guys on the guide wires, but even though it was getting close to being upright, it was still leaning at too much of an angle, not yet near where we could pull it into place. It began to fall. "LOOK OUT!" I yelled, as the whole of it came crashing down over a nearby cement wall and on to the dirt road outside the compound. Right where we would have parked our vehicles. Everything was either badly bent or broken into a hundred pieces.

There we stood with our mouths wide open looking at each other. I collected myself and said, "Praise the Lord! What has happened to us today is for the advancement of the gospel!" They all thought that I was nuts! The radio and studio staff thought I was speaking out of shock. I didn't blame anyone, but shared with them what the Lord had shared with me that very morning, just a couple of hours earlier. We all just put our arms around each other in a nice circle and thanked the Lord for what he was about to accomplish… and that no one was hurt.

This must have been in late 1994 or early in 1995. The radio had been going strong. Many people were listening daily to our broadcasts, but now, suddenly, there was no signal, no radio transmission. People began blaming the government of Kinshasa that they had shut us down again.

In the meantime, we realized that we could not fix the transmitter. We would have to send it back to HCJB in the US to have it repaired. After a brief time, we found a way to do this and requested a new antenna at the same time. Within the week we received a visit from the National radio and TV stations saying that they would give us free time on national radio and free time on national television to explain what had happened and explain that the government had not shut us down! They did not want to be blamed again for this closure. Amazing! This was God's doing!

Funds Came In

We went on the air and television and explained what had happened and then launched a campaign for the people of Kinshasa to give for the "furtherance of the Gospel."

"America gave the first amount and received the blessing," we announced. "Now it is time for the city of Kinshasa to give to the Lord and receive His blessing." That was the gist of the announcement.

We waited to see what God would do. For four months the people came with their meager gifts, in a time where there was much starvation in the city. They gave the equivalent of 5000 US dollars the first month. And then the same for the next three months which gave us the sum total of $20,000 US. We were not only able to buy a stronger transmitter (500 watts), but also a new and stronger antenna as well as a badly needed air conditioning unit to keep the place cool and out from under the stifling humidity. We were also able to have more broadcasting material and pay our DJ's to work longer hours. [76]

Discipleship lessons

We would receive many letters from listeners on how a program on the radio had affected their lives. I always enjoyed reading these accounts. One account really stood out to me as it was written by a

---

[76] Later, there was a fire and the radio burnt to the ground, no fault of our own. But there again the Lord provided, and the ministry grew to be greater than it was before. What the enemy means for destruction, the Redeemer turns it out for our good!

young gal, living at home. She wrote to the station and gave us this story (a dynamic translation).

"I was kneeling at my bed writing down some notes from a message on the program on discipleship which I always listened too. My father forbade me from using the home radio to listen to the Christian station, but I was able to procure a little pre-tuned solar powered radio that RSM gave out [sent to SSM from GALCOM]. *I would go into my small room turn the radio softly on and then make notes on discipleship, as I heard it on the radio.*

One evening as I was doing this I heard a noise in the other room, but didn't pay much attention to it. However, it was a group of thieves that had broken into the house and began emptying it of all good furniture and household items that they could steal. They had piled the things outside ready to make their escape when they opened the curtain and saw me kneeling beside my bed, they thought I was praying, and then they heard the voice of the radio talking about God. They got just enough of the message to make them completely petrified and I heard them saying to each other that this was God's home and they better not tamper with God! They fled in fear, leaving all the stuff outside of the house."

The young girl then wrote that when her father saw all that had happened he asked if he could believe in such a God as would scare off the thieves.

She finished her letter by saying that she was now teaching her father the lessons on discipleship which she had copied down from listening to the radio! She also wrote that the whole family is now listening to RSM on the family radio (but still giving great thanks for receiving that little solar powered one).

Articles and Blurbs in The Alliance Magazine

At various times the radio ministry made news in Kinshasa newspapers and that was good publicity for us in the Congo. But sometimes our ministry even made it to the official Alliance Magazine of the CMA in the USA. Here are a few blurbs and articles from the Alliance Witness or Alliance Life:

Number 1: Zaire: New Name, Old Problems

Since the recent fall of General Mobutu's 32-year regime, Zaire tentatively has been renamed the Democratic Republic of Congo. But problems persist for both the people and the church in this land of 45 million people, including about 13 million evangelical Christians. Thirty-Five C&MA missionaries are buried here. The country suffers from ethnic conflict and 1,000 to 3,000 percent inflation annually. Pray for a successful transition to good government, an end to corruption, for the doors to remain open for the gospel and for God's continuing protection over the church and **Radio Sango Malamu ("Good News").** The Kinshasa station, operated by Alliance field director Jim Sawatsky and a staff of nationals, uses a suitcase-size transmitter to broadcast the gospel to a potential audience of more than 4 million. During the rebel takeover of the capital city, Alliance missionaries were able to go to a safe place, and the radio station and churches were left largely unmolested.

"Our radio has been on the air, bringing hope to the people of the city," said Jim. "I have encouraged them to do live intercession times on the radio, calling all believers to prayer on the city's behalf. I believe we need to be light to a very darkened and discouraged populace at this moment."

Number 2: Congo-Kinshasa: Radio Station Able to Broadcast

Praise God that Radio Sango Malamu has been able to continue to broadcast even though electricity in Kinshasa has been limited (see Kingdom Concerns, 9/23 issue). Station director Jim Sawatsky says "The Lord answers prayer, again! And again! It was even more than we could have thought to ask for. We not only have a license and an assigned frequency for our station, but we have retained licenses and frequencies for eight other cities." Continue, however, to cover this project in prayer. The situation in Kinshasa is still difficult and food is scarce. Pray that God will supply the needs of believers there.

Number 3: Let the Earth Hear His Voice

The actual article was photocopied and is reproduced here below. Pictures are updated to be clearer.

Let the Earth Hear His Voice

By JAMES R. SAWATSKY

A Christian radio station in Zaire? That is impossible, Lord. For more than 30 years there has been only the national station in Kinshasa. The government would never give us a license."

years ago when the Lord first planted in my heart the desire for a Christian radio station in Zaire's capital.

A year or so later, a businessman with considerable wealth and influence looked over our audio production center in Zaire.

"Jim," he said, "you have the infrastructure here to start a radio station. What is holding you back?"

My response was the same one I had given God. "The government would never give us a license."

The man discounted my pessimism. "I believe it would," he countered. "In fact, I will use my influence to help you get a license."

That was 1991, just before the pillage in Kinshasa, which eventually spread to the rest of Zaire. Most missionaries were evacuated from Zaire, including my wife, Dawn, and me. While at home in Canada, I had a call from Richard MacDonald, who also had been forced from Zaire. He told me he had a radio station in Bukavu. If we wanted to, we could begin an extension of his Bukavu station "anywhere in Zaire, including Kinshasa," he said.

The Beginning

That was exciting news! I wasted no time contacting pioneer missionary broadcasters HCJB, negotiating for a 100-watt stereo FM transmitter, complete with antenna. We returned to Kinshasa in 1992 prepared to go forward on an extension to the Bukavu station.

Inasmuch as all the papers and documents MacDonald sent us were in order, it took us only a little more than a year to wade through the government red tape, secure a frequency, find a building for the station and install and test the FM transmitter from HCJB.

January 1, 1994, we were on the air with four full hours of broadcasting. We were elated! So, obviously, were the citizens of Kinshasa, who welcomed this new listening option enthusiastically. Surveys indicated that we were reaching 2 to 3 million listeners regularly.

But not for long. By March the government had shut us down. They offered a number of reasons for their action, but two were the most prominent. "We don't know who you are," and, "Whoever heard of a capital city having an exten-

Continuation of the Article…

[Continued from previous page]

sion radio station? If you want a radio station in Kinshasa, you need to apply for one on your own, originating here in Kinshasa."

The Lord encouraged us, assuring us that before long we would again be on the air. So we introduced new papers, asking the government to license our own Radio Sango Malamu (Radio Good News—RSM) at the same frequency.

Although we complied with all the regulations, the government refused to issue us a license. As we continued to pray and hold the Lord to His promises, we saw that a new minister of information and press had been appointed. At once we requested an audience.

By Prayer

Two associates, one of them Pastor Babaka, vice president of Studios Sango Malamu, and I would call on the minister. On the way to his office I mentioned to the two men with me that I thought we should pray with the minister even before we talked about our purpose for being there. (Little did any of us know that the minister had agreed to speak with us only because his wife had become an avid listener to our earlier broadcasts!)

After we were seated in the minister's luxurious office, I asked him if we might first pray. To my amazement, the minister jumped to his feet.

"OK," he said excitedly, "let's pray!"

Pastor Babaka began to pray. He prayed that God, in the name of Jesus, would bind the forces of evil, neutralize the fetish influences and liberate the minister to make the right decisions. I thought the minister might throw us out of his office. But the pastor concluded with a blessing upon the minister. When he finished, we all sat down.

The minister was deeply touched. It was the first time, he said, that anyone had come into his office and prayed for him and blessed him in his government ministry. He added that we were absolutely right in praying as we did. If we wanted our own radio station, we needed to continue to use the power of prayer. The forces against us, he acknowledged, were not primarily political but spiritual.

We thanked him sincerely and returned to our studios to pray.

We waited—and prayed—for about a month and then requested another interview. This time the minister received us with open arms. After we had again prayed together, the minister informed us that he was free to grant Radio Sango Malamu a temporary license. We could begin broadcasting immediately!

Radio Sango Malamu On—and Off—the Air

We went on the air in August, 1994 with the same 100-watt FM transmitter, same frequency and same makeshift studio. But this time we had our own name and our own call letters.

We began with eight hours of programming each day, not four. It wasn't long before the local newspapers were reporting that two-thirds of Kinshasa was tuned to RSM, "Your Christian radio station."

But then tragedy struck. I got an urgent call from the station reporting that the transmitter was not functioning as it should. Indeed, I already was aware of the situation because I could barely receive the signal on my personal radio. I rushed over to the station.

It didn't take us long to determine the problem. Due to serious fluctuations in the municipal electric current, our air-conditioning that keeps the transmitter cool had failed. The transmitter had overheated.

At first it seemed like a small problem. Simply replace the "cooked" parts with similar ones—if we could find them. We sent a message to HCJB engineering describing our problem and offering our solutions. Before receiving HCJB's reply, we already were doing our best to get the transmitter up and running. Meanwhile, this downtime seemed like a good opportunity to raise the antenna and install the new triangular support structure that had been given to us.

It was a Saturday morning in mid-September. With the antenna job before us, I was meditating on Philippians 1:12. My translation of the French said, "The things that have happened to me are for the progress of the gospel."

I called Poto, our maintenance man,

into my office at the studio.

"Can we pray together before we start?" I asked. I showed him the verse God had just impressed on my mind. "I don't know what the Lord means for us, but I surely don't want anyone to get hurt." The two of us prayed for God's protection and blessing.

We got the antenna down and connected all the new parts. It only remained for us to set the assembly in place. I motioned to the crane operator to bring the whole system to an upright position. Everything was supposed to fall into place. But as I looked up, I saw 80 feet of unsupported antenna at a 60-degree angle. The crane operator had already let his hook drop. Like an enormous tree, the antenna toppled to the ground, breaking into a hundred pieces.

We stood there—all six or eight of us—stunned and speechless. The transmitter was down and now the antenna was useless. What a jolt! And then the Lord brought back to my mind Philippians 1:12.

"Guys," I said, "this is for the progress of the gospel." Little did I know at that moment how true my words actually were.

A Need for $10,000

Meanwhile, HCJB engineering had responded.

"Do not touch the transmitter," they cautioned. "If you do, you will only make it worse." Regrettably, they were right. We had touched it, and we definitely had made it worse.

They directed us to send the transmitter to them immediately. As we prepared to do so, we received another communication from HCJB. They just "happened" to have another transmitter available. It was a match for the now-useless one except twice as powerful. And it had a much more efficient antenna. Would we be interested?

We had no money, but surely this was the "progress of the gospel" that God had promised us. God would somehow provide.

"Send it," I replied.

What we needed, a local businessman adviser told us, was about $10,000 to pay for the equipment, fix the air-conditioning and do everything correctly. The businessman also suggested we

18

The first equipment RSM used to broadcast was a 100-watt FM transmitter. Today the station's equipment covers a 50- to 70-mile radius, including two capital cities: Kinshasa, Zaire, and Brazzaville, Congo.

look for the money in Zaire.

"If you go to Europe or North America," he said, "*they* will get the blessing of giving. Why not keep the blessing here in Zaire? Allow our Zairian brothers and sisters the opportunity to receive the blessing of abundant giving. We need to make this radio ministry our own."

Meanwhile, we were preparing to go on national radio and television explaining to our listeners what had happened. The government generously accorded us free time, perhaps to dispel any public notion that this RSM downtime was another political move.

And Then a Miracle

So we went on government radio and television explaining our problem. We also mentioned the financial need we faced to replace the damaged equipment.

Almost at once, we began receiving calls from various churches. The Association of Protestant Pastors in Kinshasa insisted that Radio Sango Malamu was *their* station. They determined that all church offerings on the first Sunday of October would be set aside for RSM.

While the transmitter was on its way,

people began stopping by with money. Individuals. Groups. Some with small packets of money; some with large. In a country considered to be in economic collapse, where annual inflation is 12,000 to 16,000 percent and where unemployment is 80 percent, that first month we received the equivalent of $5,000! It was amazing.

And the flow continued. The second month, another $5,000. And the third month, another. By the fourth month, we had received $20,000 in all! It was nothing short of a miracle. These funds not only gave us ample provision for all the necessary equipment, they enabled us to double our broadcasting time to 16 hours each day.

The new equipment sends out a much more powerful signal. We cover a 50- to 70-mile radius, including two capital cities: Kinshasa, Zaire, and Brazzaville, Congo. We estimate our potential listening audience to be 6 million. And if the newspapers are accurate, about two-thirds of that number—perhaps 4 million people—are listening to RSM every day!

What a tremendous answer to the word the Lord gave me that awful Saturday morning when the antenna col-

lapsed: "What has happened to me has really served to advance the gospel."

Our Thanks

We at Radio Sango Malamu in Kinshasa, Zaire, are grateful to HCJB, particularly those in its engineering department. They patiently have borne with our ignorance and willingly supplied just the equipment we needed. We thank God, too, for Hilfe fur Bruder, a German organization that has funded a professional broadcast studio for RSM. And we are grateful to The Christian and Missionary Alliance for its monthly financial allotment, without which we could not function.

Above all, as Paul put it in Second Corinthians 2:14, we thank God "who always leads us in triumphal procession in Christ and through us spreads everywhere the fragrance of the knowledge of him."

Long may Radio Sango Malamu proclaim the good news of Jesus Christ! ▣

Rev. James Sawatsky, a missionary to Zaire since 1972, reports that RSM is now broadcasting 18 hours a day. Plans are in progress for two more radio stations in populous areas of Zaire as well as a Christian TV station in Kinshasa.

Chapter Twenty-Eight: More Evacuations

God did greatly bless the radio. As I look back now on that accident, it is amazing that no one was hurt, no building or vehicle damaged and the solid brick enclosure withstood the heavy blow of that falling metal without hardly a scratch! But difficulty of a different kind was on the horizon.

The Rebel Army

In 1997, a rebel by the name of Laurent Kabila was marching across the Congo with his rag-a-muffin army, taking control of all the eastern provinces as he was passing through.

On May 17,1997 General Laurent Kabila and his troops reached the capital Kinshasa, sent Mobutu into exile, and renamed Zaire the Democratic Republic of the Congo. On that day, Kabila was named President of the Democratic Republic of the Congo, which he held until his assassination in 2001.

Since Mobutu had said there would be blood running in the streets like water, Radio Sango Malamu called all its listeners to prayer and fasting for peace for the country and the capital. Intercessory prayer on behalf of the people was given day and night on the radio. And, I believe because of this, there was very little opposition and very little blood spilt that day as Kabila marched into the capital. He was actually welcomed with open arms by the populace of Kinshasa.

I really didn't want to leave the city at that time and felt sure all our missionary staff would be safe. Yet, due to the fact that I was the Field Director, I needed to take into consideration the opinions and welfare of the other CMA missionaries—the Hotalen family and the two single women.

Some of our former missionaries had already been redeployed to Brazzaville, starting a new field there as the CMA in the Republic of Congo. We kept radio contact with them and found out that all the families there banded together and figured that they had room enough for all of us from Kinshasa. Just to play it safe, as a team, we decided it would be the best part of wisdom to leave Kinshasa for a short time. We weren't sure what was going to happen. We went for a short "sabbatical" to Brazza, while Kabila marched into Kinshasa.

The Good Samaritans

I believe we were there for almost a month while things settled in Kinshasa. However, we saw little fireworks across the river, so presumed that God must have answered prayers of His people.

The Brazza team was very gracious to us all and gave us good accommodations. We had good visits, good debriefing and good opportunity to help them in teaching some of the TEE classes. We got to know missionaries working with Wycliffe Bible Translators and some others as well. At one point, we all thought it would be good to have a picnic together and took a drive outside the city to a remote area, not far from the Congo River. We had a great time, but it was on the way home that we saw the tragedy.

Coming around a curve in the little car, we came face to face with a horrendous accident. There were human bodies strewn all over the road and on the side of the road. Some were already dead, others were in very poor condition and needed serious medical attention. The sight will be forever etched in my mind. I think we were the last in the convoy of cars and watched as the first vehicles wound their way around bodies and then carried on to Brazzaville fearing that if they stopped they might get blamed for the accident. I wasn't driving, but Gramma and I and nurses Anne and Marion (from our Kinshasa team) were also in the car. It was already pretty full. What to do?

Both Anne and Marion spoke up and commanded the driver to stop, they couldn't leave this scene without doing what they could. After all they were nurses; they could quickly assess the situation. They immediately got out and began ministering what aid they could to those on and at the side of the road. Apparently, a taxi pickup, overloaded with people and merchandise, was going too fast around the curve and lost control, hitting another vehicle before landing on its side in the ditch, but not before ejecting bodies in a 50-foot radius.

They ended up with two women that needed to get to the hospital immediately or they wouldn't make it. They said, "We have to make room, we can't just leave them here to die!" So, we made room for one in our car and found another car that would take one as well. Both girls administered aid as best they could, trying to immobilize broken bones and endeavoring to stop bleeding. Then we headed as fast as we dared straight to the Brazzaville hospital. There the "our nurses" paid the admission fee for these women, bought what medicine that was needed and made sure they were comfortable and secure in hospital care.

I marveled at their action. When others passed by, these gals made sure we stopped! They ministered aid which probably saving these women's lives. They brought the injured to the hospital, paid for their expenses, contacted their families and prayed with them. Not until those hospitalized were on the road to recovery did our missionaries feel that their mission had been accomplished. I saw that day true "Good Samaritans" in action and said to myself, "Yes, that is what Jesus would have done!"

Back to Kinshasa

It wasn't long after that incident that I felt I should go across the river and touch base with the national church. We have been away almost a month and the CMA had financial obligations that needed to be fulfilled towards the national church and its leaders. I was able to contact MAF and they agreed to come and pick me up. Gramma would stay until I felt all was clear and then I would give the signal for the rest to come.

When I landed at the big international airport in Kinshasa, it was absolutely vacant! There was not even a customs officer available to stamp my passport. I had to hunt one down! The MAF pilot took me home and I could not believe how bare the streets were. But all was calm! I immediately sent word for Gramma and the other missionaries to come with all their stuff and arranged for MAF to bring them back

The next day 33 showed up at our house for lunch.

to Kinshasa. I left the next day for Boma and meetings with the church president, Rev. Albert Paku.

However, Gramma was the only one who came that next day and even was able to bring the big keyboard that I had brought over with me. All our stuff came with her on the MAF airplane and was all tucked away in our house when, a few days later, all bedlam broke loose in Brazza. This story has been written up in another book, but missionaries, ours included, barely escaped with MAF as they were dodging bullets shot at the plane. While I was in Bas-Congo, it was Gramma's turn to now play host to some 30-people flooding in from Brazzaville. She fed them all and then helped them find places to stay. Some finally left for their home countries.

The Stadium "Stade des Martyrs"

It was in the beginning of November of that year (1997), after the Kabila gov't was well established, that Radio Sango Malamu (RSM) woke up to the fact that we needed to give thanks to God for sparing us a blood bath. We called all the intercessors, all the radio audience, to come to a big celebration of thanksgiving. We needed to give thanks to God for how He answered our prayers. We announced, "Come and spend the day with us—a day of thanksgiving and prayer." This was put on uniquely by RSM, it was to be a non-denominational gathering of all who had been praying and all who desired to come and give thanks. We would start at 11:00 a.m. and terminate at 6:00 p.m. on December 31st (1997).

Many thought we were a little too bold (to put it mildly) to go for the stadium, but we didn't want to turn anyone away. The first time

RSM called people together we thought we would have 500. But we had 5000 trying to cram into campus of Evangelism Resources, the home of SSM. Many had to be turned away. The next time we went to a nearby church that held 5000, but there again we shot too low--10,000 tried to cram in and many were turned away. We had to turn away lots of people both times. This time we thought we will not turn anyone away. Even if we have only 30,000 in attendance, that's OK, we won't turn anyone away.

The day was well announced on our radio and on national radio and TV. Up to this point RSM was only nominally known by the non-Christian and government populace, but that day God made us known, by his intervention and for His glory. He put it in the hearts of people to come and spend almost the whole day worshipping Him, praying to Him, giving thanks to Him, confessing their wrongs before Him and praying blessing on the land and people. We also heard from Him through powerful, anointed preachers. The Holy spirit was so present that when people came in late they sensed so forcefully the presence of God in the place that many of them just burst into tears (including some important and wealthy men from Brazzaville).

There was a lot of music and an abundance of instruments, brass bands, worship bands, choirs of all sorts making music in the hearts and aloud to God with honor and thankful hearts for bringing the city through a very tough time without bloodshed. Our hearts were full of gratitude and thanksgiving to God for answering our prayers. All the music was great, but when the people sang it could be heard for miles around. Then people started running to the stadium.

It is interesting to know that President Mobutu never filled the stadium with his presentations and political rallies, the football clubs never filled the stadium with their competitions, the most popular Congolese bands never filled the stadium with their concerts, but that day, December 31, 1997, God filled that stadium to overflowing with His people. We aired the whole program live from the stadium and we finally had to announce that the stadium was more than full. We had to lock the doors and turn people away. The stadium was built to legally hold 80,000 people, but some speculated that there were up to 120,000 in attendance. There was not a spot available in the stands,

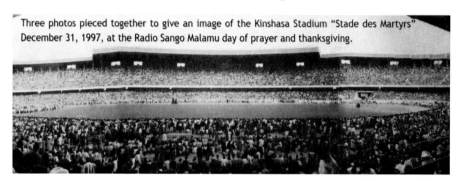

Three photos pieced together to give an image of the Kinshasa Stadium "Stade des Martyrs" December 31, 1997, at the Radio Sango Malamu day of prayer and thanksgiving.

nor on the track—we were not allowed to go on the grass. God was honored that day in Kinshasa and Radio. Now everyone in Kinshasa knew of Radio Sango Malamu, including the president of the country.

Now we were a spiritual force to be reckoned with and the whole of the 10 million people in Kinshasa, at that time, knew it… for the glory of God the Father had descended. Every year since that time, on December 31st, RSM calls people together for a day of celebration, and prayer.

A few years later, RSM and Studios Sango Malamu Ministries, were able to open up radio stations in three other locations and also open up a television station in Kinshasa. It continues its broadcasting and telecasting until this day.

The Surprise Trip to South Africa

It was during mid 90's, while a lot of unrest was carrying on in the country, that a good friend and director of Faith Comes By Hearing and the project that we were working on for him came to Kinshasa to check on how we were doing. We had run into some snares, but at the time the program was doing well, just a little behind schedule. Morgan was on his way to Cape Town, South Africa. Before his time with us at SSM had come to a close he had persuaded me to come with him to Cape Town and Johannesburg. The Studio agreed and asked that I purchase some equipment there that we had been saving for. Not only that, Gramma agreed! She indicated it would be good from me to get away. So away I went.

When we got to Jo-burg, a little late, the plane to Cape Town was full, even though we had reservations. Morgan had an appointment the next morning, so we had to get there, but the airline insisted that there was no room. He was beside himself, so I prayed. It seemed we had no choice but to stay in Jo-burg overnight. On the way out of the airport we heard our names being called. We ran as fast as we could to the gate  and just made it on the plane. To Morgan's pleasant surprise, we were put **in first class**.

When we got to the hotel, the manager said he was terribly sorry, but our room had already been taken. How was that possible! I prayed; Morgan stewed. After all, it was his business trip. A few moments of "stewage" went by and then we heard, "However, I can upgrade you to a more plush and roomy suite for the same price!" Now Morgan was saying, "I need to bring you along with me more often!" The next morning, he went to his appointment and I snooped around Cape Town—a beautiful city.

When Morgan came back in the afternoon he came with an invitation from the Director of the Bible Society to dinner that night. He said I was included and it would be just a small restaurant somewhere. Little did he know. We were taken to a revolving restaurant at the top of the city which gave us the most splendid view all evening long. I ordered antelope.

Before we left for dinner, I was putting on my best shirt when I felt something in the pocket. I fished it out and it was a 100 US dollar bill.

Where it came from I didn't know and never found out, but this affirmed to Morgan that God was really giving me a special "vacation". First class all the way! Morgan was to leave the next morning and I was to meet him the next day in Johannesburg to spend the weekend there with friends.

That night I just ate at the hotel restaurant, not wanting to spend too much I just had a very small meal, but I asked around if there would be someone that could take me to see the sights of the area. They brought a taxi driver over to me who said he would take me around for $200 for the whole day. Well, that wasn't going to work, as I didn't have that much to spend, but I did have the $100 that I found in my shirt pocket. So, in good African style, I just said that was way too expensive for me. I couldn't afford that much. I thanked him for being open to helping me, but didn't have that kind of money to spend.

Well, we got talking about Kinshasa and what I did there and in course of our conversation he came out with, "I'll do it for $100." I considered it, but wouldn't have anything left to eat if that was the case, so I didn't take him up on the offer.

He didn't leave, but probed more into what I was doing in Kinshasa and figured out that I was a missionary. He immediately said that he had a sister who was a missionary on a big boat that went from port to port and he knew that missionaries didn't have much money, so he came down to $50 for the entire day. That sounded better, but still didn't commit.

We talked some more and were very interested in each other's story. During the conversation I had decided to take him up on his offer. I was about to accept his 50-dollar for the day offer when he came out with, "Look, what I would like to do is take you around the whole area for the whole day and you just pay the gas. How about that?" I couldn't refuse.

We had a great time together and saw where the Indian and the Atlantic Oceans meet, saw the penguins, checked out another Christian radio station and generally went all around the Cape. In the evening I treated him to a big lobster meal and we were both happy and enjoyed each other's company. I thought I might have the opportunity to lead him to accepting Jesus into his life, but he wasn't quite ready for that. So, I left that up to his sister.

The next day, Saturday, he picked me up and took me to the Cape Town airport for the regular fare and a big tip. I met Morgan and his friends at the airport in Johannesburg. We had a great "Barbie" in the back yard of his friend's place and a good swim in the pool.

Sunday was a good church day and Monday, our hostess, the wife, said she would take me around Jo-burg to find the piece of equipment that I was looking for. Morgan flew off to America and we went out on the town. We visited another Christian radio station and checked many stores but did not find the right item. She suggested I stay another day and we could look some more, but I had a feeling that I had to get home immediately.

Tuesday saw me on the plane for Kinshasa.

Burglars in the House

By the time I arrived at home I was worn out, super-hot and sweaty. I didn't take long for me to have a shower and get into bed for a relaxing sleep. I kept the AC on as that would keep me cool, perhaps turn it off later. We generally did not sleep with the AC on. We just opened the window and took in a cool evening breeze.

Unbeknownst to us, due to the noise of the air conditioning unit, a group of thieves with their guns began to break into the house. They had tied up our night watchmen, face to the ground and arms tight behind their backs, tied to each other. They found a hacksaw in my garage and started cutting through the iron bars around the veranda. It took them a couple of hours to get through the bars and then shook the inside door so hard that the paddle lock that I had just inserted (but not closed) in the door fell to the ground and they were in. They found our suitcases in an empty room and began to load them with as much electronics as they could carry (I was working on a project in the house for the studio and had a fair bit of electronics--video and sound equipment). They looked all over for money. Took everything out of the fridge to see if we had stored some there and went through all the other bedrooms-—while we were peacefully sleeping.

Suddenly, there were bursts of gunshots just outside our bedroom door. I shot up perpendicular in bed as if release from a heavy-duty spring. Not knowing what was going on, but hollered, in French, "In the name of Jesus be calm!" Some more gunshots rang out, this time coming through the door and our chest of drawers, ricocheting around the room. One came to rest in a book right beside Gramma's head. I shouted all the louder (again in French), "In the name of Jesus be calm!" They calmly entered the room, didn't harm us, but calmly ripped us off—everything they could carry in the suitcases that they had found.

Seeing Eyes Blind!

The leader with rags around his head (they all had their faces covered) pointed a gun to my head and said to me in French, "Give me your dollars. I want dollars. If I don't get dollars someone is going to die." He then started ripping off my gold wedding ring and my gold chain (which I wore in those days). I said that I had no dollars of my own, took my wallet from my brief case and showed him I had only 5 dollars left. There was another wallet there with $1000.00 in it, but that money belonged to the studio. It was "God's money", saved up for some special equipment that I didn't find or buy for the Studio Ministry. I immediately prayed a similar prayer to that of brother Andrew, in the book *God's Smuggler*, "Lord you made blind eyes to see when you walked on this earth, but now I'm asking you to make seeing eyes blind!" I added, "This is your money!"

Brother Andrew - God's Smuggler – "When You were on earth, You made blind eyes see. Now, I pray, make seeing eyes blind."

Seeing the look on the leader's face, the scoff and the five dollars and the gun at my head, Gramma immediately said, "I have dollars, I have dollars!!" And produced fist full of money. I didn't know about this! From her drawer she took a couple hundred dollars in small bills that she had just that day taken from the mission in order to give it away in small portions to the many poor that came to our door. But, she said, "This is God's money!"

The thief replied, "I'll take care of God, just give me the money!" Another of the thieves began grabbing at her rings, but her rings were so tight that they would not come off. The leader suggested the rings be left as they were taking too much time and it was almost getting light outside (according to the night guards, they had come around 2 am and it was now 4 am when people in the neighborhoods start to stir).

Another thief, for the second time, came once more and rifled through my open briefcase, sitting on the floor beside my bed, in order to find more money, but didn't touch the wallet. This was amazing as it was in plain view from where I was sitting. They finally left with all their loot, suitcases on top of their heads, walking through the iron door of our big iron gate.

The neighborhood was quite upset when they heard that we had been robbed at gun point. Of course, we reported everything to the authorities, but they had no means of following up the robbery. Our neighbors, on the other hand, were not going to let this event slip through the cracks. They said, "This is our white man! He fixes the water pipes when they break, he fixes the electricity when there is a break in the transmission lines and he finds a way to repair the roads when needed. We will not let this happen to him without us looking into it."

They immediately went through the neighborhood asking the people if they saw men walking very early in the morning with suitcases on their heads. Many did. They were led straight to the house and caught the ring leader with his girl in the house with all our stuff. We never got our stuff back, but the leader of the group was wanted for murder in the next big city and was taken to the police station where they beat him within an inch of his life. He and many others learned that day that you don't trifle with God's money!

Group Sango Malamu II—during the 1990's we sang in concerts, travelled to Holland and sang at the stadium with c.120,000 people attending. All have gone on to professional music ministries of their own. From left to right: Joel Bumba, Kool Matope, Samy Biay, Runo Moyo and Jim

Part VII - The Post Kinshasa Years

Chapter Twenty-Nine: Medical Evacuation

Malaria Plus, Plus, Plus, Plus!

In 1998 I was medically evacuated. By this time our missionary team was very small. Although we were responsible to the CMA in USA, we were four Canadian and two Americans missionaries left on the field plus four children. As Field Director, I was responsible for keeping in good contact with the National church leaders, especially the president of the national church. I had done some travelling in the Bas-Congo region where the headquarter of the Alliance was, had meetings with the president, presented our financial obligations to the church and also travelled right to the coast of Muanda—on official church business. I remember being bitten by some pretty pesky mosquitos, but thought nothing of it at the time.

About two weeks after I had arrived home in Kinshasa, I felt that I was coming down with Malaria and asked Gramma if she had a Malaria cure. She had some special medicine which she kept on hand for the "street boys" she looked after and gave it to me. A few months before this, I sensed the Lord was telling me to take a prophylaxis (regular anti-malaria medicine), so I was already taking malaria medicine, but I thought that a cure couldn't hurt. As it turned out, the cure that Gramma gave me helped save my life.

It was Friday and all the other CMA missionaries were gathering together for our "Team Meeting" --a time of study, worship, "catchup", prayer and fellowship as we regularly did on Fridays. After a good time of sharing and prayer over our personal ministries, which was so important to us all, we would all meet again around two p.m. at the Portuguese club for tennis, a swim and a dinner together, often with other missionaries as well (some would bring a lunch and stay right on through to the two o'clock rendezvous). Fridays were the times that really kept our team together--loving, caring, praying, interacting, playing and eating together. None of us wanted to miss this special day. But due to my feeling not so great, I opted out that day.

Even though I was taking a regular malaria cure, and had already taken another cure, around dinner time that evening, I was feeling very poorly. I had thrown up and had quite a high fever, so I decided to call someone on the radio in hopes that some missionary would hear, answer and get word to Dawn at the club to come home. I was thinking this is beginning to get quite serious.

I called on the FM portable radio that we had, with little hope of reaching anyone because I knew all would be at the club (called A.S.K.). It is always so interesting in hind sight to see how God orchestrated events. I have no doubt that the enemy of our souls wanted to take me out that day. However, here is what happened as I recall it.

When I got up to call on the radio, I found that a young Congolese woman had come into the house. She just came walking in and said that she was going to stay in one of our bedrooms and started taking off her clothes. She was not in her right mind; I could tell that immediately and sensed she was being manipulated by Satan and his evil spirits. That's when I thought I was really being attacked by the enemy on many fronts. I called the night guard, who was there by this time, and asked him to see that this gal quickly left the premises and persuaded her in the Name of Jesus to leave. It wasn't easy, but she left, and I locked the door.

I then went to the radio to call, hoping against hope that someone might hear. "Sky five, here, anybody out there on this frequency? Sky five calling…" After a few attempts, Stan Hotelan came on the radio. "Hi Jim, this is Stan. I'm just in my car going home from the club to get something and then I'm going right back. What's happening?" Stan and family lived only a few minutes from the club in the mission duplex and compound, where the single women also lived, on the other side of the duplex. How grateful I was that he "just happened to be there" and heard my call. I asked him to let Dawn know that I was doing very poorly and requested that she come home with one of the nurses. The message got through.

Just after I said, "Over and out!" I heard a banging on the door. I thought it might be that same gal trying to come in again, but heard the young voices say, "Papa Jim, Papa Jim." I knew it was my neighbor kids whom I considered my adopted family and loved them very much. I had spent a lot of time with them, playing, singing with them, teaching them computer stuff, and even paying for their school fees. They "just happened" to come over. I went and opened the door, but felt the immediate need for bed or I was going to collapse. They saw my plight and when I asked for their mom, who was a head nurse in the local hospital, they said that she "just happened" to turn the corner of their yard when they were coming over. I asked them to run and fetch her for me and left the door open. I immediately went to my bedroom.

Mama Azita was not going to be home, according to her testimony. She had planned to visit her married daughter in another part of the city after her shift, but felt a strong urge to go home immediately. She didn't know why, but changed her plans in mid-stream and headed straight for home. She had hardly reached her house when the children ran home and called her to come quickly, "Papa Jim needs you!"

She came as quickly as she could, but by this time I was on the floor in my bathroom. I had just thrown up profusely and didn't have the energy to move, so lay flat on the tile floor beside the toilet. It was cool on my body, especially on my face, and I thought it was good for me to stay there for a while, until I got some strength at least. Mama Azita and the kids found me there. She immediately told them to go and get their father.

Now Dr. Azita was practically never home. This was probably one of the reason for which three or four of their six children were always over at our place. Mama Azita and Mama Dawn (Gramma) had become good friends too. Every room of our house was known to them and they were welcome anytime, without knocking. However, Papa Azita was not so well known as he was always on the road as an itinerant doctor for the state. He had at one point been president Mobutu's doctor, but for some reason that had changed and he received this itinerant posting. He was a good and very intelligent doctor and he "just happened" to be home as well that evening.

When he came he knew immediately that the situation was serious and told everyone to clear the area and asked for a stethoscope and a cuff to take my blood pressure. He would not let me get up. He sent the children over to the ER compound, just behind our place, to ask for a nurse who we knew was there, evacuated from Brazzaville Congo. She too was not feeling well and had stayed in the house they were renting until they could return to their home in Brazzaville. Despite her own sickness, nurse McCabe came over immediately with her apparatus. She "just happened" to be there for "such a time as this" for when she gave the stethoscope and cuff to the doctor he found that my blood pressure was 40 over zero. He was right in not letting me get up.

At the same time, Camille and Esther Ntoto (just recently married), who were also renting a house on the ER compound, had "just happened" to return home from being on their way to a church meeting.

On their way, she remembered she had left an important item at their house, so they turned around. It was while they were returning that the children saw them and said, "Papa Jim is seriously ill. Come quickly he needs you." In the kids' minds, I needed them as they were leaders in our Sango Malamu Ministry. It didn't take them long to arrive through the gate in the carport and asses the matter. The doctor gave them strict orders to go immediately to get the important medication that he needed to get my blood pressure up and stabilized. They "just happened" to be using our pickup and had wheels to go quickly to get the medication which happened surprisingly fast. (We found out later that when they went to the nearest drugstore/pharmacy, the pharmacist saw the panic on their faces and immediately gave them all they requested.) In short order they were back, an amazing happening in Kinshasa. Normally it would never happen that quickly. Generally, they would have to go from pharmacy to pharmacy to get all that they needed, but this one pharmacy "just happened" to have ALL that the doctor prescribed.

Meanwhile, on the floor I was gasping for breath. I had found it difficult to breath as it seemed that all functions were shutting down. I told Joyce McCabe that I was leaving them, that a dark cloud was coming on my brain and that my feet were numb. I said, "I'm on my way out, say goodbye to Dawn." As I write this it reminds me of a song that I enjoyed by Andraé Crouch, "It Won't Be Long."

> *"It won't be long*
> *When we'll be leaving here*
> *It won't be long*
> *We'll be going home."*

I thought sure that I was leaving and going home. Fortunately, Joyce McCabe (the nurse) had presence of mind to give me a bag to breathe into. I revived. She said that I was hyperventilating because I was taking such short breaths. I was in shock as well.

Some other missionaries, tall and strong, had come over when they heard of my serious condition. Dr. Azita took complete charge and commanded them to lift me up horizontally and take me to the couch in the front room where he gave me an injection and improvised a make-shift intravenous hook up for the other medications. The couch was moved close to the window and with an old coat-hanger he found a way to hook up the intravenous bag to the top of the window.

When Gramma came with Marion Dick and Anne Stephens, the two single missionary nurses, they found me on the couch, hooked up that way and attended to by Dr. Azita and nurse Joyce. After the bag was empty and my blood pressure had come up, the doctor insisted that they take me to the Belgian clinic and have me taken care of there. So, again I was lifted horizontally and laid to rest in the back of an old bronco and taken downtown. At the clinic, I was loaded on a stretcher and put in a bed off in a corner. Gramma stayed with me. I kept her awake by throwing up all night long. Even though they gave me quinine intravenously it still had its adverse effects. I was released the next morning, having finished the heaves, though still very weak. I was taken home in another vehicle, this time perpendicular, but I almost passed out on the way home. I was still very sick and consequently had to stay mainly horizontal for the next ten days when I finally had strength enough to resume my duties.

I have put quotation marks around "just happened" because I don't believe it just happened. I am firmly convinced what would appear to be a coincidence was all orchestrated by God. I was near death's door. I found out later that two other white men working with Gulf Oil, who had been in the same area in which I was working, had died with cerebral malaria about the same time I was taken to the hospital. Is that another coincidence? I think not. God prepared me for this and also taught me some valuable lessons:

1. Listen to the voice of the Holy Spirit--that inner voice. I felt the Lord saying to take a prophylaxis and I'm sure glad I did. The doctors said that taking that daily dose plus taking the cure and having professional medical help nearby saved my life. When I arrived home on medical evacuation, the doctor in Toronto said that I was probably one of the few who had cerebral malaria and lived to talk about it. He also mentioned how wise the doctor was who treated me in Kinshasa. He said if Dr. Azita had let me stand up with such low blood pressure, I would have had massive heart failure and would have died on the spot.

2. Don't hesitate to call for help when you really need it. Calling for help saved my life as well. It brought people around me that knew what to do.

3. God has a plan for our lives and when we listen to Him the enemy cannot thwart it.

4. The prayers of God's people are very powerful.

5. It is true that the enemy of our souls goes about as a roaring lion seeking whom he may devour!

A Relapse

A few days after I was up and around, I organized the installation of an antenna for the radio station we were setting up in a new location and new building. It was on the top of a three-story building with a metal structure made to support a high, heavy tower. We hinged the bottom of the tower in place on the second story. The top end was on the ground. Using an electric winch, we pulled the tower up until it was perfectly vertical and braced against that metal support structure. It worked perfectly, but took us all day to get everything into place. I was in the hot sum most of the day and because of getting overheated the malaria bug became active again. I didn't know that I had to wait at least a month before I could go into the sun again. I was back in bed again with Malaria, but this time with typhoid fever as well. My resistance was so low, my immune system so attacked that I couldn't ward it off (typhoid often likes to piggy-back on a Malaria attack). On top of that I had serious headaches and my head was twirling like I was on a tilt-a-whirl at the fair. I had serious vertigo.

When the US doctor whom we knew examined me again (for after the original crisis Dr. Azita was off again on his rounds), he said the best thing he could recommend is to go home; be medically evacuated for further medical examinations and treatment. He didn't know what caused the dizzy spells and was afraid that the cerebral malaria had caused damage somewhere in the brain.

A Prayer for Healing

The day after his recommendation, we had a Field Team meeting and all agreed that I should leave and be treated in Canada. I didn't want to go, but succumbed to the majority decision. We asked Esther and Camille to stay in our house. That next evening with tickets in hand, we were in our home waiting to leave for the airport and catch an overnight flight to Switzerland. Our missionary team was there, a few other friends and missionaries from ER were there and someone said they should pray for me. This was all good. They had good intentions, but the prayer, I felt, was more perfunctory than really meeting with God. I wasn't healed, but perhaps God had other "things" in mind.

Shortly after, just before Gramma and I were about to leave, the general director of our ministry, brother Futi, knocked on the door and came in. "What's this I hear about your leaving?" he said. I had asked him to come over earlier as I knew I had to talk things over with him, but he had a speaking engagement and was not able to come right away. I explained what the doctor said and then we discussed the program of the SSM ministry. Thinking that I wouldn't be gone too long, we didn't go into too much detail. Futi Luemba was a great leader and I knew the ministry was in very capable hands.

After our discussion I asked him to pray for me and in the midst of people milling around and chatting, we sat on the couch and he put his hands on me and prayed. Futi knew how to pray and I was glad he had come. It wasn't a long prayer, but it was powerful and straight to the point. It was a prayer of faith. He left then as quickly as he had come. The friends standing around encouraged me to get ready to leave for it was time we made a dash for the airfield of N'djili. As we were leaving I whispered to Gramma, "I believe God has healed me, I don't need to go!" However, that wasn't an option at this point. All the wheels were already set in motion.

They put me in the VIP lounge at the airport and went looking for a wheel chair to roll me out to the plane. They couldn't find one, so the airline officials sent me on ahead saying just take your time. I walked about 125 meters on the tarmac to the plane, slowly but I thought I was gaining strength with every step. I was so weak before that it was all I could do to stand for a while. I climbed the long stairs into the plane and felt good.

The stewardess came and made me comfortable. She could see that I still wasn't in the greatest of health. She said, "Don't worry, we will take good care of you. Nothing has ever happened on our Swiss Air flights and we will be on the ground in Switzerland before you know it." It was something like that; trying to reassure me of a good flight.

The Airline Surprise

Around eleven o'clock in the evening we touched down in Lomé, Togo. Greater Lomé, being the capital of the country had a population of about a million people at that time. It was an active center with a lot of international industry and oil. The airplane did not stay long at the airport and soon we were on our way again. As we were climbing to the destined altitude, at about 25,000 feet, there was a small explosion.

It seemed to me that someone had left the WC door open and flushed the toilet which was completely stuck open. There was a mighty rushing-sucking whooshing sound. However, none of the attendants were seen, no one was moving to do anything about it. Suddenly, the oxygen masks came down with the instruction from the pilot to put them on immediately as he dropped the plane to 10,000 feet. I grabbed my mask and put it on in a jiffy, but Gramma was busy trying to help the inebriated woman next to her, so I shouted, "Put your mask on first and then help her before you pass out!"

It all happened so fast and I was so worried about Gramma that I didn't even feel the plane descend. The next minute the pilot came over the intercom with the words that a seal had broken in the door (just opposite us) and that we were now at a height which would equalize the pressure. The broken seal was what made that big vacuum cleaner-like noise and that is why nobody came to check the door. They would have been sucked out immediately if the door had not held and they knew it. Good thing we both had our seat belts on. Well, we didn't need the masks anymore and the pilot announced that we were looking for an airstrip on which to land. Nigeria wouldn't take us, so we went back to Lomé.

The three-star hotel in Lomé could accommodate us all, the announcer said. I had my doubts, but we all were transported to the hotel and we waited. Around five in the morning we were fortunate enough to be given a key to a room. A man had just left, the bathroom was all wet from his shower, the bed clothes were all crumpled and awry from his sleep and nothing was in order. I said to Gramma, just turn the pillow cases inside out, smooth the bed out and we'll lay on top of it and get some sleep, which we did.

Now during all this kafuffle and upset, I kept on saying, "I'm getting stronger and I'm getting better! I can feel it." I had no more vertigo and was feeling like strength was pouring into my body. We finally left that afternoon for Zurich and arrived there in the evening. Swiss Air put us up (at the airlines expense, of course) in a first-class hotel complete with slippers and bath robes and all the other amenities of a five-star hotel. The eiderdown comforter and pillows were a real treat… and all the time I continued getting better.

By the time we finally landed in Toronto, I was ready to walk off as a normal person. In Zurich I was transported via wheel chair and then an electric cart as the airlines had tagged me and I was not allowed to walk. The same thing happened in Canada. They wouldn't let me walk off the plane. When they wheeled me out to meet the people from headquarters in Toronto, even though I was in a wheel chair, they were surprised to see that I was looking so good.

I felt that I had to explain to the CMA receiving committee that I had been prayed for just before I was about to leave and I felt the Lord's healing touch in my body. Auntie Ruth and Uncle Norm took us to their home and we were able to meet with all the doctors and take in all the medical appointments that had been arranged for us without difficulty. That's when the doctor in Toronto said to me, "You probably had cerebral malaria and if you had stood up from the bathroom floor you would have had a massive heart attack and you wouldn't be here now!" He and others, found nothing the matter with me, except that I was still weak.

Before leaving Toronto for Vancouver, we were taken for lunch by "the brass" of the CMA in Canada. We had a wonderful time and a great meal. I was quite thirsty and ordered a glass of coke, not realizing that there was much more sugar in the coke in Canada than there was in Congo. And not realizing again, that coke and all that sugar really dumps your immune system, I enjoyed it. And yes, it did dump my immune system. The vertigo came back, the weakness came back, the fever came back, and it took me another week or more of bed rest before I was able to travel again. Boy, did I regret that! I don't think that I ever had a Canadian coke again after that experience.

More Surprises

We were invited to stay with our good friends Bev and Merl Francis in White Rock, BC. White Rock seemed to be our home away from home (in Kinshasa) as we had always gone there for our home assignments. We had been asked to be missionaries in residence at Peace Portal Alliance Church up to this point for all our time spent in Canada after our first home assignment year at CBC/CTS. My parents, your great grandparents, were both home in heaven. Gramma's mother was there too, but Dad Layland (grandpa George) had remarried and was living in the White Rock area as well. We were delighted to be able to stay a few months with Bev and Merl while recuperating.

In 1998, God gave us a beautiful spring and He granted us privilege of walking every day on the beach. At first, I was exhausted after walking only about 100 meters, including the return trip. But as we continued walking each day I was able to enjoy further walks on the pier and along the beach. Later, I was even able to run a bit and so it seemed to us that therapy in Canada had done the trick.

After six months of west coast healing sea air, I was fully recovered, ready to return to Kinshasa. We were packed; tickets purchased. The day of our scheduled departure we got a phone call from the airlines, "Mr. Sawatsky, I'm afraid I must inform you that the Kinshasa airport has been surrounded by rebel forces and all flights to Kinshasa have been cancelled indefinitely.[77] Your tickets will be refunded immediately." What a shock! We had heard nothing. Kinshasa was in blackout and all we could find out was a little bit of info from Reuters.

Shortly after that, while we were waiting in limbo, Grandpa George's wife, Muriel, went into the hospital never to return. We didn't know how long Muriel would be under supervised care, but Grandpa George needed to be looked after as dementia was just setting in and he couldn't cook for himself. Gramma now felt it was time for her to take care of her father. He had been a staunch supporter of our ministry, but now could not live well on his own. So, Gramma stepped up to the plate. Also, she felt the Lord tapped her on the shoulder and said, "Now, this will be your new ministry—taking care of your father." Gramma never did make it back to Africa.

Wrapping Things Up

After the government in the DRC (Democratic Republic of Congo) had finally quieted things down, as the Field Director I really needed to get back to Kinshasa and the national church as they had been without communication from us and without funds that were generally supplied for specific ministries. Fortunately, all the missionaries had left just before this uprising in Kinshasa had occurred. Hotalens had returned for a year of home assignment and it "just so happened" that Marion (Dick) and Anne (Stephens) had also returned to Canada for special ministries. As Hotalens were not going back, we had our final Congo field leadership team conference in Red Deer, Alberta.

---

[77] War broke out in August 1998, when Kabila tried to expel Rwandan military forces that had helped him overthrow Mobutu. Anyone can read more on this on the internet. There were a lot of atrocities committed and I was glad none of our missionaries had to go through that stress again. You might be interested in the following article, http://www.independent.co.uk/news/rebels-fall-on-streets-of-kinshasa-1174727.html

I had a very good light leather jacket given to me by Uncle Norm Wylie which had a "million" pockets in it. I decided to wear that leather jacket all the way to the Congo and stuffed over 10,000 dollars in cash and checks in all the different pockets—most of them concealed. All were funds for the Congolese Alliance church. Seeing I had been away for some time, the funds which CMA in North America had promised each month to the Congolese national CMA church had mounted up and were carried in for immediate deployment. I arrived in Kinshasa without incident, but the plane had been late. We should have arrived a six p.m. but we didn't get to Kinshasa until after ten p.m.

By the time we cleared customs, it was after eleven p.m. The government had imposed an eleven o'clock curfew on the city and no one but military was to be travelling after that hour. We had no choice. We couldn't sleep at the airport and we had a pickup full of people. My neighbor kids had come to welcome me back (the ones who found me on the floor in my bathroom), my secretary had come, our director for Studios Sango Malamu, Futi Luemba, had also come to welcome me back and our "son" and chauffeur, Poto, was also there to drive us all in our vehicle. It was a great reunion and we decided to chance it and go straight home. All lived in the same general area.

We took the "ring road" around Kinshasa to get to our home on the opposite side of the city thinking that this might be the most secure. Not a good choice! In a place where there were absolutely no street lights, we came across a seven-ton military vehicle parked right across the road, packed with soldiers and their AK-47s. It seemed like we were in deep trouble.

I began to pray as the soldiers piled out of their truck and held us at gun point. We tried to explain who we were (everyone knew of Radio Sango Malamu in the city), but these guys wouldn't listen to reason. They rifled through our stuff, told us to get back into the double cab pick-up as they piled in as well and told Poto to start driving. You don't argue much with AK-47s and so we all obeyed. On the way, escorted by the big military vehicle and the rest of the soldiers, we were told that they were taking us to jail for having disobeyed the curfew order. For some reason they made several stops on the way to the military HQ and the jail, which was not very far from our home.

At each stop they were arguing with my secretary, Anne, who was fluent in Swahili. It seemed that they were Kabila's soldiers from the east and they only spoke Swahili. Anne was trying to reason with them and let them know that we were God's servants only, part of the Christian radio station RSM, and were only on the road because the plane that brought in the mundele missionary, president of this well-known ministry, was late. There was nothing we could do, but go home.

Most of the soldiers who climbed in our vehicle, had taken over the seats in the double cab so the rest of us were standing (some sitting) in the box at the back, with a few other soldiers. As we were travelling, I took off my jacket and gave it to Hiton, my neighbor's daughter. She was about 12 or 13 at the time (she was there with her two younger siblings to meet Papa Jim) and said, "You put this on, don't let anybody take it from you and you go home immediately. They won't put you and your siblings in jail, so just scurry home with the jacket. It has a lot of money in it!" She put it on and it hung down to her knees. The night air was a bit cool as we went flying down Ring Road, so the soldiers thought that I was just giving the child some extra protection from the wind.

At the last stop, before we were to turn the corner to the jail, Anne began arguing again with them. Futi saw the uselessness of it all and sat in the back of the pickup and started singing praises to the Lord. I quickly jumped in and joined him. I thought, "Yeah, that is what you do **before** you get to prison. Why wait until you get locked up before singing praises to God, as did Paul and Silas. Let's do it now!" So we did!

It didn't take long for all to get quiet, then Poto and Anne literally ran to the car, got in it and started moving, without saying a word. A few military also jumped in the back of the pickup with us and away we went. I banged on the top of the cab and leaned over and asked Poto through the open window, "Where are we going in such a hurry?"

He replied, "After you started singing, the leader turned to me and told me to take you all home as quick as I could. He gave me five minutes to take you home and come back with the soldiers as they had to go back to their post immediately."

Praise the Lord! It only took five minutes to get to our house where we all immediately jumped out of the vehicle. As Poto was turning the pickup around I found a bunch of Sango Malamu tapes that I had stashed away for an occasion like this and threw them to the soldiers in the back of the pickup. At this their whole demeanor changed and gave friendly waves, like old friends, as they drove out of the yard.

Poto was back in another 5 or 6 minutes with our pickup, empty and ready to head to his home for a good night's sleep. By this time, it was after midnight, but all were able to get home without a problem. Before Hiton headed next door, she took off the jacket and handed it to me.

When Futi started singing, I just knew that this was what needed to be done and joined him in full voice. I found out later that the frequent stops and arguing were meant to produce money (a bribe) for letting us go. I also found out that they dared not ask straight out for it because if word ever got back to their commander, it would literally mean their heads. President Kabila had said that corruption is to be annihilated and anyone who is caught accepting a bribe will be terminated. So, when we started singing praises to the Lord, they knew we were not going to give them any money to keep us from going to jail. They also didn't want to tangle with God, so they told us to leave IMMEDIATELY! And we did! We sang praises all the way home.

An Upsetting Surprise

The Area Director for Africa from the CMA in the USA came to Kinshasa a few days later. We had good meetings in Kinshasa and then flew to Boma to meet with the church leaders. It was at that meeting in Boma where I experienced the surprise of all surprises. The new president of the CMA had turned all the church leaders against me and accused me of a number of wrong doings, but all were outright lies! They had these grievances against me, accused me and wrote me a letter of *persona non grata* (that of being an unacceptable or unwelcome person). My director heard all of these accusations and knew that they were not in the least founded, but suggested we leave and not try to argue with the executive committee at this time. When he got back to the USA, he wrote a letter to the CMA Congo church president honoring me, stating that there was no such action against the church on my part and paid me the highest compliments of integrity. I was very glad to have received a copy.

Yet, it seemed that the church president did not share that letter with anyone, I'm presuming this because he sent my letter of *persona non grata* to all the church officials of the Congo and all the heads of state, in the whole political arena, stating as well that I was not to be let back into the country.

I was devastated, to say the least! I had to abruptly leave all my Congolese friends, leave the CEAC church (pastor and deacons that I had worked so closely with), our Studios Sango Malamu Ministry and everything that I had worked for, for 30 years of ministry. To make it worse some Congolese leaders, whom I thought were friends, were among those who also signed the document.[78]

Back at home, I was completely despondent and stressed out, so much so that not long after that experience, while working with the Pacific District as Missions Consultant, I had a heart attack. I enjoyed my work at the district as Missions Consultant, but it was an interim assignment. My heart was still in media in Africa.

Actually, I was on my way back to Africa, as the newly appointed Media Consultant for Africa for the Christian and Missionary Alliance in Canada when the heart attack occurred. I had set up meetings with leaders in Pointe Noire and Libreville with the view of planting radio stations in these two key cities.

I was at my friend Merl's place doing some last-minute laptop computer adjustments when I felt heavy duty indigestion and numbness in my left arm. He immediately recognized the symptoms and told me I was having a heart attack and rushed me to the hospital. I had to cancel all meetings and was peacefully ready to meet the Lord. It was a close call as one of my main arteries was completely blocked, but God still had His reasons for keeping me around. I got better and actually made many subsequent trips to Africa, including Congo-Kinshasa. However, sad to say, my trips were never to see the CMA church in the Congo or the CMA Congo church leaders. My trips there were always just to help in the ministry of SSM. I was never given any problems getting a visa or coming into the country. At all times, when the officials recognized me as the president-founder of Studios Sango Malamu (and Radio Sango Malamu), they were very glad to help me in any way (and I always had a tape in hand of our original music to give them). They

---

[78] *I couldn't understand why the church leaders would fabricate these lies about me and treat me as a persona non grata when I thought that we had a very good relationship. I was finally able to piece together (via the grapevine) an understanding. The newly elected CMA national church president was goaded by the ECC president to run this little Canadian missionary out of town and take over the radio station. If the missionary was gone, all would fall into the hands of the CMA National Church. Radio was very powerful, and they wanted that power!*

Needless to say, this didn't work. God gave me good insight, right at the beginning of SSM to make it a separate, independent ministry. Thanks to the New SSM president, Pastor Babaka (a former magistrate), who knew the legal status of SSM and would not back down.

even went as far as direct me to the airport VIP lounge, although I never travelled first class to the Congo. It seems the Lord has His own way of looking after His children.

Validated and Vindicated

As Media Consultant for Africa, I had now set up several radio stations and had been able to meet all the African CMA church leaders. Although not everyone of the seven or eight nations in which the CMA was working had Christian radio, all the CMA national churches were interested in using this means of evangelism. Some felt that this was the only effective way to reach their people who had deep roots in other world religions. Social contact of any kind was often forbidden between followers of other religions and followers of Jesus Christ, but many would listen to their radios and hear the messages of the prophet Jesus.

At one point, I was invited to a conference for all these CMA African leaders. It was to be held in Abidjan, Cote D'Ivoire and I was to speak about radio and its benefits in propagating the gospel in West Africa. All the key CMA Africa church leaders were to be there.

I came into one of the main churches on a Sunday morning, just to go to church before the conference was to begin on the Monday. Someone came up to me and told me that the pastor of this large CMA church in Abidjan was asking me to come into his office before the church was to begin. I respectfully declined, saying that I was content to sit in the congregation. The messenger came back with a more forceful invitation; I was expected in the office right away. I complied.

As I came through his office door, there sat all the presidents of the CMA African Churches—from Mali, Burkina Faso, Guinea, Cote D'Ivoire, Gabon, Congo-Brazzaville and another man who I didn't recognize, but thought might have been from Niger or Benin. They all immediately stood to their feet at this surprise entrance and we all laughed and greeted each other in a loving embrace, African style, one after the other. We prayed together and then went and sat on the platform together. It was only after some time that I found out that the "other person" there, whom I didn't know, was from the Congo (DRC) and was the president's representative as the president himself was "indisposed". The Lord seemed to say to me, again, "See, I have vindicated you before those who have done you wrong and validated your ministry. Just leave it to me, I will take care of you." Which, as I write, reminds me of the song, "God Will Take Care of You" (through every day or' all your way). He has certainly done that!

The Reconciliation

Some twenty years later, one day I got a call from Paul Tsasa, the younger brother of our trio, saying that he had heard that the CMA in the Congo was calling us, the original Kinshasa Trio or Trio Sango Malamu, back to the Congo to do a legacy tour with the CMA church there. They wanted to honor us for the ministry that we had there over the span of at least 10 years (not including the second group). We were all able to go, except for Big Joe (Joseph Tama Tsasa) the older brother. Joe was our lead singer, our lead guitar player and the writer of many of our songs, but he had just had a stroke that impaired his left side and was not yet able to travel, play or sing. But he sent his son Rodney (an excellent keyboard artist) and I took with me my son (-in-law) Brian Thiessen, a professional musician, on the guitar and other stringed instruments.

We met Paul and Rodney in Kinshasa and then also met Edo Bumba (who had sung with us in the past and who had worked with me at the studio as a sound engineer). Although Edo had to come from Sweden on his own, he wasn't going to miss out on this historic occasion! Then Dodo Miranda showed up from Angola, Kool Matope came from Gabon and Samy Biay, still living in Kinshasa, soon appeared on the scene. We had several generations of Sango Malamu on board and did we ever have a great time. Even brother Kibutu was able to come and be the main speaker for us--our evangelist some thirty years earlier. Many came to the Lord through our meetings and it was a pure delight for us all to minister together again.[79]

After the meetings, I was called along with Brian to meet with the CMA church leaders. I was a bit apprehensive as the last meeting I had attended with the CMA Congo church leaders didn't go that well. But we went, and I'm sure glad we did. The new church president, Doctor Kenzo Mabiala, understood what the problem had been between my family and the church and together with his leaders before my family

---

[79] In Boma, over three nights of meetings, approximately 10,000 people turned out and some 1000 people made decisions to follow Jesus. We did the same thing in Kinshasa, but the turnout was not like that in Boma. Nevertheless, God still blessed in marvelous ways. Kibutu's brother, for many years opposed to the gospel, gave his life to Jesus. What a celebration that was!

(Brian) apologized for the ways in which I had been treated by the CEAC in the past and asked for forgiveness. Of course, forgiveness was given, love was expressed and there where hugs all around. I went away from that meeting with a light and joyous heart. Here is an edited part of the letter I wrote to Dr. Kenzo after our meeting that day:

I praise the Lord and bless all those who had a part in bringing the group "Sango Malamu" again to the Congo. What a marvelous eye-opening experience that was.

...The second thing that really affected me personally was the warm and heart felt welcoming fellowship that I felt coming from you and the leaders of the CEAC. As you well know, the past administration had ruptured my relationship with the CEAC church, for reasons only known to them. ... After having poured my life into ministry with the CEAC for almost 30 years, this rupture was devastating to me and my family. At first, I was sick in heart, then sick in spirit, then literally sick physically, but that didn't help me overcome the darkness of my soul.

Although... most of my life I have been a person truly desiring to follow God, [I must admit that I was] continually "thinking outside of the box", ...and although headquarters in Canada and the USA always stood behind me, I felt that the CEAC church in the Congo did not understand my ministry. I... finally came to grips with this and forgave them as Christ had forgiven me and forgives us all as we need that forgiveness. BUT I wasn't free... the sorrow of that ruptured this relationship was still a dark cloud in my life.

However, I praise our Father in heaven and His Son Jesus that through the ministry of the Holy Spirit this recent trip has dispelled that darkness of soul. After the crusade in Boma, our meeting with the CEAC church leaders, together with my family (represented by bokilo Brian) was definitely unexpected. When asked to meet with you, I wasn't sure what to anticipate, but the kind words spoken were indelibly imprinted on my heart. Forgiveness was requested; forgiveness was given and again expressed. Love, understanding and grace were extended and received in an emotional and physical embrace ...and my spirit soared! Something within me felt like a bird let loose from its cage and only sometime after did I realize that the "dark cloud [over my soul]" was lifted! May the Lord be praised!

I write this letter moved, as the apostle Paul wrote to Timothy, not from a "spirit of fear" of but from a spirit of ... love (emotion) ... from the very core of my existence where the Holy Spirit is present.

[This letter is] to you, to the church of the CEAC and its leaders in the DR of Congo. Amen.

Gratefully yours,

Jim Sawatsky
Retired Missionary with the CEAC in the Congo.

This 2014 tour was my last visit to the Congo.

Sango Malamu Legacy Group in Boma on stage and in Kinshasa before departing.

Rodney (Joe's son), Samy, Jim &Paul, drummer, Edo, Dodo & (bokilo)Brian

Chapter Thirty: Media Consultant

It was in the early 2000's that CMA Canada asked if I would become the Media Consultant for all of their African fields and install radio stations and recording studios in other parts of West Africa as I had done in the Congo. It was with great delight that I accepted this position. As a result, we set up stations in Pointe Noir, Republic of Congo; Libreville, Gabon; Conakry, Guinea; Bobo Dioulasso, Burkina Faso as well as in the capital city of Ouagadougou and in more remote areas of the country and in Mali. We established some solar powered stations in Mali and worked with others in Niger, Guinea, Cote d'Ivoire, and Benin. At the same time, with the agreement of CMA Canada, I was able to work with Trans World Radio as their program director for Africa. In 2004, I was about to do a radio workshop for TWR in Madagascar and Mauritius when Gramma became extremely ill. So ill in fact that I had to retired from all ministry and take care of her. This was a bit disheartening for me at the time, but I remembered that God had promised to work out all things for our good and I believe for His honor. Before I retired, however, I was able to see some wonderful things happen in radio in West and Central Africa, giving "the winds a mighty voice that Jesus Saves". I'll share just two of those experiences.

Radio in Pointe Noire, Congo

The first radio station that we set up, apart from RSM in Kinshasa, was the Good News Radio station in Pointe Noire, Republic of Congo, in 2001. Some special groups in America had raised the sum of $30,000.00US for this special project in Ponte Noire and we were asked to buy the equipment and come and set it up. Which we did, together with a good digital recording studio for recording their own programs and also some small music groups.

Next to Brazzaville, the capital of the Republic of Congo, Pointe Noire was the second most important city of the country. Being a port city right on the Atlantic, Pointe-Noire was the main commercial center of the country and at that time had a population of around 700,000 people.[80] Radio Sango Malamu in Kinshasa was being heard in many parts of Brazzaville, then about 1.5 million people. Pointe Noire, a

---

[80] *Wikipedia*

commercial center and the next most populated city in the RC, seemed to be the next best choice for Christian Radio reaching the masses.

I asked bokilo, Uncle Brian, to come along and help set up the recording studio and teach operators how to use the equipment while I concentrated on the radio station itself. Once we got there, missionary Stan Hotalen would be a tremendous help as well. Brian and I came to the Vancouver airport with 13 big suitcases and boxes plus our carry-ons, to bring along all this equipment with us as personal baggage to Brazzaville. We had prayed much over the equipment and the whole project, but still didn't know how we would be able to get everything to our destination.

The tickets we had gave us two bags each, first to Paris and then on to Brazzaville. Pointe Noire's ticket would have to be purchased in Brazzaville as it would be a local flight. We could figure that one out once in Brazza with the help of the mission agent, but our main goal now was to get everything to Brazza. With two bags each on the tickets that left us with 9 other big bags and boxes to bring along as excess bags at $200.00 a piece that would cost us $1800, which of course we didn't have!

Miracle #1

We prayed for favor with the airline personnel and continued that prayer as we showed up before the ticket agent with thirteen big suitcases (including some big cardboard boxes) and only $200 cash for extra luggage. The agent almost had a fit when she saw us with all the luggage and sent us immediately to a special counter where we met the managing director for all sales and extra luggage. He was just arriving as we were approaching his area and upon seeing all the luggage we had in tow asked us, "What is the problem here?" I explained that all this was special equipment going to Brazzaville, Congo, Africa, and that it was a church related not-for-profit project. And then I asked if he could help us get a special rate. I could just see the wheels turning as he looked at us. He finally said, "OK, [still thinking]…but you'll have to pay some extra baggage fees." After having figured out in his own mind what he could do (no doubt in my mind, influenced by God Himself!), he continued, "We'll let you check 10 bags all the way through to Brazzaville. For the other three, you'll have to pay."

"Thank you so much, sir, for your kind generosity, but will everything be checked straight to Brazzaville? We really don't want to handle this again in Paris."

"All bags will be checked straight through to Brazzaville, but you'll have to pay $200 cash for the other 3 bags."

"Oh, thank you Jesus!" I exclaimed under my breath. We were happy with that as we had just that amount of cash in hand! God was at work. We praised the Lord all the way to Brazzaville and didn't see our luggage again until we landed there. God's grace and favor was present. Prayer was answered!

Miracle #2

We just about missed our flight to Brazzaville while in Paris as the flight was loading 2 hours ahead of schedule due to a pending strike. Now, about to land in Brazzaville 2 hours early (that never happens in Africa) was a real problem. There was no one there to meet us. All our stuff came through okay, except for one bag (which has often happened to us travelling in, to or from Africa). We quickly put a tracer on it and prayed that it would come through with the next airplane from France.

All was all smooth "sailing", without a hitch from Vancouver, but now here we were in Brazzaville, with the 12 bags and boxes piled high against the wall, trying to keep them out of the way while waiting for our contact person to show up. Then we heard that the President of the Country (The Republic of Congo) was coming through the airport and everyone and everything had to be cleared out immediately— especially bags and boxes piled high against the wall!

Brian and I were anxiously awaiting the arrival of Nicaise—the mission agent—to come and do his magic and get all the bags through customs without hassle. But he didn't arrive early, true to normal African procedure, and there we waited. The customs officials were a little lenient in allowing us time to wait for our contact man, but when the "front man" for President Sassou Nguesso came by to clear the airport and tie up loose ends, he certainly had questions about all that baggage against the wall.

When he walked in, all the other passengers had already left, we were the only ones still behind customs twiddling our thumbs!

"What's with all these bags against the wall?" he demanded in good French. "Who owns all this stuff and what is it doing here? It all has to be cleared out immediately!"

We didn't have much of choice. We owned up to the fact that all the bags and boxes were ours and that we were waiting for our contact man to show up. I didn't want to tell him that it was all radio equipment for we didn't even have a license to bring it into the country let alone operate a private radio station in his country. What we understood was that we were invited by the CMA Congolese church and by the missionaries to bring it all in and they would get it through customs. But no one was there to meet us!

Just as we were about to begin dragging all our luggage through customs, where all the customs agents had been eyeing us and just waiting for us, something like vultures waiting for their part of a lion kill, Nicaise showed up. He came rushing in, but before he could hardly greet us, he was recognized by the Colonel and was greeted heartily by him. Suddenly, the atmosphere in the room changed. All was quiet as these two men began chatting. Nicaise finally introduced us and then explained who we were and what was in the boxes and suitcases. It was all for a Christian radio station in Pointe Noire.

Quickly and quietly the Colonel, under presidential orders, gave direction for all the men present, the "bagagistes"[81] to load everything onto motorized carts and take them to the Pointe Noire plane that was now loading its cargo for takeoff in an hour or so. No one asked questions, no one inspected the boxes, and no one interfered with the loading of all the luggage onto the awaiting plane. All was done in a brief period and we were free to go. Brian went with Nicaise and all the equipment while I stayed in Brazzaville for further business. The next day the missing bag came, and I flew with it to Pointe Noire.

When I got there, I heard the story. Apparently Nicaise's father and the Colonel were good friends (both military personnel) and the Colonel had been in his house many times. For that reason alone, he acted promptly enough to get everything out to Pointe Noire as quickly

---

[81] A "bagagiste" is French for a baggage handler or a person who loads and unloads luggage.

as possible. He also would not shrink from helping the son of his old friend. When the equipment arrived in Pointe Noire, word must have been passed on that all this stuff was under presidential orders and did not need to pass through customs. The airline personnel told the missionaries to bring their pickups right beside the airplane, on the tarmac, and all twelve bags and boxes were gently loaded in place. The chauffeurs drove off the runway with all the boxes, bags and suitcases in plain sight and brought everything directly to the mission house, where the radio station buildings were located, without so much as a whisper as to who we were, what were the contents of bags and who was it for.

God's plan is marvelous!

Miracle #3

The next day was Sunday and I was expected to preach in one of the largest CMA churches in Pointe

Pointe-Noire

Noire. Before the message, I explained why we were there and asked the people to pray that against all odds we would be able to have the radio station set up and running and, also, have a license to broadcast by next Sunday. That would be a miracle for sure! We all prayed, the whole congregation, all at one time, and then waited for God to continue to show us his favor.

During that week, we were able to get everything organized and in place and completely set up, including the antenna, with the help of Stan. We did a test "run" to see if we could hear anything on our FM car radios. We could hear the station well all over the city and beyond. We were delighted.

Stan knew the head of security for the city of Pointe Noire and the surrounding area, so invited him and his wife for dinner (to see if he could give us some good advice as to how to proceed). While he was there, we showed him the station and played some music for him to prove that it was up and running and ready to broadcast.

He was astonished! We then asked him how we should go about getting a license and who we should contact in order to do that, hoping he would intervene for us. His answer to us was something like, "Oh, just begin broadcasting and as long as you have no commercials and just play Christian music it will be all right. By the time the government determines who is broadcasting you will already have a following and they would have to give you license to save face." And then he tagged on to these remarks that the Prefect, the President's representative (who would be like a governor of a state or even the Premiere of a province), would be the only one who could grant us a license. "But," He added, "Good luck in trying to get to see him!"

The radio committee met together and prayed over what we should do. Even though this man was head of security, I was very leery of following his instructions. I didn't sit right with me. After our prayer time, it was agreed upon that we should not in fact follow the chief security advisor's advice, but that we should ask to see the Prefect and make an appointment with him.

The next day was Friday and we asked Nicaise and another pastor to go to the office of the Prefect to see if he would give us an audience. He granted our request and gave us an exact time to meet him in his office the next day and he would hear us out. The request to see him was explicit. It was concerning getting a license for a Christian radio station to broadcast.

The next day, Saturday, a delegation from the Radio committee went to meet with the Prefect. He wasn't there! He was called out to deal with a major issue that had come up, but gave explicit instructions to his secretary to give us what we wanted. We asked for a license to broadcast and to our complete surprise the documents were drawn up immediately. The Prefect would sign them when he got back later that evening. And he did. By late Saturday night, we were completely legal and by Sunday morning, early, we were on the air! Things just don't happen that fast in Africa!

Another Miracle!

That next Sunday I walked into the same church and stood in front of the congregation with a small transistor radio in my hand. When I addressed the congregation I said, "Last week when I was here we all prayed that we would be able to set up the Christian radio station and have a license to broadcast within just one week. If this would happen, we would know for certain that God was in this ministry of Christian radio for the city and it would be a definite miracle from His hand."

Then I turned on the radio and said, "Listen to this." Over the radio came Christian music and then the call letters. The announcer said,

"You are listening to Good News Radio at 104.5 FM!" There was a cheer that went up that could be heard outside the building and around the community.

As in Congo Kinshasa, so in Congo Pointe Noire, Christian radio was the first private radio station to be on the air—at least since their independence.[82]

Radio for Libreville, Gabon

This was another exciting project. I had already made several trips to Libreville to cast vision, help them set up a non-profit organization and to find a suitable spot for a radio station and recording studio. The main CMA church had buildings and extra rooms attached to the Sanctuary that really weren't being used. We asked to use one large room for a recording studio with a ground entrance and three rooms upstairs for our radio station. The committee was composed of mostly CMA people but not all. Nevertheless, the radio committee was in agreement that this CMA church was the best available spot—on a high hill overlooking the city. Good rooms were available and a good area on the property just outside the building was available to set up a high antenna. The church agreed, and we began to make preparations.

Funds came in from various sources, but mainly from the CMA USA.[83] Soon all the equipment was put together, purchased, and brought over for both the radio and sound production studios. This was amazing enough, but the part that I really want to tell you about is the

 purchase of the antenna tower; for radio is no good without a good radio tower and antenna. The antenna we had

---

[82] I must add that when the authorities heard that a private radio station was on the air without their knowledge, they went to the Prefect to demand that they find the station and confiscate all the equipment. The Prefect calmed them all down and said it was all very legal and that he had himself signed the license for this Good News Radio station to operate. You can imagine what would have happened had we listened to the advice of the Chief Security Officer.

[83] The original Sango Malamu Trio, sang again at the CMA USA nationwide conference in the early years of 2000 and raised money for radio in Africa. We raised, I believe, around $100,000.

already purchased with the transmitter and other equipment, but what were we going to use for a tower?

While the Good News Radio committee was working on getting a license I was keeping my eyes open for an antenna tower. On one of my visits to South Africa, due to my working with Trans World Radio and their ministry in Africa, I was following a tip that I got from networking with radio people in Johannesburg. A pastor who I had met expressed his interest in Christian radio in Africa. I called him up and we agreed to meet for coffee in a special mall in a suburb area of Jo-burg. I had been in Cape Town and in the Fish Hoek area gleaning from their experiences in Christian radio and now I was having talks with Trans World Radio in Jo-burg gleaning info from them on their ministry across Africa and sharing what we had done in Kinshasa and Pointe Noire and Bobo-Dioulasso. In fact, this was going to be our 2nd meeting. The pastor and one of his elders were going to buy me coffee this time and it seemed that they had some exciting news to share.

Miracle #1

When we met it didn't take long for the pastor to introduce his church elder, who "just happened" to be an engineer in the designing and building of radio towers. I was very glad (to say the least) to hear that and began questioning him on how a hundred-foot high antenna tower could be built and how much it would cost to build one etc. As we were discussing prices for buying a ready-made antenna as opposed to the cost of building one ourselves, he said, "Wait a minute. I wanted to tell you that a complete antenna was fabricated for a radio station in South Africa (somewhere), but they refused it for some reason and it is still boxed up and sitting at our factory ready to be sent." He went on to say that the down payment was forfeited, and he thought that we (meaning the Good News Radio in Libreville, Gabon) could get it for a very low price. Actually, for next to nothing!

The tower was engineered and built especially for a private radio station, but they didn't go through with the deal. The engineering company had already received a good part of the costs and were now looking to unload the antenna for a very low price. He thought that if it was explained that this was for a non-profit Christian Radio station in Gabon, they could possibly let it go for an even cheaper price than they would for another radio station. As we were talking, I was explaining that the only hang up would be in how to send it to Libreville.

"No problem!" came the immediate response. The engineer stipulated that it was already crated for shipping and all we would have to do was give him the address and pay the shipping and he would send it. What a surprise!

This is when the pastor interjected and said that he and his church would take charge of the shipping and would pay all the costs necessary to get the antenna to our radio station in Libreville. Another major surprise!

As we talked more, I asked the engineer if he would entertain the idea of coming and helping us set it up, seeing he was the designer and builder of this particular antenna. Another surprise! He said he would and he and the pastor felt that the church would fund his return ticket as well. Boy, was I now walking on air!

Before we left that meeting, phone calls were made, confirmation of the sale was given, the purchase of the tower was made and the possibility of sending it to Libreville via a reputable shipping agent had all been accomplished. I couldn't believe it. Within an hour or so, I had purchased the exact tower we needed, negotiated a very good price (due to low value of the Ren verses the US dollar), received confirmation from the engineer that he would come and set it up. ...and had witnessed the pastor confirming that his congregation would raise all funds necessary to send the tower and the engineer to Libreville to set it up correctly. What a miracle of God! I could hardly believe it myself. Where the antenna would cost something like 10 grand or more in Gabon, it was purchased in a mall in Johannesburg, SA, for less than $1000 dollars US, which (because of a local church involvement) included shipping and professional set up!

Walking away from that meeting, I shook my head in disbelief, did all this really happen? It really did! We all followed through with our commitments and the antenna tower was purchased for the exact prices indicated; the church sent the tower via steamer and paid for all the expenses; the customs in Gabon let it go without duty as it was for a Christian non-profit organization; the engineer came and set it up as he promised, and the Libreville church provided the rooms and they were prepared as promised. For me it was another marvelous God story to see how God provided all the funds and the people necessary for the complete installation of this Good News Radio station in Libreville. Not only that, an engineer from Holland was contacted and he volunteered to come and bring all the sound recording equipment from

Holland, set it up and train some men to operate it. There was no doubt about God's presence in all of this.

Miracle #2

One more God story! Now that everything was in place; the radio people were being trained, the tower in the process of being set up (by well-paid locals) with the engineer on the job, the question was, "Who could I get to help me climb up this 100-foot tower to put the antenna in place?" It was going to be too difficult for me to do it alone. I needed help, but who would volunteer. Most Africans I know are afraid of heights!

The engineer from SA finally said that he would help. That was a relief, but he got up to about 20 feet and said that was as far as he could go. Well, that wasn't much help after all. He was a great engineer, but couldn't take heights. Who else would help? No one volunteered. But Again, God provided! I wrote the following article about this:

When all was ready to set up the antenna equipment on the tower that had just been built, I was on the lookout for people to help me bring cables and equipment up the 30-meter tower. I was much in prayer over this as there was not one volunteer. Some tried, but were too scared and immediately came down. Finally, a young man who was in-training as a radio station operator volunteered when the group of trainees was asked.

"Are you sure?" I asked. It is pretty high up there. He seemed to indicate that it was no problem. When I gave him his first assignment, he scampered up to the top and in no time at all finished his part of the installation. I was just coming up with the heavy cable and attachments when he was already coming down. We soon put all the bays up for the 4-bay antenna and all was installed in record time. I asked him after it was all done how he could do that so fast, without fear, when everyone else had declined.

"Oh" he said, "I didn't want to tell you this at first, but I used to be a high wire act in the circus! I'm used to heights."

Where in the world, in all of Africa at least, would I find a "high wire" acrobat? Well, to me at least, this was a miracle, a provision of God himself, which permitted us to install the antenna in record time.

It was amazing how God provided in every area. He even brought to us a whole crew of Muslims in Mali to help us set up the antenna just outside of the Christian church. This was in an outlying village where we set up a solar powered radio station. They were so proud of this station that they claimed it as their own even though it broadcasted only the gospel of Jesus Christ. Later I heard that a chief of the area was so impressed with the music and messages of the radio, though Muslim, gave his life to Jesus.

As Media Consultant I was exploring many unique areas in which to set up Christian Radio. It was an exciting adventure to see how God opened doors and how "giving the winds a mighty voice" affected the whole listening area.

 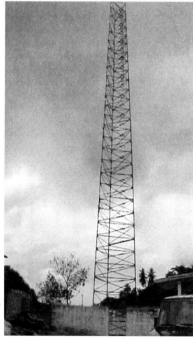

While the men were still building the tower, I began setting up the antenna. But I needed help!

Chapter Thirty-One: Some Concluding Thoughts

SSM Involvement

In 2005, we inherited some money from Gramma's Auntie Blanche that had been in trust, but was designated for ministry with SSM. Gramma was now well enough to take care of herself, so early in 2006 I went back to visit SSM with a gift for ministry of $10,000—raised partly from the interest of Auntie Blanche's funds given to the CMA and partly through our home church of PCC[84]. It was during that visit that the SSM board of directors asked if I would accept the appointment of being President again. God had already alerted me to this possibility and I already had some serious conversation with Him about this. I had written out a couple of pages of things that would have to take place if I would be at the helm again. The SSM board accepted the conditions and unanimously voted me as president of the ministry again. I commuted back and forth as long as special funds were available through the legacy of Auntie Blanche Palmer. During this time, I was able to revamp the Audio recording studio, with the help of Uncle Brian (Thiessen) and Audio technician Samy Biay of SSM, buy the radio and television ministry a large 50,000-kilowatt generator and revamp the radio and television stations with new equipment—all with donations from supporters of our GNI ministry and a special Congolese banker friend now living in the USA. SSM was heavily in debt at the time, but we were able to negotiate the many debts and restructure the organization to bring us completely out of the red.

Part of the restructuring was the ability to finally reorganize the legal structure of our organization under a new name, "Studios Sango Malamu Ministries" which gained for SSMM the legal right to operate permanently in any part of the Congo. The legal document was called the "Personalité Civile". Due to many obstacles, including religious and political, we were never able to secure that nationwide legal status before, but after approximately 20 years, in 2008, we finally had the official document in hand. A few days later, due to my own health concerns I had to say goodbye to the Congo for good.

SSM Ministries carries on under new leadership until today.

---

[84] *Pacific Community Church, Cloverdale, BC*

Business Opportunities

On many occasion I saw how easy it would be for me to make money in the Congo. There were opportunities on every hand. Now, as I look back I see how God kept me from even dipping into this allurement. In fact, everything I barely tried, like just "sticking my toe in the water", went south immediately—even some investments that I tried here at home never worked out. It seemed that God was saying, "Keep your focus on Me. I have promised to bless you. I will take care of you!" Over time this message to me became even more clear: I was NOT to be involved in making money! I had no special Biblical Word from God on that other than His Kitimat promise and a sense that He was calling me to this kind of "no business" commitment. However, sometimes this was hard for me to understand, but I finally got the picture when everything that I would invest in seemed to flop.

In Kinshasa (around 1974-5), I bought ten big Red Horn laying chickens from a missionary "farmer" and made a great chicken coop and nests for them …and everything. I even bought some laying feed, thinking that I would have enough eggs for ourselves and even sell a few (eggs and chickens) on the side. One night they all got stolen which brought an abrupt end to my chicken ranching …and just about the time they were ready to lay!

I was given a piglet and thought that I could at least raise one pig, then maybe have others (we had a large yard). However, after a few short months, it just had to be eaten—that was the end of my pig farming days.

We were given a goat and brought it home on the top of our suburban all the way from Kwimba, some 500 kilometers or more from Kinshasa. I thought that I might be able raise a few goats for food and for sale! But the goat too had to be eaten, all too soon!

We have had not a few vehicles (and motorcycles) of various makes and models, in Canada and in Africa—most of them very inexpensive and some of them were even given to us. On each occasion when it came to sell, I would think of the best price I could get for the vehicle. I don't remember ever getting the best possible price for any of them. Sometimes, the Lord just said that He wanted me, in turn, to give the vehicle away to someone needy! Other vehicles I felt I could sell, but when they didn't sell, I would say, "OK Lord, what price should I put on this vehicle?" When I did that, He would give me a price, which was always a little lower price than my original idea …and it always sold in short order!

Having an entrepreneurial mind set, it was and still is hard to pass up a worthwhile investment opportunity. Later, after having left the Congo, I got sucked into several schemes that seemed really legit, but every one of them came to a discouraging end. Some funds were able to be recuperated, but overall, most of everything that was invested had to be written off. It seemed to me the Lord was repeatedly saying, "Don't worry about the future or making money, I will take care of you." It took me a long time to get that angst out of my britches, but I finally concluded that business and investments were not for me!

Only one time was I able to embark on an investment that made a little profit—that of buying houses, gutting and remodeling them for a quick resale. It happened twice and that was during the time that I had just fully retired from the CMA (2004). It was a time when Gramma was seriously ill and we needed money desperately. A very close friend of mine (Rudy) had the bucks to buy the house; I had enough of a line of credit to supply all the materials and did most of the work. Rudy also helped here and there and so did other friends and relatives, but the bulk of the renos were in my hands. We were able to clear a modest profit which we divided evenly after all expenses were paid. The bulk of my revenue mostly went into medical bills, medications and food supplements. God provided in a wonderful fashion, just like He had always promised.

After having said all of that, I must conclude with the more important truth of just trusting the Lord for daily supply and for the future as well. He had promised to bless us, so we rested in that. The Lord very specifically said to Gramma one day that if she took care of His children, He would take care of ours. That was a precious promise and we hung on to that throughout our career days and still do. With this background of promises, we really didn't think much of retirement and what that would mean.

After our children left for boarding school, I had visions of being in Africa for the rest of our days and probably wouldn't even get to see much of our children, or even our grandchildren.

But God had other things in store for us. About 5 years before Gramma got seriously ill and I had to retire to take care of her[85], we had experienced a wonderful blessing of God. It started many years earlier when Gramma's father, Great Grandpa George, had indicated that he wanted to leave his house in White Rock to us. Both her siblings agreed with that, which is amazing in itself, and even helped dad and us make that a reality.

When we couldn't go back to the Congo, Gramma moved in with Grandpa George to take care of him. It wasn't long after that Muriel, his second wife, passed away in the hospital. We then were looking for the best for us to take diligent care of him. Just before Dad Layland began falling into serious dementia, we were able to sell his house in White Rock, with his permission and signature, and buy a large enough house to hold 4 generations. We bought a newer house in Cloverdale, together with daughter Loralee and Brian and their three, so that we could all look after grandpa George—as he became known to us all.

After 10 great years of wonderful community living (which was in complete contrast to my vision of dying in Africa without seeing much of my kids or grandkids), we all agreed that it was time to either find a larger house, perhaps live on acreage together somewhere. By this time Aunt Loralee and Uncle Brian had 5 children. But Gramma wasn't too sure about us moving. She liked Cloverdale, our church community and other friends who live relatively close by. Consequently, with the help of a financial advisor, we were able to buy out our kids who in turn purchased a 6-bedroom home in Abbotsford.

I never cease to be amazed at God's wonderful provision. We have had precious times with you, our 11 grandchildren (never realizing that this might even be possible), we have a wonderful house in which to live, in a quiet neighborhood, we have good transportation and enough food and clothing for each day—and even have a cruiser motor bike. It is totally amazing! We never saved up for this, we never even imagined this, but God in His great grace has given all this to us. He promised to bless us and He surely has!

---

[85] *Her illness and he healing is another story, for her to tell, but it proved to us again of God's marvelous grace and faithfulness to us.*

Oh yes, one more thing. I am so grateful that God had given us wonderful friends over the years in Africa. I have come to understand that relationships with faithful and good friends and family are so important. Now that we are retired, one of our greatest treasures is not houses or lands or material things, but the wonderful relationships and the friendships we have. God has given me, besides my family, three godly men that I can share anything and everything with. Two of them have been friends since high school. That to me is one of God's greatest blessings!

Gramma,   (Caroline) Gracen,   Rudy (Donna),   Merl (Bev)

When Gramma was sick, my buddies got me got me back into riding cruisers in Canada. This was around 2003.

Addendum

I don't want to belabor this idea of not getting into business and investments, but not long ago, I believe the Lord revealed to me, through my reading of 1Timothy 6 why I was not to be involved in trying to get rich on my own. It was a revelation for me and I thought I would share it with you. Perhaps it may help you in making some of your life decisions.

I had never been given a scripture on this, but only felt the still small voice in my spirit—which I had the audacity to challenge from time to time. Now here is the "rhema"—what God's Word said to me, personally!

1 Timothy 6:5-19

*Teach and urge these things. If anyone teaches a different doctrine and does not agree with the sound words of our Lord Jesus Christ and the teaching that accords with godliness, he is puffed up with conceit and understands nothing. He has an unhealthy craving for controversy and for quarrels about words, which produce envy, dissension ...constant friction among people who are depraved in mind and deprived of the truth, <u>imagining that godliness is a means of gain</u>. Now there is great gain in **<u>godliness with contentment</u>** for we brought nothing into the world, and we cannot take anything out of the world.* **But if we have food and clothing, with these we will be content.** *But those <u>who desire to be rich fall into temptation, into a snare, into many senseless and harmful desires</u>...*

<u>But as for you, O man of God, flee these things</u>. Pursue righteousness, godliness, faith, love, steadfastness, gentleness. Fight the good fight of the faith. Take hold of the eternal life *to which you were called and about which you made the good confession in the presence of many witnesses...*

As for the rich *in this present age, charge them not to be haughty,* **nor to set their hopes on the uncertainty of riches, but on God, <u>who richly provides us with everything to enjoy</u>.** *18 They are to do good, to be rich in good works, to be generous and ready to share, 19 thus storing up treasure for themselves as a good foundation for the future, so that they may take hold of that which is truly life.*

In reading and studying this passage, God flatly told me that "godliness" does not mean "gain". If there is a teaching out there somewhere that says that you will be rich because you are godly, it is false teaching.

On the other hand, there is *great gain in **godliness with contentment***. The fact that there could be "godly gain" in being content in whatever situation I would find myself, suddenly became to me a new, revealing and wonderful fact of the Christian life. Whether being wined and dined in a very expensive hotel or sleeping on a dirt floor with rats running over my head, there can be contentment. And there is "gain" in that. But that gain is not primarily of the monetary type, rather it is the amazing sense of a fulfilled life of bringing pleasure to our God and glory to His Name. This "gain" I believe is in the using of the "gifts" He has given to us and sensing His pleasure when we use them .nd then, He says, "everything else will be added to us."[86] If we have enough to eat and proper clothes to wear we should be content. God himself will give us that contentment when we look to Him as a child looks to the father with a contented heart because he has been provided for. What else is there then but to experience the love of the Father, His faithfulness, His grace and to revel in it?

I believe my heavenly Father was saying to me, I have kept you from falling into temptation, from falling into a snare of many harmful desires when you have been content with me and what I have supplied for you.

"OK, I get it now. Thank you, Father!"

I always thought I could handle being wealthy, but God knew better.

He is saying now, "What my instructions have been for you was to flee from being rich, not run towards it, and pursue the right way of living—pursue the instructions that I have for you, which include being like Me, depending on only Me, in faith, with love, with persistence and with a gentle spirit."

"Yes Lord, I see it all now from a different perspective and I thank You for being so patient with me and often putting a corral around my erring thoughts and actions. I see You have put up 'road signs' in different areas at various times in my life and when I have obeyed them it has been a blessing for me. When I haven't, I have had to reap the

---

[86] *(Matt.6:33) But seek first the kingdom of God and His righteousness, and all these things will be added unto you.*

full repercussions of disobedience. But all these experiences have brought me into a closer relationship with You.

"You promised to bless me, and You have, in countless ways. Your blessing has been the undeniable and fantastic "gain of godliness with contentment" towards one who has been most fallible and broken, yet patched together to be a vase in some way fit for the Master's use. Thank you Lord for keeping me close to Your chest! Amen."

The Best Biking Buddies and their wives. Rudy (Donna), Gracen (Carline) (Dawn) and Jim have been friends since 1956 in Chilliwack Sr. High School BC.